THE ONCE AND FUTURE KING

F. H. BUCKLEY

THE ONCE AND FUTURE
KING

The Rise of Crown Government in America

Encounter Books New York • London

First American edition published in 2014 by Encounter Books,
an activity of Encounter for Culture and Education, Inc.,
a nonprofit, tax-exempt corporation.
Encounter Books website address: www.encounterbooks.com

Manufactured in the United States and printed on
acid-free paper. The paper used in this publication meets
the minimum requirements of ANSI/NISO Z39.48 1992
(R 1997) (Permanence of Paper).

FIRST AMERICAN EDITION

LIBRARY OF CONGRESS CATALOGING-IN-PUBLICATION DATA
Buckley, F. H. (Francis H.), 1948-
The once and future king: the rise of crown government in America /F. H. Buckley.
pages cm
Includes bibliographical references and index.
ISBN 978-1-59403-719-1 (hardcover: alk. paper)—ISBN 978-1-59403-720-7 (ebook)
1. Executive power. 2. Presidents. 3. Constitutional history. 4. Comparative government.
5. United States—Politics and government. 6. Great Britain—Politics and government.
7. Canada—Politics and government. I. Title.
JF251.B83 2014
321.8'7—dc23
2013020656

For Esther and Sarah

Contents

Preface

A good many people helped me with this book, and I am very grateful. Chris DeMuth, Philip Hamburger, and Ron Rotunda read the entire book, and their comments were very valuable. Several other friends, including Joe Bast, Jake Goldberg, Tom Lindsay, and Jim Pfiffner, read chapters of the book, and gave me helpful comments. I am especially grateful to Ed Whelan for his advice about the inner workings of American government used in chapter 5. With good comments, one adds a page to a book; with great comments, one deletes a page. I thank Ed for his great comments.

Michael Barone, James Ceasar, Jack A. Goldstone, Hon. Edith Jones, Jeffrey Jenkins, Tom and Lorraine Pangle, George Thomas, Hon. John Tyson, and John Yoo gave me valuable comments on American constitutional history. I am especially grateful to Sandy Levinson, who not only provided wise insights into American constitutionalism, but also gave me a commemorative plate bearing the likenesses of the Canadian Fathers of Confederation.

Jane Atzenstat, Hon. Michael Duffy, Rod Macdonald, O.C., Christopher Moore, and Alastair Sweeny helped me better understand the Anglo-Canadian model of government. Had I turned to them earlier,

I might not have waited so long to appreciate the discrete charm of Canadian constitutional history.

Robert McGuire pioneered the application of econometric methods to the study of the Framers, and I am most grateful for his assistance. For their help on the empirical portions of the book, I am also very grateful to Peg Brinig, Keith L. Dougherty, Jon Klick, Pippa Norris, and Eric Rasmusen. Jason Sorens was particularly helpful, as were my colleagues David Levy and the Hon. Joshua Wright.

Senator Duffy and his executive assistant, Melanie Mercier, permitted me to gain access to materials at the Library of Parliament in Ottawa, where Reference Archivist Ilene McKenna assisted me, and where Barbara Pilek, Chief of the Branch Libraries and Information Service, went out of her way to help. Sara McDowell, Coordinator of Library Instruction for Faculty and Graduate Students at the Robarts Library of the University of Toronto, helped me to research Canadian materials and access Early Canadiana Online. I am very grateful to them all.

Paul Haas, at the George Mason Law Library, was extremely helpful in getting interlibrary loans and finding online materials for me. I wonder whether he found time to assist anyone else on faculty. Researching eighteenth- and nineteenth-century materials today is immeasurably easier because of the web. All of Hansard is online, as are the most obscure biographies and memoirs from the period.

I also thank participants at workshops at the Universities of Buffalo, Georgia, and Texas, as well as participants at the federal Fifth Circuit Court of Appeals annual conference.

Liberty Fund conferences permit academics from different disciplines and beliefs to discuss the foundational questions of liberty and responsibility, and does so without pushing an ideological agenda. I could not have written this book had I not participated in many of their conferences on the Founders, and am very grateful to them. Liberty Fund also profiled a précis of the book in their Law and Liberty forum, at http://www.libertylawsite.org/liberty-forum/, and I am grateful to Hans

Eicholz and Richard Reinsch for organizing the panel, and to James R. Rogers and John Yoo for their comments.

George Mason law students Dan Schneider, Chris Gardner, Robert Hopkins, and Chris Mufarrige provided excellent research assistance, and if you're a judge or lawyer, you'd do very well for yourself were you to hire one of them.

A form of chapter 2 appeared in 1 *British Journal of American Legal Studies* 349 (2012), and a portion of chapter 7 appeared in the September 2012 *New Criterion*. Some matter appeared in essays I wrote in *The American Illness: Essays on the Rule of Law* (New Haven: Yale University Press, 2013). I thank their editors and referees, particularly Ann Richardson Oakes, for their valuable assistance. Some of my ideas first appeared in *The American Spectator* and the *National Post*, and I thank Wlady Pleszczynski and Jonathan Kay for their advice and friendship.

I also thank George Mason School of Law and George Mason's Mercatus Institute for their generous support.

I owe yet more debts to the fine editors at Encounter Books, who do their jobs exceedingly well. I sent an advance copy of the manuscript to the very entrepreneurial Roger Kimball, simply to get his comments, and received an offer of publication the next morning. Executive director Nola Tully, production director Heather Ohle, and production manager Katherine Wong shepherded the book along quickly, and Lauren Miklos and Sam Schneider employed their immense marketing talents to bring the book to the attention of readers. Finally, I would have been lost without the assistance of Lesley Rock, who was tremendously helpful in designing and shepherding this book through to completion.

The impulse to add fresh, late-breaking material must at some point end, if a book is ever to be published. As I write, Congress is debating whether to launch a war against Syria, a debate which very likely would not have taken place had not Prime Minister David Cameron felt obliged to seek Parliament's consent for his war plans—and thereafter failed to receive it. This would seem to illustrate, for all to see, the difference between executive accountability in parliamentary versus presidential regimes, and to my mind the superiority of the former.

Finally, this book would not have been possible without the encouragement and invaluable organizational and editorial assistance offered from the very beginning by my wife, Esther Goldberg, whose help I cannot ever adequately acknowledge.

F. H. Buckley
Alexandria, Virginia
September 9, 2013

-I-

The Fall and Rise
of
Crown Government

Rex Quondam, Rex Futurus

The prejudice of Englishmen, in favor of their
own government . . . arises as much
or more from national pride than reason.
—THOMAS PAINE, COMMON SENSE

Over the last 250 years there have been four American constitutions. Each has resulted in a different form of government. We have seen three thus far, and now are on the cusp of a fourth.

The first constitution, in the prerevolutionary thirteen colonies, was one of Crown government, in which royal governors exercised enormous powers. This was swept aside by the American Revolution, and (after the interregnum of the Articles of Confederation) the Framers, at their Convention in Philadelphia in the summer of 1787, produced the second constitution, one designed to correct the flaws of Crown government and the Articles of Confederation. What they proposed was a form of congressional government, with power centered in a Senate and House of Representatives.

The third constitution was one of separation of powers, of power divided between the legislative and executive branches. Its seeds were found in the second constitution, and matured over the next fifty years, as the president came to be popularly elected, and his office emerged as the modern executive—commanding, decisive, and possessing all the authority of the only person elected by the nation at large. Contrary to popular belief, this was not what the Framers had intended. It was not even what James Madison had wanted at the Philadelphia Convention, although it is often referred to as the Madisonian Constitution because of his defense of separationism in the Federalist Papers.[1] Instead, the separation of powers between the executive and legislative branches is much more a creature of the unexpected rise of democracy.

We have now entered into a fourth constitution, one of strong presidential government. The executive has slipped off many of the constraints of the separation of powers. The president makes and unmakes laws without the consent of Congress and spends trillions of government dollars; and the greatest of decisions—whether to commit his country to war—is made by him alone. His ability to reward friends and punish enemies exceeds anything seen in the past. He is *rex quondam, rex futurus*—the once and future king. And all of this is irreversible.

The long arc of American constitutional government has bent from the monarchical principle of the colonial period to congressional government, then to the separation of powers, and finally back again to Crown government and rule by a single person. The same pattern can be observed in Britain's Westminster system of parliamentary government, which was exported first to Canada, and then throughout the Commonwealth. As in America, there have been four British constitutions since the Revolutionary War.

First came the "personal government" of George III, who chose his ministers and was supported by a large block of "King's Friends" in Parliament. While sharing power with Parliament, the King dominated the government, and the American Revolution was itself a consequence of his unpopular resistance to the colonists' demands. George III was not a tyrant, however. His rule did not represent a sharp break from the constitutional practice that prevailed after the 1689 English Bill of Rights, and his ministers could not long survive when opposed by a determined majority in the House of Commons. Nevertheless, this was still a form of Crown government.

This changed in 1782 after the fall of George III's prime minister, Lord North, when the monarch's power lessened and that of the House of Commons increased; and this I call the second British constitution. It was one in which power was shared between King and Parliament, and looked at from the distant prospect of Philadelphia, it seemed to the Framers to feature a separation of powers between the executive branch, in the form of the monarch, and the legislative branch in Parliament.

Over the next fifty years, as the American Constitution evolved from congressional government to the separation of powers, the British constitution also changed, though in the opposite direction. By the time of the Great Reform Act of 1832, the monarch and House of Lords were well on their way to political insignificance. What there was of a separation of powers was abandoned, and of Britain's third constitution all that remained was an all-powerful House of Commons. There was a similar evolution in Canada, with a movement from rule by governors general and fractious assemblies to government by the House of Commons alone. The three countries had crossed paths, with America moving from legislative government to the separation of powers, and Britain and Canada moving from the separation of powers to legislative government.

A fourth constitution is now emerging in Britain and Canada, one that parallels the move to the strong presidentialism of America's fourth revolution. Under Britain's third constitution its government was led by the ruling party's principal politicians, and was labeled "cabinet government" by the nineteenth-century essayist Walter Bagehot.[2] Today, however, this has given way to rule by a prime minister who dominates his cabinet and Parliament.

What more than anything explains the move toward Crown government in all three countries is the growth of the regulatory state, where the role of legislation has diminished and that of regulatory rule making has expanded, with the regulators responsible to the executive branch and not to the legislature. Modernity, in the form of the regulatory state, is the enemy of the separation of powers and diffuse power, and insists on one-man rule. As in America, moreover, this is unlikely to change in Britain and Canada.

Crown government might seem to be coded in the constitutional DNA of monarchies such as Britain and Canada. For Americans, however, the return to one-man rule may appear a betrayal of the Revolution and its promise of republican government. So it seemed to George Mason, who complained at the Philadelphia Convention that a popularly elected president would "degenerate" into an "elective monarchy,"[3] which was worse, he thought, than the real thing. A hereditary king like George III lacked the legitimacy conferred by voters, and therefore had to share power with the legislature. An elective president would not be so constrained, and would thus be more dangerous to liberty.

To paraphrase John Stuart Mill, he who knows only his own country knows little enough of that.[4] One who seeks to understand American government should therefore also know something of other political systems, especially those of similar societies such as Britain and Canada. Where there are similarities, one looks for an explanation beyond the realm of constitutional law from something outside the system, such as a common British heritage in the eighteenth century, the rise of democracy in the nineteenth century, and the growth of the regulatory state in the twentieth century. Where there are differences, one looks for evidence that one constitutional regime, more than the other, is better adapted to the demands placed upon it. That is how constitutions are evaluated. One is apt to think one lives under the best of all possible governments, but unless one is willing to put it to the test, this is little more than the prejudice of Thomas Paine's hypothetical Englishman.

AMERICA AND BRITAIN CHANGE PLACES

Everyone knows how America came to adopt the separation of powers in government. The delegates to the Philadelphia Convention who drafted the Constitution were sophisticated legal theorists. They had studied "the celebrated Montesquieu" and wisely applied the French Enlightenment philosopher's defense of the separation of powers. "When legislative power is united with executive power in a single person or in a single body of the magistracy, there is no liberty," said Montesquieu,[5] and the American Framers would follow him and protect liberty through a Constitution in which a separately elected president, Senate, and House of Representatives would each have to consent before a bill was enacted.

I tell a different story in chapter 2. The modern presidential system, with its separation of powers, was an unexpected consequence of the democratization of American politics, and not a prominent feature of the Framers' Constitution. It was a near run thing, decided only on day 105 of a 116-day convention. The delegates debated the presidential appointment process on twenty-one different days, and took more than thirty votes on the subject, with sixteen roll calls alone on how to select the president. In six of these (one unanimously), they voted for a president appointed by Congress, a system that would have resembled a parliamentary regime. Once they voted 8 to 2 for a president appointed by state legislatures. On one thing they were wholly clear: they did not want a president elected by the people. That question was put to them four times, and lost each time.

The Framers wanted a government with a much weaker separation of powers. James Madison came to Philadelphia with a proposal that came to be called the Virginia Plan, in which an elected House of Representatives would appoint senators, and the House and Senate together would appoint the president. Such a system would have more closely resembled the British Westminster system of parliamentary government, and the gridlock that characterizes Washington today would largely be absent. The party that won the White House would typically win the legislative branch, giving us the winner-take-all government of parliamentary systems.

The delegates rejected the Virginia Plan, but not to vindicate the principle of the separation of powers. What instead was at issue was the division of power between the states and the federal government, with supporters of states' rights from the smaller states and nationalists from the larger ones on opposite sides. Delegates favoring states' rights took the first trick, on the membership of the Senate. The states would appoint senators and each state, irrespective of size, would have two. States'-rights delegates feared the centralization of power in the federal government, and believed that a senate so constituted would prevent this from happening. They might have had a point.

As for the presidency, the nationalists wanted a president chosen by the people, as he would be the only person elected by voters across the country and would thus have greater legitimacy to resist encroachments by the states. Once again, however, states'-rights supporters voted this down. What they chose instead was an elaborate system in which state legislatures would determine how presidential electors would be chosen, but in which the electors would not choose the president unless they gave him a majority of their votes. This, the Framers thought, would seldom happen, since they did not expect that, after George Washington, candidates with national appeal would emerge. In the case where no candidate received a majority of electoral votes, the election would be thrown to the House of Representatives, voting by state. What the Framers expected, then, was that the House would almost always choose the president, just as Madison had wanted in the Virginia Plan. Congressmen could not serve as president or sit in the cabinet, but responsibilities would be mingled and Congress would dominate the government. What the Framers envisaged was a separation of persons more than of powers.

In time all of this changed, as a consequence of the growth of political parties and political pressure to let voters elect politicians directly. Presidents came to be chosen by popular ballot, as the nationalists had wanted, rather than by electors selected by states. National candidates emerged and received a majority of electoral votes, so that after 1824 the choice of president never fell to the House. After the Seventeenth Amendment was adopted in 1913, senators were elected by popular vote; and even before this, people had voted for their state legislators with an eye on how they would pick senators. The American system of separation of powers was more an unintended by-product of the growth of democracy than the deliberate choice of the Framers.

Where one did find contemporary support for separationism was in Britain, as I note in chapter 3. The eighteenth-century Westminster system required the assent of King, House of Lords, and House of Commons to enact a bill. Over the ensuing half-century, the monarch and House of Lords lost power to the House of Commons, and by the passage of the 1832 Reform Bill the House of Commons had emerged as the dominant branch of government. A determined House of Commons could now insist on getting its way, and might require the King to appoint new peers to the House of Lords to overcome any objections from that body. Looking backward in 1867, it seemed clear to Walter Bagehot, writing in *The English Constitution,* that the "efficient secret of the English Constitution may be described as the close union, the nearly complete fusion, of the executive and legislative powers."[6] Time's arrow moved always in the direction of democracy, but while it dispatched separationism from Britain, it delivered it to America.

Naturalized citizens sometimes assert their superiority to native citizens, who did not choose their nationality. In the same way, the Canadian adoption of a Westminster system, which I discuss in chapter 4, might be thought more deliberate and voluntary than Great Britain's, for the Canadians had choices. Britons could not become Americans, but that was always an option for Canadians. They could have adopted an American separation of powers, or they could simply have moved next door when the wage differential exceeded their attachment to the monarchical principle. That possibility always weighed on one's mind, as Canadian humorist Stephen Leacock noted. He wrote of an elderly Ontario politician who announced that he would soon go to that place to which all men must go, and none returns. The politician expected some sign of emotion from his audience, but there was none—they thought he was planning to move to the States.[7]

The attraction of America was so great that it took an act of will for Canadians to resist their dangerous neighbor. In negotiating the 1871

Treaty of Washington, America sought Canada as compensation for the damage to American shipping inflicted by the Confederate raider *Alabama*, and the British (who had let the ship be built in England) would have been happy to give the country away. Only one delegate to the conference, the Canadian prime minister, stood in the way and insisted on his country's independence.

Some Canadian radicals wanted to adopt an American-style constitution, with a president and a separation of powers. Most Canadians disagreed, however. They valued the British connection and the British traditions of liberty with which they were familiar. They also feared that, were they to adopt the American presidential system, this would lead the country down the slippery slope to outright annexation by the United States. Why have a separate country, if the political principles are the same?

More than anything, Canadians were familiar with the American system of government, and didn't like what they saw. The United States had split apart in a Civil War, and Canadians thought that delegates at the Philadelphia Convention had created a nation that had become far too decentralized and unstable. They also observed the costs of the American system of separation of powers in the inefficiency of its government, and wanted none of it. In their debates, the Fathers of Canadian Confederation anticipated Bagehot, and articulated reasoned arguments for the superiority of parliamentary government. In the end, they showed how an organic constitution, created over centuries in one country, could be grafted onto another country quite different in its religious, linguistic, and social institutions. The Canadian example of a peaceful accession to independence with a Westminster system of government came to be followed by fifty countries with a combined population of more than two billion people, and that is no small thing.

THE CONVERGENCE TOWARD CROWN GOVERNMENT
Within the last twenty years political power has been centralized in the executive branch of government in America, Britain, and Canada, like a

virus that attacks different people, with different constitutions, in different countries at the same time. Something other than the different systems of government must have produced the change; and there are three plausible explanations. First, power naturally gravitates from disorganized groups (such as Congress) to a single person (such as the president). The group must struggle to get its act together; not so the single person. Second, the imperatives of the regulatory state require a large bureaucracy that is primarily responsible to the executive; the legislative branch must delegate rule-making authority to regulators whose rules are so varied and extensive that they resist legislative oversight. That leaves the executive branch, which hires the regulators, promotes and demotes them, and generally tells them what to do. Third, political campaigns have been transformed by the media, which makes rock stars of presidents and prime ministers. What all this has produced is something very close to George Mason's elective monarchy, a form of Crown government more centralized still than the personal government of George III against which the Framers had rebelled.

In chapter 5 I describe the growth of Crown government in the United States and Canada. In Canada, cabinet members now take a back seat to the political advisers in the Prime Minister's Office, who are responsible solely to the prime minister; and the civil service is centralized around a Privy Council Office, with whose head prime ministers plan their agendas. In the United States power has been centralized in the presidency, even more than in Canada. The separation of powers, which was meant to restrict the president's authority, has instead served to shield him from congressional oversight. With the moral authority of the only person elected by the country as a whole and a fixed term of office, a president can make laws by regulation and unmake them by refusing to enforce the law, with an independence from Congress that prime ministers could never have from Parliament. The president also has what prime ministers lack, the power to begin or continue a war without regard to the wishes of the legislature.

In the first five chapters, which form Part I of this book, I describe the historical evolution of the constitutions of America, Britain, and

Canada, and their recent convergence around a strong executive power. In the five chapters of Part II, I discuss the dangers this might pose, and the manner in which parliamentary regimes are better equipped to preserve peaceful, ordered, and good democratic government.

THE PITFALLS OF PRESIDENTIALISM

Echoing Montesquieu, James Madison thought the separation of powers a necessary bulwark of liberty: "The accumulation of all powers, legislative, executive, and judiciary, in the same hands, whether of one, a few, or many, and whether hereditary, self-appointed, or elective, may justly be pronounced the very definition of tyranny."[8] That has not been our historical experience, however, as I show in chapter 6. There are a good many more presidents-for-life than prime-ministers-for-life. For example, nearly every country of the former Soviet Union that adopted a presidential system is now an autocracy. Lithuania apart, only their parliamentary systems remain full democracies. The U.S. Constitution seemingly was not made for export. If it has not led to autocracy, is that because it is American, and not because of the separation of powers?

A democracy may more easily descend into a dictatorship when the head of government is also head of state, as he is in a presidential regime. As heads of government, presidents are the most powerful officials in their countries. As heads of state, they are also their countries' ceremonial leaders, and command the loyalty and respect of all patriots. Not so in a parliamentary system, which keeps the two functions separate. Prime ministers are not heads of state and do not symbolize the nation. The difference, as I explain in chapter 7, is protective of liberty in parliamentary regimes.

Parliamentary systems also have safety valves that presidential systems lack. Presidents have a fixed term; prime ministers may be turfed out at any time by a majority in the House of Commons. Presidents are largely immunized from parliamentary accountability; prime ministers must face Parliament and respond to questions from the Opposition on a daily basis when Parliament is in session and the prime minister is in the country. In chapter 8 I discuss how these differences help presidents who would become dictators, and also how they bring a different kind of leader to power. A president may be a demagogue, unskilled in debate, impatient and vexed when questioned, cocooned from the public. A successful prime minister is a very different sort of person. He must be thick-skinned, and able to tolerate catcalls in Parliament and on the hustings. He, more than presidents, is assisted by a sense of humor and wit. Delusions of Gaullist grandeur are fatal for prime ministers, but can be an advantage for presidents.

The separation of powers in presidential regimes is thought to serve two purposes. By placing a check on the power of a president, it is said to protect liberty; and by subjecting legislation to the scrutiny of three different branches of government, it screens out bad laws. As I show in chapter 9, however, the deadlocks produced by divided government in a presidential regime may encourage a power-seeking president to disregard the legislature and rule by decree. The claim about better government is similarly suspect. While separationism might prevent bad laws from being enacted, it also impedes the repeal of bad laws. The choice is between *ex ante* screening, before a law is enacted in a presidential regime, and *ex post* reversibility thereafter in a parliamentary one, and I argue that the advantage lies with Britain and Canada.

Presidential regimes lend themselves to would-be dictators, and alarmists might perceive a fatal tendency to dictatorial, one-man rule in the United States. There is little reason to expect that to happen in the near future, since the democratic traditions of the United States remain among the strongest in the world. Nevertheless, any predictions about the shape of American politics twenty to forty years hence are speculative, and in the last chapter I examine three ways that strong presidentialism might turn into an even stronger form of executive governance: through the criminalization of political differences, through changes in the Supreme Court, and through demographic changes. I conclude with a brief look at how the balance might be tilted back in the direction of congressional government.

The Framers' Constitution was an improvement over the contemporary British constitution. However, neither it nor the modern American Constitution is an improvement over the British or Canadian constitutions of today. When compared with presidential government, modern parliamentary systems more strongly hold misbehaving leaders to account before a House of Commons. Since it lacks a separation of powers, parliamentary government also avoids what Woodrow Wilson identified as the inconveniences of divided government. American government "lacks promptness because its authorities are multiplied," he wrote. It "lacks wieldiness because its processes are roundabout, lacks efficiency because its responsibility is indistinct and its action without competent direction."[9] Parliamentary systems have few of these difficulties, and at the same time better protect political freedom. An American is apt to think that his Constitution uniquely protects liberty. The truth is almost exactly the reverse, and this calls for a reconsideration of the limits of executive power in America, not for the purpose of vindicating the principle of separation of powers, but rather to expand congressional power.

Among historians, a developing historical literature examines the family resemblances in ideology, culture, customs, and architecture among countries on either side of the Atlantic.[10] This book is in that tradition, since it discusses constitution making in three similar North Atlantic countries, each of which looked over its shoulder to see what the others were doing. In recent years, however, American constitutional scholars have shown little attention to or understanding of the parliamentary governments of Britain and Canada. This is not surprising. Like them, we are all patriots first and philosophers second. That is just as it should be, and Americans will rightfully resist an argument that their country should adopt the parliamentary regimes of other countries (a constitutional impossibility, in any event). However, one need not look to other countries for models on how to resist Crown government, since the

Framers wanted a form of congressional government, and would have been shocked by the rise of George Mason's elective monarchy. Fidelity to their intentions and to the form of government they wished for America would further the cause of freedom.

THE AMERICAN PRESIDENT

We are not indeed constituting a British Government,
but a more dangerous monarchy, an elective one.

—GEORGE MASON

The delegates who met in Philadelphia in the summer of 1787 drafted Article II of the Constitution, which as amended governs modern presidential elections. What they had in mind was a different form of government than our present one, with a weaker separation of powers between the executive and legislative branches and with very different ideas about presidential elections. If one examines what the delegates said, as Lincoln did in his 1860 Cooper Union speech, one quickly discovers that separationism was not the principal theme of the Philadelphia Convention, and that the delegates very nearly adopted a system not unlike the parliamentary regimes of Great Britain and Canada.

The delegates were divided between coalitions of nationalists and states'-rights supporters, and what they finally agreed on was a compromise, with something for everyone. As the nationalists had wanted, the new Constitution would be much more centralized than the Articles of Confederation that had governed the country from 1781 to 1789. The states'-rights delegates won most of the other points, however, and the Constitution would be much more decentralized than the nationalists had proposed. States would appoint senators, who would serve at the heart of the federal government, the better to resist its encroachments on states' rights; state legislatures would determine the method by which the president would be appointed, and in the republic's early years most states simply picked presidential electors themselves. The delegates also expected that the choice of president would generally fall to the House of Representatives, with each state delegation getting one vote. Such a system could and did give rise to sectional conflict, with states disagreeing among themselves over slavery and tariffs. What one wouldn't have expected to see was the deadlock within the federal system apparent today. People today might support the principle of separation of powers for a variety of reasons, but fidelity to the intentions of the Framers isn't one of them.

Getting the history right matters to originalists who take the intent of the delegates as the touchstone of constitutional interpretation.[1] When confronted with a constitutional problem, a growing number of federal judges have begun to look for guidance from the Framers. Their Constitution should be our Constitution, they say. Originalism remains controversial, however, and among those who reject it, some assert that it is impossible to derive a single (or even any) meaning from the Framers' deliberations, given the fractious nature of the debates, the sharp conflicts among the various coalitions, and the many times the delegates changed their minds. It is at times indeed difficult to say what they meant. But it is not impossible, as I show here; and sometimes it's not difficult at all.

Besides, the debates are so fascinating—so much the leading documents of American government—that they more than repay the effort to study them. They have the high drama of an extended argument among an extraordinary group of politically astute and educated leaders who did not know what the outcome of the debate would be. Would a unified country emerge from the Convention? Would the country fall apart, divided into separate sections, or even return to Britain? Would the American Revolution itself be undone? There are other documents from the Founding era—the Federalist Papers, the debates in state conventions held to ratify the new Constitution—but these are very much of secondary interest. The Federalist Papers were seldom read outside of New York; the principal essays were written by two people, James Madison and Alexander Hamilton, who had not gotten the constitution they wanted but who accepted it as better than nothing. Nor do the ratifying conventions provide great guidance. What the Framers had proposed at their Convention was a take-it-or-leave-it constitution that the ratifying conventions could only adopt or reject, without amendments. And since rejecting it would be so devastating, that was not on the cards.

THE CONVENTION

The delegates who gathered in Philadelphia were, in the popular imagination, a set of brilliant political philosophers who produced what a hundred years later Gladstone called "the most wonderful work ever struck off by the brain and purpose of man."[2] For the British prime minister, the delegates were supreme political theorists who produced a compelling system of government to rival that of Westminster. While taking a rather more sober view of things, many modern accounts of the Philadelphia Convention emphasize the high theory of republican government. But theorists among the delegates, people such as Madison and Hamilton, were few in number; and when the Convention was over both men left Philadelphia less than happy with the result. It was better than the alternative of the Articles of Confederation, but was nevertheless a missed opportunity.

The Constitution was more the work of lesser-known men who possessed a larger fund of practical wisdom and, compared to Madison, a much greater ability to compromise. And compromise was what was needed, for there was nothing like a consensus about the form the government would take. In particular, there was no agreement about the scope of executive power. Pennsylvania's James Wilson remarked, "This subject has greatly divided the House, and will also divide people out of doors. It is in truth the most difficult of all on which we have had to decide."[3]

The delegates sought to create something entirely new, a charter for a republican government to be formed from states loosely united under the Articles of Confederation. For models they had nothing wholly serviceable. They prized the virtues they saw in the ancient world, but saw a hodgepodge of confusing institutions when they examined the constitutions of republican Greece and Rome. They admired the constitution of Great Britain, with which they were more familiar, but had fought a revolution to replace it; and most thought it ill-suited for what they called the genius of America. They had the Articles of Confederation, which provided for what passed as a central government; but these had proved unsatisfactory, and the purpose of the Convention was to correct their defects. Finally, they had the constitutions of the states, most of which were reformed during the Revolution; but they were of limited assistance in designing a constitution for a compound republic composed of all the states.

What nearly all of the delegates did know was that they had come to the end of the line with the Articles of Confederation. These had created a "firm league of friendship" among sovereign, free, and independent states, with the thinnest of central governments. Congress could not levy taxes directly on the people, nor could it compel the states to pay their share of national expenses. It could issue paper currency—which rapidly proved almost worthless, giving us the expression "not worth a Continental." Europe today is more of a country than America was under the Articles.

At their Convention, the delegates complained that government under the Articles had broken down. Important decisions were left unmade, and it was increasingly difficult to assemble a quorum in Congress. Whatever government might exist, said Alexander Hamilton, it was "dissolving or already dissolved."[4] At a critical moment, when the delegates seemed hopelessly divided, the country's leading deist, Benjamin Franklin, suggested that they appoint a chaplain and pray for guidance.[5]

Had the Convention adjourned at that point, the country might easily have broken apart.[6] Its fate, recalled Gouverneur Morris, hung by a hair.[7]

It was also difficult to raise funds for investment projects because the states had treated creditors shabbily, and the country was in a depression. "In every point of view," wrote Madison in 1785, "the trade of this Country is in a deplorable Condition."[8] Perhaps things were not quite so desperate as that,[9] but what the delegates saw when they looked about were states with devalued currencies and massive deficits. So deep was the crisis, so profound the financial problems, and so great the unwillingness of politicians to deal with them, that the economic difficulties were every bit as bad as those facing America today.

The problem, the Framers thought, came from the mercenary new men who now inhabited the statehouses in America. A good part of the colonial elite, especially from the northern states, had been exiled by the Revolution; many of those who were left served as delegates at the Philadelphia Convention or in the Continental Congress in New York. That left what the delegates saw as a second string of ill-educated populists to serve in the state legislatures.[10] What would be needed, some thought, was a strong national government to trump them and correct these ills.

Very early in the Convention the delegates made several procedural decisions that importantly affected the outcome. On May 25, the first day, they unanimously elected Washington as its president, and appointed Virginia's George Wythe, America's first law professor, to chair a committee to draft the rules of procedure. Adopted on May 28, the rules impressed upon the delegates the solemnity of their undertaking. A delegate wishing to speak was asked to stand and address the president; and while one delegate was speaking the other delegates were not to read a book or speak to each other. When the meeting was over, the delegates were to stand until the president left the room.

Crucially, the delegates agreed that votes would be taken by state, with a majority of states deciding an issue, and a majority of delegates within each state deciding how the state would vote. A quorum was set at seven states, so that four states might in theory decide an issue. Nationalists from the relatively populous Pennsylvania delegation objected to giving an equal voice to small-state delegations, but were persuaded by the Virginians that this was the only way to get everyone on board.[11] After this, many of the most contentious issues at the Convention were foreordained. Because small states outnumbered large states, states' rights would be protected. And because issues were decided by majority vote, and not the unanimity that would have been needed to amend the Articles of Confederation, there was likely going to be a deal.

The delegates also decided to hold their deliberations in Committee of the Whole, which freed them from most parliamentary rules. This permitted them to return to subjects previously discussed, and undo prior resolutions. And so they came back again and again to the same question, changing their minds back and forth on how to select a president, and dropping long prepared speeches into the debates. They decided to keep their deliberations secret, and for the most part adhered to this. The only time Washington was heard to express anger was when he discovered that a set of Convention notes had been left on the floor for anyone to pick up. He kept silent about this until the end of the session, but then stood up and, like a stern headmaster, reminded everyone of the rule of confidentiality. "I know not whose paper it is," he said, "but there it is" (throwing it down on the table), "let him who owns it take it." Washington bowed, took up his hat, and strode from the room "with a dignity so severe that every Person seemed alarmed."[12] No one had the courage to claim the notes.

To these procedural rules might be added a social convention that promoted amity and cooperation. Philadelphia was a smallish town of forty thousand people, and the delegates could not help but see each other socially at their homes and clubs. They might gather around the mulberry tree in Franklin's yard, or dine at the India Queen inn, the Convention's unofficial club, where many of them stayed. On Sundays they took trips together to visit Valley Forge or Bartram's Garden. At their request, Washington might join them for dinner, to elevate the tone.

Many of the delegates knew each other from past congresses, or from the Revolutionary Army. Those who had been strangers quickly fell in with each other to cut the deals that kept the Convention from falling apart.

THE DELEGATES

Virginia led the way in planning for the Convention. It appointed a delegation that included George Wythe, George Mason, James Madison, and George Washington. Mason was the author of the June 1776 Virginia Declaration of Rights, from which much of the Declaration of Independence had been cribbed. Washington was the Indispensible Man, without whom the Revolution would have failed. Having retired to Mount Vernon at a time when he might easily have assumed a dictatorship over the country, he was a world figure, regarded by his countrymen with awe.

Besides the prominent Virginians, the delegates included John Dickinson, Benjamin Franklin, Alexander Hamilton, Robert Morris, Gouverneur Morris, and James Wilson. When he learned their names, Jefferson described them as "demigods" in a letter to John Adams.[13] They included sixteen lawyers, four judges, seven politicians, four planters, and two physicians.[14] Twenty-nine of them had undergraduate degrees, including nine from Princeton, four each from Yale and William and Mary, and three each from Harvard and King's College (Columbia). Three had attended college in Great Britain, at Oxford, St. Andrews, and Glasgow. Six had been trained at the Inns of Court in London.[15] Most would have been seen as the natural aristocrats of American society, and half were on Mrs. John Jay's dinner invitation list, which was the social register of the time.[16]

That said, some of the more prominent delegates took little part in the proceedings. Wythe's wife took ill and died, and he left after a week. Franklin was 81 years old, and often had to be carried on a litter the three blocks from his home to the Convention, by prisoners from the local jail. His speeches were read for him, and he seldom spoke closely on an issue. As the Convention's elder statesman, his primary concern was to smooth over disputes and produce compromises, and this he did most effectively; but since he rowed with muffled oars, most historians have discounted his contributions. Hamilton was absent for much of the Convention and did himself no favors by freely advancing his strong conservative views. He wanted a strong national government, loathed democracy, and saw little difference between it and the kind of republic the delegates were considering. It was "pork still, with a little change of the sauce," New York's Robert Yates heard him say.[17]

Many of the delegates are deservedly obscure today. Half of them failed to make a contribution to the discussion, and some absented themselves from Philadelphia for long periods. Forrest McDonald described a group of dirt farmers, religious crackpots, and impecunious bootlickers straggling into town to represent their states.[18] "You may have been taught to respect the characters of the members of the late Convention," said George Mason.

> You may have supposed they were an assemblage of great men. There is nothing less true. From [New England] there were knaves and fools and from the states southward of Virginia they were a parcel of coxcombs and from the middle states office hunters not a few.[19]

One delegate, it seems, sold information about the proceedings to British agents.[20]

Fortunately, the politicians most opposed to tampering with the Articles stayed away from the Convention. Backwoods populists such as William Findley refused to travel to Philadelphia when told they wouldn't be reimbursed for their expenses. Radical demagogues such as John Hancock and Patrick Henry also stayed home. Henry had been appointed a delegate but declined to travel to Philadelphia, saying "I smelt a rat."[21] Samuel Adams thought himself too old to travel and stayed in Boston, where he served as president of the state senate. More than any other state, Rhode Island had cheapened its currency to benefit debtors; and no one from that state showed up. An apologetic Rhode Islander told Washington that most of the state's legislators were "licentious . . ., destitute of education, and many of them, Void of principle."[22]

THE VIRGINIA PLAN

As the delegates arrived in Philadelphia, one thing was clear to all of them, and most of all to those from Virginia: as the most populous state, the Old Dominion would play a leading role in the Convention. Virginia was the oldest overseas colony of Britain, and until the early 1780s laid claim to all the land from Kentucky to Manitoba. It supplied much of the revolutionary leadership and four of the first five presidents. Without Virginia, the American Revolution would have been an isolated revolt by Massachusetts hotheads, easily suppressed by Britain.

In addition, the impetus for the Convention had come from Virginia. Under the Articles of Confederation the national government lacked the power to regulate interstate commerce, and after the Revolution the states began to levy tariffs on each other's goods. Virginians, including George Washington and George Mason, wanted to open the Potomac up to trade, but the river lay almost entirely within the borders of Maryland, and navigation rights were disputed between the two states. A trade agreement made sense, and delegates from the two states met in Alexandria in March 1785 to relax trade barriers (even though the Articles of Confederation prohibited interstate treaties of this kind).

The conference was so successful that, when it ended at Mount Vernon, the Virginia delegates proposed a further conference of all thirteen states. This was held in Annapolis in September 1785. John Dickinson from Delaware was chosen president; James Madison and Hamilton attended. Eight states stayed away, however, and five states was too small a quorum for a national agreement. A third conference would be needed, and was called for May 14, 1787, in Philadelphia. Hamilton drafted the Annapolis conference report. The delegates, he said, were unhappy with the "important defects" in the Articles of Confederation, which had rendered "the situation of the United States delicate and critical."

The Philadelphia Convention would be charged with remedying these defects, a task that would require "an exertion of the united virtue and wisdom of all the members of the Confederacy."[23]

The Virginians arrived in Philadelphia before any of the other out-of-state delegates. James Madison was there on May 5, and the rest of the Virginians arrived by May 17. A quorum of seven states was not in place until May 25. Had everyone arrived on time, the Convention would likely have begun cautiously; but having arrived early, the Virginians used the opportunity to steal a march on the other delegates. Madison later recalled that "on the arrival of the Virginia Deputies at Philada, it occurred to them that from the early and prominent part taken by that State in bringing about the Convention some initiative step might be expected from them."[24] And so they met as a group for two to three hours a day to prepare a plan for a new constitution.[25]

The first day of substantive business was May 29. The delegates arrived at the Assembly Room of the Pennsylvania State House (now Independence Hall), where eleven years before eight of them had signed the Declaration of Independence. Shuffling in, they took their places at Windsor chairs arranged by state in semicircles around a raised dais, before tables covered in green baize, in a room small enough that every delegate was visible and every ordinary conversation audible. The delegates looked about, at the room, at each other, with anxious surmise, knowing that everything for which they had struggled, as far back as the Stamp Act, had led to this place and this time, and that all their efforts might be for naught if they failed to reach an agreement.

At ten o'clock, the door was closed behind them by sentries who stood watch to ensure that none but the delegates could enter. Washington had been unanimously elected the president of the Convention, and he ascended the dais to open the session. James Madison took a seat next to him to take notes of the proceedings. Stately, plump Edmund Randolph, Virginia's governor, stood up, and Washington nodded at him to speak. What Randolph would read came to be known as the Virginia Plan. It proposed scrapping the Articles of Confederation, and the debate over it dominated the Convention for its first six weeks.

Randolph was a member of one of Virginia's most prominent families, and a second cousin of Thomas Jefferson. He was bluff and well-spoken, but seemed almost apologetic as he began to read off the resolutions the Virginians had prepared. The plan was not from Randolph's pen, but principally from that of Madison, the man at Washington's side, and Randolph did not wish to claim the credit for drafting it. But Madison was halting in speech and spoke so lowly that his voice was often lost. At five and a half feet, he was a full head shorter than George Washington. Clearly, he was not the man to present a plan for a wholly new constitution for the country.

Few of the other delegates were prepared for the Virginia Plan. When Congress had joined the call for the Convention, in February 1787, it proposed that the delegates meet "for the sole and express purpose of revising the Articles of Confederation and reporting to Congress and the several legislatures such alterations and provisions therein as shall when agreed to in Congress and confirmed by the states render the federal government adequate to the exigencies of Government and the preservation of the Union."[26] This was a call to tinker with the Articles, nothing more. Some delegates argued that, since it exceeded the mandate from Congress, the Virginia Plan was out of order. As the Convention continued, bitter words were exchanged. Several delegates threatened to walk out in protest, and some indeed did so.

Nevertheless, the delegates continued talking. The prestige of the Virginia delegation, and the presence of Washington, made it difficult to ignore the Virginia Plan. It was also that which had sorely been lacking: a plan, a serious attempt to amend the defects of the Articles of Confederation, prepared by the thoughtful James Madison. And it was backed by a core of nationalists from Virginia and Pennsylvania, the two largest states.

Madison had outlined his thoughts about government in an essay entitled *Vices of the Political System of the United States*, written a month before the Convention began,[27] and the imprint of the essay can be seen throughout the Virginia Plan. The problem, he argued, was that government under the Articles was both too decentralized and too democratic. The ultimate authority rested with the states, and the decisions of Congress were little more than recommendations. In addition, state governments were excessively democratic, and the honest delegate too often "the dupe of a favorite leader, veiling his selfish views under the professions of public good, and varnishing his sophistical arguments with the glowing colours of popular eloquence." Sadly, the voice of (ahem) "individuals of extended views, and of national pride" were silenced by the demagogues.

For an answer to these ills, Madison borrowed two ideas from David Hume, whom he had studied at Princeton.[28] Hume had proposed, in a 1754 essay on the *Idea of a Perfect Commonwealth*, a highly artificial scheme of government that began with a division of Great Britain and Ireland into one hundred counties, each with one hundred parishes, and built up from there with parish meetings, county-town assemblies, county magistrates, and senators. It would be difficult to imagine anything more at odds with Hume's empiricism, with his belief that political arrangements were the product of messy historical quarrels that owed more to contingent conventions and accidental arrangements than to abstract reasoning; and one is permitted to wonder whether the essay was only half-serious, and meant in part as a satire on political theorizing—a possibility that surely would have escaped the humorless Madison.

And yet Hume's essay was something more than a satire. He believed that some constitutions were better than others,[29] and that speculations about the best kind of constitution were "the most worthy curiosity of any the wit of man can possibly devise." It would be foolish to propose radical changes to existing, benign constitutions, like that of Britain, he thought. But what if the opportunity to start afresh arose elsewhere, "either by a dissolution of some old government, or by the combination of men to form a new one, in some distant part of the world"? When Madison read this, he must have heard Hume speaking to him directly.

The time had come to dissolve the old government, and the combination of delegates in distant Philadelphia now had the responsibility to devise a new one.

In his essay, Hume had suggested two principles of constitutional governance, both of which Madison thought admirably suited to America. The first was a theory of refinement, or *filtration*, of representatives, in which higher levels of representatives would be chosen by those at lower levels, rather than directly elected by the people. Ordinary voters would elect local representatives, who would then elect a higher level of representatives, and so on up the ladder. Madison adopted the filtration theory in his *Vices* essay, which envisaged "a process of elections" designed to ensure that the most senior places in government would be occupied by "the purest and noblest characters" in society. Such a system would "extract from the mass of the Society" those who "feel most strongly the proper motives to pursue the end of their appointment, and be most capable to devise the proper means of attaining it." In the Convention he described this as a "policy of refining the popular appointments by successive filtrations."[30]

Hume offered a second thought on democracy that Madison seized on as well. The public good is more likely to be promoted in large republics, said Hume; and Madison saw this as an argument to transfer power from the states to the *extended republic* of a national American state. Hume had turned on its head an argument that Montesquieu had made in *The Spirit of the Laws*. Montesquieu believed that republics should be small in size, because he thought that powerful interest groups would promote their private ends in large states.[31] Just the opposite, said Hume. Large republics are protected from "tumult and faction," since the very size of the country would make it harder for factions or interest groups to unite in a common plan. "The parts are so distant and remote, that it is very difficult, either by intrigue, prejudice, or passion, to hurry them into any measures against the public interest."[32]

Madison had seen corrupt voters back in Orange County, Virginia, and experienced the turbulence of small-state politicians in the state's

House of Delegates. He expected something better from a national American government, and eagerly adopted Hume's defense of extended republics. With Hume, he recognized that a well-organized state would seek to prevent a majority from oppressing a minority; and this, he thought, a large state could do more easily than a small one. Madison wrote in his essay that in an extended republic,

> *the Society becomes broken into a greater variety of interests, of pursuits, of passions, which check each other, whilst those who may feel a common sentiment have less opportunity of communication and concert. It may be inferred that the inconveniences of popular States contrary to the prevailing Theory, are in proportion not to the extent, but to the narrowness of their limits.*

Madison had added a wrinkle to Hume's theory. Hume had thought that a majoritarian faction could never assemble in a large state. Madison agreed with this, but said that it wasn't the size of the state that prevented this; rather, it was the multiplicity of the factions, and their ability to check each other.[33]

Madison dropped the extended republic theory into a speech he made to the Convention in answer to Connecticut's Roger Sherman. As a states'-rights supporter, Sherman had wanted state legislatures, and not the voters, to choose members of the House of Representatives, and as a nationalist Madison opposed this. In a large nation, argued Madison, members of the lower house might safely be elected by the people; there is a danger of majoritarian oppression, but this is less likely in an extended republic.

> *The only remedy is to enlarge the sphere, & thereby divide the community into so great a number of interests & parties, that in the 1st place a majority will not be likely at the same moment to have a common interest separate from that of the whole or of the minority; and in the 2d*

place, that in case they shd have such an interest, they may not be so apt to unite in the pursuit of it.[34]

That gives us two methods of dealing with the problems of democracy—filtration and extended republics—and as political scientist E. E. Schattschneider noted, this might seem like one method too many.[35] If democracy is not to be feared in an extended republic, why should presidents and senators be filtered through appointment by elected representatives, and not directly elected by the people? This was a point that supporters of democracy would grasp in time, but Madison was not yet one of them.[36] Instead, he thought the two strategies would reinforce each other, and that both were necessary.

The Virginia Plan incorporated Madison's filtration principle: the idea that superior men will reach the exalted seats of power when the upper legislative ranks are appointed by lower bodies, and not by the people. While providing for a formal separation of powers between the branches, the plan proposed that the legislature appoint the executive. The "first" or lower house, today's House of Representatives, would be popularly elected, and would be "the grand depository of the democratic principle of the government," according to George Mason. "It was, so to speak, to be our House of Commons."[37] The second or higher branch, our Senate, would be coequal in power, but its members would be selected by the first branch, from a list of nominees provided by the state legislatures. Together, the two branches would elect the president, called the "national executive." This was spelled out in the plan's Resolution Seven:

> *Resolved that a National Executive be instituted; to be chosen by the National Legislature for the term of ___ years, to receive punctually at stated times, a fixed compensation for the services rendered, in which no increase or diminution shall be made so as to affect the Magistracy, existing at the time of increase or diminution, and to be ineligible a second time; and that besides a general authority to execute the*

National laws, it ought to enjoy the Executive rights vested in Congress by the Confederation.[38]

Had the Virginia Plan been adopted, America would have had an essentially parliamentary system. The crucial power would lie in the House of Representatives, which would appoint the members of the Senate, and which, together with the Senate, would appoint the president. A powerful lower house could be expected to appoint a president subservient to its wishes, not one likely to defy it.

Resolution Seven also would have limited the president to a single term. That might have seemed an uncontroversial fetter on the office, since term limits were a feature of the Virginia Constitution (which Madison, along with Mason, had drafted); and governors are still term-limited in Virginia. However, the restriction expressed a concern about presidential power, even beyond the filtration principle.

When compared to the Constitution that the delegates finally adopted, the Virginia Plan would have limited the president's power in yet another way. The Constitution grants the president the power to veto bills for any or no reason, subject to an override by a two-thirds vote of Congress. In Resolution Eight of the Virginia Plan, however, the presidential veto power was shared with a quasi-judicial Council of Revision.

Resolved, that the Executive and a convenient number of the National Judiciary, ought to compose a council of revision with authority to examine every act of the National Legislature before it shall operate, & every act of a particular Legislature before a Negative thereon shall be final; and that the dissent of the said Council shall amount to a rejection, unless the Act of the National Legislature be again passed, or that of a particular Legislature be again negatived by ___ of the members of each branch.[39]

The idea of a president sharing his veto power with members of the Supreme Court will seem strange to us.[40] It made sense to Madison, because he did not have a thick conception of executive power or of a separation of powers in which the president might routinely oppose the will of Congress. He did think the veto might be employed to strike down the debtor relief schemes he feared, "those unwise & unjust measures which constituted so great a portion of our calamities."[41] Nevertheless, the structure of the Virginia Plan would not lead one to expect this to happen very frequently, for the reasons Madison gave in his *Vices* essay. Pro-debtor factions would be weaker in an extended republic than in state governments, and the appointed Senate would wisely constrain immoderate measures from the House in an application of Madison's filtration theory.

If Madison wanted judges on the Council of Revision, it was because he saw the veto more as a judicial than a political act, to be employed when the legislature overstepped its constitutional bounds. Maryland's Luther Martin recognized that the courts would rule on the constitutionality of legislation,[42] but the doctrine of judicial review lay in the future, and what Madison saw in its place was the Council of Revision.

Madison's Council of Revision was not adopted. Instead, the delegates compromised on a full veto power, exercisable in any case of political disagreement, but one that a supermajority in Congress could override. Nevertheless, the president's veto power was understood in constitutional terms for much of the nineteenth century. Madison gave an example of this in his last act before leaving the presidency, vetoing legislation for internal improvements because he thought the federal government's commerce power did not include the power to build roads and canals.[43] Similarly, near the end of the century, Grover Cleveland vetoed a farm relief bill for which he said he could find no warrant in the Constitution.[44]

In sum, the Virginia Plan would have created a chief executive very different from the one we know today. Appointed by Congress, the president would be its creature, charged with doing its will but seemingly with little discretion about how to do so. He would have a veto over legislative acts, but this would be shared with members of the bench, and for the most part limited to passing on the constitutionality of bills. The crucial power would be vested in the House of Representatives, Mason's "House of Commons," which would appoint the members of the Senate, and which, with the Senate, would appoint the president, who would thus be doubly insulated from the people. If anything, Madison's president would have lacked the power of a modern prime minister, who typically dominates his party and Parliament.

The fear of executive misbehavior led some delegates to propose an extraordinary variation on the office: a three-man presidency. The Virginia Plan contemplated a single president, but Edmund Randolph argued that a troika could better represent what were then the three sections of the country: New England, the middle states, and the South. Besides, said Randolph, a single executive is "the foetus of monarchy."[45] Madison opposed the idea, and the Convention voted it down, but George Mason agreed with Randolph, as did another ten delegates.[46] At the end of the Convention Mason and Randolph refused to sign the Constitution, in part because they feared the power it vested in the executive.

WHY DID THEY WANT PARLIAMENTARY GOVERNMENT?

Presidential government is taken for granted by Americans. Why then were the Framers so taken with parliamentary government? The simplest answer is that this was the system they knew best. They had lived under a form of it during the colonial period, with royal governors and elected assemblies, and saw it from afar in Britain. And while they might have abhorred government *from* Westminster before the American Revolution, once it was over they fell over themselves in praise of the government *of* Westminster.

Conservatives such as Hamilton, Dickinson, and South Carolina's Charles Pinckney confessed their admiration of Britain's constitutional monarchy,[47] and even their opponents saw the virtues of the British system. "There is a natural inclination in mankind to Kingly Government," observed Franklin.[48] Only a republican system of government would do for the United States, said Randolph; otherwise, he said, he might well be prepared to adopt the British system in America.[49] North Carolina's Hugh Williamson saw an American monarchy as inevitable,[50] and some delegates, including Hamilton and Gouverneur Morris, might have welcomed this.[51] Maryland's John Mercer copied out a list of twenty delegates who, he laughingly said, favored an American monarchy. Mercer was an opinionated 28-year-old who saw monarchists under his bed, but some delegates took him seriously.[52] As historian Gordon Wood noted, monarchy prevailed almost everywhere else, and "we shall never understand events of the 1790s until we take seriously, as contemporaries did, the possibility of some sort of monarchy developing in America."[53]

The magnetic pull of parliamentary government may be seen in the constitutions the states adopted immediately after the Revolution. Save for Connecticut, all of the states reformed their governments, and in nearly every case the new constitution featured a governor chosen by the legislature. The most influential state constitution, and the first one to be adopted, was that of Virginia; it provided for a governor, or chief magistrate, to be chosen annually by joint ballot of both houses of the legislature.[54] Only in New York, Massachusetts, and New Hampshire were governors elected directly by the people.

Many constitutions, like Virginia's, formally provided that the legislative, executive, and judicial powers were to be separate, and that legislators could not serve as governors. This, however, was the thinnest kind of separation of powers, one that scarcely deserves its name. In every state but New York the legislature appointed an executive council that could countermand the governor's decisions. "The Executives of the States," noted Madison, "are in general little more than Cyphers; the legislatures omnipotent."[55] For the Framers, then, parliamentary government was the default position.

Some of the Framers wanted a parliamentary government for a reason that seems very dated today. If a president were to be popularly elected, would voters know much about a candidate from outside their state? "Of the affairs of Georgia," said Madison, "I know as little as those of Kamskatska."[56] That was an argument for a president appointed by Congress, said Sherman, since legislators would know the presidential candidates better than the voters would.[57] All this would soon change, and indeed was changing, with advances in transportation and communication technology.[58] On August 22, 1787, inventor John Fitch made the first successful trial of a steamboat on the Delaware River, in the presence of several delegates to the Convention. Nevertheless, the delegates did not foresee the rapidity of such change, or the rise of national parties, which would shortly address the problem of voter ignorance.

There were two more important reasons why many delegates opposed a democratically elected president: First, they were fearful of democracy; and second, they were apprehensive of presidential power. Put the two together, in the form of a democratically elected president, and one had the fetus of monarchy of which Randolph had complained.

Nearly all of the delegates mistrusted democracy, and given a choice between the popular election of the president and a congressional appointment, they preferred the latter. Like Madison, they liked the idea of a selection filtered by an intermediate level of elected officials. The defects of the Articles period could be traced, they thought, to an "excess of democracy,"[59] with its "turbulence and follies."[60]

Because they kept their deliberations secret, it was easier for the delegates to express a contempt for democracy that at times made them seem like French aristocrats peering through their lorgnettes at *la canaille.* Elbridge Gerry, fresh from Shays's Rebellion in western Massachusetts, observed that "the worst men get into the Legislature. Several members of that body have lately been convicted of infamous crimes. Men of indigence, ignorance and baseness, spare no pains, however dirty to carry their point against men who are superior to the artifices practiced."[61] Roger Sherman agreed. "The people . . . immediately should have as little to do as may be about the Government. They want information and are constantly liable to be misled."[62] For his part, George Mason thought that "it would be as unnatural to refer the choice of a proper character for chief Magistrate to the people, as it would, to refer a trial of colours to a blind man."[63]

Madison had spent the previous winter boning up on the republics of antiquity, a study that did nothing to reassure him about democracy. He feared "the transient impressions into which [the people] might be led," and wondered whether they might propose land reform schemes like those of the Gracchi in Republican Rome.

An increase of population will of necessity increase the proportion of those who will labour under all the hardships of life, & secretly sigh for a more equal distribution of its blessings. These may in time outnumber those who are placed above the feelings of indigence. According to the equal laws of suffrage, the power will slide into the hands of the former. No agrarian attempts have yet been made in this Country, but symptoms of a leveling spirit, as we have understood, have sufficiently appeared in a certain quarters to give notice of the future danger.[64]

What were they thinking? we are tempted to ask. Without the support of the ordinary people they now denigrated, America would not have won its independence a few years before. But the patriot's passionate attachment to absolute liberty during the American Revolution had led to lawlessness and violence, and while this was condoned (and even encouraged when directed against Loyalists), it was quite another thing when the mob turned its attention to the new American governments.

Serious rioting broke out in many of the major American cities in the 1780s. The Revolution had clothed public protests in a mantle of legitimacy, and state authorities, who had relied on extralegal groups during the Revolution, were reluctant to resist the same groups when the war was over.[65] Knowing this, the delegates feared that what popular suffrage would produce would mirror the Massachusetts election of May 1787, when conservative Governor James Bowdoin had lost his bid for reelection because he had called up the militia to suppress Shays's Rebellion. Madison told the delegates that "the insurrections in Massachusetts admonished all the States of the danger to which they were exposed."[66]

In the midst of their deliberations, the delegates were treated to a vivid example of mob rule when an elderly woman was stoned not five blocks from their meeting place. Know as the "Widow Korbmacher," she had first been set upon on May 5, before the delegates arrived, by a mob suspecting her to be a witch. On July 10 the crowd struck again, shouting insults, carrying her through the streets, and pelting her with stones. She died of her injuries on July 18,[67] the day after the delegates voted 9 to 1 against the popular election of the president.[68]

Some delegates knew mob violence at first hand. In 1779, lawyer James Wilson had narrowly escaped from a gang of rioters after he successfully defended Loyalists whose property had been seized. The mob had been whipped up by Pennsylvania's populist governor, who himself lived in a confiscated Loyalist house. Wilson barricaded himself in his home, two blocks from Independence Hall, with twenty or so of his colleagues (including two delegates to the future Philadelphia Convention, Robert Morris and Thomas Mifflin). The mob was in the process of aiming a cannon at the house when it was dispersed by cavalry led by the military commandant of Philadelphia, Benedict Arnold. Six people died in the affair, but the rioters were afterward pardoned. Wilson had to flee Philadelphia for a few weeks, and his house came to be called "Fort Wilson."[69]

The fear of democracy was especially pronounced when the subject of a popularly elected president arose. Roger Sherman thought that "an Independence of the Executive on the supreme Legislative, was . . . the very essence of tyranny."[70] Similarly, George Mason argued that "if strong and extensive powers are vested in the Executive, and that Executive consists only of one person, the government will of course degenerate (for I will call it a degeneracy) into a monarchy."[71] What delegates feared was that a president elected by the people would threaten liberty more than would a hereditary monarch who lacked the legitimacy conferred by a popular election. "We are not indeed constituting a British Government," said Mason, "but a more dangerous monarchy, an elective one."[72]

Sherman wanted Congress to impose severe limits on a president's authority. The president, he said, should be nothing more than the legislature's agent. His job would be to execute the laws passed by the legislature, without exercising much (or any) discretion about how this was done.[73] This was a theory of separation of powers, though not one now familiar to us. The legislature would make the laws, but not apply them; the executive would apply them, but not make them; the separation of the two powers would preserve liberty and the rule of law.[74]

This was an old-fashioned view of executive authority. A hundred years earlier, a more modern John Locke had argued that the executive should have broader powers. Under the royal prerogative, the King had the discretion to interpret or even vary legislation when the public good so demanded; Locke thought this a valuable right, since legislators are not "able to foresee, and provide by laws, for all that may be useful to the community."[75] However, Sherman and other Framers hearkened back to even earlier fears of the prerogative originating with the English Civil War, and parliamentary jealousy of the use Charles I had made of the prerogative to dissolve Parliament and rule autocratically.

Sherman's views about the dangers of such a prerogative were those of a member of a "country" party, in contradistinction to a "court" party, with the distinction between the two derived from the court and country parties of early modern British history.[76] During the English Civil War, the court party favored the Crown prerogative, at the expense of Parliament; the country party sought to restrict the royal prerogative, and saw Parliament as the guarantor of English liberties.

The two parties also differed on the need for civic virtue in a republic. Country party members thought that republican government could not be preserved unless the citizens had a disinterested desire to promote the public good, shorn of any attachment to their private or factional interests. "Cabal," "corruption," and "faction," where private interest trumped the public good, were seen as mortal ills for a state.[77] By contrast, court party members scoffed at the idea of a special kind of republican virtue.

With Hume they agreed that "all plans of government, which suppose great reformation in the manners of mankind, are plainly imaginary."[78]

Apart from Sherman, country party members likely included Elbridge Gerry of Massachusetts; John Lansing and Robert Yates of New York; Benjamin Franklin and Jared Ingersoll of Pennsylvania; Gunning Bedford and Richard Bassett of Delaware; Luther Martin, Daniel Jennifer, and John Mercer of Maryland; Virginia's Edmund Randolph and George Mason; Hugh Williamson of North Carolina; Pierce Butler and Charles Cotesworth Pinckney of South Carolina; and Abraham Martin and William Few of Georgia.[79] The court party was represented by Hamilton; Gouverneur Morris, Robert Morris, and James Wilson of Pennsylvania; and John Rutledge of South Carolina.[80]

Madison may also be counted as a member of the court party at the Convention. His *Vices* essay argued that self-interest would blind voters to the common good. "Place three individuals in a situation wherein the interest of each depends on the voice of the others, and give to two of them an interest opposed to the rights of the third? Will the latter be secure?" As an answer, Madison devised a constitutional regime whose purpose was to blunt the majoritarian excesses of an unconstrained democracy. In Federalist Paper No. 51, Madison famously expanded on the idea that republican virtue would not suffice. Men are not republican angels, he said, but self-interested seekers of private gain, and government should channel self-interest in such a way that it serves the public good. "Ambition must be made to counteract ambition," so that the overweening pursuit of advantage by one group is checked by other groups in the competition for power.

In general, country party members wanted a relatively weak executive and opposed a popularly elected president, while court party members preferred a president elected by the people, recognizing that this would clothe him with greater political legitimacy. But the distinction between the two parties blurs over an influential group of delegates, including Washington, who adhered to country party ideas about republican virtue, but who nevertheless wanted a strong national government—and who, sooner or later, saw a popularly elected president as a way to strengthen the national government.[81] And then there was Madison, a court party nationalist whose filtration principle nevertheless led him to propose a congressionally appointed president. How he and country party nationalists such as Washington were led to support the method of electing presidents stipulated in Article II of the Constitution, and what they understood this to mean, is one of the greatest and least understood dramas of the Convention, and of American government.

JAMES WILSON'S MAN OF THE PEOPLE

The delegates came from very different backgrounds. Some were conservative, some not; some were rich, some not. Surprisingly, it was the conservative or wealthy delegates—Hamilton, James Wilson, Gouverneur Morris, and John Dickinson—who wanted a president elected by the people; the more republican delegates, whom one would have expected to be most sympathetic to popular elections—Roger Sherman, George Mason, and John Rutledge—sought an appointed executive. As Hamilton observed, "the members most tenacious of republicanism . . . were as loud as any in declaiming against the vices of democracy."[82]

James Wilson had most cause to fear the "excesses of democracy," after the "Battle of Fort Wilson." Like Hamilton, Wilson wanted a strong central government; unlike Hamilton, Wilson sincerely believed in popular sovereignty, and subscribed to that most benign of legal fictions, the idea that in America, sovereignty vests in the people.[83] Of all the delegates, he came closest to championing the present constitutional regime, one with a popular election of members of both houses of Congress, as well as the president. He had signed the Declaration of Independence and served on the Supreme Court, but deserves to be remembered principally for his role at the Convention.[84]

What Wilson had recognized, before anyone else, was how a democratically elected president would strengthen the strong national government he yearned to see. An elected president would be the only member of the government chosen by all the people of the United States, and would provide the leadership to resist parochial parties from different states. That was not a politic thing to say before the defenders of states' rights at the Convention, but Wilson could be more candid at the Pennsylvania ratifying convention later that year. The president, he said, would be "THE MAN OF THE PEOPLE," and as such would "consider himself as not particularly interested for any [one part of the United States], but will watch over the whole with paternal care and affection."[85]

Wilson recognized that, for most delegates, a direct election of the president was a bridge too far. Nevertheless, the idea of democracy might be made more palatable if presidential electors were interposed between the president and the people; what Wilson proposed was the electoral college: Voters would elect members of the college, who would then choose the president. This was a clever method of addressing the fears of democracy, since it suggested that the electors might exercise an independent judgment if the voters chose poorly. However, Wilson's motion was defeated 7 to 2 in roll call 11,[86] with only Pennsylvania and Maryland supporting it. The delegates then voted 8 to 2 for a president appointed by the legislature.[87] Wilson had failed, but over the course of the Convention he and his allies would create a minority coalition of nationalists who supported a strong presidency.[88]

THE STATES'-RIGHTS DELEGATES COUNTERATTACK

A second group of delegates, led by Elbridge Gerry, opposed the Virginia Plan's proposal of a congressionally appointed president. These were states'-rights supporters who were troubled by the degree of centralization implicit in both Wilson's democratically elected president and Madison's congressionally appointed president, and who wanted the states to appoint the president.[89] A congressional appointment, argued Gerry, would lead to "corruption."[90] For country party members, this was a code word for pampered courtiers trading favors at the feet of a monarch, and Gerry said the Virginia Plan would result in the same kind of underhanded deals between the president and legislators. A state-appointed presidency, Gerry argued, would give us better presidents than those whom the people would elect, in keeping with Madison's filtration principle.

Very early in the Convention the states'-rights delegates watered down the Virginia Plan, with a unanimous vote on June 7 for a Senate appointed by state legislatures.[91] This had been proposed by John Dickinson as a means of giving states a voice in the federal government. This was also, he said, an application of Madison's filtration theory, since state legislatures could be expected to choose more wisely than voters in a popular election. Only Madison, still wedded to the Virginia Plan, spoke against this. The system of state legislatures appointing the Senate continued until 1913, when the Seventeenth Amendment instituted the popular election of senators. Dickinson had wanted to empower the states; by reversing his system of appointment, the Seventeenth Amendment is thought to have shifted power from the states to the federal government.[92]

The small-state delegates pressed their advantage a week later, when William Paterson presented the New Jersey Plan to the delegates.[93] The Virginians had caucused behind the scenes to produce a plan that shocked the small-state delegates, who thought it would result in an excessively strong national government. In response, the small-state delegates had caucused privately too, to produce a rival scheme of government. The New Jersey Plan was a bombshell. It modified the Articles of Confederation, but unlike the Virginia Plan did not junk them. Congress would have a taxing power, but would continue as a unicameral house, with each state given a single vote. When Paterson introduced his plan, John Dickinson turned to Madison and said, "you see the consequence of pushing things too far."[94] There were now two radically different plans on the floor, and the debate between them would consume the deliberations and passions of the delegates for the next month.

To resolve the crisis, on July 2 the delegates appointed a Committee of Eleven, with one member from each state in attendance at the time, to settle on a compromise. At Franklin's suggestion, the committee devised the plan of representation now found in the Constitution: representation by population in the House of Representatives, and equal representation for states in the Senate. The delegates had previously agreed that state legislatures should appoint congressional senators; now they agreed that small states should have the same representation as large states in the Senate. Delegates from the larger states objected, but were outvoted on July 7;[95] on July 16, the Convention ratified the committee's entire proposal.[96] This came to be called the Connecticut Compromise, but the label is misleading, for it was less a compromise than a defeat for nationalists from the large states.

The large-state delegates met the morning of July 17 to see whether their plans for a Senate appointed by the House of Representatives might be salvaged, but decided that the game was lost.[97] When the Framers convened that day, the small-state delegates returned to the attack, this time against another of Madison's pet ideas, a congressional veto over state laws. On Madison's extended republic theory, the national government would be less prone to factions and interest-group inefficiencies than state governments; the Virginia Plan's Resolution Six would therefore have given Congress the power to "negative," or veto, state laws that it thought contravened the Constitution.[98] The delegates had voted this down once, on June 8;[99] but lest any doubt remain, they rejected it again on July 17.[100]

Until then there had been broad agreement that the president should be appointed by Congress. If anything, the New Jersey Plan tilted in the direction of parliamentary governance, since it reopened the question of whether there should be more than one president at a time, and would have permitted Congress to remove the president at the request of a majority of state governors.[101] Now, however, the Pennsylvanians counterattacked; Gouverneur Morris moved that the president be elected by popular suffrage. But when it came to a vote, only Pennsylvania supported the resolution.[102] Maryland's Luther Martin then proposed that the president be chosen by electors appointed by state legislatures, but delegates were still wedded to appointment by Congress, and voted 8 to 2 against, with only Delaware and Maryland in favor.[103] The delegates finally voted unanimously for a congressionally appointed president.[104] Even the dissenters had given up, and everyone must have thought that the issue was at last settled.

That afternoon, on July 17, the delegates broke early. A group of them, led by Washington, visited Gray's Ferry, where one could observe the exotic plants of Bartram's Garden, drink tea, or fish in the Schuylkill.[105] The leafy walks may have prompted reflection about the office Washington soon would hold, for two days later, on July 19, the delegates suddenly reversed themselves. On a motion by Gouverneur Morris, they unanimously agreed to reconsider the method of installing a president.

GOUVERNEUR MORRIS—THE MAN OF THE CONVENTION

Morris was a representative of the rising merchant class and a member of the court party. He was as fearful of democracy as any delegate, but now he sought to persuade country party nationalists to support the democratic election of presidents. What Morris wanted was a president who, clothed with the authority conferred by a popular election, would strengthen the central government.[106] That was not an argument that would appeal to many delegates, however. Ingeniously, Morris argued that the lower classes needed a tribune of the people, and this could only be the president. Congress would come to represent the rich and powerful, and if it could appoint the president, "legislative tyranny" would ensue. What was needed was a separation of powers between the executive and legislative branches. "If the Legislature elect," said Morris, "it will be the work of intrigue, of cabal, and of faction."[107]

Morris had cleverly sought to appeal to several constituencies among the delegates. The call for a tribune of the people would appeal to the pro-debtor crowd, who wanted a new Tribune Gracchus to redistribute wealth. Morris also sought to enlist the support of country party members with the buzzwords of intrigue and cabal. And the reference to congressional tyranny would appeal to states'-rights supporters, notably Elbridge Gerry, who had expressed fear of corrupt bargains if the legislature appointed the president.[108] Finally, Morris sought to appeal to that man of theory, James Madison, who Morris knew would hear echoes of Montesquieu in an argument for separation of powers.

The two men had known each other for some years. They did not overlap in the Continental Congress, but both were in Philadelphia in the early 1780s. For the first month of the Convention they saw little of each other. Though he was present at its start, Morris had left after a few days, not returning until July 2, when he wasted no time in making up for his absence by launching into a patronizing speech in favor of a Senate composed of American aristocrats.[109] In his brashness, he had failed to take the measure of the delegates, and Madison was especially annoyed. On July 11 he admonished Morris for continually insisting on the "political depravity of men, and the necessity of checking one vice and interest" against another.[110] It wasn't so much what Morris had said, however, as the way he had said it. Madison didn't think men were angels, but Morris had spoken like a brassy New Yorker, and this had irritated the Virginian.

Morris was everything Madison was not. The New Yorker was tall, confident, ebullient, and witty. He had lost a leg, and his right arm was withered, but this scarcely slowed him down. By contrast, Madison was a hypochondriac who outlived every other member of the Convention. He was especially shy with women, while Morris enjoyed a remarkably successful career as a rake. While the story that Morris owed his peg leg to a jump from a window to escape a jealous husband is probably apocryphal, we do know something of his many affairs, thanks to his candid diaries and correspondence. The letters that Mme Chaumont wrote to him are too heated to be quoted, sniffed a prim Morris biographer.[111] More discreetly still, Morris's granddaughter complained of the lady's "ceaseless annoyances."[112] With a touch of envy, a French diplomat described him as "*sans moeurs, et, si l'on en croit ses ennemis, sans principes.*"[113]

At the Convention Morris was the master of the strategic compromise, the adroit suggestion, the art of the deal. A Georgia delegate described him as:

one of those Genius's in whom every species of talents combine to render him conspicuous and flourishing in public debate:—He winds through all the mazes of rhetoric, and throws around him such a glare that he charms, captivates, and leads away all the senses of all who hear him.[114]

As for Madison, the Georgian recalled his scholarship, industry, sweet temper, and "great modesty."[115]

This was a trying time for Madison. When he heard of the New Jersey Plan, he had felt "serious anxiety."[116] Before the Connecticut Compromise of July 16, he and the other delegates had feared that the Convention might end in failure, and tempers had run high. Within a few days, however, the crisis had passed, and Madison seems to have made up his differences with Morris. Years later Madison remembered the New Yorker not unfondly. "To the brilliancy of his genius, [Morris] added, what is too rare, a candid surrender of his opinions, when the lights of discussion satisfied him, that they had been too hastily formed, and a readiness to aid in making the best of measures in which he had been overruled."[117] Evidently Morris had seen the need to flatter Madison, who was only too happy to receive the attention of his more sophisticated colleague.

At the same time, Morris brought Madison around to the idea of a popularly elected president. When he arrived in Philadelphia Madison had subscribed to Hume's theory of filtration, with its appointed executive, but without investing the deepest thought or feeling on the subject. A month before the Convention he confessed his uncertainties to Edmund Randolph. "A national Executive will also be necessary. I have scarcely ventured to form my own opinion yet, either of the manner in which it ought to be constituted, or of the authorities with which it ought to be clothed."[118] It was now prudent to drop Hume's filtration theory, but Madison needed a new theory to do so; and that was what Morris handed him, by invoking the separation of powers. At some level Madison must have recognized, with the Pennsylvanians, that the nationalist cause he supported would be served by a powerful president, one who could stand up to the states as American presidents have done since then. Moreover, a filtration scheme in which Congress appointed the president would make less sense to a nationalist if state-appointed senators would assist in the filtering. However, practical considerations were little more than an empty breeze to Madison, who yearned for the rock of a good hard theory. Happily, he was a supple theorist, who could amend his theories when the need arose.[119]

The penny, so carefully inserted by Morris, now dropped. Madison had authored the Virginia Plan's proposal for a congressionally appointed president, but after listening to Morris he did a nimble volte-face. As a nationalist, Madison was dismayed by the Connecticut Compromise and senators appointed by state legislatures, and as a nationalist he was now brought around to the idea of a popularly elected president. Like Morris, he recognized that a president so elected would strengthen the national government, and like Morris he veiled his argument in separationist, rather than nationalist, terms: A separation of powers between legislative, executive, and judicial powers was essential to preserve liberty, and the three branches could be separate only if they were independent of each other. "A dependence of the Executive on the Legislature, would render it the Executor as well as the maker of laws; & then according to the observation of Montesquieu, tyrannical laws may be made that they may be executed in a tyrannical manner."[120]

Morris had consolidated the nationalist faction at the Convention. Until that point the nationalists had differed among themselves about democratic elections and the presidency. Some had supported the congressionally appointed president of the Virginia Plan, others wanted a president elected by the people. Now the nationalists would present a united front in favor of a popularly elected president.

A FINAL COMPROMISE

The nationalists were not a majority, however, and Morris and his allies moved cautiously. On July 19, Connecticut's Oliver Ellsworth and Delaware's Jacob Broom proposed that the president be appointed by electors.

This was an ambiguous motion: it could have led to a motion that the electors themselves be elected by popular ballot, as James Wilson had proposed on June 2;[121] or it might be tacked on to a motion that the electors be chosen by state legislatures, as Elbridge Gerry had suggested,[122] and as Jacob Broom and Maryland's Luther Martin had proposed.[123] What Morris, Ellsworth, and Broom hoped to create was a coalition of all those opposed to congressional appointment, for they only had no use for electors.

The tactic succeeded. The motion passed 6 to 3, with only the three southernmost states holding out for a congressionally appointed president.[124] Ellsworth and Broom were states'-rights supporters, and they next moved that the electors be chosen by state legislatures. This passed 8 to 2 in roll call 183, with Madison's Virginia in dissent and Morris's Pennsylvania voting yes.[125] The Pennsylvanians had bowed to what they saw as inevitable, a states'-rights coalition that had won one trick after another that month.

This came close to the solution that the delegates eventually adopted in the Constitution's Article II, Section 1, clause 2, which specifies how state legislatures would choose electors. Under Article II, the states are permitted to let voters elect the electors, and within fifty years most states did just that. That possibility was not open to the states under roll call 183; what then would a presidency have looked like? The states would be stronger, of course. There would also be a much-weakened separation of powers, since state legislatures would appoint both the president and the Senate. The party structure of American politics would be based at the state level, and this would likely have carried over to elections for the House of Representatives. A winning coalition of states would carry all before it, and the gridlock that characterizes the federal government today would largely be absent.

In short order, the delegates had voted twice against what we understand as the separation of powers, in both cases by overwhelming margins. On July 17, in roll call 167, they had voted unanimously for a congressional appointment of the president; two days later they had voted 8 to

2, in roll call 183, for a president appointed by electors appointed by state legislatures. In both cases they had rejected the popular election of the president, and affirmed his dependence on legislatures.

That should have put an end to it. But on July 24 a Georgia delegate, arguing that it would be difficult to find capable men to serve as electors in distant states, once again moved that the president be appointed by Congress. The motion passed 7 to 4 in roll call 215, with Virginia and Pennsylvania voting no.[126]

Roll call 215 may have seemed decisive, but the delegates remained troubled, and the next day considered a proposal to split the difference. The president would be appointed by Congress for his first term, but if he sought a second term, he would be appointed by electors appointed by the states. This motion failed, seven votes to four.[127] That left the Virginia Plan on the table. On July 26 George Mason moved that the president be appointed by Congress; this again passed, 6 to 3, in roll call 225, with Washington and Madison voting no.[128]

At this point the delegates had voted six times on proposals for a congressionally appointed president. Its supporters had assembled a caucus composed of those, including Randolph, Sherman, Mason, and Charles Pinckney, who thought liberty best defended by the legislature, and who feared that a strict separation of powers would make a monarch of the president.[129] The supporters also included those, including Gerry, Sherman, and Pinckney, who simply didn't think that the people were up to the task of electing a president.[130] Rounding them out were the delegates from the three southernmost states of North and South Carolina and Georgia, who, representing slave states that opposed an end to the slave trade, had their own reasons to fear a concentration of power in the national government. They were opposed by a smaller group of states composed of Pennsylvania and (depending on who showed up that day) Maryland, Delaware, and Virginia.

The delegates now thought they were nearly done. At the end of the day they turned over the draft constitution, with its appointed president, to a Committee of Detail for fine-tuning, and adjourned for ten days.

The committee reported back to the Convention on August 6, with a draft constitution that departed significantly from the Virginia Plan, but which still retained a congressionally elected president.[131] That question, it was thought, had been settled.

It wasn't, though. On August 24, the delegates returned to the question. Daniel Carroll of Maryland, one of the two Catholics at the Convention and an ardent democrat, proposed that the president be elected by the people, and not the legislature. Only Pennsylvania and Delaware supported the motion, and it failed, nine votes to two, in roll call 355.[132] The coalitions that had been assembled for roll calls 11 and 215 continued to hold, if less strongly than before. But then Gouverneur Morris spoke up, warning of legislative tyranny if the president were dependent on the support of Congress, and proposing that the president be appointed by electors themselves elected by the people. This gained three more votes, including that of Virginia; but the motion still failed, 6 to 5, in roll call 359.[133]

A motion to postpone the issue failed, as did a motion to refer the matter to a committee of all the states. Gouverneur Morris then proposed that the president be chosen by electors, as an abstract matter. The delegates would have understood that the electors might be either democratically chosen or appointed by the states. Had the motion passed, it would have amounted to a rejection of a congressionally appointed president. However, the delegates were split 4 to 4, and the motion was taken to have failed.[134]

This was the high tide of separationism at the Convention. Morris had won Connecticut and New Jersey over to his side, but still had not assembled a winning coalition. There were now three proposals on the table: one for presidential appointment by the states, one for congressional appointment, and a third for election by the people. As can be seen in tables A.1, A.2, and A.3 of appendix A, the first two proposals secured majority support in various roll calls. Only the third, with its popularly elected president, failed to pass every time it was put to the delegates.

The delegates arrived at their final compromise two weeks later, on September 6, in what became Article II of the Constitution. Two narratives might explain how they finally settled on the manner of choosing a president. The first is that there was a last-minute conversion, in which democratic delegates persuaded their colleagues to accept a popularly elected president by appealing to the need for a separation of powers. This is the commonly accepted view of the Convention, but I think it mistaken. A fair reading of the Framers' debates (assisted by the empirical study of appendix A) reveals a different understanding of what they intended, and what they expected from the Constitution they drafted. The preferences and coalitions that emerged over the first three months of the Convention were too strong for what would have been a radical change of heart.

On August 31 the delegates referred the question of presidential elections to the Committee on Unfinished Parts, with one delegate for each state. Those who favored a democratically elected president were represented by Madison, Gouverneur Morris, Dickinson, Carroll, Rufus King of Massachusetts, and possibly Hugh Williamson of North Carolina.[135] They were opposed by New Hampshire's Nicholas Gilman, South Carolina's Pierce Butler, and Georgia's Abraham Baldwin. The two remaining members of the committee, Roger Sherman and New Jersey's David Brearley, had supported an appointment by Congress, but their states had voted a few days earlier, on roll call 359, for popular election.

The committee was well aware that whatever solution it might propose would have to commend itself to the delegates. The Convention was now three months into its deliberations. Everyone sensed that it must come to an end shortly. Years later Madison recalled that the decision about how to choose a president, made so late in the day, "was not exempt from a degree of the hurrying influence produced by fatigue and impatience."[136] They were out of time and voted for the plan with a minimum of discussion. What they devised was the basis for the Constitution's Article II. It was this or nothing.[137]

WHAT DID IT MEAN?

On September 4, Gouverneur Morris presented the committee's plan to the Convention. Many of the committee's members, he said, had wanted a popular election of the president, but that was not what the committee had recommended. Instead, Morris said, the committee was proposing a change that would eliminate the prospect of intrigue and faction were Congress to appoint the president.[138] The committee's plan also would make it possible to reelect the president to a second term and eliminate term limits, which would deprive the country of an experienced president.

This was an argument for a form of separation of powers, and it seemed to win over Butler.[139] But it would be a stretch to claim that the other members of the committee or the Convention subscribed to it, or understood it to mean our current understanding of separationism. They didn't anticipate a powerful executive branch, and thought that the choice of president had been removed from the people in three ways.

First, the delegates who had been skeptical about democracy and who subscribed to Madison's filtration theory would have noted that an electoral college was interposed between the voters and the president under Article II, Section 1, clause 2:

> *Each State shall appoint, in such Manner as the Legislature thereof may direct, a Number of Electors, equal to the whole Number of Senators and Representatives to which the State may be entitled in the Congress . . .*

This plausibly helped bring Madison on board; he thought that the electors would exercise an independent judgment, arguing before the Virginia ratifying convention that a choice by electors would be "more judicious" than a vote by the people.[140] The author of the Virginia Plan continued to think it necessary to filter the impurities of democracy. In Federalist No. 64 John Jay agreed with him, as did Hamilton in Federalist No. 68:

> *It was equally desirable, that the immediate election should be made by men most capable of analyzing the qualities adapted to the station, and*

acting under circumstances favorable to deliberation, and to a judicious
combination of all the reasons and inducements which were proper to
govern their choice. A small number of persons, selected by their fellow
citizens from the general mass, will be most likely to possess the informa-
tion and discernment requisite to so complicated an investigation.

That wasn't the only reason for supporting an electoral college. In debating representation, delegates had reached the Three-Fifths Compromise, which gave slave states additional representation by counting slaves as three-fifths of a person. In addition, some were concerned that a state might inflate its votes by broadening its franchise.[141] However, all of these concerns might have been addressed without interposing a group of people between the voters and the president; nor was it necessary to defend their independent discretion, unless there was something suspect about choices made in popular elections. Similarly, the delegates would not have thought the clause's ban on congressmen serving as electors necessary, unless they thought the electors would exercise independent judgment.[142] Today the American electoral college, unique in the world, lingers on like some stray piece of DNA that once served a long-forgotten need and now is devoid of purpose. But it was put there for a reason.

Second, most delegates thought that they had agreed on a congressional appointment of the president. If, under clause 2, electors failed to give a candidate a majority of votes, clause 3 threw the election to the House (originally the Senate, in the committee's draft).

The Person having the greatest Number of Votes shall be the President, if
such Number be a Majority of the whole Number of Electors appointed;
and if there be more than one who have such Majority, and have an
equal Number of Votes, then the House of Representatives shall immedi-
ately chuse by Ballot one of them for President; and if no Person have a
Majority, then from the five highest on the List the said House shall in
like Manner chuse the President. . . .

This is what happened in the elections of 1800 and 1824, and most of the Framers thought it would almost always happen this way, since they did not expect that, after George Washington, national candidates with countrywide support would emerge. George Mason thought the election would be thrown to the legislature 95 percent of the time,[143] and many of the most prominent members of the Convention, including Madison, Wilson, Hamilton, Dickinson, Randolph, Charles Pinckney, Rutledge, and (likely) Sherman, agreed that this was likely.[144] Almost the only delegate to disagree was Gouverneur Morris,[145] who more than anyone had put the winning coalition together.

This would have come down to Madison's Virginia Plan; and in case anyone missed the point, he repeated it in Federalist No. 39, contrasting elections for members of the House with elections for senators and presidents. Members of the House would be elected "immediately" by the people, while senators and presidents would be chosen "indirectly from the choice of the people." That, he said, was the way in which governors were appointed in state governments—that is, by the legislature.

A third coalition, composed of small-state delegates, might have thought *they* had won the electoral debate. They had just won the Connecticut Compromise, which gave them an equal number of seats in the Senate, and they were on a roll. Letting state legislatures choose the method of selecting presidential electors might have seemed like one more notch on their belt. Six weeks before, the delegates had voted 8 to 2 for electors chosen by state legislatures, and some delegates would have expected that that is just what their states would do, given the choice. That indeed is how most states selected electors in the first presidential election, of 1788–89, and in 1812 half the states still chose their electors in this manner. One-fourth did so in 1824, and South Carolina continued to choose electors in this way until 1860.

Small-state delegates would also have understood that each state would have as many presidential electors as the number of its senators and representatives, giving smaller states a greater clout than they would have had if the number of electors were based on state population. Moreover, in the event electors failed to give a majority of their votes to a single candidate and the choice of president fell to the House, each state, large or small, would have one vote, a measure proposed by the astute Sherman.[146] But for this, recalled Rufus King (a nationalist member of the Committee on Unfinished Parts), small-state delegates would not have agreed to the compromise.[147]

The delegates had voted for a form of separation of powers, but just what did this mean to them? Madison's encomium to separationism in Federalist No. 47 is often taken to refer to the modern American presidential system, but that is not what he had in mind. In the same paper, he held up the 1776 Virginia Constitution, which he had had a hand in drafting, as an example of separationism. We wouldn't think it so today. The Virginia Constitution declared that "the legislative, executive and judiciary departments, shall be separate and distinct," but then made the governor the creature of the legislature. He was not popularly elected, but instead was appointed by the legislature. Just in case he forgot who appointed him, the legislature also appointed an executive council that could veto the governor's decisions. The constitution went on to prohibit the governor from exercising "under any presence . . . any power or prerogative, by virtue of any law, statute or custom of England." That might have been too great a concentration of power in the legislative branch, thought Madison, but (as the educated reader of 1787 would have understood the Constitution) this was nevertheless "the sense in which [the separation of powers] has hitherto been understood in America."

What the delegates would not have anticipated is the kind of separation of powers we have today. Their presidents would nearly always be chosen by the House of Representatives, like its Speaker, making splits between the executive and legislative branches far less likely. The choice would be made by state delegations in the House; state legislatures would also choose both presidential electors and senators. Politics would be centered at the state level, and a party that won one branch of government would in most cases make a clean sweep of the presidency and both houses of Congress.

Few, if any, delegates thought that, by adopting Article II, they were voting for the popular election of the president. And yet, for the minority of democrats at the Convention, this was as close as they would come. That was how Dickinson remembered things in 1802, fifteen years later. He recalled that he came late to the Committee on Unfinished Parts one morning and found the other members on their feet, about to leave. As a courtesy, they read their draft plan to him, which again featured a president appointed by the legislature. Dickinson remonstrated with the other committee members. "The Powers which we had agreed to vest in the President, were so many and so great, that I did not think, the people would be willing to deposit them with him, unless they themselves would be more immediately concerned in his Election."[148] The work of the entire Convention would be lost, and the country would revert to the wholly unsuitable Articles of Confederation, with little chance of a successful revision. He recalled what happened next.

> *Having thus expressed my sentiments, Gouverneur Morris immediately said—"Come, Gentlemen, let us sit down again, and converse further on this subject." We then all sat down, and after some conference, James Maddison took a Pen and Paper, and sketched a Mode for Electing the President agreeable to the present provision. To this we assented and reported accordingly.*[149]

Throughout their deliberations, the delegates were well aware that whatever they proposed would count for nothing if it did not commend itself to the voters. George Mason observed that "notwithstanding the oppressions & injustice experienced amongst us from democracy; the genius of the people is in favor of it, and the genius of the people must be consulted."[150] More than anyone, Dickinson was sensitive to the need for a constitution that the people would support. "When this plan goes forth," he told the delegates, "it will be attacked by the popular leaders. Aristocracy will be its watchword: the Shibboleth among its adversaries."[151] The only successful method of conferring such powers on a single individual would be if he were a man of the people.

During the Convention, Dickinson was the great compromiser. He was the first to propose that the Senate be elected by state legislatures, and more than anyone voiced the moderate Federalist position that carried the day. And it was he, plausibly, who brokered the compromise that gave us Article II.[152] There is of course the possibility that his memory was faulty. Fifteen years after the fact, he recalled insisting at the Convention that the president would entirely owe his election to the will of the people. There would be electors, but they would be mere ciphers. "There was no Cloud interposed between [the president] and the people."[153] But in 1788, just a year after the Convention had concluded, he had argued that electors would exercise an independent discretion, and this in *The Letters of Fabius*, written to persuade voters to support the Constitution. Here the Fabian conservative underlined that, while the power of the people pervades the Constitution, the people do not elect the president.

> *This president is to be chosen, not by the people at large, because it may not be possible, that all the freemen of the empire should always have the necessary information, for directing their choice of such an officer. . . .*[154]

The electors might throw away their votes on an unworthy candidate, but they might also, "justly revering the duties of their office, dedicate their votes to the best interests of their country."[155]

If there was a pure democrat at the Convention, that honor belongs rather to James Wilson. Wilson was the first to propose the popular election of the president, and his persistent appeals to democratic principles and political realities must have had an influence on other delegates. He believed that the legitimacy of government derived from the mutual consent of free men, and from the theory of a sovereign people he derived the right of popular sovereignty.[156] Defending the Constitution before the Pennsylvania ratifying convention, he asserted that in principle the new government was entirely democratic,[157] and that the choice of president "is brought as nearly home to the people as is practicable."[158] If Wilson's ideas did not succeed in 1787, they in time came to define the fundamental principles of American constitutionalism.

And then there was the wily Gouverneur Morris, who saw democracy as a threat to republican government, but who nevertheless supported a popularly elected president as a bulwark against populist and democratic state governments. Like Hamilton, he was above all concerned to promote American commerce, which he saw as a source of political stability as well as wealth. "Take away commerce, and the democracy will triumph."[159] And what commerce needed was a strong national government, with an elected president at its head. He it was who cleverly turned that man of theory, James Madison, supplying him with a convenient new theory of separationism that permitted him to abandon inconvenient old filtration theories, and who thus persuaded the nationalist Virginian delegates to abandon the idea of a congressional appointment of the president. Without this, we today would have a form of parliamentary government in the United States.

That leaves Madison. Though he came to be called the "Father of the Constitution," this was not a sobriquet earned at the Convention, where he often dug in his heels to defend losing propositions. Nor did the final document bear the imprint of his cherished ideas. He had wanted a president appointed by Congress; a Senate appointed by the House of Representatives; seats in the Senate allocated on the basis of population; a congressional veto over all state laws; and a Council of Revision, composed of the executive and judicial branches, with authority to veto congressional bills; and on every one of these, he was voted down. He was a member of the Committee on Unfinished Parts, but once Morris presented his plan for the election of presidents, Madison raised several objections that went nowhere. Madison was so frustrated at this point that he supported Mason's call for an executive council, composed of members nominated by the states, to fetter the president's authority.[160]

By the very end of the Convention, Madison had reverted to his earlier opposition to a strong presidential system.

With Hamilton, Madison was the principal author of the Federalist Papers, which glossed over the battles in the Convention and passed silently over the objections the two of them had to the new Constitution (and with each other). Hamilton confessed his disappointment with the Constitution at the Convention, telling the delegates he would support it only because it was "better than nothing."[161] Madison too emerged from the Convention unhappy with the result. In a letter written on the same day that the delegates voted to adopt what has come down to us as Article II, Madison told Jefferson that "the plan . . . will neither effectually *answer* its *national object*, nor prevent the local *mischiefs* which everywhere *excite disgust* agst. the *State Governments*."[162] He had lost, and he knew it.

The Federalist Papers themselves seem to have had little effect on the ratification debates,[163] which were rather the work of the politicians in each state. Of these, Madison was a tireless worker. He had pushed for the Convention, secured Washington's presence in Philadelphia, and provided the impetus to replace the Articles of Confederation with an ambitious Virginia Plan. In the Continental Congress that followed the Convention, he successfully argued that the Constitution be sent to state conventions for ratification; and at the Virginia ratifying convention, he stood up to antifederalists such as Mason and Patrick Henry. If he *is* the Father of the Constitution, however, this is one of those cases, not unknown in delivery rooms, where the child bears little resemblance to the father.

In the end, democrats won the day. The rickety machinery they devised for the election of presidents was a sealed car speeding through the first decades of the republic, darkened in obscurity on departure, but emerging in sunlight on arrival to transform American politics. Presidential electors came to be chosen by popular vote, not by state legislatures, and the electors became the mere ciphers that Dickinson assumed they were in 1802. Presidential candidates with national appeal arose, so that elections were not kicked over to the House of Representatives.

The president became the principal symbol of American democracy and equality, and the most effective counterpoise to state governments. Not only was he democratically elected, he was the only person so elected by the entire country. Even before the advent of democracy presidents had discovered the power of executive orders, and Jefferson had found that his republican principles did not require him to leave the Louisiana Purchase on the table.[164] Thereafter, in times of crisis, a Lincoln or Franklin Delano Roosevelt might emerge to defend or lead a unified county. With a legitimacy derived from both the Constitution and the democratic process, the president became the spokesman for the welfare of the nation as a whole. He might thus oppose the will of Congress, and in doing so strengthen the separation of powers.

Nevertheless, it is historically inaccurate to view the Constitution through a separationist prism. The delegates had sharply disagreed on the division of powers between the federal and state governments, and what they devised was a compromise between the highly decentralized Articles of Confederation and the Virginia Plan's strong nationalism. They arrived at a method of choosing senators not to promote an abstract principle of separation of powers within the central government, but to give states a measure of control over the central government. As for the executive, states'-rights supporters were given a president selected by a method chosen by the states, and (or so they thought) the ultimate choice would be made by state delegations in the House of Representatives, with one vote per state. To adhere to the Framers' understanding of the Constitution, the doctrine of separation of powers should thus be demoted from its position as a foundational principle of constitutional interpretation.

-3-

THE BRITISH PRIME MINISTER

No great historic problem has ever been
settled by means of a brilliant idea.
—SIR LEWIS NAMIER

In their debates, the Framers of the American Constitution looked to other models they might follow. A few spoke self-consciously of ancient Greece's Amphictyonic Council, the Hellenistic Achaean League, Charlemagne's Empire. That was largely window dressing, though, an ostentatious display of scholarship. Only one model seriously commanded their attention: that of Britain. Their debates were an extended commentary on the British constitution—which they admired, but which they rejected as unsuited for America.

To what did they object, when they looked to the government of Westminster? We wouldn't think it a democracy. The franchise was severely limited, large cities went unrepresented in Parliament, many members of Parliament were appointed by a local aristocrat, and George III exercised a very strong influence over the government. But the absence of democracy wouldn't have bothered very many of the delegates, and Britain wasn't entirely undemocratic either. From the fourteenth century onward, a Dick ("Turn again") Whittington could travel to London to seek his fortune, and there was a remarkable degree of mobility between the social classes.[1] A Norfolk parson's son might rise to command the Royal Navy and ascend to the peerage as Lord Nelson; a coal merchant's son might become the arch-Tory Lord Chancellor, Lord Eldon. Through trade, a person might climb the social ladder with a freedom unknown in most of the rest of Europe. "England knows not democracy as a doctrine," observed Lewis Namier, "but has always practiced it as a fine art."[2]

Britain was the freest country in the world at the time of the American Revolution. Though he might dominate the government, George III ruled as a constitutional monarch, and knew that he governed through Parliament, even if the colonists might have forgotten it. Before the Revolution some Americans had argued that, in their quest for self-government, they might bypass Parliament entirely. "The British Empire is not a single state," wrote Benjamin Franklin. "It comprehends many . . . We have the same King but not the same legislatures."[3] The government of an American province, thought Franklin, was constituted by George III and the local House of Assembly, and only it—not Parliament at Westminster—had the power to levy taxes.

What Franklin objected to was the doctrine of parliamentary sovereignty, under which the "King-in-Parliament"—King, House of Lords, and House of Commons—has supreme legal authority. Statutes passed by both houses of Parliament and to which the King assents are "absolute and without control," as William Blackstone wrote in 1765, the same year in which the Stamp Act was passed.[4] There was nothing new in this. Parliamentary sovereignty had been a well-established constitutional principle at least as far back as the Glorious Revolution of 1688; and earlier constitutional doctrines, in which a Charles I might rule without relying on Parliament, or in which the common law as interpreted by the courts trumped Parliament, were left behind by the 1689 Revolution Settlement. Nor was there anything novel in Parliament's assertion of authority over America. As far back as 1696, Parliament had declared that colonial laws were invalid if inconsistent with Acts of Parliament.[5]

Britons had come to see Parliament as the safeguard of their liberties, and found the American appeal to royal government a puzzling throwback to the earlier, illiberal regime of Charles I. Before long, Americans, too, abandoned the idea of a direct connection to the King with a Declaration of Independence that labeled George III a tyrant.

George III exercised a powerful influence over the government's policies. He had a broad right to select whomever he wanted to serve as prime minister, and through a system of patronage controlled the votes of many members of Parliament. He was not, however, the tyrant the Patriots took him to be. Ironically, he might have been one had he tried to rule over America directly, as Franklin proposed. The prime minister, Lord North, recognized this in answering charges by the Whig leader, Charles James Fox, that North's ministry was Tory. "The aim of toryism was to increase the [King's] prerogative," said North. "That in the present case, the administration contended for the right of Parliament, while the Americans talked of their belonging to the Crown."[6] But while George III adhered to the 1689 settlement, he also dominated the government, and was the most steadfast opponent of American independence. He remained so even after his ministers recognized that the cause was lost, and this precipitated a British constitutional crisis that put an end to the personal control he had exercised over Parliament. Both in America and in Britain, the American Revolution hastened the growth of democratic government.

THE ORDEAL OF LORD NORTH

Lord North was the prime minister of England from 1770 to 1782, with a period of continued leadership unmatched by all save two prime ministers since then. There was a reason for this. He was an amiable and effective leader who disarmed his opponents with his wit and good humor. No man was less given to enmity, or better able to bury a quarrel with a jest. Years later he told an old antagonist that, notwithstanding their differences in Parliament, "there are not two men in the kingdom who would now be more happy to see each other." Both were blind at the time, and led about by attendants.[7]

If we remember North today, however, it is as the blunderer who lost America during the Revolution. "Lord Chatham, the king of Prussia, nay, Alexander the Great, never gained more in one campaign than the noble Lord has lost," thundered Whig statesman Fox. "He has lost a whole continent."[8] That was a judgment North sought desperately to avoid; he knew early on that the Revolution was not going Britain's way, and frequently asked George III to let him resign. In 1779 he described his agony to the King:

> *I have been miserable for ten years in obedience to Your Majesty's commands . . . I must look upon it as a degree of guilt to continue in office, while the Publick suffers.*[9]

The King refused North's pleas and North remained in office, faithful to the constitutional principle that a King was entitled to choose his ministers. The seals of office may have been in North's hands, but it was the King who supervised the conduct of the war, and North reported to him as an employee to his superior. However, North's government could not carry on unless it enjoyed the support of Parliament, and this grew thin as the war continued. Fox argued that there were now two parties in the country, "His Majesty's ministers, supported by the influence of the crown, against all Britain."[10]

No one desired victory over the colonists more than the King, but after the 1777 British defeat in the Battles of Saratoga, it had become clear that the war would be a protracted and costly affair. The government was forced to increase taxation to meet the expenses of the campaign, and the House was bombarded with petitions to cut government spending. More than eight thousand freeholders in Yorkshire signed a petition demanding government reform, annual elections for Parliament, and an increase in the number of parliamentary county seats. Matters came to a head in 1780, when John Dunning's motion that "the influence of the Crown has increased, is increasing, and ought to be diminished" was carried by 233 votes to 215.[11]

Thereafter the North ministry stumbled on, with the news from America becoming progressively worse. Word of Lord Cornwallis's surrender at Yorktown in October 1781 came to Lord North on November 25. "Oh God," he repeated aloud, "it is all over!"[12] He realized that he must make peace or his government would fall, but George III disagreed. On November 28 he wrote North, "I have no doubt when Men are a little recovered of the shock felt by the bad news . . . that they will then find the necessity of carrying on the war, though the mode of it may require alterations."[13] This meant keeping North in office, as the Whig leader, Lord Rockingham, had refused to serve as prime minister unless the King agreed to American independence, and to the dismissal of his current ministers.

North's government struggled on for the next few months, temporizing about its plans and losing supporters. On February 22, 1782, a motion to end the American war was defeated by a single vote.[14] A month later, on March 17, a motion of nonconfidence in the government was defeated by only nine votes. Everyone knew that North's opponents were days away from defeating the government. Yet still the King resisted turning over power to the Rockingham Whigs, implying that he would abdicate before doing so. "I am resolved not to throw myself into the hands of Opposition at all events," he told North, "and shall certainly, if things go as they seem to lead, know what my conscience as well as my honour dictates as the only way left to me."[15] The idea of a "Loyal Opposition," of a party loyal to the King but opposed to the government, would be a nineteenth-century innovation. With George III as the de facto head of government, opposition to the government was opposition to the King.

The next day North finally persuaded the King to let him resign. At 4:30 on the afternoon of March 18, a packed House of Commons met to debate the fate of the government. As the session opened, the Earl of Surrey rose to move nonconfidence in the North ministry; at the same moment, North stood up to announce his resignation. "Each noble lord seemed determined not to give way to the other," wrote the reporter. "This created a great deal of confusion, one side of the house crying out loudly for earl Surrey to speak first; the other side as loudly calling out lord North."[16] At last North was heard to say that he wished only to save Surrey from making a wholly unnecessary motion. Surrey had wanted to dismiss the ministry—but the ministry was no more.

Fox tried to pursue the matter, to establish the principle that a government might fall through a motion of nonconfidence. However, North conceded the point, and in a gracious and emotional speech thanked the House for its many years of support. He moved for an adjournment, to which the House consented, and walked out, much relieved that his ordeal was over. It was snowing, and the other members stood at the door waiting for their carriages. North had known that, with his resignation, it would be a short session, and unlike his enemies had his carriage at the ready. He saw a few friends gathered at the exit and said, "Come home and dine, and have the credit of having dined with a fallen minister on the day of his dismissal." With them he stepped aboard his carriage; and to his opponents, huddled in the snow and awaiting their own carriages, he bowed and said, "Good night, gentlemen, you see what it is to be in [on] the secret!"[17]

Lord North had not lost a motion of nonconfidence, but he had lost the support of the House, and his government would certainly have fallen had he not resigned. This was the first example of a change of ministry as the immediate result of a vote in the House of Commons. It was also the first recognition of the vital principle of collective responsibility, in which all members of the inner cabinet would fall with the prime minister. "In the disasters of the American revolution," concluded constitutional historian Sir David Keir, "the eighteenth-century constitution sustained its death-blow."[18]

WILLIAM PITT'S CONSTITUTION

Constitutional changes in Britain are incremental, for the most part. While most historians believe, with John Dunning, that the influence of the Crown had increased on the accession of George III, a school of historians led by Sir Lewis Namier argued that the King had not departed from the generally accepted constitutional principles of the reigns of the first two Georges.[19] North's fall was not the first time that a government had left office because it had lost the support of the House of Commons; in 1741 a motion of nonconfidence had been made against the government of Sir Robert Walpole, in the form of an address to the King to remove Walpole. Walpole declared this to be "one of the greatest encroachments that was ever made upon the prerogative of the Crown," and the motion was defeated by a large majority.[20] However, in the general election that followed, many of Walpole's supporters were defeated and he voluntarily resigned his office.

Even after North's fall in 1782, George III continued to take an active part in British election campaigns and in the choice of who was to lead his government. The King was the "font of honour," and could award peerages and knighthoods to his supporters. He also controlled the Civil List, a fund of moneys he could spend freely to secure the loyalty of the "King's Friends" in Parliament.[21]

In succeeding North, Lord Rockingham had imposed his own policies and ministers upon a resentful King. When Rockingham died in July 1782, the King happily chose the more amenable Earl of Shelburne as prime minister. But when Shelburne was faulted for conceding overgenerous terms to the Americans in the 1783 Treaty of Paris, his ministry was replaced in April of that year by an improbable Fox-North coalition. Lord North had been George III's principal supporter in Parliament; Charles James Fox was the principal opponent of the King's power. This seemed a union of both ends against the middle, but now North recognized that he had had quite enough of overbearing monarchs, and told Fox that "the King ought to be treated with every sort of respect and attention, but the appearance of power is all that a king of this country can have."[22] The much-abused North had come around to Fox's constitutional theories of a purely ceremonial royal power.

George III detested Fox, whom he blamed for corrupting his son, the Prince of Wales, and sought out anyone who might keep Fox from office. A son of the Earl of Chatham (Pitt the Elder), the 23-year-old William Pitt, was the chancellor of the exchequer, and the King asked him to form a government. The time was not right, and Pitt refused, as did his uncle, Thomas. Get me "Mr. Thomas Pitt or Mr. Thomas Anybody," cried the desperate King.[23] He once again considered abdication, but at last concluded that it was easier to swallow Fox as secretary of state than the dissolute Prince of Wales as his successor.

One of the new government's first acts was a motion to create a government-appointed board to oversee the oppressive East India Company, then ruled by the first governor general of Bengal, Warren Hastings. While this passed the House of Commons by a large majority, there were those who thought a board appointed by the wildly profligate Fox might not be a great improvement over Hastings. Fox possessed what Irish MP Henry Grattan called a "negligent grandeur,"[24] an ability to inspire the deepest affection of his followers, while giving the impression he longed to be at the gaming table. He was without guile and artifice. The historian Edward Gibbon thought that "perhaps no human being was ever more perfectly exempt from the taint of malevolence, vanity or falsehood."[25] Nonetheless, few people were less suited to administer the fabulously wealthy East India Company than Fox, of whom Horace Walpole left a memorable picture:

> As soon as he rose, which was very late, [Fox] had a levée of his followers, and of the members of the Gaming Club, at Brooks', all his disciples. His bristly black person, and shagged breast quite open, and rarely purified by any ablutions, was wrapped in a foul linen nightgown, and his bushy hair disheveled.[26]

His friend Sir Brooke Boothby said that Fox loved three things: women, gambling, and politics,[27] and it seemed in that order. He had gambled away his father's inheritance, and in an age of rakes and spendthrifts, set the tone for a high society of men of pleasure.

For the King, Fox and the India bill were targets too tempting to resist. George first persuaded Pitt to serve as prime minister were the government to fall. The King then contrived to kill the India bill, and thus defeat the Fox-North ministry. He gave Pitt's cousin, Lord Temple, a letter to circulate to his fellow peers in the House of Lords, in which the King called the India bill unconstitutional and subversive of the rights of the Crown, and said he would consider all who voted for it as his enemies.[28] The bill was accordingly defeated in the House of Lords on the evening of December 18, 1783, and George III immediately required Fox and North to deliver up the Seal of State, without even deigning to meet them. "I choose this method," he wrote North, "as Audiences on such occasions must be unpleasant."[29]

The next morning, December 19, a delighted George III invited Pitt to kiss hands and become prime minister. Pitt accepted, and that morning faced the most hostile of Parliaments. When his appointment was announced to the House of Commons, the members of the Fox-North coalition burst into laughter at the idea of a 24-year-old prime minister. They called Pitt's new government the mince-pie administration, so certain were they that it could not last beyond Christmas. Behind the laughter was anger that the Fox-North government had fallen through an extraordinary assertion of royal power, with a new government, installed solely through the King's influence, that thumbed its nose at the House of Commons.

What followed was gridlock. The House of Commons immediately defeated the government in two votes, with majorities of 39 and 54 against. Pitt had the support of the King and the House of Lords, but had few allies in the House of Commons, and no bills could be passed. The King offered to dissolve Parliament and hold a new election, which might have given Pitt more support in the House of Commons, but Pitt refused to go to the people until he had a chance to stare down Fox and North. On January 13, 1784, after a debate that lasted until seven in the morning, the House of Commons resolved by a vote of 296 to 54 that the King's efforts to defeat the Fox-North government had been unconstitutional. There followed a series of nonconfidence motions, but with the King's encouragement, the preternaturally calm and self-assured Pitt hung on. If not made to be loved, noted his fellow MP Nathaniel Wraxall, he had a remarkable ability to guide and command.

> *In his manners, Pitt, if not repulsive, was cold, stiff and without Suavity or Amenity. He seemed never to invite Approach or to encourage Acquaintance . . . Smiles were not natural to him, even when seated on the Treasury Bench . . . From the Instant that Pitt entered the Door-way of the House of Commons, he advanced up the Floor with a quick and firm step, his Head erect and thrown back, looking neither to the right nor to the left, nor favoring with a Nod or a Glance any of the Individuals seated on either side.*[30]

Faced with Pitt's unblinking gaze, Fox's majority continually shrank. Nor was Pitt unwilling to influence MPs with the tools now at his command. The floodgates of patronage were opened, and the Pittites suddenly found themselves endowed with titles and royal pensions. They sensed the country behind them, ready for a fresh start after the disastrous American war conducted by Lord North, Fox's ally. On March 8, 1784, Pitt lost a vote in the House by only one vote. Fox had staked all on ultimate victory, but victory had eluded him; and now, finally, Pitt called for an election. The polls remained open for forty days, during which drink and cash, promises and threats were liberally applied to sway the voters. In Westminster the lovely Georgiana, Duchess of Devonshire, was said to have kissed voters who pledged to vote for her lover, Fox.[31] He won his seat, but Pitt won the House, with the largest majority any government had received in that century. With an eye to the Protestant martyrology, the government's supporters went down to defeat as "Fox's Martyrs."

What Fox had sought was a revolution in constitutional governance, in which all power would devolve on Parliament and with the prime minister assuming the role of executive. "Had not a majority of the House of Commons almost from time immemorial governed this country?" he asked.[32] But that was not the constitution of George III and William Pitt. What Fox wanted was Roger Sherman's constitution, in which the legislature was supreme. By contrast, the Pittite constitution featured a form of the separation of powers that James Wilson and Gouverneur Morris would urge upon Americans. Pitt and the King had the better understanding of the British constitution, but Fox had a more accurate sense of the direction of constitutional reform. In one of the ironies of history, however, the Framers proposed a constitution that came to resemble the Pittite constitution more than that of the forward-looking Fox.

Americans regarded the political turmoil with great interest. Some ministers were better disposed toward Americans than others, and it mattered who would negotiate the peace treaty between America and Britain, and carry out its terms. No one was more sympathetic to the Americans than Fox, who wore their blue-and-buff uniform to Parliament to show his support for their Revolution. Gouverneur Morris was especially interested in English politics. His stepbrother had fought for the British, and had become a member of the House of Commons. At the Philadelphia Convention, Morris recognized how the prime minister had nearly assumed the executive power in Britain. "If [Fox] had carried his India bill, which he was very near doing, he would have [been] made the Minister, the King in form almost as well as in substance."[33]

In time prime ministers became the ruler that Morris had foreseen, but this was far in the future. For the fifty-year period between the fall of Lord North and the British Reform Act of 1832, the Pittite constitution represented an intermediate stage, in which the prime minister had more power than he did in the early part of George III's reign, but less still than a modern prime minister. The King would give full support to Pitt as an administrator, and would agree to major reforms, including economic measures that curbed the King's spending power. Gradually, responsibility for public money was taken from the King and placed in the hands of the prime minister. The modern cabinet also began to develop, as a body that owed its appointment and continuance in office to the prime minister, and not the King. But Pitt did not advance a legislative agenda the way modern prime ministers do, demanding loyalty from their cabinets. Instead, matters were decided by free votes; cabinet ministers might disagree with Pitt over major issues such as parliamentary reform, abolition of the slave trade, and repeal of religious tests without losing their jobs. The doctrine of collective cabinet responsibility, under which members of the cabinet must publicly support all governmental decisions, even if they do not privately agree with them, was a thing of the future.

The King was more than a figurehead, however, and remained a real factor in government. The royal veto, which had last been used to torpedo a public bill in 1708,[34] was not a dead letter, and George III threatened to employ it against Catholic emancipation in 1799, a measure Pitt had proposed. He went further, and publicly declared that he would consider as his personal enemy anyone who proposed the measure. In 1801 an exasperated Pitt suggested that he might resign if he were not permitted to introduce Catholic emancipation, and five days later George accepted his resignation.[35]

Prime ministers continued to depend on the support of the House, but political parties were in their infancy. In rare cases, such as 1784, the nation might divide into two camps upon a constitutional crisis, but for the most part Parliament was composed of shifting political coalitions, and not stable parties. There was still a core of King's Friends, but Pitt's economic reforms had reduced George's influence, and over time the center of political gravity shifted from the King in Windsor to the politicians in Westminster.

REFORM

The Parliament of the eighteenth century was based upon the electoral system of 1660 (with the addition of Scottish seats after the 1707 Act of Union), and reflected where people had lived at that earlier time. During the reign of George III the growing cities of the midlands were greatly underrepresented, while "rotten boroughs" with few inhabitants continued to send disproportionately more members to Parliament. The great County of York, with sixteen thousand voters, was represented by two members—the same number of seats accorded the fifty electors of Thirsk. Similarly, Old Sarum, which had flourished in Norman times, was an uninhabited mound of earth in the nineteenth century; while Dunwich, a thriving capital in the Kingdom of East Anglia, was now almost washed away into the sea. Many of the ridings (or electoral districts) were "pocket boroughs," smaller districts dominated by one major landowner who effectively controlled its members of Parliament. Seats were bought and sold, noted journalist William Cobbett, and Parliament refused to do anything about it.[36]

We might wonder how such a seemingly irrational system survived. The greater wonder was the reform movement that swept it away, for the prereform system had an entrenched core of supporters who were its beneficiaries. Privileged bodies have never been in the habit of reforming themselves; in our own times, political incumbents devise powerful obstacles to any threat to dislodge them. Moreover, many of the House's most distinguished members first came to Parliament from a pocket borough: Fox (while still a minor), Pitt the Younger, Charles Grey, Henry Brougham, Thomas Babington Macaulay, and even the young William Gladstone (on the strength of an antireform speech in the Oxford Union).[37] Pitt the Elder served as the member for Old Sarum, as did John Horne Tooke, the parliamentary reformer. For many bright young men, fresh from the Grand Tour (or, in Grey's case, still on it), the unreformed Parliament provided an entry to politics that a more democratic electorate might well have denied.

Many eighteenth-century Britons thought that their system of "virtual" representation, with its unrepresentative Parliament, served them well—that apart from moments of crisis they were prosperous and well-governed, and the incentives of the great landed families that controlled parliamentary seats were aligned with those of a primarily agricultural country. Given this, they would have agreed with Samuel Johnson that American colonists had no reason to object to taxes imposed by Westminster. The Americans were not directly represented in Parliament, but then neither were most Britons. If virtual representation worked for Birmingham, why not for Boston?

The first proposal for general reform of the electoral system came from John Wilkes in 1776.[38] A more democratic system would not, he said, have permitted the ministry to carry on its campaign to subjugate America. "We ought in every thing, as far as we can, to make the theory and the practice of the constitution coincide."[39] A sensible proposal, one might have thought; and yet it was laughed away. "Lord North was very jocular," according to the reporter (who sadly omitted the jokes),[40] and no one else spoke on the subject, which was voted down without a division.

Having once been raised, however, the cause of reform refused to go away. After his landslide victory in the election of 1784, Pitt felt the country at his back, and proposed to buy up the small boroughs from their electors and redistribute the seats to the new, unrepresented cities. Fox objected to compensating the electors, an expense the celebrated wit Sydney Smith later compared to reimbursing highwaymen when their poaching grounds in Finchley Common were enclosed.[41] Fox nevertheless voted for the motion, as did reformers such as William Wilberforce; but most Foxites opposed it, as did North's supporters, and it was defeated 248 to 174.[42]

There were two more parliamentary attempts at electoral reform before the great reform movement of 1832. In the first, an Irish member introduced a bill for reform in 1790, but by then the French Revolution had made the idea of reform odious to many members. The then secretary of war, William Windham, spoke against the motion, which never came to a vote. "What!" he said, "would he recommend you to repair your house in a hurricane?"[43] Two years later, Charles Grey emerged from his devouring affair with the Duchess of Devonshire to take up the cause, replying to Windham in a notice of motion for electoral reform.[44] It was precisely *when* radicals, inspired by the French Revolution, threatened the British constitution that every reasonable cause of complaint should be addressed, he said. Now, however, Pitt spoke out against reform, and Edmund Burke warned of radical Jacobins in their midst. Reform had few friends in the House of Commons, and the matter died on the order table.

The cause of reform thereafter languished for forty years. Grey took his seat in the House of Lords on his father's death in 1807, and the House of Commons lost its strongest advocate for reform. Ten years later Wellington recalled how Grey's voice was missed. "Nobody cares a damn for the House of Lords," he told the diarist Thomas Creevey. "The House of Commons is everything in England, and the House of Lords nothing."[45] Deprived of a sympathetic and energetic audience, Grey became despondent, and in 1810 suggested that parliamentary reform be deferred while the Napoleonic Wars continued.[46]

With Parliament a dead end, radicals such as William Cobbett agitated for reform through pamphlets and mass meetings. Corresponding societies were formed to promote reform, and were duly suppressed by the government. Horne Tooke was put on trial, and Cobbett himself was imprisoned for two years. Even after Napoleon's defeat, the example of the French Revolution made reform appear threatening. In *The Masque of Anarchy*, Percy Bysshe Shelley imagined that conservatives would be shamed by the 1819 Peterloo Massacre, in which Yeomen cavalry, supported by the 15th Hussars (fresh from Waterloo), charged a peaceful assembly of reformers in St. Peter's Field in Manchester and left a dozen men and women dead. Instead, the principal speaker at the assembly was sentenced to thirty months in prison for sedition, and Parliament made it illegal for more than fifty people to attend a political meeting without the approval of authorities.[47]

Because Peterloo was a working-class protest, it had failed to excite the sympathy of reformers in Parliament. By 1830, however, the cause of reform had begun to revive. The landed aristocracy who controlled the pocket boroughs no longer seemed to provide a rising middle class with effective virtual representation, particularly when it came to the objections free traders had to the protectionist Corn Laws. The Catholic Emancipation Act of 1829 had brought a new kind of Irish MP to Westminster, one whose support would make a crucial difference in the struggle for reform. The excesses of the French Revolution were now forty years in the past, and the 1830 July Revolution that made Louis-Philippe King of the French proved that the middle class might safely make a revolution. To English Whigs, France's July Revolution recalled England's 1688 Glorious Revolution, and the diarist Charles Greville reported that people felt an "electrical reciprocity" between the two countries.[48] Finally, King George IV had died in June, and his brother, the new King William IV, was regarded as much more open to reform.

At that time, parliamentary elections were called on the death of a king. While the Tories under the Duke of Wellington were returned to power in the general election of 1830, the party lost fifty seats. It had opposed reform, and continued to think it had no lessons to take from the French. When Gladstone, then a moderate Tory, cited the example of the July Revolution to an English workingman, he was told, "Damn all foreign countries. What has old England to do with foreign countries!" A chastened Gladstone later recalled that "this is not the only time that I have received an important message from a humble source."[49] The Duke of Wellington himself declared his unwavering opposition to reform in an unnecessarily candid speech before the House of Lords. He did not think that the unreformed Parliament could be improved upon, he said, and therefore would always oppose any attempt at reform.[50] Sitting down, he asked his neighbor, "I have not said too much, have I?" "You've announced the fall of your government, that's all," was the reply.[51]

His ministry fell at once, and in December 1830 Grey was asked to form a government. He announced that his government would bring in a reform bill, and gave the task of drafting it to his impossibly peevish, self-righteous, and impetuous son-in-law, John "Radical Jack" Lambton,

Lord Durham. What emerged from Durham's pen was far more sweeping than anyone had imagined, for he proposed to eliminate 168 seats in a House of 638 members. The bill was tabled in a two-hour speech by the diminutive Lord John Russell on March 1, 1831. When Russell proposed that sixty English rotten boroughs would be disenfranchised under the measure, a member called out "name them!," and as Russell did so, the magnitude of the change sank in. The parliamentary reporter described how Russell "was frequently interrupted by shouts of laughter, cries of 'hear, hear,!' from Members for these boroughs, and various interlocutions across the Table."[52] There was a desire for reform, but had Durham gone too far? Many thought that, had the Tories had the presence of mind to demand a vote at that point, the Grey ministry would have fallen.[53]

On March 21 a packed House of Commons took up the bill on second reading. "Such a scene as the division of last Tuesday I never saw, and never expect to see again," wrote Macaulay.

> *The crowd overflowed the House in every part. When the strangers were cleared out, and the doors locked, we had six hundred and eight members present,—more by fifty-five than ever were in a division before. The Ayes and Noes were like two volleys of cannon from opposite sides of a field of battle. When the opposition went out into the lobby, an operation which took up twenty minutes or more, we spread ourselves over the benches on both sides of the House: for there were many of us who had not been able to find a seat during the evening. When the doors were shut we began to speculate on our numbers.*

They had, as it turned out, 302 votes on their side. But how many would the Tories muster?

> *Everybody was desponding. . . . First we heard that they were three hundred and three; then that number rose to three hundred and ten; then went down to three hundred and seven. . . . We were all breathless with anxiety, when Charles Wood, who stood near the door, jumped up on a*

bench and cried out, "They are only three hundred and one." We set up
a shout that you might have heard to Charing Cross, waving our hats,
stamping against the floor, and clapping our hands. The tellers scarcely
got through the crowd; for the House was thronged up to the table, and
all the floor was fluctuating with heads like the pit of a theatre.[54]

The reform bill had passed, by a majority of one vote: 302 to 301. Thirty members from rotten boroughs had voted to abolish their ridings, and a further thirty-two members had voted to have their representation reduced by half.[55] Had one of them switched their vote the Grey ministry would have fallen, and the cause of reform would have been deferred once again.

Second reading of a bill amounts to assent in principle. But the details were yet to be worked out, and on April 19, 1831, the government was defeated on an amendment to the bill. Grey despaired of victory, and decided to take his case to the voters. That required the consent of the King to dissolve Parliament, and William IV seemed at first unable to make up his mind. However, the Tories, who wanted neither an election nor passage of the Reform Act, overplayed their hand. In the House of Lords, the Tory Lord Wharncliffe announced that he would move an address to the King against dissolution.[56] More than anything, William IV did not like to be pressured, and this infuriated him. He decided to dissolve Parliament, and to ensure that Wharncliffe would not have time to make his motion first, declared that he would go to Westminster immediately. Told that the Horse Guards were not ready, that the horses' manes were not plaited, he said, "I'll go, if I go in a hackney coach!"[57]

As the King arrived, the Tory leader in the House of Commons, Sir Robert Peel, was furiously declaiming against the "very worst and vilest species of despotism—the despotism of demagogues," and against something worse still, the despotism of journalism.[58] In the middle of his harangue he was interrupted by the parliamentary Usher of the Black Rod, who appeared at the Bar of the House and announced, "I am commanded by his Majesty to command the immediate attendance of this hon. House in the House of Lords, to hear . . . his Majesty's Speech for the Prorogation of Parliament."[59] When they arrived there, a loud voice was heard to say "God save the King." At that moment the large doors to the right of the throne were thrown open, and William entered the House, his crown awry. Grey followed, bearing the great two-handed sword of state, as if defying the Tories to object.[60] In a short speech the King declared Parliament dissolved, and the contest was removed from Parliament and handed to the people. In the ensuing election the pro-reform Whigs won a majority of 130 to 140 seats.

A second reform bill, little changed from the first, received second reading in July 1831 and third reading on September 22, when it passed by 346 to 237 votes. However, the bill still required the assent of the House of Lords, and there the 67-year-old Grey introduced it on October 3, reminding the peers that he had advocated reform for nearly fifty years in Parliament. The bill was enthusiastically supported by most Britons, who had given the Whigs their large majority in the House of Commons; but the Tories commanded a majority in the House of Lords, and passage was anything but assured. Such was the excitement over the debate that the reporter noted the unwonted presence of "a considerable number of Peeresses, and their daughters, and relations . . . [who] displayed all the enthusiastic ardour of the sex in their sympathy with the sentiments of the different speakers."[61]

What the Tories objected to were the democratic principles they detected in the bill, and which the Duke of Wellington decried in almost the same words that Madison had used in 1787.

A democracy has never been established in any part of the world, that it has not immediately declared war against property—against the payment of the public debt—and against all the principles of conservation, which are secured by, and are, in fact, the principal objects of the British Constitution, as it now exists. Property, and its possessors, will become the common enemy.[62]

Wellington appealed to the principle of the separation of powers, to government by "King, Lords and Commons." The House of Commons was not entitled to get its own way should the other branches of government disagree with it, he said. The House of Commons had voted for reform; the House of Lords demurred. The situation, said Wellington, was no different from 1783, when Pitt, with the support of George III and the House of Lords, had resisted the majority of Fox and North supporters in the House of Commons. The reform bill could not proceed, and Grey should have accepted this; instead, he had persuaded the King to dissolve Parliament, and in so doing had denied the principle, at the heart of the Pittite constitution, that the King was entitled to choose his own ministers. Grey had proposed a revolution in constitutional theory by appealing to the democratic principle that the ministry should be chosen by voters who elect the House of Commons. He had adopted the idea that James Wilson had enunciated at the Philadelphia Convention, that the legitimacy of the government depended on the consent of the voters. Wellington's arguments carried the day, and the House of Lords voted 199 to 158 against the bill.[63]

The two houses of Parliament were now in deadlock, but Grey had a stratagem to break the gridlock which Americans lack when the House of Representatives and the Senate disagree. On the advice of his ministers the King could appoint new peers who would vote with the government, and this had been done in 1711, when the Tory ministry needed to overcome the opposition of Whig peers to the Treaty of Utrecht. With this precedent in mind, Grey had Parliament prorogued (or suspended), and a third reform bill was introduced on December 12, 1831. This included several amendments that had been proposed by the Tories, and was carried on second reading by 324 to 162 votes, exactly two to one. For the bill to pass, however, Grey needed the support of a nervous William IV, and the riots that had broken out across England on the defeat of the second reform bill had done little to calm the King, who personally did not much care for parliamentary reform.

As the King shilly-shallied, Grey's cabinet let William know that they would resign if new peers were not created. To their surprise, William took them at their word, and approached Wellington to see whether the Tories might form a government. They lacked the support to do so, however, and the Whigs remained in office. At this point, the gridlock embraced all three branches of the British government. Now, however, the King gave in, and signed an agreement with the Whigs that he would create as many peers as they wished. Faced with the degradation of their institution, the House of Lords blinked. In the midst of debate fifty to sixty Tory peers walked out, Wellington in their lead, giving the Whigs their majority; and so the Great Reform Act at last was passed.[64]

The Reform Act extended the franchise, but stopped well short of giving everyone the vote. Only male householders living in properties worth at least £10 a year were enfranchised; even so, this increased the British electorate threefold. The new voters were the members of the middle class whom Lord Brougham memorably described as:

the genuine depositaries of sober, rational, intelligent, and honest English feeling. . . . If they have a fault, it is that error on the right side, a suspicion of State quacks—a dogged love of existing institutions—a perfect contempt of all political nostrums. . . . . Grave—intelligent— rational—fond of thinking for themselves—they consider a subject long before they make up their minds on it; and the opinions they are thus slow to form, they are not swift to abandon.[65]

These were the voters who elected governments that abolished slavery in the Empire, adopted free trade, and gave Britain limited-liability company laws. Over time, as people become wealthier, the £10 property restriction became less of a barrier, and voting rolls increased from 652,000 in 1833 to 1,056,000 in 1866.[66] Grey had not sought to broaden voting rights beyond the £10 householder, but the extension of the franchise led to further calls for reform, and to the far more democratic Reform Acts of 1867 and 1884.

Of greater consequence were the constitutional changes effected by the 1832 Reform Act. Unlike Pitt in 1783, Grey was chosen to lead the country by the voters, and not by his King; and in that sense, he was the first modern British prime minister.[67] The King might retain discretion about the choice of ministers during periods of minority government, but had to give way when facing a prime minister supported by a decisive majority in the House of Commons. The House of Lords also found its power much diminished. It retained the power to advise, even to delay, but not to block legislation that the lower house was determined to enact. If the House of Lords was not the "nothing" Wellington had called it in 1817, it was clearly of secondary importance. The House of Commons was not "everything," but it had gained an ascendancy, through the support of the voters, that the King and House of Lords could never have. The new extended franchise also permitted political parties to appeal to voters across the country, and strengthened a party system that ensured the ultimate supremacy of the electorate.

Looking backward in 1865, Walter Bagehot described the revolution that the 1832 Reform Act had brought to British constitutional law. The eighteenth-century constitution had been one of separation of powers, of checks and balances; and this was retained in what Bagehot called the "dignified" part of the constitution, in which the British monarch was the head of state and the House of Lords shared legislative powers with the House of Commons. After the Reform Act, however, there was a chasm between the dignified part of the constitution and the "efficient" one, in which real power was located. The House of Commons was now all-powerful, and since it determined who would serve as prime minister, the legislative and executive branches of government now were merged in the lower house. The efficient secret of the English constitution was the abandonment of separationism.[68]

Bagehot preferred parliamentary to presidential government. One of the features of the British system that appealed to him was the way in which it would filter out unworthy candidates, just as Hume and Madison had proposed. Bagehot knew that the Framers had wanted electors to perform a filtering function, exercising an independent judgment about who was the best man for the job. By his time, however, America's electors had lost this power, and presidents had come to be elected directly by the people. Because it preserved the filtration function, Bagehot thought the British system superior. Prime ministers are not elected by the people, but by the representatives of the people in Parliament; and this system of "double election" could be trusted to select a better set of leaders than those chosen by popular election.[69]

Over the crucial half-century between the American Revolution and the rise of democratic politics, a dignified constitution had given way to an efficient constitution in both America and Britain, and in so doing the two countries had traded places. In America, the Framers' Constitution, with a president appointed by electors themselves appointed by state legislatures—a president ultimately selected by the House of Representatives—had yielded to a popularly elected president and a reinforced separation of powers. In Britain, a system of checks and balances had been replaced by a doctrine of parliamentary sovereignty in which the nonelected parts of the constitution—the House of Lords and the monarch—ceded power to the House of Commons and the prime minister. By the time of the raucous 1829 inauguration of Andrew Jackson in America, and the 1832 Reform Act in Britain, the transformation had been largely completed in both countries. To the rest of the world they presented two different models for democratic self-government, one with a separation of powers and one without; and what remained to be seen was which would be followed by other countries.

-4-

EXPORTING WESTMINSTER

The word 'Parliament' shall mean the . . .
Parliament of the Kingdom of Canada.
—EARLY DRAFT, BRITISH NORTH AMERICA ACT

On July 1, 1867, the British colonies of Canada (today's Ontario and Quebec), Nova Scotia, and New Brunswick were united under the British North America Act.[1] The geographically improbable new country of Canada wasn't much of a nation, as nation-states go. Ontario and Quebec were little more than a third their present size. The new country lacked a common language and religion, and didn't have the unifying ideology of its neighbor to the south. Its own people knew little of each other, and the colonies' isolation was magnified by harsh winters and the vast distances that separated them. Nor was the BNA Act a declaration of independence. It was a statute of the British, not the Canadian, Parliament, and the British monarch remains the Canadian head of state to this day. Britain continued to set Canadian foreign policy for many years after 1867. When Britain declared war on Germany in 1914, for example, Canada was at once at war too, without the need for a separate declaration of war.[2] True, Canada was self-governing in its internal affairs, but that was nothing new either; the colonial assemblies had won the right to set their own internal policies almost twenty years before the British North America Act.

What was new was that this was the first time a colony had peacefully remodeled its constitution and united with other colonies in doing so. Had the Canadian colonies failed to unite, they likely would have been submerged in an American republic that was blessed with broader markets, and that had on several occasions invaded them. Many Americans of the time, including William Seward, Charles Sumner, Andrew Johnson, and Ulysses Grant, had expected Canada to fall like ripe fruit into their laps. Had that happened, the Canadian model of acceding peacefully to independence with a British constitutional regime would have failed, and the competition this offered to the presidential regime of the United States, with its separation of powers, would have been lost. Since the Canadian example was followed by the rest of what now is called the Commonwealth, the BNA Act and Canada's path to independence had a significance that extended far beyond its borders.

THE COUNTERREVOLUTIONARY STATE

As described in chapter 2, Gladstone praised the American Constitution as the supreme product of rational deliberation. By contrast, the British constitution had grown like Topsy and was "the most subtle organism which has proceeded from the womb and the long gestation of progressive history."[3] That might seem to give the advantage to Americans when it came to exporting a constitution to another country. How might the organic British constitution, formed over centuries in one country and responding to its particular needs, be made to work in another, very different country? That was the problem with which Parliament had grappled in its first attempt to do so, the Canada Act of 1791.

Canada scarcely existed in 1791. It comprised a small part only of today's country: the shrunken provinces of Quebec, with a population of one hundred fifty thousand people; and of Ontario, with about fourteen thousand Loyalist exiles who had fled America after Britain's shattering defeat in the Revolution. Britain had lost the war, and more importantly, seemed to have lost its nerve. After the defeat at Yorktown, British forces still held New York, Charleston, and Savannah, and America's French allies had departed; all of the midwestern forts remained in British hands. Nevertheless the Shelburne ministry, which had come to power on the death of the Marquess of Rockingham in July 1782, yielded to nearly all of the demands that the A-Team of American diplomats—Franklin, Adams, and John Jay—had made in negotiating the 1783 Treaty of Paris. Britain retained Canada, but relinquished all the land it held in the thirteen colonies. Under Article V of the treaty, Congress would "earnestly recommend" that the states reimburse American Loyalists whose property had been seized by American Patriots, but no one expected anything to come of that, and indeed the Loyalists had been cynically abandoned.[4] Further, Britain's Indian allies beyond the Appalachians felt betrayed by the treaty's recognition of the Mississippi as the western boundary of the United States.

As a youth, Shelburne had been converted to free trade by Adam Smith, and saw an independent and prosperous America as good for Britain. Let the Americans have their thirteen colonies, then, and the old North-West as well, all the land between the Appalachians and the Mississippi. The more territory America possessed, the greater the market for British goods, provided Americans could be persuaded of British goodwill. What Shelburne did at first resist was American independence. He wanted what his mentor, Lord Chatham, had proposed six years earlier, and what Canadians won sixty years later: a right to self-government in internal affairs, and rule by Westminster in foreign affairs. It was too late for this, however, for the Americans insisted upon complete independence, and Shelburne was forced to recognize that Britain had lost all control over the United States. On this he had no choice, but his generous peace terms were resented at home, and in April 1783 his government was toppled by the Fox-North coalition. North might have lost the war, but Shelburne had lost the peace.

The British defeat was humiliating, but not as shameful as the abandonment of the Loyalists. This amounted, said Edmund Burke, to a "gross
libel on the national character" of Britain, one that "manifested our own
impotency, ingratitude, and disgrace."[5] The departure of the last group
of Loyalists from New York in November 1783, aboard a British fleet
bound for Nova Scotia, was for Britons what the fall of Saigon in 1975
was for Americans, a scar on the national psyche, from which Britain
might regain a measure of dignity by the support it gave to the Loyalists. Their adherence to the Crown had made exiles of them, and their
properties in America were forfeit to the implacable new country. Britain
had no legal obligation to them, but their moral claim was compelling,
and the Pitt ministry that succeeded the Fox-North government allocated
£3 million to their compensation.

The ministry's sense of obligation extended beyond the Loyalists to
the new colonies in Canada. These Britain supported generously, and
from the ashes of the first British Empire and the loss of America arose a
second British Empire, one more powerful than the first.[6] In proposing
a constitution for Canada, Pitt noted that the appropriate lessons had
been drawn from the American Revolution. "To avoid the occasion of
a misunderstanding, similar to that which had formerly taken place, no
taxes were meant to be imposed by the Parliament respecting Canada."[7]
There would be no Stamp Acts from Westminster, and any domestic
taxes would be levied by the government of Canada itself. In addition,
the costs of defending Canada from the United States would be heavily
subsidized by Britain, as would the costs of executive and judicial sala-
ries, with the result that Canadians paid virtually no taxes. And while
American settlers had to pay speculators for land, free land and building
supplies too would be given to the Loyalist settlers.[8]

Historian Steven Watson would describe the Canada Act as the most
important measure of Pitt's government.[9] It divided Canada into Upper
and Lower Canada (corresponding to today's Ontario and Quebec), and
gave to both a government framed on the British model. Americans had
adopted a republican constitution only a few years earlier; now Britain

would establish a new country, with a rival constitution, at America's doorstep. A lieutenant governor would represent the King and exercise the same powers the monarch had in Britain. An elected assembly would take the place of the House of Commons, while an appointed or hereditary executive council would serve as a Canadian House of Lords. There was a much broader franchise than in Britain, even after its 1832 and 1867 Reform Acts; and there would be no rotten boroughs in Canada. As in Britain and America, the power to tax and to authorize expenditures was vested in the lower house, but this was a less than effective power when the budget was largely furnished by the British government.

The Loyalists who settled in Upper Canada and the eastern townships of Lower Canada carried with them memories of ill-treatment by the Patriots and a strong antipathy to republican government. That did not, however, make them Tories as we now understand that term. They were not Burkean conservatives *avant la lettre*, and their philosophy of government, to the extent they had one, did not differ greatly from that of the Patriots.[10] They thought that political legitimacy rested on the consent of the governed, and were not disposed to accept what Pitt had proposed in the Canada Act, the "aristocratical principle . . . of our mixed government."[11] Pitt had higher hopes for francophone Lower Canada, with its quasi-feudal, seigneurial system. In that fertile ground, he thought, an aristocracy might take root.

Fox thought otherwise, and made the Burkean point that it would be "peculiarly absurd" to graft a British aristocracy upon a Canadian tree. Was this, Fox asked, the government's answer to the French Revolution? If France had become republican, was French Canada to maintain the distinctions of Louis XVI's *ancien régime,* and were "those red and blue ribbons, which had lost their luster in the old world, . . . to shine forth again in the new?"[12] But if the *ancien régime* wouldn't serve, then whither should one look for a model constitution? Fox was an ardent reformer, and had gone out of his way to express his admiration for the new constitution of revolutionary France, which he though "the most stupendous and glorious edifice of liberty, which had been erected on the foundation of human integrity in any time or country."[13] Was that what Fox wanted for Canada? If so, Burke would denounce him.

Burke's *Reflections on the Revolution in France* had been published five months earlier, and Fox, who had privately expressed his disapproval of the book's conservatism, now voiced his public objections. Both were Whigs, and Burke had been Fox's mentor in Whiggism, but Burke profoundly disagreed with Fox about the French Revolution, and now the two men would break with each other in the debate over the Canada Act. Fly from the French Revolution, Burke cried, even if this meant a loss of Fox's friendship—as indeed it did, publicly, in a tearful scene on the floor of the House of Commons.[14] Thereafter, the two former friends never spoke, save on rare social occasions when obliged to do so. The disagreement over the French Revolution split the Whig Party and postponed parliamentary reform in Britain for another forty years. It would take longer still in Canada.

Burke was less than fair to Fox, who disclaimed any intention to foist the constitution of revolutionary France upon Canadians. What he wanted instead was a "popular" government, one that more closely resembled that of the United States, including the elected upper house that he thought the Americans had adopted. "Canada must be preserved to Great Britain by the choice of its inhabitants. But it should be felt by the inhabitants that their situation was not worse than that of their neighbors."[15] Fox had recognized that states compete for people through their laws, an insight that Frederick Jackson Turner would later employ in his Frontier Thesis.[16]

Pitt also recognized that Canada and the United States would compete for people, but thought that Canada would be better able to do so with a more conservative constitution. If Americans had adopted a republican form of government, Canada would be monarchical and (he hoped) aristocratic. If American politics were turbulent and at times violent, Canada was promised peace and good government. The Americans had objected to taxation without representation. They now would have both, while Canadians would have little of either. Loyalists would be reimbursed for property seized by the Americans, on average at thirty cents on the dollar. With all of Canada's disadvantages—in climate, in size of population—Britain would do what it could to launch the new country as a competitor to its lost American colonies.

The early governors of Upper Canada certainly felt themselves in competition with the Americans. Sir Guy Carleton (later Lord Dorchester), the first governor general of the two Canadas, and Sir John Graves Simcoe, the first lieutenant governor of Upper Canada, had both fought in the Revolutionary War and expected to see a renewal of hostilities. Dorchester had been commander-in-chief of all British forces at the end of the war, and had supervised the evacuation of Loyalists from New York in the fall of 1783.[17] These included the ex-slaves who had fought or sought shelter with the British, and whom the Royal Navy brought to Nova Scotia against the strong objections of George Washington. Dorchester ordered that no British troops should leave New York until the last Loyalist, white or black, who had sought the Crown's protection was safely aboard ship, and was himself the last British officer to embark. After several years in England he returned to Canada as its governor, where he prepared for what he regarded as an inevitable war with America. Until the Jay Treaty of 1794, he retained the British forts in the American Northwest, which he justified because of America's failure to honor Loyalist property claims stipulated under Article V of the Treaty of Paris.

During the Revolution Simcoe had commanded the Queen's Rangers, a highly efficient regiment of Loyalist light cavalry and infantry. The war over, Simcoe served in Parliament and, still bitter about the British defeat in the Revolution, expressed a strong desire to visit the Canadian hinterland. The new republic to the south, based upon the repugnant doctrines of equality and democracy, must come a cropper, he thought; and as lieutenant governor of Upper Canada he might assist in its demise. "The establishment of the British Constitution in this Province . . . [offers] the best method gradually to counteract, and ultimately to destroy, or to disarm, the [American] spirit of democratic subversion."[18] He knew he could not accomplish this worthy goal by force of arms, but thought he might nevertheless restore America to the Crown through the superior example of an Upper Canada made "as nearly as may be a perfect image and transcript of the British Government and Constitution."[19]

His thoughts turned first to Vermont, that dagger pointed at the heart of Connecticut. He knew its people well. "The Inhabitants of Vermont are a brave, virtuous, and English race of People, descendants of the best families in the Country, . . . Episcopalians and Enemies to the New Yorkers and Congress."[20] Alas, the Green Mountain Boys proved not to be the monarchists he took them to be, and in 1791 Vermont's shortsighted leaders gave up the advantages of rejoining the British Empire, and it became the fourteenth state of the United States.

A setback, to be sure, but Simcoe did not abandon hope of persuading Americans to forsake their vain republican delusions, and welcomed the "Late Loyalists" who emigrated to Canada in the 1790s as converts to monarchical principles. The duc de La Rochefoucauld-Liancourt was there when one group of Americans arrived with their oxen in hopes of free land. "Aye, aye," the governor told the puzzled family,

"you are tired of the federal government; you like not any longer to have so many kings; you wish again for your old father," (it is thus the Governor calls the British Monarch when he speaks with Americans); "you are perfectly right; come along, we love such good Royalists as you are, we will give you land."[21]

Simcoe saw Upper Canada as an explicitly counterrevolutionary state, formed by Loyalists who had rejected the principles of the American Revolution, and governed under a constitution that gave the lieutenant governor all the cards. He could prorogue the legislature and veto its bills; and his veto, unlike a presidential veto in the United States, could not be overridden by a supermajority of the assembly. He also nominated the members of the executive council, who, unlike the House of Lords, served at his pleasure. Before long, however, the council and its supporters were seen as oppressive and antidemocratic. In Upper Canada its members were said to belong to a "Family Compact," while in Lower Canada they were called the "Château Clique." Before a bill could be passed the assembly's consent was required, but it, too, could be brought into line through the lieutenant governor's patronage.

The Restoration Europe of Prince Metternich and Joseph de Maistre, from the fall of Napoleon in 1815 to the 1830 July Revolution, is remembered as a reactionary period of high conservatism, a time when *trône* united with *autel* to suppress the democratic freedoms of an exuberant and sanguinary Revolutionary Age. Upper Canada was there first, a province whose subjects were on the losing side of a revolution a decade before the fall of Louis XVI, and for whom revolution had meant mob rule and lynch-mob justice. The problem with America, Pitt and Simcoe thought, was an excess of democracy. Very well, then; there would be less of it in Canada. The new American Constitution barred the federal government (though not the states) from establishing a religion. Very well; in Upper Canada, one-seventh of all Crown lands would be set aside as clergy reserves for the support of the Church of England. Conservative at its birth, Upper Canada became yet more conservative after America invaded Canada in the War of 1812—Mr. Madison's War, in which the United States came in a strong second. When he visited its capital, Toronto, thirty years later, Charles Dickens discovered a society far more conservative than his own. "The wild and rabid toryism of Toronto is, I speak seriously, *appalling*."[22]

Conservative though it was, Canada was still able to attract American migrants after the Revolution. It offered a more ordered society and at least as much freedom from government as Americans had. Land was free, and because of the British subventions, the tax bill weighed lightly upon Upper Canadians. The Indians who had sided with the British against the Patriots also found a welcome home in Canada, and one of Governor Simcoe's first acts was to propose the abolition of slavery. For the Loyalists, whether on the Royal Navy ships that left New York in 1783 or in Upper Canada, antislavery was present at the creation. Henceforth, Canada would be free of slave catchers, and would become the terminus of the Underground Railway. In Lower Canada the Catholic Church was almost an established religion, and Canadian Catholics enjoyed more liberties than anywhere else in the Empire, as well as a toleration and social acceptance increasingly denied them in the United States. Historian Maya Jasanoff describes the Loyalist conception of ordered liberty as the "Spirit of 1783," a worthy competitor to the American Spirit of 1776.

RESPONSIBLE GOVERNMENT

The second British Empire offered its subjects personal liberty, ordered government, and low taxes. On occasion, however, it appeared to act on the principle that any featherbrained member of the upper class who looked good on a mount would make a good colonial ruler. One such person was Sir Francis Bond Head, who to his great surprise was appointed lieutenant governor of Upper Canada in 1835. How he came to be chosen remains something of a mystery. The position was offered to several worthy candidates, all of whom found a reason to say no, until someone suggested that the job be offered to "Young Head." But which Head was this? Sir Edmund Head was a classical scholar who might usefully bring his knowledge of the aorist tense to Upper Canada, where indeed he was posted as lieutenant governor eighteen years later. But the colonial secretary understood "Young Head" to be Edmund's cousin Francis, the author of such popular travel books as *Bubbles from the Brunnens of Nassau*. But perhaps Francis Head was the right choice all along, for had he not earned a knighthood by showing William IV how to use a lasso?

When Head arrived, he found that Canadians had begun to chafe at the absence of democratic government. The Loyalists had had a tradition of self-government in the thirteen colonies before the Revolution, and the Late Loyalists who moved north for free land after the Revolution were not quite the monarchists that Simcoe had taken them to be. In Upper Canada, the most radical of reformers was William Lyon Mackenzie, a stunted Celt of furious mien who admired American democracy and bore a Scot's dislike of the English in general and the Family Compact in particular.[23] He and Head could not have been more unalike. The new lieutenant governor was an English snob who was inordinately vain about his appearance, especially his fine head of curly blond hair. Soon after arriving, he met with Mackenzie and quickly summed up his opponent. "Afraid to look me in the face, he sat, with his feet not reaching the ground, and with his countenance averted from me, at an angle of about 70 degrees; while, with the eccentricity, the volubility, and indeed the appearance of a madman, the tiny creature raved about grievances here and grievances there."[24] Things went downhill from there.

As lieutenant governor, Head was determined to oppose "the insane theory of conciliating democracy,"[25] which he believed had cost Britain its American colonies. What was needed was a firm hand, one that Head was only too happy to supply. He almost immediately fell into a dispute with his executive council, which resigned en masse; and with Torontonians, who protested Head's autocratic ways. His principal supporter in Upper Canada was its chief justice, Sir John Beverley Robinson, an arch-Tory who had fought the Americans in the War of 1812. Robinson's father had served in the Queen's Rangers under John Graves Simcoe; his grandfather was the speaker of the Virginia House of Burgesses who had cried "Treason, treason!" after Patrick Henry's provocative speech on the Stamp Act. But even Robinson realized that, in Head, the Tories had too much of a good thing, declaring, "The man would make a rebellion anywhere."[26] And so he did.

Mackenzie was the mayor of Toronto, and was five times elected to the Upper Canadian assembly (and four times expelled from it). At first he proposed something closer to the post-Reform Act British constitution, in which political power resided in the elected legislature. Adopting John Dunning's 1780 motion in Parliament, he argued that "the power of the Crown has increased, is increasing and ought to be diminished."[27] In time, however, he despaired of parliamentary governance, and came to prefer the American system, with its elected president and separation of powers. The last straw for Mackenzie came in 1836, when he lost his seat in the assembly after Head interjected himself in a provincial election. Thereafter, an exasperated Mackenzie began to agitate for an armed uprising. He drafted a declaration, modeled on the American Declaration of Independence, and met with fellow rebels to drill in the use of muskets. Head welcomed this, hoping to charge Mackenzie with treason; and to tempt him to rebel, Head sent the provincial militia two hundred miles away, to Kingston. So encouraged, the rebels gathered a few miles north of Toronto in December 1837, with plans to march on the city and stage a coup d'état. However, not all of the rebels were prepared for bloodshed—unlike the Loyalists, who from every corner of the colony assembled in Toronto to stop them. The veterans of the Peninsular campaign, the chief justice with his musket, the schoolboys from Upper Canada College, a young lawyer named John A. Macdonald, and Head himself, with a brace of pistols under his belt, all marched out, accompanied by a band playing the Royal Navy's "Heart of Oak." After a short skirmish the rebels fled, and Mackenzie sought refuge in the United States.

As happens too often, Head's loyal service went unrecognized by an ungrateful British government. In two short years, he had provoked a rebellion and angered the American government, which saw Mackenzie as a kindred republican and Canada as a suitable target for what shortly would be called America's "manifest destiny." The colonial secretary accepted Head's offer of resignation, and failed to offer him a new position. An aggrieved Head took his case to the prime minister in Downing Street, and was brought in to see Lord Melbourne while he was shaving. Head began to explain himself, but Melbourne put down his razor and cut him short. "You see, Head, you are such a damned odd fellow."[28] Melbourne rebuffed Head's pleas for another posting, and instead appointed Lord Durham governor general of the Canadas, with a mission to report on the causes of Mackenzie's rebellion and a Lower Canada rebellion that same year.

Durham was a quick study.[29] He spent five months in Canada, during the summer and fall of 1838, but only ten days in Upper Canada.

He passed through Toronto in less than a day, during which he had a twenty-minute conversation with a leading moderate reformer, Robert Baldwin.[30] From that brief visit he wrote the leading state paper on British colonial policy, the Durham Report, which adopted Baldwin's suggestion that Canada be granted responsible government. What that meant was two things. First, the governor would be "responsible" to the elected assembly, in the sense that he would be required to defer to the wishes of a majority of its members. Second, the government, constituted by the party with a majority of seats in the assembly, would be "responsible" for the policies that the governor adopted, at the government's request. The result would be a democratic cabinet government, in which the appointed governor was a figurehead. This was the efficient secret that Walter Bagehot later discovered in the British constitution—a largely ceremonial governor, and a government run by an elected cabinet with the support of the assembly.

Durham recognized that Canada was losing its competition for settlers with the United States. It now had a population of more than one million, but too often Canadians were moving south to a larger, more prosperous, and democratic America. The Canadian practice of retaining Crown land in the hands of the lieutenant governor, to be parceled out to his friends, proved in time to be less efficient than the market-driven approach of America, with its land speculators. In promoting internal improvements such as roads and canals, the Canadian government also lagged behind the American one. Americans had their imperfect separation of powers, but this was nothing compared to the gridlock of a lieutenant governor and House of Assembly constantly at loggerheads.

G. M. Trevelyan thought that, in his report, Durham had "saved Canada and the Empire."[31] While that lays it on thick, this was the first state document to propose exporting the British system of democratic self-government, which in Canada would thereafter compete with American republicanism. Louis-Joseph Papineau, the leader of the 1837 rebellion in Lower Canada, had in 1834 boasted that "instead of Europe giving kings and kingdoms to America, the day is not far distant when America will give presidents and republics to Europe."[32] Durham had risen to Papineau's challenge, and offered British North America and the Empire not presidents and republics, but prime ministers and parliaments.

For an answer to Canada's difficulties, Durham looked not to the American but to the British constitution. "Since the Revolution of 1688, the stability of the English constitution has been secured by that wise principle of our Government which has vested the direction of national policy, and the distribution of patronage, in the leaders of the Parliamentary majority."[33] In Britain, the House of Commons was both responsible and representative. It was responsible because it was vested with the plenitude of legislative authority; and it was representative because (after the Great Reform Act which Durham had helped to draft) it was elected by the people at large. By contrast, Canadians had representative but irresponsible government. The assembly was popularly elected, with an extensive franchise, but the colony lacked responsible government because the executive could generally ignore the assembly's wishes. Lacking responsibility, the assembly was also irresponsible, in the sense that its members voiced extravagant views that they knew would be ignored.

The result was gridlock and rebellion, and Durham's proposed solution was to grant responsible government to Canada. A simple matter, he said. "It needs no change in the principles of government, no invention of a new constitutional theory, to supply the remedy which would, in my opinion, completely remove the existing political disorders. It needs but to follow out consistently the principles of the British Constitution."[34] Britain would retain the power to legislate over matters of imperial interest, such as foreign policy; but as for matters of provincial interest, Canada would be self-governing. This was the solution that Shelburne had offered Americans in 1783, and while they had turned it down, Durham now proposed it for Canadians. No great revolution would be needed, he said. All that would be necessary was a "single dispatch" by the Colonial

Office to the governor, requiring him to entrust his administration to the party holding the majority of seats in the assembly.

Thereafter, the Anglo-Canadian system of parliamentary governance and accession to independence by gradual means was followed in the mature dominions of Australia, New Zealand, and South Africa. It provided the model, after much bloodshed, for the early twentieth century's Irish Free State, and in the decolonialization period that followed the Second World War, for the former British colonies in Asia and Africa. Betrayed on occasion by unscrupulous politicians and military juntas, it remains a model for liberal, democratic governance that rivals that of the American presidential system.

In the case of Canada, however, there was a wrinkle, for Durham was unwilling to repose much confidence in a parliament of French Canadians, whom he scathingly (and falsely) described as a people of "no history, and no literature."[35] The French were a majority in Lower Canada, and Durham therefore proposed to dilute their power by uniting the two Canadas into a single province, with an assembly in which the less populous Upper Canada would have the same number of members as Lower Canada. "I had expected to find a contest between a government and a people," he wrote. Instead, "I found two nations warring in the bosom of a single state: I found a struggle, not of principles, but of races."[36] Were the two Canadas united, he hoped, the French Canadians would eventually adopt the language and culture of England. That was not to happen, of course; but the subsequent merger of the two colonies into the Province of Canada under the 1840 Act of Union gave the impetus for the subsequent union of all of the British North American colonies as provinces of Canada.

The 1840 act preserved many of the differences between the two Canadas. Each would retain its distinctive legal system, and the privileged positions of the Anglicans in Ontario and Catholics in Quebec would be maintained. The united province lacked a single powerful prime minister, and effective power was shared by two leaders, one from each region: the attorney-general of Canada West and the attorney-general of Canada East. Clumsy as this was, it nonetheless led to broad political parties that spanned the two regions and bridged linguistic and religious divides. Without this, it would have been far more difficult to create the united country that emerged in 1867 with the British North America Act.

The 1840 Act of Union did not usher in the responsible government that Durham had proposed, and this came only in 1849.[37] Before then, the governors who followed Durham mostly thought themselves able to ignore the assembly's wishes, and are chiefly memorable for the effect that Canada had upon their health. Durham himself was ill during his visit, and died shortly after his return. His successor, Lord Sydenham, served two years as governor and died in 1841, afer a fall from his horse while visiting his mistress. Sydenham's successor, the conciliatory Sir Charles Bagot, served a further two years before he too died. Bagot's successor, Sir Charles Metcalfe, suffered from facial cancer, and was blind and disfigured when he resigned in 1845. Only Sir Francis Bond Head escaped the common fate of Canadian governors of the period, riding to hounds at 75 and dying at 83.

Responsible government was adopted only after the arrival of Lord Elgin as governor general in 1847. Elgin was the son of the 7th Earl of Elgin (who had made off with the Elgin Marbles, now in the British Museum), and the son-in-law of Lord Durham (who himself was the son-in-law of Lord Grey of the Reform Act, the Whig Party being very much a family affair). In 1848 a Reform government was elected in Canada, led by Robert Baldwin as attorney-general West and the Napoleon lookalike, Louis-Hippolyte Lafontaine, as attorney-general East. In 1849 the new ministry passed the Rebellion Losses Bill, which compensated French Canadians who had lost property in their 1837 rebellion against colonial government. Elgin was personally opposed to the bill, but nevertheless gave it his consent. His decision was highly unpopular with English Montrealers, and Elgin was pelted with rotten eggs by (of all things) a Tory mob, which for good measure went on to burn the Parliament buildings.

This was a test case for responsible government. Elgin had accepted the principle that he served as a figurehead, and must sign bills he personally opposed. There was one further barrier, however, and that was in Westminster. The Rebellion Losses Bill became law when it was passed by the assembly and signed by the governor general. But Westminster retained the right, under the 1840 act, to disallow a Canadian statute within two years of its passage; and the House of Commons debated whether Britain should do exactly that in the case of the Rebellion Losses Bill. Gladstone objected to the bill and strenuously defended the disallowance power in principle,[38] but few took him up, and the last obstacle to responsible government and home rule was quietly allowed to fall into desuetude. By 1859, a self-confident Canadian government imposed tariffs on British goods and boldly denied that Westminster could legitimately exercise its disallowance power.[39]

In its second Empire, Britain had adopted a far more conciliatory attitude to colonist demands. What then had changed, between the time of the American Revolution and the grant of self-government to Canada? First, the Revolution had taught the British that, in administering their mature colonies, compulsion should yield to persuasion. As Canadians could not realistically be forced to accept government from the Colonial Office, Britain would seek to show the colonists that they might wish to retain their British connection even if they ran their own affairs. The British might not have thought that, as a matter of theory, government depended for its legitimacy on the consent of the governed; but as a matter of prudence, they wanted that consent anyway.

Second, responsible government in Canada was seen as nothing more than an application of the democratic principles of the 1832 (but not the 1776) British constitution. During the American Revolution, Britain could not export democratic government, not having it itself. By 1849, however, a very different form of government had been installed at Westminster, one the Canadians looked to as a model. The Canadian Lafontaine-Baldwin ministry understood this, as did Whigs in Britain. The colonial secretary at the time was the 3rd Earl Grey, son of the Lord

Grey of the Reform Act (not to mention the namesake for Earl Grey tea, and the uncle of a future governor general, the 4th Earl Grey, who fifty years later gave Canadians the Grey Cup trophy for football). Pitt had said that he wanted to give Canada the same government that Britain had. Now, said the reformers, we ask for no more than this.

Third, Britons had tired of their costly responsibilities to Canada, and "Little Englanders" began to turn inwards toward their own country. After negotiating a tiresome fisheries squabble between Canada and the United States, Disraeli wrote that "these wretched colonies will be independent too in a few years, and are a millstone round our necks."[40] The sentiment was shared by many in Parliament, Grey wrote Elgin.

> *There begins to prevail in the House of Commons, and I am sorry to say in the highest quarters, an opinion (which I believe to be utterly erroneous) that we have no interest in preserving our colonies and ought therefore to make no sacrifice for that purpose. Peel, Graham, and Gladstone, if they do not avow this opinion as openly as Cobden and his friends, yet betray very clearly that they entertain it, nor do I find some members of the cabinet free from it.*[41]

Britain's moral debt to the Loyalists had been paid, and now, after the repeal of the protectionist Corn Laws and the rise of free trade, Britons were more concerned with their profitable exports to the United States. Canada was thought by many a *damnosa hereditas*, a burdensome inheritance.

Finally, the stumbling block of sovereignty had been quietly removed. During the American Revolution, Britons had thought there was room for one sovereign only, and that a sovereign America could not coexist as a colony of a sovereign Parliament. That was a theoretical problem to which there was no answer, but in practical terms, nothing more was needed than the single dispatch that the colonial secretary, Lord Grey, sent to Lord Falkland, the Nova Scotia lieutenant governor. What must be made apparent, said Grey, is that "any transfer which may take place of political power from the hands of one party in the province to another is the result, not of an act of yours, but of the wishes of the people themselves."[42]

More than a century later, Daniel Patrick Moynihan raised a storm of controversy by arguing that racial questions in the United States deserved a period of "benign neglect." Moynihan thought he was quoting from the Durham Report, but the phrase was Moynihan's, not Durham's. It was Moynihan's way of summarizing what Durham thought British policy toward Canada should be on the grant of responsible government. And indeed, the more responsible Canada was, the less responsible Britain was for Canadian affairs. After everyone had adjusted to the Rebellion Losses Bill, Grey wrote to Elgin that "people here are beginning to forget Canada, which is the best thing they can do."[43] With responsible government, Canada became self-governing in its internal affairs, and this provided the impetus for the next act in Canadian constitutional history: the union of Canada and two Maritime provinces under the British North America Act.

CONFEDERATION

September 1, 1864, was a day of high excitement in Charlottetown, the little capital of Prince Edward Island. Slaymaker and Nichols' Olympic Circus was in town, the first circus to visit the island in two decades, and the town's twenty small hotels were full of people who had come to see the acting dogs and monkeys, Mlle Caroline (*"maîtresse de cheval"*), and Mr. John Allen, the "Celebrated Nestor and Wit Extraordinary." No one paid much attention to a meeting of politicians from the Maritime colonies of Nova Scotia, New Brunswick, and Prince Edward Island, who themselves were eager to see the elephants. Less attention still was paid to the 200-ton steamship with a man-of-war cut that pulled into the harbor that morning, bearing with it two-thirds of the Canadian cabinet, for the surprise visitors were gate-crashers. With everyone else otherwise occupied, a lone provincial secretary rowed out in a bumboat to greet them.[44] The Charlottetown conference had been called to discuss the union of the Maritime provinces, and the Canadians had dropped in to propose a union—which people were beginning to call a confederation—of all of the British North American colonies.

The Charlottetown conference had been convened by the lieutenant governor of New Brunswick, Arthur Hamilton Gordon. As a youth, Gordon had been coddled by his father, Lord Aberdeen, and according to his admiring biographer was left with "personality defects that he never completely overcame."[45] He had, he confessed, "an excessive desire to be eminent,"[46] and as he did not think he would achieve this in Britain, he thought he might do so in the smaller pond of Canada. His quandary he described in the form of a dialogue between his ego and alter ego.

Alter ego: "Dost thou not feel that thou canst and will rule?"
Ego: "Alas, Alas. I do."[47]

After a desultory career as a backbench MP and minor diplomat (where he managed to snub the king of the Belgians), he was appointed lieutenant governor of New Brunswick in 1861. On arriving in its capital of Fredericton, however, he found the job less than rewarding. It was a bore to be surrounded by one's inferiors; nor had he, in an era of responsible government, the political power his father had enjoyed as prime minister of Britain. No doubt he received some satisfaction from the instruction he gave to the local Anglican clergy that, after calling down God's blessing upon the Queen, they should ask Him to remember "Thy Servant Arthur."

Thy Servant Arthur, as Canadians came to call him, wanted to play in a larger field. In 1860 New Brunswick had a population of a quarter million, Nova Scotia 330,000, and little Prince Edward Island 80,000. Put them together, thought Gordon, and they might amount to something. They were dwarfed by Ontario (Canada West) with its population of 1.4 million, and Quebec (Canada East) with its 1.1 million inhabitants, to say nothing of the 31 million Americans; but Gordon did not want his little backwater to be swamped by pushy Canadians, and resisted anything more extensive than a union of the Maritime colonies.

For their part, Canadians were eager for the federal solution to which the awkward structure of their government inclined them. Lord Durham, who had proposed a federation of all of the British North American colonies, had hoped that French Canadians would be assimilated into the broader English-speaking world that surrounded them. While that was not on the cards, the 1840 Act of Union gave anglophone Canada West equal representation in the House of Assembly, even though it had fewer people than francophone Canada East. By the 1860s, however, this had been reversed, and the radicals of Canada West, now in the majority and not entirely free from anti-Catholic bigotry, demanded "representation by population" and an increase in the anglophone Ontario members of the assembly. Francophones in Quebec stoutly resisted "rep by pop," fearing that were it adopted, French Canada would go the way of Louisiana, its language and institutions dissolved in an English sea. Equal representation in the legislature, which had been adopted to reduce French-Canadian political power, was now seen to protect a shrinking francophone population.

The Act of Union also produced gridlock, as it became impossible to pass legislation without support from both sides of the United Canadas. John C. Calhoun's theory of "concurrent majorities," formed in defense of slavery and rejected in the United States, was adopted in Canada to protect French Canadian institutions. A "double majority," or a majority vote from both Canada East and West, was assumed to be necessary to pass legislation, so that a majority on one side could always block a majority on the other side.[48] Important legislation was held up, including an 1861 militia bill proposed to respond to the threat of an American invasion. To the great annoyance of Britain, which had sent fourteen thousand men to defend Canada, the Canadians could not agree to do what was necessary to defend themselves. This, thought the Anglo-Canadian intellectual Goldwin Smith, was the real motive behind the desire for a new constitution. "Whoever may lay claim to the parentage of Confederation, . . . its real parent was Deadlock."[49]

What was needed was a compromise, and this came in June 1864 when a Canadian coalition government adopted the principle of federalism as a way out, with rep by pop for the central government in Ottawa, and provincial rights for a francophone Quebec. Federalism also offered a basis for a grand union of the British North American colonies: the Maritime colonies in the east; British Columbia in the west; and between it and Ontario, the vast Rupert's Land of the Hudson's Bay Company, and the North-Western Territories.

The great compromise was the work of Toronto reformer George Brown, the owner and editor of the Toronto *Globe*. Brown was a bigoted partisan who had little sympathy for French Canadians, or respect for their religion.[50] He also had an inflexible sense of political entitlement and a large capacity for moral indignation. Goldwin Smith observed that "Of liberality of character and sentiment, of breadth of view and toleration of difference of opinion, no human being was ever more devoid" than Brown.[51] Nevertheless, he had recognized the possibility of a grand bargain with the hated Tories, led by John A. Macdonald and George-Étienne Cartier; and the coalition they formed created the Canada of today. When the coalition was announced, French Canadian representatives gathered around Brown to embrace him, to his great embarrassment.

Like the Reform Baldwin-Lafontaine government of the 1840s, the Tory Macdonald-Cartier ministry was an Anglo-French partnership between the two sections of the United Canadas. Macdonald was a lawyer from Kingston, Ontario, and a political natural. Of him, Goldwin Smith wrote admiringly that "the study of his life from his earliest years had been the manipulation of human nature for the purposes of party. In that craft he was unrivalled."[52] He had an infectious zest for life, and at age 71 rode 150 miles through the Rocky Mountains on the cowcatcher of a Canadian Pacific Railway locomotive, ordering the train to stop over a three-hundred-foot trestle to admire the view of the torrent below.[53] He was also an alcoholic who, in a crisis, was apt to disappear into a bottle. In dismissing the Irish-

Canadian Thomas D'Arcy McGee from his cabinet, Macdonald is supposed to have said, "You'll have to quit drinking, McGee. There's room for only one drunk in this government." He made no secret of his binges, and to a heckler who accused him of being drunk, replied "Yes, but the people would prefer John A. drunk to George Brown sober."[54] As indeed they did. People loved him for the evident delight he took in the simple tasks of politics, the hustings and the cabinet making, and for his ready wit. To a woman who asked him how it was that he, a man, could vote, while she could not, he pretended to ponder, and then replied, "Madam, I cannot conceive."[55] He was devoid of meanness and possessed gifts of friendship and empathy that Brown and the Reformers (now called Liberals or "Grits") wholly lacked. One day in Parliament he met a Grit MP who had been seriously ill. "Davy, old man," said Macdonald, "I'm glad to see you back. I hope you'll soon be yourself again and live many a day to vote against me—as you always have done." The sick man, who had been greeted curtly by the leaders of his own party, later recalled, "I never gave the old man a vote in my life, but hang me if it doesn't go against my grain to follow the men who haven't a word of kind greeting for me, and oppose a man with a heart like Sir John's."[56]

His opposite number, Cartier, was an ebullient French Canadian who combined a Gallic charm with the smarts of a corporate lawyer who had served as general counsel for the Grand Trunk Railway. He had taken part in the 1837 Lower Canada rebellion, but over time had decided that the ultramontane *Parti bleu* offered the best defense of French Canadian nationalism. In France, he was once asked how it was that, separated from *la patrie*, French Canadians had managed to maintain their identity. We did so precisely because we were cut off from France, he answered. Had Quebec gone through the convulsions of the French Revolution, without the free institutions its citizens had received from England and the protection these offered their church and language, they would have been lost to history as a nation.[57] Reformers such as Durham and Brown would have improved French Canada out of existence. With Macdonald's Tories, then, the conservative *bleus* made common cause; and if Cartier was more of a proponent of provincial rights than Macdonald, the two complemented each other, and together their government offered Canadians a balance between conflicting centripetal and centrifugal impulses.

Nothing could be more dissimilar than the way in which Americans and Canadians made their constitutions. The Americans were children of the Enlightenment who debated the first principles of government before the stern eye of George Washington. The Canadians were mid-Victorians, bred in the traditions of parliamentary government, who read John Stuart Mill and *The Economist*. They did not aspire to begin the world anew, and did not think constitution making inconsistent with an epic lark. On their way to Charlottetown, the Canadians stopped in New Brunswick and Nova Scotia to entertain the locals. There was a great feast in St. John, New Brunswick, and a dinner and reception in the provincial capital of Fredericton. There followed a week in Halifax, Nova Scotia, with festivities that included picnics and a dance on the deck of HMS *Duncan*. Charlottetown was a series of banquets and balls. The French Canadians, whom the Maritimers were apt to find a little intimidating, put on a great show of bonhomie, singing *"À la claire fontaine"* and pretending to paddle *voyageur* canoes as they did so. The Canadians had brought with them a small fortune in champagne, and as they uncorked the bottles, said a Canadian historian, the road to confederation truly began.[58]

The Canadians quickly took charge of the conference. Thy Servant Arthur had been shunted aside by the Maritime politicians, who now found themselves taking a back seat to their more worldly visitors. The Canadians had prepackaged their proposal before they left home, and each session of the conference was devoted to their plans for a federal government and the assumption of provincial debt. At the last banquet, a delegate, champagne glass in hand, called out, "if anyone can show just cause or impediment why the Colonies should not be united in matrimonial alliance, let him now express it or forever hold his peace." To which there was silent acquiescence.

What remained to be done was to hammer out the details of the union, in what became the British North America Act; and for this, the delegates gathered a month later, in October 1864, in Quebec City. The Framers had spent 116 days drafting the American Constitution; the Quebec City delegates spent two weeks on theirs, with much of the time spent on dinners and dances. By now the stolid Maritimers had entered into the spirit of the thing, and brought with them their wives and marriageable daughters, with all their crinolines and hoop skirts, for the grandest balls of all. There they met their opposite numbers, the flirtatious French Canadian ladies, who danced the energetic polkas and sensuous waltzes, and according to a delegate made "no difficulty in falling in love—or appearing to do it—with a dozen gentlemen at a time."[59] The highlight was the Bachelors Ball, where the members of the Canadian cabinet showed themselves to be indefatigable dancers. "They are cunning fellows," complained the Charlottetown *Examiner*. "They know that if they can dance themselves into the affections of the wives and daughters of [Prince Edward Island], the men will certainly be an easy conquest."[60]

The guiding principle of the Quebec Conference was the need for a British constitution and a continued connection to the monarch and the mother country. Macdonald believed that, had Canada decided upon independence, Britain would have willingly acquiesced.[61] So indeed Walter Bagehot had said, when the BNA Act came before Parliament.

Why should we miss so grand an opportunity of declaring publicly, what every British statesman secretly acknowledges, that this country reigns over her grand North American colonies by their own consent alone; that on the day when a two-thirds vote for independence becomes possible in both Houses, our right and our desire to reign over them will end, and Great Britain will simply become a cordial and powerful ally.[62]

For that reason, Macdonald went out of his way to affirm Canada's allegiance to Queen Victoria and the British connection.

Britain saw Canada as an inconvenient colony, said Macdonald, one that had not paid its way.[63] Canada had expected Britain to absorb most of the cost of Canadian defense, and on top of this had slapped a tariff on British goods. There were some in Britain, Macdonald noted, who would not have been saddened by a Canadian declaration of independence. Let the country be strong and united, however, and things might be different; for then the Canadian connection might be seen as an asset, and not as a liability. The Canadian provinces had a population approaching four million people, about as many as the United States in 1787 and Australia in 1900. Canada's merchant fleet was the third largest in the world, and westward expansion would soon make it second only to Russia in size. It was now ready to take its place in the world as a country free from war, disorder, and high taxes. In the future, said Macdonald, Britain would be thankful for Canada's support.

> *Instead of looking upon us as a merely dependent colony, England will have in us a friendly nation—a subordinate but still a powerful people—to stand by her in North America in peace and war. The people of Australia will be another such subordinate nation. And England will have this advantage . . . that, though at war with all the rest of the world, she will be able to look to the subordinate nations in alliance with her, and owing allegiance to the same Sovereign, who will enable her again to meet the whole world in arms, as she has done before.[64]*

It would take seventy-five years, but Macdonald's prophesy came to pass in 1940, when Canada paid its debts to Pitt and Burke, Dorchester and Simcoe, Durham and Elgin, and a Britain at war with almost the rest of the world. When France fell to Germany in World War II and the Anglo-French army was besieged in Dunkirk, the Home Counties lay unprotected but for a newly arrived Canadian army.

Canada's Fathers of Confederation were sincere monarchists. In Quebec, the delegates unanimously resolved, upon a motion by Macdonald, that the executive authority should be vested in the British monarch "and be administered according to the well understood principles of the British Constitution by the Sovereign personally or by the Representative of the Sovereign duly authorized."[65] Macdonald had wanted the new country to be styled the Kingdom of Canada, but gave the choice of appellation to Queen Victoria, whose ministers preferred to designate it as the Dominion of Canada, lest Americans be offended by a monarchy next door. When he went to London to shepherd the British North America Act through Parliament, Macdonald had a private audience with Victoria. He knelt and kissed her hand, and was told that she was aware of the loyalty the British Americans had shown. "We have desired in this measure," he answered, "to declare in the most solemn and emphatic manner our resolve to be under the Sovereignty of Your Majesty and your family forever."[66]

While the Queen was to be head of state, she would not be the head of government. To designate the monarch as the executive, as the British North American Act did, was simply to adopt the principle of responsible government to which Canada had acceded fifteen years before, and which was Bagehot's efficient secret of the British constitution. "We cannot limit or define the powers of the Crown in such respect," said Macdonald. "See our Union Act. There is nothing in it about Responsible Government. It is a system which we have adopted."[67] What the Dominion of Canada would have is what the United Canadas had after 1849—government by elected politicians, and not by the Crown or appointed governors.

As a democracy, the government of Canada would resemble that of its neighbor to the south, which Macdonald himself admired. Macdonald had carefully read Madison's notes on the Philadelphia Convention, and brought a copy of them to the Quebec conference. Anticipating Gladstone, he called the American Constitution "one of the most skilful works which human intelligence ever created; it is one of the most perfect organizations that has ever governed a free people. To say it has some defects is but to say it is not the work of Omniscience."[68] What Canada would have, however, would be a very different constitution, one more like what Madison and Hamilton had first proposed in Philadelphia than what they defended in that selling document, the Federalist Papers.

Canada would be as monarchical as Hamilton might have wished. Madison's filtration theory from the Virginia Plan, in which the House of Representatives would appoint, or "filter," the president and senators, also found a place in the Canadian constitution. Under the BNA Act, the House of Commons would choose the prime minister, who in turn would appoint senators. George Brown defended this in terms of filtration, saying there was no need to elect senators, since their selection would ultimately rest with members of an elected lower house, who would choose from among the best candidates they could find. If inferior legislators ended up in the Senate, the members of the lower house would have to answer to the voters.[69]

Other parts of the Virginia Plan, rejected in Philadelphia, found a home in Quebec. Madison's national veto, under which the federal government had the power to disallow state or provincial legislation, was voted down by the Framers but was incorporated in the BNA Act. The Canadian federal government would also have the "residuary power" over all matters not delegated to the provinces, just as Hamilton had proposed for the United States. Canada's senators, appointed by the prime minister, would serve for life, as Hamilton had wanted. Americans fondly characterize their Constitution as Madisonian, but the Canadian constitution, with its national veto, its elected lower house, and appointed Senate and prime minister, might perhaps with more accuracy be so described. For his part, Hamilton would unquestionably have preferred the BNA Act to the Framers' Constitution.

How did the two countries, which shared a common British inheritance, democratic institutions, and a porous border, come to adopt such different constitutions? Canadian monarchism supplies one reason. Another was a simple desire for a distinctive Canadian brand. Macdonald and the Fathers of Confederation sought to create a self-governing country, and as nationalists they recognized that, without a British constitution, there would be insufficient reason to resist the annexationist impulse to join the United States. "The moment we found our Constitution upon the American principle," argued a New Brunswick legislator, "we will gradually settle into the United States. If we become American in practice, we will very soon become American in fact."[70] A monarchical constitution would provide a form of product differentiation, like the red serge with which Macdonald would clothe the North-West Mounted Police, to distinguish them from the blue-clad cavalry to the south, with their Indian wars.

The lure of annexationism was never entirely absent in nineteenth-century Canada. After burning their Parliament building in 1849 in protest of the Rebellion Losses Bill, English Montrealers had proposed a union with the United States as a solution to the constitutional crisis. More recently, George Brown had briefly toyed with the idea of annexation as a means of satisfying the democratic impasse to which the Act of 1840 had led. Prominent intellectuals such as Goldwin Smith regarded annexation by the larger republic as inevitable. From the United States came calls to seize Canada by force, as America had sought to do during its Revolution and the War of 1812. The American armies of the time had proven inadequate to the task, but with the swollen ranks of the Union forces of the Civil War, Canada and Britain would have found it far more difficult to defeat a third invasion. Americans liked land, noted D'Arcy McGee. "They coveted Florida, and seized it; they coveted Louisiana, and purchased it; they coveted Texas, and stole it; and then they picked a quarrel with Mexico, which ended up with their getting California."[71] The American Secretary of State William Seward threatened to conquer Canada in 1861, and the United States might have done so but for Lincoln's desire to fight only one war at a time. It was thus as a Canadian nationalist that Macdonald boasted, "A British subject I was born and a British subject I will die!"

None of the Fathers of Confederation favored joining the American republic, of course. Macdonald was one of the very few to have anything good to say about the United States. More than two-thirds of them had been born in Canada, with parents who had lived through an American invasion fifty years before, during the War of 1812. Many had Loyalist grandparents who had been forced to flee America after the Revolutionary War. One of the Fathers, Sir Leonard Tilley, had heard his grandmother describe her arrival in a desolate New Brunswick in 1783. She had climbed to the top of a hill and watched the departing Royal Navy ships that had brought her there from New York, "and such a feeling of loneliness came over me that, although I had not shed a tear through all the war, I sat down on the damp moss with my baby on my lap and cried."[72] For such people, a non-American constitution that served to distinguish the two countries would be desirable for its own sake.

Canadian nationalists sought to weaken provincial powers, and this supplies a third reason for the differences between the American and Canadian constitutions. What the nationalists at the Philadelphia Convention had lost, the nationalists in Quebec had won: a national veto over provincial legislation, and the residuary power over matters not delegated to the provinces. In time, the fears of a George Mason that power would gravitate from the states to the American federal government were realized; but in 1864, the Quebec delegates who looked over their shoulder saw what seemed to them an excessively decentralized constitution, one that had led to a civil war. That was not a model for Canada, they thought.

On the first of September, 1864, the day the Charlottetown Conference began, Confederate General John Bell Hood ("the gallant Hood of Texas") burned the supply depots of Atlanta and abandoned the city to Sherman's Union army. While the delegates were still in Quebec, a group of Confederate soldiers in Montreal raided St. Albans, Vermont, just across the border. The raid became a major crisis when the dean of Montreal's McGill University Faculty of Law persuaded a Montreal magistrate that he lacked jurisdiction to try the belligerents, and the raiders were released, along with half the money they had robbed from the banks of St. Albans.[73] The Union quickly responded. For the first time, America began requiring passports from Canadian visitors. It also threatened to withdraw from the 1817 Rush-Bagot treaty, which had banned warships from the Great Lakes after the war of 1812. Then, early in 1865, Congress informed Canada that the Canadian-American Reciprocity Treaty (or free trade agreement) of 1854 would not be renewed. All of this made the Civil War a pressing domestic problem for Canadians, and reinforced their fear of excessive decentralization and desire for broader markets across the different colonies of British North America.

Monarchism, product differentiation, and nationalism provided three reasons why the Quebec delegates rejected the American constitutional model. The fourth reason was the Canadian desire to avoid what were seen as the defects of the American Constitution, with its excessively powerful presidents. Unlike a prime minister who had to face a House of Commons, presidents were dangerously insulated from accountability. A century before American writers began to detect signs of an "imperial presidency," Macdonald warned of the threats to liberty from presidential government.

> *The President, during his term of office, is in great measure a despot, a one-man power, with the command of the naval and military forces— with an immense amount of patronage as head of the Executive, and with the veto power as a branch of the legislature, perfectly uncontrolled by responsible advisers.*[74]

The Canadian delegates also rejected the principle of separation of powers, with all the gridlock it produced. They had seen enough of gridlock in the battles between lieutenant governors and elected assemblies prior to the institution of responsible government, and in the "double majority" doctrine after the Act of 1840, and they didn't want any part of it. A Canadian prime minister would be dependent upon the support of the House of Commons, and might be replaced were he to lose it. By contrast, said Macdonald, gridlock was built into the American Constitution.

There would be an upper house, called a Senate, but unlike the American Senate, the Canadian Senate would have few powers. Its members would be appointed by the federal government, and while they might delay legislation, they would finally have to yield to a determined House of Commons, even as the House of Lords had done to enable passage of the Great Reform Act. Had senators been popularly elected it would have been otherwise, which is precisely why Macdonald wanted an appointed body.

> There is no fear of a dead lock between the two houses. There is an infinitely greater chance of a dead lock between the two branches of the legislature, should the elective principle be adopted, than with a nominated chamber—chosen by the Crown, and having no mission from the people.[75]

As an elected body, the Senate might have claimed as much legitimacy as the House of Commons; but as an appointed body, it could not resist the popular will as expressed by the lower house.

Macdonald had anticipated Bagehot's efficient secret, with its all-powerful House of Commons, three months before Bagehot's first article on the English constitution appeared in the *Fortnightly Review*. The two men admired each other, and met at least once. On one of his visits to England Macdonald dined at the house of a man whom he scarcely knew, in the company of people unknown to him. Macdonald was questioned about the British constitution, and replied that Walter Bagehot was the best authority he knew. "I am glad to hear you say that," said his neighbor, "for I am Mr. Bagehot."[76] But perhaps Macdonald knew this all along, for he always played a deep game. Bagehot paid close attention to confederation, and was delighted to see a Westminster-based constitution adopted in North America. Thereafter, he said, that continent's two different constitutional models would usefully compete with each other, side by side.[77]

The Quebec conference wasn't the end of the story. The plan of union still had to be approved by three colonial assemblies, and this took some heavy lifting in New Brunswick and Nova Scotia. In New Brunswick, it required a stiff note from the Colonial Office to Thy Servant Arthur, and two elections, before the plan was approved.[78] Thereafter, the plan still required enactment by Parliament in Westminster. In 1867, however, British politicians had little on their mind save the Second Reform Act, and, Macdonald later recalled, the British North America Act was treated by the colonial secretary as if it were "a private bill uniting two or three English parishes."[79] Indeed, after the second reading of the BNA Act, the House of Commons turned its attention to the vastly more interesting question of the Tax on Dogs Act.[80]

Still, the Fathers had a grand old time in England. Macdonald and Brown went to The Derby, and returned from Epsom in a carriage with war reporter William Howard Russell, armed with peashooters and a bag of peas. Macdonald collected an honorary Oxford degree, and returned to Canada with a new wife. Brown skipped Oxford to go shopping, and returned to Toronto with new silverware and crystal. On the eve of confederation, June 30, 1867, he stayed up all night writing a nine-thousand-word editorial for the *Globe*. "We hail the birthday of a new nationality," it began. "A united British America . . . takes its place this day among the nations of the world."[81]

The new country was primarily the work of three men: George Brown, George-Étienne Cartier, and John A. Macdonald. Brown was defeated in the 1867 Canadian general election and never again held elective office. He died in 1880, from a wound he suffered at the hands of a disgruntled *Globe* employee. Cartier died in 1873 in London, where he had gone (along with his wife and mistress) to consult a Harley Street specialist. In previous visits he had been lionized in London, which had become a second home to him. He had been entertained by the Prince of Wales, Lord Palmerston, Gladstone, and Cardinal Manning, and as a guest at Windsor had chatted in French with the Queen. When Macdonald received word of his death, he announced the news in the House and said simply, "I feel myself quite unable to say more at the moment." He then sank to his seat and, his arm over the empty seat of his former colleague, wept silently. Macdonald went on to survive a campaign finance scandal, and but for a five-year interregnum was prime minister of Canada from 1867 until his death in 1891. During that time he oversaw the creation of a transcontinental railway, and the expansion of Canada from the Atlantic to the Pacific and from the United States to the Arctic Ocean.

Thy Servant Arthur left New Brunswick in 1866 and went on to serve as governor general of five other British colonies, all with better weather than Canada. After the turbulence of New Brunswick, with its obstreperous and impertinent politicians, he had a preference for colonies where he might rule as well as reign, and was probably most happy as governor of Fiji. Tempering justice with mercy, he found it necessary to hang only twenty-six natives after an uprising, and entirely suppressed the local custom of burning rebel villages and raping the women.

-5-

The Rise of Crown Government

Only the president represents the national interest.
And on him alone converge all the needs and
aspirations of all parts of the country.
—JOHN F. KENNEDY, JANUARY 14, 1960

Over the last 250 years, America, Britain, and Canada have moved from monarchical to democratic government. In America, this resulted in a strengthened presidency and the separation of powers between the executive and legislative branches. In Britain and Canada, democracy extinguished what there was of a separation of powers, and resulted in the unitary government of an all-powerful House of Commons. But if the forms of government diverged with the rise of democracy, they are all now beginning to converge around a powerful executive, in the persons of the American president and the British and Canadian prime ministers. The modern state is guided less by legislation than in the past, and more by what Hamilton, in Federalist No. 70, described as executive "energy." The government is led by a single person, and not by party elders or a cabinet. The change can be seen as a return to Crown government,[1] not a hereditary monarchy, but rather George Mason's elective monarch.

Had this occurred in one country only, one would seek an explanation particular to that country. Since the change has arisen in all three countries, at about the same time, an explanation for the rise of Crown government must be sought in economic changes and technological advances common to all three countries, and not in their different forms of government.

CROWN GOVERNMENT IN AMERICA

There is a lengthy literature on the recent expansion of American presidential power. Thirty years ago, political scholar Theodore J. Lowi condemned what he saw as a "plebiscitary republic with a personal presidency" in the Reagan administration.[2] Other writers, more partisan than Lowi, discovered signs of presidential overreach only when their man lost and the other fellow won. Arthur M. Schlesinger Jr. proudly served as a Kennedy adviser, but subsequently condemned Richard Nixon's abuse of his presidential powers, and called for a return of power to the congressional branch in a book entitled *The Imperial Presidency*. *Plus ça change*, the book was reissued in 2004, in time for Schlesinger to expatiate on George W. Bush's alarming assertions of presidential authority. In between, Schlesinger bemoaned the political weakness of the Carter administration and the House's impeachment of Bill Clinton.[3] At times, the changing of gears can be amusing. The most celebrated scholar of the subject, Richard E. Neustadt, published *Presidential Power* in 1960, decrying executive weakness and suggesting ways in which a presidential hero like Kennedy could amass more power. Twelve years later he found himself approached by a clean-cut young Nixon aide at a conference. "I'm glad I met you," Jeb Magruder told him. "I read your book a couple of years ago, indeed I had to. Bob Haldeman made each of us read it as soon as we joined the White House staff."[4] When Neustadt next heard of Magruder, he and H. R. Haldeman were being indicted for their roles in the Watergate scandal.

What nearly everyone agrees is that the role of the president has expanded, and that of Congress has receded. As this happened, the executive branch grew, and now numbers 2.5 million people (including workers at federal agencies, but excluding the military). The president can assert a large measure of control over the agencies, by appointing political loyalists to head them, and by staffing them with as many as six thousand political appointees in senior management positions. Unlike civil servants, who are hired through a competitive process, the authority to hire political appointees rests solely with the president, who may direct their actions and remove them if he sees fit.

In recent years, the proportion of political appointees throughout government bureaucracy has expanded. In the State Department, career Foreign Service officers comprised 24 percent of top leadership positions in 2012, down from 61 percent in 1975. This makes government more democratic, for a popularly elected president can ensure through his political appointees that his policies will be followed throughout his administration. At the same time, however, a top-down bureaucracy is less likely to provide nonpartisan, expert advice, as perhaps one saw in the mismanagement of Iraqi reconstruction. A group of former diplomatic corps officials have concluded that the politicization of the Foreign Service "spawns opportunism and political correctness, weakens esprit de corps within the service and emaciates institutional memory."[5]

The presidential appointment power has expanded through the use of "czars," who are not cabinet members and thus do not require Senate confirmation, but are nonetheless charged with major oversight responsibilities. The czars report directly to the president, as members of his staff, and ensure White House supervision and control of government operations.[6] They are part of the president's immediate staff in the Executive Office of the President, which today consists of an estimated two to three thousand people.

Political appointees can also be expected to see that regulatory burdens are imposed in a partisan manner. That very possibly explains the IRS scandal, in which the Internal Revenue Service slow-walked applications for charitable 501(c)(4) status from Tea Party groups. Donations to 501(c)(4) groups are not deductible, but such groups do not have to pay taxes and are permitted to keep their donor lists private, and that's important to them.

In the past, the IRS had granted 501(c)(4) status to applicants with a political agenda, but for conservative groups that practice stopped before the 2010 and 2012 elections. What held things up were the instructions IRS field agents were given in processing applications. Groups with troublesome names such as "Tea Party" or "Patriots" or that advocated education about the Constitution were pulled out of the pile for additional scrutiny, and that scrutiny carried the administration through two elections. Applications from several dozen progressive groups were also held up, but the focus was clearly upon conservative groups. In follow-up questions from the IRS, such groups were asked for their donor lists, and in one case for the content of their prayers.

The IRS stonewalled the scandal until just before the IRS's inspector general issued a report revealing the story, and has not been especially forthcoming since then. Remarkably, the head of the IRS's tax-exempt division, Lois Lerner, pleaded the Fifth Amendment rather than testify before a congressional committee. How high up the scandal went remains something of a mystery, therefore, but it doesn't take a particularly suspicious personality to see the influence of politics in all of this. In particular, suspicion has centered on the direction given the IRS chief counsel's office, which is headed by an Obama political appointee.[7]

Political considerations influence administrative decisions throughout the U.S. government, from decisions about who will be audited or investigated to decisions about who will be sued. Major Nidal Malik Hasan was known by his fellow soldiers at the Fort Hood army base to be an unstable Islamic extremist who justified suicide killings of American troops. Nevertheless, he was permitted to carry on as an army psychiatrist because none of his colleagues wished to seem politically incorrect. On November 5, 2009, Hasan walked into the base's processing center where wounded soldiers returning from Afghanistan were being treated. Shouting "*Allahu Akbar*," he opened fire on the soldiers, sparing civilians. Before he was taken down, he killed thirteen people and wounded thirty more. Though it would be difficult to imagine a clearer case of terrorism, the Defense Department characterized the attack as "workplace violence" and offered survivors psychological counseling, but not Purple Hearts or combat-injury pay. For political reasons, the administration had created a climate that disavowed the threat of domestic Islamic terrorism, and then, adding insult to injury, denied to its victims that it had occurred.

The President's Legislative Powers. Article I, Section 1 of the Constitution bars presidential lawmaking by specifying that "[a]ll legislative Powers herein granted shall be vested in a Congress of the United States." Nevertheless, Congress has quietly acquiesced in the expansion of presidential power, by drafting major legislation in the most general terms, with details to be penciled in by federal agencies under the supervision of the executive branch; and this can be seen as a grant of legislative powers to the president. Presidential lawmaking of this kind amounts to a return to the monarchical prerogatives that Roger Sherman and the other Framers so feared.

The 2010 Dodd-Frank financial reform act is a striking example of how Congress may delegate broad authority to federal agencies, and through them to the president.[8] The act created two new agencies, the Financial Stability Oversight Council and the Consumer Financial Protection Bureau, each with enormous powers over large sectors of the American economy.

The FSOC was created to regulate every American financial institution, with many of the details left to be worked out by regulators. It is tasked with identifying "systemically important" (too big to fail, or TBTF) nonbank financial companies, bringing them under the scrutiny of the Federal Reserve, and recommending heightened prudential standards for the Fed to impose on them. Bank holding companies with more than $50 billion in assets are automatically determined to be too big to fail, and the council may include other firms in this category based on unspecified risk factors that FSOC regulators formulate. These banks need not have been designated as systemically important, so long as the council determines that they are in danger of default, and could threaten the stability of the system. The statute was touted as eliminating the need for future bailouts like the Troubled Asset Relief Program, but in fact it institutionalizes bailouts by giving the Fed the power to extend credit to a TBTF bank, or to buy its assets. The FSOC has also increased the likelihood of future bailouts by designating several nonbanks such as AIG and GE Capital as TBTF.

The FSOC gives the president, through his appointees, a broad control over the American economy. This is especially true of the financial firms the FSOC has deemed systemically risky, such as the insurance giant AIG, which it effectively nationalized in 2008 when the Treasury Department made a rescue loan in return for AIG's nonvoting preferred shares. It then converted these shares to voting common shares (sidestepping the need for shareholder consent through a reverse stock split). The loan was for $85 billion at 14 percent interest, at a time when the prevailing market interest rate was 1.5 percent, and was secured by a first claim over AIG's $800 billion in assets. Subsequently, AIG's new management transferred $63 billion to various banks, no strings attached. All of this was done covertly, to hide the fact that a huge government-run financial institution was being used as a conduit to flood the market with capital, and that the recipients were really getting a disguised bailout. There might have been other ways of rescuing AIG, but they were off the table after the government stepped in.[9]

Just how aggressive the government might be in asserting its financial clout became clear when solvent banks were pressured to take unwanted TARP funds by threats that a Federal Reserve Board audit would report that the bank, though entirely solvent, did not comply with the Fed's safety requirements. BB&T CEO John Allison explained why this happened. "At the time that TARP was instituted, there were three large financial institutions that were under stress, but [Federal Reserve Chairman Ben] Bernanke didn't want to bail those three out, because it'd be obvious he was helping them, so he used regulatory, I mean, intense regulatory pressure, to encourage all the $100-billion-and-over institutions to participate."[10]

The Dodd-Frank act's Consumer Financial Protection Bureau has a mandate that includes credit card and consumer real estate mortgage transactions. The bureau can punish lenders who offer loans that the CFPB later deems to be "unfair, deceptive or abusive."[11] Mortgage originators are barred from steering consumers to loans that "the consumer lacks a reasonable ability to repay" or "has predatory characteristics or effects (such as equity stripping, excessive fees, or abusive terms)."[12] These vague and open-ended standards place little discernible limits on the regulators' powers.

The blank check the act handed to the CFPB might easily be cashed with a favored political constituency. For example, in 2012, the bureau announced it would adopt "disparate impact" standards in enforcing the antidiscrimination provisions of the Equal Credit Opportunity Act.[13] Under such standards, a home mortgage lender could be found to have discriminated against a racial group even if it did not intend to do so, so long as it employed a screening test that statistically disadvantaged the group. There are safe harbors if the test serves a sound business purpose, and there isn't a better alternative. That is not easy to prove, however; and the threat that bankers and mortgage lenders might have to bear the cost and embarrassment of defending themselves against charges of discrimination has led them to lower their lending standards.

Some will think these desirable policies (even if similar policies fueled the subprime loan market, and are said to have been a cause of the 2008 financial crisis). Similarly, the strong-arm tactics employed to force all banks to take TARP moneys might be thought a prudent response to a financial emergency. But the point is that these were decisions taken by an administration through its regulators, and Congress was out of the picture. The examples also illustrate how an unscrupulous president might extract special payoffs from particular companies.

The CFPB is immunized from Congress's power to oversee spending because it receives more than $400 million from the Federal Reserve each year, and Congress is prohibited from reviewing that budget. Under the classic conception of the separation of powers, things like this aren't supposed to happen. Legislators aren't supposed to give away power to the executive. Instead, ambition in one branch is expected to counteract ambition in the other, as Madison asserted in Federalist No. 51. That doesn't begin to describe the alliances between members of the same party in different branches, however. In the December 2013 negotiations over raising the nation's debt ceiling, for example, Senate Democrats urged President Barack Obama to ignore Congress and act unilaterally.[14] Madison also failed to take account of how one Congress might seek to legislate over time. There is no single institution called Congress, but rather a shifting group of players inhabiting the Capitol from time to time; one Congress might rationally seek to fetter a successor. There is the 111th Congress, the 112th Congress, and the 113th Congress—and they are all different. As a formal matter, one Congress can't bind a future Congress; but when government is divided under the separation of powers, it may prove exceedingly difficult to repeal an act passed by a prior Congress. Dodd-Frank was passed by a Democratically controlled Congress on July 15, 2010, and it didn't take a genius to recognize that, while the presidency would remain in Democratic hands, control of the House of Representatives likely would flip to Republicans four months later, and it might be prudent to tie the hands of subsequent congresses to fiddle with the statute.

The Independent Payment Advisory Board, set up by the 2010 Patient Protection and Affordable Care Act (now called Obamacare by both sides), is the most remarkable recent congressional grant of rule-making authority to an agency. The IPAB consists of fifteen members, appointed by the president subject to Senate confirmation, and is charged with containing medical care costs, which constitute about 18 percent of the U.S. economy. If projected spending exceeds certain targets, the statute requires the IPAB to issue binding recommendations to reduce spending, which the secretary of health and human services must then implement unless Congress steps in. Should Congress try to curb the board's powers, moreover, Obamacare provides for restricted debate, short deadlines, and supermajoritarian voting requirements. Not surprisingly, all this has led to charges that the IPAB will ration medical care. Indeed, in a belated recognition that Sarah Palin's concerns about Obamacare were well-founded, Paul Krugman said that the "death panels" will be needed to solve the country's looming fiscal crisis.[15]

Were that to happen, we might not find out about it until long afterward. To bring some discipline to the rule-making procedure, the 1946 Administrative Procedure Act requires that, before they become effective, new rules be made public in order to permit the public to comment on them. But there is an exception to the notice-and-comment requirement "when the agency for good cause finds . . . that notice and public procedure thereon are impracticable, unnecessary, or contrary to the public interest."[16] Agencies heavily rely on the good-cause exception, and from 2003 to 2010 did not publish a notice in a third of the cases involving major rules (costing more than $100 million a year).[17]

Presidents have always been able to shape regulatory policies by appointing their allies to head or supervise agencies, and executive oversight powers have increased with government efficiency laws that created the Office of Management and Budget and the Office of Information and Regulatory Affairs. The OMB evaluates the effectiveness of agency programs and policies to ensure that they are consistent with the president's budget and policies. OIRA (pronounced "Oh-Ira") is a branch of the OMB charged with conducting a cost-benefit analysis of proposed new agency rules. Both OMB and OIRA increase a president's control over federal agencies, as well as control by agency heads over their underlings.

OIRA is an especially consequential office, as the question of what counts as a benefit or cost is highly subjective. Just what is the value of a human life, for example? A conservative president might thus charge the office with rolling back the regulatory policies of a prior, more liberal administration. Even in the Obama administration, OIRA killed a good many regulations, such as a proposed update of child agricultural labor standards. The decision came from Cass Sunstein, the über-qualified OIRA head, but the *New York Times* reported that "the ultimate decisions in those cases were made by the president, his senior political advisers or cabinet officers."[18]

The president's control over an agency is especially strong when it is headed by a single person whom he appoints, such as the head of the CFPB or the administrator of the Environmental Protection Agency. The EPA is among the most politicized of agencies, with policies that turn on a dime when a different party wins the presidency. Other agencies that report to a multiperson commission drawn from both parties, such as the Nuclear Regulatory Commission, are more likely to cut things down the middle. The NRC model recognizes that reasonable men, with different political views, may differ about the best set of policies. By contrast, the EPA model assumes that some issues are beyond political dispute, and rest on a basis of incontrovertible, sound science.[19] That is not the history of the EPA, however.

In 2008, then candidate Barak Obama said that he wanted to ban new coal-powered energy plants under proposed cap-and-trade legislation. Once in office, however, the Obama administration spent its political capital on health-care reform, and found that it was unable to tackle global warming even when Democrats controlled both branches of Congress. Stymied on the political front, the administration then turned to the EPA. The Supreme Court had ruled in 2007 that, under the Clean Air Act, carbon dioxide and other greenhouse gases were "air pollutants" and might be regulated by the EPA if it found them a threat to health.[20] The EPA made that finding in 2009, and in 2012 crafted rules that would essentially make it impossible to build new coal-fired plants, a decision upheld by a federal appeals court.[21] While EPA decisions are to be made on the basis of the best scientific evidence, George W. Bush's EPA had argued (unsuccessfully) before the Supreme Court in 2007 that greenhouse gases were not air pollutants, only to be contradicted in 2012 by Obama's EPA, whose head had worked to curtail greenhouse gases in New Jersey prior to her appointment by Obama in 2009. What cannot be done by legislation is now increasingly being done by regulations in which the executive's hand weighs heavily on the scale.

Whatever the makeup of an agency, presidents from Clinton on have asserted the authority to require its head to take specific actions that, it was argued, Congress had implicitly authorized in its legislation, or that inherently are within the scope of the executive branch.[22] As Clinton adviser Paul Begala put it, "Stroke of the pen . . . Law of the land. Kind of cool."[23] By all accounts, we are to expect more of this in the next few years.

Against this, what might Congress do to reassert its legislative powers? Its principal power is that of the purse. Congress can show its pleasure for or displeasure at an agency in the budgetary process, by increasing or decreasing its funding. The degree of supervision can be very precise, as where Congress provided that the Fish and Wildlife Service is banned from spending any money to add any new species to the list of endangered animals. In divided government, however, any such efforts at control will be muted, and in general the effectiveness of congressional oversight has been doubted.[24] The possibility of oversight also pales before the innumerable new regulations that regulators issue each year.

Another thing Congress might do is curtail an agency's power by specifying its duties in greater detail. As the Dodd-Frank example shows, however, Congress is often content to delegate the broadest possible rule-making powers to agencies. At one time this might have been thought to run afoul of the nondelegation of powers doctrine. *Delegatus non potest delegare*, and congressmen (being delegates themselves) are not permitted to delegate their powers. However, the last time a statute was held unconstitutional under the nondelegation doctrine was in the 1935 "sick chickens case," *Schechter Poultry Corp. v. United States*, where the National Industrial Recovery Act was laughed out of court.[25] Congress had given the New Deal's National Recovery Administration (the "Blue

Eagle") the power to authorize and regulate industrial cartels, and the Supreme Court held that the NRA's poultry-industry regulations were based on an improper delegation of legislative authority. Since then, the nondelegation doctrine has withered away. The grant of authority is upheld so long as the court can find an "intelligible principle" that might guide the agency in its exercise of discretion, and that has proven the weakest of obstacles.[26] The end result has been a judicial gift of authority to the executive that has greatly weakened the separation of powers.[27]

Were an agency to embark on a regulatory frolic that bore no relation to its underlying legislation, the courts might nevertheless intervene. One such case was *FDA v. Brown & Williamson Tobacco Corp.*[28] Congress had granted the Food and Drug Administration the authority to regulate "drugs," and in 1996, at Clinton's request, the FDA so defined tobacco. The Supreme Court struck this down, holding that Congress could not have intended to define tobacco as a drug, as that would have given the FDA the power to ban it altogether. Congress had separately rejected such measures in the past, and had enacted its own tobacco-specific statutes. Tellingly, a prior FDA commissioner had told a congressional committee that the agency did not consider tobacco a drug, and courts do not look fondly on agency policy reversals.[29] Before the agency could begin to regulate a major American industry, something more was required from Congress.

The *Brown & Williamson* case is exceptional, however. Under the Supreme Court's 1984 *Chevron* standard,[30] the courts will seldom second-guess the reasons an agency gives for its interpretation of a statute. The deference shown by courts is hardly surprising, since they are not equipped to decide scientific issues themselves and must rely on an agency's experts. That said, "arbitrary and capricious" agency decisions have been impeached in a few cases.[31] In *American Petroleum Institute v. EPA*,[32] for example, a federal appeals court tossed out that agency's mandates for cellulosic biofuels under the Renewable Fuels Standard, finding that they were based not on sound science and neutral measures of costs and benefits, but rather on unfounded aspirations about what the future might bring. The EPA had required the petroleum industry to use an increasing amount of biofuels, or face fines. The problem was that the EPA's rosy predictions about biofuel production proved false. The agency predicted production volumes of 5 million gallons, 6.6 million gallons and 8.7 million gallons in 2010, 2011, and 2012, respectively. In reality, no cellulosic biofuels were produced in the United States in 2010 and 2011, and only 20,069 gallons were produced in 2012. Despite this, the industry had been fined for failing to use nonexistent fuels, and the court held that this was an improper exercise of the EPA's authority. Things are seldom that black and white, however, and *American Petroleum* stands out as one of the few cases in which a court has set aside a regulation. So great is the deference to federal agencies that a scholarly review of the "arbitrary and capricious" standard suggested that it resembles a mere "façade of lawfulness."[33]

A third thing Congress might do is fetter the president's power to remove federal agency heads. As we will see in chapter 8, Congress almost invariably defers to the president on his power to choose his executive-branch officers under the Appointments Clause of Article II, Section 2, clause 2 (the president "shall nominate, and, by and with the Advice and Consent of the Senate, shall appoint Ambassadors, other public Ministers and Consuls, Judges of the supreme Court, and all other Officers of the United States"). The thinking is that the president is entitled to appoint his team. But what if the president seeks to fire a subordinate, and Congress objects? Or if Congress seeks to remove an official it dislikes?

Congressional efforts to reassert control over federal agencies in this way have been frustrated by the courts. In *Myers v. United States*,[34] the Supreme Court ruled in 1926 that Congress could not interfere with the president's exclusive power to appoint (and hence fire) the plaintiff postmaster. Nor can Congress arrogate to itself the power to fire administration officials. Thus in *Bowsher v. Synar* the Supreme Court struck down the 1985 Gramm-Rudman-Hollings Balanced Budget Act, which had given the comptroller general the power to mandate spending reductions and made him removable only by Congress.[35] Those decisions might have rested on the firm grounds of the Appointments Clause, but in both cases, the court invoked a broader principle of separationism.[36]

Congress may nevertheless restrict the president's power to fire top officials in independent agencies. On setting up the Federal Trade Commission in 1914, Congress had provided that the president could not remove its commissioners except for good cause. When FDR fired a commissioner over a simple difference of policy, a conservative Supreme Court, in *Humphrey's Executor v. United States*, held that the FTC was meant to be independent of politics and that Congress had properly limited the president's termination powers.[37] In *Myers*, the president had fired a postmaster, clearly a federal official; in *Humphrey's Executor*, the FTC commissioner was a member of a quasi-judicial or quasi-legislative body, and that was the difference. Similarly, in *Bowsher*, Congress had attempted to give *itself* the right to fire the official; while in *Humphrey's Executor*, Congress had given the *president* the termination power, subject only to the conditions Congress had imposed.

Recently, the Supreme Court has limited Congress's ability to restrict the presidential power to fire lower-level officials, even if they are members of a quasi-judicial or quasi-legislative body. After the 2001 Enron scandal, Congress enacted the Sarbanes-Oxley law, which created the Public Company Accounting Oversight Board (or PCAOB, pronounced "peekaboo") to oversee and regulate accounting firms. The board's members were not government employees and were removable by the Securities and Exchange Commission only for cause. As for the SEC commissioners, they also could only be dismissed for cause. This attempt at double insulation was struck down by the Supreme Court in 2010, in *Free Enterprise Fund v. Public Company Accounting Oversight Board*.[38] The court found that if the president could remove an SEC member only for cause, and the SEC could remove a PCAOB member only for cause, this trenched on Article II's vesting power and the president's duty to "take care that the laws be faithfully executed." What had perversely bothered the court, in an era of Crown government, was the possibility that presidential power might be weakened.

The Supreme Court also relied on the principle of separationism in 1983 to strike down a legislative veto by a single house of Congress, in *Immigration and Naturalization Service v. Chadha.*[39] In a legislative veto, Congress first makes a broad grant of authority to the executive, then subsequently clips his wings by vetoing executive regulations to which it objects. Since it takes both houses of Congress to pass a bill, a veto by one house alone might be thought effective, and the INS statute so provided. In this case, the House of Representatives had vetoed the Attorney General's suspension of an INS deportation proceeding, and regrettably, the court held that the one-house veto violates the principle of separation of powers. Subsequent attempts to impose greater legislative control over agency rule making with a two-house veto have proven ineffective. It is simply too difficult to get both houses of Congress to agree, not to mention a president who is unlikely to want to overturn a regulation adopted by his administration.[40]

In relying on the Framers to justify these decisions, the court misread the records of the Convention, privileging the few delegates who supported a strong separation of powers and a presidential form of government, and ignoring the larger number who wanted something more closely resembling legislative government. Those who had warned of legislative usurpation were the familiar trio of Gouverneur Morris, James Wilson, and (after he was turned by Morris) James Madison,[41] and, as I show in chapter 2, they were in the minority. Worse still, the Supreme Court has abdicated its role as the policeman of the balance of power. It has ignored the rise of the executive branch, and become the enabler of Crown government. It is like an umpire who yearns to award a 15-yard penalty against the hapless team that is down 49–0 at the half.

The President's Nonenforceability Powers. Under his legislative powers, a president may effectively make laws by decree. In addition, he can unmake laws by vetoing them or, more controversially, by refusing to enforce them. Presidents have always had the power to veto a bill, though his veto is subject to a two-thirds override by both houses of Congress. In recent years, however, presidents have enjoyed an expanded, nonreviewable kind of veto power: Without vetoing a bill and risking a congressional override, they might simply decide not to enforce it.

At the Philadelphia Convention, Hamilton would have given the president a general veto (or "negative") over all legislation,[42] without a congressional override; but this was defeated by nine votes to one.[43] The Virginia Plan had proposed a Council of Revision, which could veto bills, but the president would have shared the veto power with members of the bench, and the power was implicitly restricted to legislation where Congress had exceeded its constitutional bounds. This also was rejected by the delegates. What they finally agreed to, on almost the last day of the Convention,[44] was Article I, Section 7's veto, unlimited in scope and subject to a two-thirds congressional override.

On average, few presidential vetoes are overridden by Congress, but it does happen. Congress successfully overrode a third of George W. Bush's vetoes (four out of twelve), and Andrew Johnson and Franklin Pierce had the dubious distinction of seeing more than half of their vetoes undone in this way. A president will thus be tempted to avoid the embarrassment of an override through the simple expedient of declining to enforce laws with which he disagrees, and this can be seen as a nonreviewable veto power. The practice has come to a head over the last ten years with a resurgence in presidential "signing statements," through which a president, without vetoing a bill, issues a statement at its passage that he does not consider himself bound by it. For example, on signing the Supplemental Appropriations Act, 2009, Obama issued the following statement:

Provisions of this bill . . . would interfere with my constitutional authority to conduct foreign relations by directing the Executive to take certain positions in negotiations or discussions with international organizations and foreign governments, or by requiring consultation with the Congress prior to such negotiations or discussions. I will not treat these provisions as limiting my ability to engage in foreign diplomacy or negotiations.[45]

Signing statements became controversial under George W. Bush. Other presidents had issued them before him, and Obama has done so after him. In principle, a president's refusal to enforce an unconstitutional act is not a shocking exercise of executive power.[46] Were Congress to pass a law abridging the right to practice one's religion, for example, no one would expect the president to enforce it while waiting for the Supreme Court to strike it down. What made Bush's signing statements controversial was that the laws he challenged included bans on torture and restrictions on other counterterrorism measures. Bush had asserted broad powers to conduct war as he saw fit, powers that the Supreme Court subsequently curtailed.[47]

Under Obama, this implicit veto power has been expanded to nullify laws that are constitutionally unobjectionable, as a matter of prosecutorial discretion. Congress repeatedly rejected Obama's DREAM Act,[48] which would have given conditional permanent residency to some undocumented illegal immigrants, and so Obama issued an executive order that they not be deported. His new program provides a formalized Citizenship and Immigration Services procedure, called the Deferred Action for Childhood Arrivals, and would allow an estimated 1.7 million young, undocumented immigrants to live and work in the United States. Obama had done more than decline to enforce an old law: By executive fiat, he had replaced it with a new law. One DREAM Act sponsor enthused that "this is the single largest opportunity we've had since [the amnesty program of] 1986 to bring people out of the shadows and into documented status."[49] The executive branch obviously possesses a degree of discretion in the manner in which it enforces law, but if this permits a president to disregard broadly written laws in the face of congressional opposition, and replace them with laws of his own making, one might reasonably ask whether any limits can be set to the expansion of presidential veto powers.

The Obama administration has also released a policy directive relaxing the work requirements that were at the heart of the 1996 welfare reform law (the Personal Responsibility and Work Opportunity Reconciliation

Act), passed after a lengthy debate over how to get people off welfare. The act foresaw the possibility that subsequent administrations might seek to gut its workfare requirements, and therefore made them nonwaivable.[50] The workfare requirements would appear to have dramatically reduced welfare rolls, but whatever one thinks of them, Obama's decision to waive compliance with nonwaivable legislation was a remarkable assertion of presidential power. The expanded veto undercut the spirit, and seemingly the letter, of the major legislative initiative of the Clinton presidency.

Apart from waiving legislation, a president might delay its implementation, as Obama recently did with Obamacare's "employer mandate." Businesses with more than fifty employees are required to provide insurance or pay a fine, and employers at the cusp of that threshold had threatened not to hire more workers or to use part-time workers. Everyone struggled to understand just what a nine-hundred-page bill meant, and that was even before regulations numbering many thousands of pages were rolled out. Outgoing Democratic Senator Max Baucus, one of the fathers of Obamacare, warned that "I just see a huge train wreck coming down."[51] The legislation had specified that it would go into effect in 2014, but the administration postponed this until 2015—conveniently past the congressional elections—by simply refusing to enforce the penalties.

A president's assertion that he need not enforce a properly enacted and constitutionally unassailable statute would seem to contravene Article I, Section 1's vesting power (legislative powers are vested in Congress), and it implicitly violates the presidential veto power of Article I, Section 7 (why veto a bill, and risk an override by Congress, if a president can simply decide not to enforce it?). It also would seem to disregard Article II, Section 3 of the Constitution, which enjoins the president to "take Care that the Laws be faithfully executed," to say nothing of the doctrine of separation of powers itself. As such, the president's nonenforceability power may be constitutionally suspect, but if so, this would seem a breach without a legal remedy, since it is unclear who would have standing to sue.[52] Only a political remedy exists, in the requirement of a referendum on the expansion of presidential power in a popular election—a referendum won by the president in 2012.

Beyond the nonenforcement power is the power presidents have claimed to exempt particular individuals and firms from compliance with a law by granting them a waiver. Such waivers might usefully give a company struggling to adjust to new laws of impenetrable obscurity (such as Obamacare) more time to bring itself within their strictures. At the same time, an administration might play politics by granting waivers from onerous requirements to its special friends. Whether this happens is largely shielded from view, given the large number of waivers that are granted. For example, the Obama administration has granted more than one thousand waivers from Obamacare requirements, and of these nearly a quarter were given to the labor unions that had urged passage of the law. When questioned about this, an administration official denied that politics had played a role;[53] and who could prove otherwise? Nothing in the statute authorizes the administration to grant a waiver, but that didn't seem to matter, either.

The President's Spending Power. The principle that taxing and spending authority is vested in the legislature was one of Parliament's hard-won victories in seventeenth-century English constitutional history, which established the principle that money bills must originate in the House of Commons. The Framers adopted this in Article I, Section 7, which provides that tax legislation must first be introduced in the House of Representatives. Further, Article I, Section 9, clause 7 requires congressional approval in the form of an appropriations statute before any moneys are spent. "If it were otherwise," wrote nineteenth-century Justice Joseph Story, "the executive would possess an unbounded power over the public purse of the nation; and might apply all its monied resources at his pleasure."[54]

The Constitution nevertheless gives the president a role in spending policies, since his signature is required on all money bills. He might therefore bargain for a smaller (Reagan) or bigger (Clinton) government before agreeing to the appropriations bill Congress sends him. In a show-down with Congress, moreover, the precedent of the 1995 government shutdown suggests that voters will side with the president. After Clinton vetoed a Republican appropriations bill in late 1995, the administration ran out of money and suspended nonessential services for nearly a month. The standoff was costly for both sides, but Republicans backed down first, and Clinton went on the win reelection.

While presidents cannot spend moneys without an appropriation, they historically had the negative power *not* to spend appropriated funds. From Jefferson down to Nixon, presidents had relied on a procedure called impoundment in order to not spend moneys that Congress had directed be spent. This procedure was blocked by the Congressional Budget and Impoundment Control Act of 1974, which bars a presiden-tial rescission (a decision not to spend funds) unless this is approved by both houses of Congress within forty-five days.[55] This restriction on the president's authority was upheld by the Supreme Court, in a case where Richard Nixon had sought through a rescission to sidestep a congres-sional override of his veto of environmental legislation.[56] Nevertheless, the president's power to hold up spending, short of a formal rescission, can amount to much the same thing. The congressional appropriation for 2010 expressly prohibited canceling the Constellation space program, but the Obama administration subsequently announced that it would drop the program. When congressmen objected that this violated the law, the NASA administrator responded that NASA had not canceled the program, but was only looking into doing so.[57] Three years later the program remains in limbo. This was possibly a prudent decision, but nevertheless shows how a president may skirt a statute.

In spending decisions, Congress can tie a president's hands through "earmarks," or legislative spending mandates. Earmarks form less than 2 percent of federal spending,[58] however, and for the rest, presidents enjoy a broad discretion in how to spend allocated moneys. There was a particularly extensive grant of discretionary authority to the president under the 2009 stimulus package,[59] which appropriated $787 billion in spending. Of this, $27 billion was allocated for rail and port facilities, $8 billion for high-speed rail, and $16.8 billion for energy efficiency and renewable energy projects, with relatively little guidance about how these enormous funds were to be spent. Inevitably, this led to Republican charges of wasteful spending by the administration. In particular, the allocation for renewable energy projects was the source of the funds for the ill-fated $500-million Solyndra loan guarantee.[60] This led many to conclude with then National Economic Council director Larry Summers that the government is a lousy venture capitalist.[61] Were one to be exceedingly generous, the Solyndra loan guarantee might be thought not imprudent when viewed from an *ex ante* perspective, and complaints made after Solyndra's bankruptcy might be considered an example of the hindsight bias. The point, however, is that the president has a broad spending power. The Solyndra guarantee was not made out of the blue, but only after frequent meetings between Solyndra executives and White House officials, who had touted the bailout as an example of the president's support for green energy.

The 2008–09 GM-Chrysler auto bailout was an especially remarkable example of presidential spending power. More than $80 billion in TARP funds was used to bail out the two car manufacturers, even though this contravened the appropriation statute. Congress had authorized TARP moneys to be spent on "financial institutions" such as banks, savings and loans, credit unions, and insurance companies—not on car companies. Bush sought approval for the automobile bailout from Congress, but it failed to overcome a Senate filibuster.[62] Nevertheless, Bush and Obama went ahead with the auto bailout, showing how aggressive presidents may stare down Congress and ignore the Constitution.[63]

Dodd-Frank and the stimulus package were ostensibly neutral economic measures, but the manner in which they were carried out illustrates how a president might use his powers to advance his political agenda. Minorities, women, and labor unions are important members of the Democratic coalition, and each did well from financial reform and the bailouts. When a number of car dealerships were terminated in the auto bailout, preference was given to minority- or female-owned distributorships.[64] The Chrysler bailout, orchestrated by Obama, his Treasury secretary (Tim Geithner), and the National Economic Council director (Larry Summers), featured a preferential payout to union allies in the United Auto Workers, at the expense of more highly secured bondholders. The entire auto bailout is estimated to have cost taxpayers more than $20 billion, which was about the size of the payout to the union.[65] The president also pushed his clean-energy initiatives in the Chrysler reorganization. Fiat Motors emerged with a 20 percent interest in the new firm, to be increased to 35 percent under certain conditions that included producing energy-efficient cars for the American market.[66] One economist reported that Democratic states got more money than Republican states, union states more than nonunion ones, and wealthy states more than poor ones.[67] To assert that the bailouts were good policy misses the point, which is that the relevant decision was taken by the president, not by Congress, and that politics played an important role in the spending decisions.

The President's War Power. The Framers recognized that the president could react more quickly to a crisis than the legislature, and that he should be free to respond to a military attack on the country. Several delegates expressed the worry that this would give him too much power, but did not see their way around this.[68] The compromise that found its way into the Constitution was proposed by Madison and Elbridge Gerry: Congress was given the power to declare war, "leaving to the Executive the power to repel sudden attacks."[69] Roger Sherman summarized what most of the delegates likely took from the discussion. "The president should be able to repel and not to commence war."[70]

Among the Framers, Alexander Hamilton was at the other extreme, in his support for broad presidential powers. In a speech on June 18, 1787, Hamilton expressed a desire for a president who "dares execute his powers,"[71] one with veto powers over legislation, and lifetime tenure during good behavior. Call him an elective monarch if you want, he said, but that was what the country needed. Hamilton expanded on these ideas in Federalist No. 70, where he argued that a "vigorous" presidency was consistent with the republican form of government. "Energy in the Executive is a leading character in the definition of good government," he wrote. "Decision, activity, secrecy, and despatch will generally characterize the proceedings of one man in a much more eminent degree than the proceedings of any greater number; and in proportion as the number is increased, these qualities will be diminished."

The passage is often taken to represent the opinions of the Framers about executive power, but this ignores what they said in their debates. Hamilton was so far outside the mainstream that when he finished his speech, no one seconded it or even thought it necessary to speak against it. A few days later a delegate reviewed the various plans that had been presented, and of Hamilton, said that "though he has been praised by every body, he had been supported by none."[72] Hamilton recognized that he had marginalized himself, and this might explain why he absented himself for much of the rest of the Convention.

The Framers agreed, in Article II, Section 1 of the Constitution, that "the executive Power shall be vested in a President." They did not have an expansive view of what that power might be. They did not foresee the modern regulatory state, and imagined that government might be kept to a modest size. Moreover, they would not have foreseen the quarrels between the executive and legislative branches that we now take for granted, since both branches were to be inextricably bound up with each other. State legislatures would appoint both the senators and the presidential electors, with most presidential elections thrown to the House of Representatives, voting by state. There were safety valves, with presidential vetoes and congressional overrides, and the requirement of senatorial consent to major presidential appointments. For the most part, however, what they anticipated was cooperation, not conflict, among the branches, with Congress as the dominant branch. What they would not have understood is what has come to be called the "unitary executive" theory of presidential governance.

The unitary executive theory holds (uncontroversially) that the executive power vests solely in the president, and (more controversially) that Congress cannot interfere with the president's decisions on a broad range of executive issues, including national security. What the theory has going for it are the two compelling advantages presidents enjoy over Congress: Presidents have access to up-to-the-minute information about foreign threats that no individual congressman possesses; and presidents have the ability to act unilaterally, while Congress can act only as a group, after debate and a vote.

Congress cannot feasibly prevent a president from launching military operations, but can subsequently employ its spending power to deny funds for the prosecution of a war, and is particularly willing to do so when American troops are not engaged. After Nixon's Vietnamization policy and the 1973 Paris Peace Accords, U.S. military activities in South Vietnam ceased. What remained was U.S. military support for the South Vietnamese government. Congress cut off funding for this in 1974, after Nixon's resignation, and South Vietnam fell to communist North Vietnam less than a year later. Ten years later, another Democratic Congress cut off aid to the Nicaraguan contras, again an administration-supported war in which no U.S. troops were engaged. Rather than abandon the contras, the administration unwisely diverted funds from secret arms sales to Iran, resulting in the Iran-Contra scandal that tainted the last two years of Reagan's presidency. The need to secure spending authorization explains why presidents are more likely to threaten or employ force when their party controls Congress.[73]

When American troops are engaged, however, Congress is far less ready to step in, because this would be thought unpatriotic. The Federalist Party would have denied financial support for the War of 1812, but this helped sign the party's death notice. In 2007, a Democratic Congress was clearly unhappy with the war in Iraq, but stopped short of denying funding for it.[74] Then Senator Obama opposed the war, but consistently voted funds for it.[75]

Apart from cutting off funding, there is seemingly little Congress can do to prevent a president from embarking on a war. In 1973, a Democratic Congress overrode a Nixon veto to pass the War Powers Resolution,[76] which would prevent presidents from sending American troops into action abroad without the consent of Congress, except when the country has been attacked. Even then, troops are to be withdrawn within sixty to ninety days, unless Congress authorizes the war. Since its passage, however, every president, Republican and Democrat, has asserted that the resolution is unconstitutional. Clinton disregarded it during the Bosnian and Serbian bombing campaigns. Individual congressmen have protested this, and even tried to litigate the issue, but Congress has quietly acquiesced in the assertion of presidential power.[77]

It has thus been accepted, at least as a constitutional convention, that presidents do not require congressional approval to conduct military operations, and even to send troops into combat. In the past, some presidents have thought it prudent to secure such approval, as both Bushes did before the two Iraq wars. Democrats were able to maintain their deniability over the issue by giving the Republicans just enough support to pass the resolutions, but not a majority of their votes. Even Democrats who supported the resolutions, like Joe Biden, John Kerry, and Hillary Clinton, subsequently found themselves able to explain their votes away when the war became unpopular. They were for it before they were against it. A similar pattern was observed in 1999, with a Democratic president and a Republican Congress, over the U.S. bombing campaign in Serbia. The House authorization vote passed, 219 to 191, but while 174 of the 192 Democrats supported Clinton, 173 of the 217 Republicans opposed him.[78]

The War Powers Resolution has thus become something of a dead letter. William Howell and Jon Pevehouse report that there is no evidence that it has reduced the number of major conflicts in which the United States has engaged.[79] Congressional approval seems neither necessary to authorize a war, nor sufficient to stop the mouths of sunshine hawks when a once-popular war becomes troublesome.[80]

The conferral of war-making power on the president clothes him with immense political power, which he might abuse were he to launch a war for domestic political reasons—for example, to distract attention from political scandals at home. On October 25, 1973, the United States moved to DEFCON 3 (a level of military preparedness declared only once since then, during the September 11, 2001, attacks). This was in reaction to Soviet threats against Israel during the Yom Kippur War—but it was also only five days after the "Saturday Night Massacre," in which Nixon fired Watergate special prosecutor Archibald Cox. Attorney General Elliot Richardson and Deputy Attorney General William D. Ruckelshaus immediately resigned in protest, and pressure quickly mounted for Nixon's impeachment. The Soviet threat to Israel was real, but cynics questioned whether the saber-rattling was an attempt to busy giddy minds with foreign quarrels, as Shakespeare's Henry IV had advised his son. Similar doubts were raised about a 1998 cruise-missile strike on a Sudanese pharmaceutical factory that, it was claimed, was aiding Osama bin Laden. The evidence about the link to bin Laden was weak,[81] and the strike came only three days after Clinton had lied to a grand jury about his relationship with Monica Lewinsky, and a few weeks before the release of the Starr Report, which cited eleven possible impeachable offenses. It didn't help that all this happened at the same time as the release of a film entitled *Wag the Dog*, which portrays a president who launches a war to distract attention from a sex scandal.

While the prestige of the presidency is such that few questioned the 1998 strike, empirical studies report that presidential decisions to use military force are more closely correlated with domestic political issues than with the international environment.[82] A "diversionary hypothesis" posits that presidents embark on war to distract attention from unpopular domestic affairs, such as the Clinton sex scandal. Findings that, since the 1950s, presidents are more likely to go to war during periods of high unemployment are consistent with diversionary explanations of the exercise of the war power.[83] Carl von Clausewitz's dictum that war is the continuation of politics by other means was never more true than in recent American history.

The president's war power has expanded through new doctrines of war and new technologies of war making. In the past, presidents sought to defend the decision to go to war in terms of threats to the country's national interest. More recently, however, scholars have urged that wars might be justified even when America's interests are not directly affected. In the face of humanitarian crises abroad, it has been argued that stronger nations have not only the right but also the responsibility to protect ("R2P") people in other countries from atrocities. Obama has let other nations take the initiative in launching humanitarian wars, preferring to "lead from behind," and for this has been criticized by the interventionist wing of the Republican Party. Many will find R2P a compelling justification for military intervention, with the example of the 1994 Rwandan genocide showing what can happen when a president declines to step in. It remains to be seen whether future presidents will more enthusiastically embrace R2P, and put the country in a continuous state of war.

Technological developments, and the country's technological edge in warfare, also serve to enhance the presidential war power. The Obama administration has asserted that presidents have the unfettered power to conduct drone and missile strikes so long as there is little chance of U.S. casualties,[84] and given the changing face of high-tech warfare, this would leave presidents with broad war-making powers. The celerity of modern warfare also serves to empower presidents, for whom the sixty-day window of the War Powers Resolution may be more than enough time to intervene decisively in a conflict. NATO's 2011 Libyan war succeeded largely because the United States destroyed the country's air defense system and command structure in the opening days of the mission. Thereafter, U.S. support for the NATO air strikes was limited to operating aerial refueling tankers and intelligence-gathering drones, which the administration said did not require congressional approval.

In all these ways, a fourth American constitution has emerged in recent years, one dominated by the executive branch. Mason called this an elective monarchy; I have called it Crown government, for the president's power may be compared to that of George III from 1770 to 1782, during the period of his personal rule. The evolution is the result of broad economic and technological changes, and the best evidence of this comes from the similar experience of the parliamentary country that most resembles the United States.

CROWN GOVERNMENT IN CANADA

When Bagehot wrote *The English Constitution* in 1867, he described the British constitution as one of "cabinet government," in which the prime minister shared power with his senior colleagues in Parliament, and policy decisions were taken in cabinet meetings. This described the Canadian government as recently as the 1950s and 1960s. Today, however, crucial decisions are generally made before the cabinet meets, by the prime minister and his top aides in Canada's Prime Minister's Office (in Britain, the Cabinet Office).[85] The Canadian cabinet has become more a discussion than a decision forum, one where ministers are briefed about government policies to keep them on message and enforce cabinet solidarity. The prime minister controls the agenda, and nothing happens without a push from him. The result is what political scientist Donald J. Savoie calls "court government," with the prime minister's advisers our modern-day courtiers.[86]

Cabinet members remain important political allies, and a government may be weakened—at times, fatally—by the resignation of a prominent minister. In Britain, Geoffrey Howe quit Margaret Thatcher's cabinet in 1990 over entry into the European Union, and she resigned as prime minister three weeks later. In Canada, Douglas Harkness and George Hees resigned from John Diefenbaker's cabinet in 1963 over defense policy, and the sense that Diefenbaker's minority government had fallen apart led to its defeat in a nonconfidence vote three days later. These are exceptions, however, and the prime minister's rivals in his party, such as Britain's Gordon Brown or Canada's Paul Martin, must ordinarily wait patiently until a Tony Blair or Jean Chrétien decides in his own good time that he will step down as prime minister.

The decline of cabinet government has been hastened by the increased interconnectedness of policy decisions. In the past, a powerful minister of agriculture might rule his department like a private fiefdom, resisting any attempt from outside to second-guess his decisions. Today, however, decisions in one department might easily give rise to environmental, social, and fiscal issues across a number of other departments. This has led to a centralized government in which cabinet members yield power to the prime minister.[87]

To assist them, prime ministers have sought the assistance of about one hundred top advisers in the Prime Minister's Office, headed by the prime minister's chief of staff. The PMO resembles the much larger Office of the President of the United States, and is composed of political appointees who hold office while the government is in power, and who depart when it falls. They are not a parallel cabinet, but over the last forty years major decisions have been moved from the cabinet to the PMO, a development that occurred in the United States at roughly the same time, with a transfer of power from the cabinet to the White House and presidential czars.[88]

In similar fashion, power within the civil service has been centralized. Before the emergence of Crown government, the most senior civil servant in a government department reported to his cabinet minister, who in this way controlled the flow of information. In Canada, this began to change in the 1960s, with the emergence of the Privy Council Office (in Britain, the Cabinet Office) as the senior arm of the civil service, charged with overseeing the implementation of the government's programs in every department. The PCO has become a rite of passage for the most ambitious of civil servants, a place to network with other rising stars, with whom one can afterward deal across departments. It is headed by the clerk of the privy council (in Britain, the cabinet secretary), who is the prime minister's deputy minister and the senior official in the civil service. "Our role was not to rival or compete with the departments," reported a very able PCO clerk, "but it was our role to know all the right questions about everything coming forward and to cover them in our briefing of the prime minister."[89] Franklin Roosevelt wanted something like this for America, but this, along with other proposals to strengthen the executive branch, was denounced as a "dictator bill," and went nowhere.[90]

Both the PMO and PCO exist to help the prime minister, with advice on policy directions assigned to the PMO, and on administration to the PCO. In practice, the distinction between the two kinds of advice is difficult to maintain; and while members of the PMO are political appointees and those in the PCO are career civil servants, both work closely with each other, and occasionally change jobs.[91] Although the civil service is ostensibly nonpartisan, its members must have a finely tuned political sense to survive and rise in the ranks.[92] The idea, popularized by the BBC television series *Yes, Minister*, that the deputy minister (the permanent under-secretary in Britain) runs the show, playing Jeeves to the minister's Bertie Wooster, is merely an amusing (and reassuring) fiction.

If the cabinet has been relegated to a secondary role, backbench MPs have less power still. Two-time Prime Minister Pierre Trudeau famously described them as "nobodies,"[93] and their lack of influence was recently underlined by Paul Martin.

> *Over the last forty years or so, Canadians have seen the influence of individual members of parliament eroded as the power of the prime minister and the executive branch of government grew. . . . They vote according to the dictates of their party, and too often, when their party is in power, no one in the government cares particularly what they have to say.*[94]

Compared to American political parties, parliamentary parties are much more under the control of the party leader, whether he be the prime minister or the leader of the Opposition. American congressmen have their own power base, separate from the national party, because of the manner in which American government protects incumbents through gerrymandering and pork-barrel spending. Once elected, they are likely to be reelected, unless caught in bed "with a live boy or a dead girl," as Louisiana's Edwin Edwards once boasted (before he was sentenced to prison on racketeering charges). The average reelection rate since 1990 is 87 percent for senators and 94 percent for House members.[95] By contrast, a third of the MPs elected to the Canadian Parliament in 2011 (109 out of 309) were new to the House, and little more than a third (120 out of 309) were first elected prior to 2006.

WHY DID IT HAPPEN?

There are three reasons why one might expect today's executive to be vastly more powerful than his eighteenth-century peer in America, Britain, and Canada. The first, suggested by Jean-Jacques Rousseau, is that over time, power tends to localize in a single person. Second, the growth of the regulatory state in the twentieth century shifted power from the legislature to a bureaucracy responsible to the executive. And third, the changed role of the media has made a star of the executive, at the expense of the legislature.

The Logic of Political Power. Following Montesquieu, Rousseau thought liberty better protected in smaller rather than larger states. Montesquieu had identified what he saw as an informational problem: In a large republic, it is difficult to identify the public good, and this permits politicians to prefer wasteful, private goods (such as inefficient congressional earmarks) to public ones.[96] To this Rousseau added a further large-state pathology: A large state is necessarily one with a too-powerful executive. Large states require strong governments to control their more extensive territory, and more legislators to represent the greater number of people. As the number of legislators increases, however, each member's influence weakens until, as a group, they become ineffectual. Since a strong government is needed in a large state, a strong executive will emerge to fill the political void.[97]

In Federalist No. 51, Madison had imagined a contest in which ambition would counteract ambition, and the legislature would check excessive executive power. What this forgets, Rousseau would have objected, is that the legislature is composed of many people, and the executive of only one, and that it is more difficult for a group of people to coordinate on a course of action than it is for a single person. Charles Lindbergh made the same point when asked how it was that, all alone, he had flown across the Atlantic. "Well," he answered, "I didn't do it by committee."

Two hundred years later, Rousseau's insight would come to be called, variously, the *prisoners' dilemma* or the *common pool* problem. When it is collectively rational for people to cooperate, but each person is better off if he lets the other fellow do it, then no one might cooperate. That's the moral of the story about belling the cat: The mice will all be better off if one of them puts a bell on the cat to warn them when he is near, but just which mouse is going to bell the cat? Similarly, legislators as a group might be better off if they unite to oppose a power-seeking executive, but individually each might fail to do so. (For the best, the very best, explanation of this, simply google "Dilbert prisoner's dilemma".)

As I write, America struggles to deal with a fiscal crisis. To solve this, the president and Congress must agree on a remedy. Obama has one plan. From Congress, however, no single plan has emerged, only a swirling group of inchoate proposals. Both sides can claim the support of the voters in the 2012 elections, Obama in the White House and the Republicans in the House. But Obama is a single player, while Republicans are disorganized and divided among themselves; and as Rousseau suggested, the game favors the unitary executive.

The Regulatory State. Three features of regulatory rule making give an advantage to agencies and the executive over Congress. First, regulatory rules may be issued expeditiously by an agency head who is appointed by the president, and who serves at his pleasure (subject to the conditions on removal that Congress might have attached for quasi-legislative agencies). By contrast, congressional lawmaking happens only after a lengthy process in which both houses and the president agree on a bill. Second, regulatory rules are self-financing, since they place the costs of compliance on the private sector. If the EPA imposes a new environmental mandate on Detroit, the car manufacturers must simply comply with it. Unlike congressional laws, there are no tax and budgetary considerations, no authorizing and appropriating procedures to be followed. Third, even when agencies follow the notice-and-comment procedure, their decisions are often veiled from public view and accountability, unlike congressional action. Chris deMuth described the difference:

> *Regulatory legislation is public and symbolic—characterized by hearings, speeches, and votes where the people's representatives declare themselves for or against safe drinking water, corporate fraud, and discrimination against the handicapped. Regulatory administration, in contrast, is cloistered and quotidian—characterized by piecework rule-making, interest-group maneuvering, and impenetrable complexity.*[98]

As a consequence, the regulatory state has expanded beyond anything that the Framers could have anticipated. Many of them would have shared Roger Sherman's belief that laws could be enacted with sufficient specificity to exclude judgment calls about how they should be applied. Instead, the executive would only have to follow the legislature's instructions, rather like the way one follows the printed instructions in assembling an IKEA table. Broad grants of discretion to the executive were dangerous, for they smacked of the royal prerogative against which the Framers had fought a revolution.

Sherman's ideas about the prerogative, which seem so dated today, were shared by many of his contemporaries. Britain's Jeremy Bentham, who believed he had a genius for legislation, also subscribed to a theory of legislative supremacy. All of law, he thought, might usefully be codified by the ideal, rational legislator, one whose laws, informed by the best science of the day, prescribed the most efficient set of sanctions and rewards. Bentham's enemy was the common law judge, and specifically

Blackstone, who preferred judges to legislators and celebrated the judges who tempered the severity of Parliament's cruel criminal sanctions.[99] That wouldn't do, thought Bentham. Since the legislator has better information than judges about the best set of laws, any deviation from his intentions would simply introduce error and uncertainty. Strictly speaking, judge-made common law was not even law, he thought. Only statute law was the real thing.[100] This thinking informed the nineteenth-century codification movement, and its influence can still be seen in the U.S. Federal Sentencing Guidelines, whose purpose is to reduce a judge's discretion in criminal sentencing.

All this was easier to swallow in a thin eighteenth-century government, with fewer rules that did not intrude overmuch on personal choice. But as legal rules expanded in scope and number, and an ideology of state planning took hold, it became necessary to delegate the draftsmanship of rules to the regulators. Nevertheless, Sherman's ideal of legislative supremacy continued to attract adherents, and in particular informed Max Weber's celebration of an ideal, rational, bureaucratic government. The legislature could not provide a detailed road map, but it could provide the general laws and intelligible principles to which a Weberian civil service, composed of scientific experts, would adhere. The bureaucrat would have decree-making powers, but would regulate according to the legislator's principles, and would not be called on to exercise much personal discretion.[101]

This conception of the bureaucrat and of legislative supremacy, with its faith in public-spirited civil servants and objective, scientific management, was contested from four different directions, with arguments that bureaucrats necessarily exercise personal discretion, and that this requires that they be supervised by the executive. Writing not long after Bentham, Hegel foresaw the rise of the administrative state, and recognized that this must expand executive power. The legislator's rules cannot be applied like the axioms of geometry, he thought, but instead require practical judgment, the ability to sense how a rule might properly be applied. For example, the legislator might want to ban some forms of general behavior, such as the unfair, deceptive, and abusive acts proscribed by the Consumer Financial Protection Bureau. Determining whether one is guilty of such a practice requires the virtue the Greeks called *phronēsis*, the practical judgment that determines whether a particular instance fits under a general rule—as opposed to the methodical and technical application of the highly specific rules in the IKEA box. This means that the bureaucrat must be allowed a measure of discretion, and because of this he must be monitored by the executive.[102]

Second, technological changes have vastly increased the scope of rule making beyond anything that the legislator can handle. At the dawn of the automobile age, a car's safety features came down to the brake and the horn. Since then, developments in car technology have increased the number of safety devices by many orders of magnitude. In addition, new devices such as driving sensors and rearview cameras come on stream with a rapidity the legislator could never hope to match. Because of this, regulators necessarily exercise an enormous discretion and ability to determine public policy, and this has shifted power from the legislative to the executive branch.

Third, regulations acquire a life of their own and expand beyond anything the legislator might have imagined. The *Washington Post* recently provided an amusing example of how they breed like rabbits, with a story about how a magician was required to come up with a disaster plan for "Casey," the bunny he pulled out of his hat. The regulation began life with a 1966 statute that required scientists to obtain licenses for dogs and cats used in their research. In 1970 the law was amended to catch "exhibitors" of other animals as well. The 1966 bill was four pages long, but now the Department of Agriculture has fourteen pages of regulations just for rabbits. The magician didn't know how to come up with a disaster plan, but a professional writer of such plans volunteered her help. What she came up with added up to twenty-eight pages, which she admitted was a bit on the short side. But then we're only talking about a rabbit, she added apologetically. "It's not going to stop traffic and cause car accidents."[103]

Fourth, scholars in the public-choice school of economics emphasize the bureaucrat's private incentives, which call for the policing that only the executive can provide.[104] Bureaucrats can be expected to craft policies that increase the size of their bailiwick, even if this is not in the public interest. Fish gotta swim, birds gotta fly, and bureaucrats have to build their empires. They can also be expected to be excessively risk-averse when the costs of a wrong decision are highly public, as compared to the benefits of a right decision. For example, the Food and Drug Administration has been faulted for delaying or barring the introduction of valuable new drugs because of negligible risk factors. Excessive risk aversion will kill more people than it saves, but the FDA won't bear those costs itself, since the costs of failing to approve life-saving new drugs are not observable, while the costs of unexpected harmful side effects are highly public. The rationally risk-averse regulator has therefore an incentive to block innovation and slow down clinical development.[105] Again, this argues for the oversight that the executive can provide far better than Congress.

For all these reasons, the rise of the regulatory state has coincided with the expansion of executive power in America, Britain, and Canada. The conceit that economic processes might be planned by regulators was not a new one, for seventeenth-century *dirigistes* such as Louis XIV's minister Jean-Baptiste Colbert had similar aspirations. What a Colbert lacked, however, were the technological advances in communications and information that made central planning seem feasible—and this in an age of standardized mass production, where both industry and government seemed amenable to top-down rules.[106] New Dealers, who sought an expanded government and happily reposed confidence in scientific management by public-spirited regulators, applauded the change, while conservatives such as Lord Hewart opposed it. In 1929, Hewart famously labeled the modern bureaucratic state the "New Despotism." Recognizing how it had transferred power from Parliament to the prime minister, he lamented that it had reversed the gains Parliament had made against the Crown. After struggling for centuries to wrest power from the King, Parliament now passed general statutes that conferred quasi-judicial and quasi-legislative responsibilities upon the executive, in the person of the prime minister. It would not be amiss, thought Hewart, for a new John Dunning to propose that "the power of the Crown has increased, is increasing, and ought to be diminished."[107]

The Role of the Media. The third reason for the expansion of executive power is the change the media has made in modern politics. In 1860, Abraham Lincoln conducted his presidential campaign from the State House in Springfield, Illinois.

> *Here, Mr. Lincoln, attended only by his private secretary, Mr. Nicolay, passed the long summer days of the campaign, receiving the constant stream of visitors, anxious to look upon a real presidential candidate. There was free access to him; not even an usher stood at the door; any one might knock and enter.... He made no addresses, wrote no public letters, held no conferences.*[108]

With a better system of transportation and vigorous campaigners such as Teddy Roosevelt, this had changed fifty years later. It changed further still with the use Franklin Roosevelt made of the radio with his Fireside Chats. The greatest change, however, came with television, which focuses more on appearance than substance, on personalities more than policies. The technological changes in the media have served to endow presidents and prime ministers with star power, making them the government's central actors.

The 1960 presidential election was the first time television played a dominant role in an election. Those who listened to the debate on the radio came away thinking that Nixon had won, but the verdict of television viewers was very different.[109] Nixon looked better on radio than on TV. The same change in the mode of campaigning would be seen in the 1968 Canadian general election, in which the Liberals, under an ebullient Pierre Trudeau, defeated the Tories, led by the craggily ugly

Robert Stanfield. The cameras loved Trudeau, as they had Kennedy. They followed him when he stared down rock-throwing protestors, slid down banisters, did full gainers at the swimming pool, and performed pirouettes in palaces. Marshall McLuhan found in him the perfect leader, cool and detached, for the new medium, and this was the start of a beautiful friendship that mutual incomprehension did nothing to mar. Stanfield was no match for Trudeau. In the 1974 election, a reporter took thirty-six pictures of the awkward-looking Stanfield tossing a football. On the last catch he fumbled the ball—and that was the photo on the front page of every newspaper in Canada the next morning. Stanfield's Tories never could beat Trudeau's Liberals, and Trudeau remembered his opponent as "a quiet, decent man who perhaps entered federal politics at a time when his virtues were not appreciated."[110]

At one time it was thought that the rise of new media would prevent a president from amassing excessive personal power. That doesn't seem to be happening in America, however. Instead, the Obama White House has used social media and content creation to compete with the new media and manipulate the old media. The White House is a rival news organization, with its own video network and distribution system, and need not rely on print journalism or the television networks to get its message out. It no longer feels the need to put the president before probing reporters, preferring teleprompters and softball questions from *People* magazine. The fawning reporter is rewarded with access, the hostile journalist frozen out. *Politico* explained how this has transformed American journalism and government.

> *The results are transformational. With more technology, and fewer resources at many media companies, the balance of power between the White House and press has tipped unmistakably toward the government. This is an arguably dangerous development, and one that the Obama White House—fluent in digital media and no fan of the mainstream press—has exploited cleverly and ruthlessly. And future*

presidents from both parties will undoubtedly copy and expand on this approach.[111]

Crisis Government. A fourth and less than persuasive reason is sometimes given for Crown government: A powerful executive can react more quickly to a crisis than can the legislature. As a critique of weak executives, this takes two forms. First, it is said that a weak leader will attract foreign enemies against which the state cannot adequately defend itself. Second, weak executives, faced with an emergency, must ignore legal constraints meant to bind them, and thus will in time become the strong executives of Crown government. The first argument was made by Joseph Schumpeter, the second by Carl Schmitt.

Economist Schumpeter expressed his concerns about the weakness of Western democracies in *Capitalism, Socialism and Democracy*, a book celebrated by free-market adherents for its portrayal of capitalism's creative destruction of inefficient business, but one with an underlying pessimistic message about the future of capitalism. Published in 1942, the book argued that capitalism saps the private virtues that transcend self-interest and motivate citizens to defend free institutions, and that this invites attacks by nondemocratic enemies.[112] It might well have seemed that way to many people at the beginning of the Second World War, but so far as a political theory can be falsified by history, this one was, by the democracies' defeat of the Axis powers in that war, and the fall of Communism. The parliamentary governments of Britain and the Commonwealth and the presidential government of America proved more than able to mobilize their countries for war. These were not the Crown governments of recent years, but they were nevertheless able to bring strong leaders to the fore to fight a war.

While Schumpeter saw democracies succumbing to external threats, Schmitt identified an internal challenge. Democratic governments could make laws for normal, expected contingencies, but were unable to respond to or even plan for emergencies, which by definition were unforeseeable.

These could only be dealt with by bending or ignoring legislation by an executive with the power to suspend the law and rule personally. In exceptional circumstances, a law-bound Weimar Republic must thus make way for a dictator; and when the dictator decides what constitutes the exception, he is the ultimate power in the state. In Schmitt's famous phrase, "sovereign is he who decides on the exception."[113]

Schmitt was a German political theorist whose admiration for strong executives led him to embrace National Socialism in 1933, a creed that he never renounced after the war. While this would seem to consign him to a political bestiary, his ideas have enjoyed a revival as a challenge to liberal norms of democratic government and the rule of law.[114] That's surprising for several reasons, most obviously because the costs of dictatorship outweigh any temporary benefits of one-man rule, given the Hitlers and Mussolinis that such theories would justify. An alleged "crisis" won't persuade voters to surrender power to a dictator, unless he uses guns to convince them.

As a critique of the rule of law, moreover, Schmitt's attack unwinds from within. When the definition of an emergency expands, it becomes expected and routinized. The legislator can plan for it, erect structures, appropriate moneys. The best example of this is the Federal Emergency Management Agency, which by anticipating disasters constitutes a legislative rebuke to Schmitt's theory. In 2011 alone, FEMA stepped in 238 times for major disasters, emergencies, or fires. Such emergencies, for which the legislator has prepared a response, are a splendid opportunity for pork-barrel spending; and like the hurricanes that *The Onion* tells us are attracted to trailer parks, disasters are more likely to occur just before a presidential election.[115] The amount of disaster relief is also significantly correlated with the number of representatives the state has on congressional oversight committees.[116] We have more supposed "emergencies" today than ever in the past,[117] but this is a consequence, and not a cause, of the rise of Crown government.

Presidents frequently issue executive orders as a response to emergencies, but if this explained the rise of Crown government we would be having more real crises today than in the past. Some have indeed argued this, but such beliefs are entirely ahistorical. To suggest that the British have more emergencies today than in their bloody fifteenth century is absurd, and throughout their long nineteenth century, Americans had emergencies as trying as any today. To be sure, there are real emergencies that call for exceptional action from an executive, such as the Pearl Harbor and 9/11 attacks. These are the most serious emergencies America has faced in the last one hundred years; and in both cases, presidents sought and received congressional approval for their responses within days, with the declaration of war against Japan on December 8, 1941, and the congressional resolution on the Authorization for Use of Military Force Against Terrorists on September 14, 2011. It is obviously a mistake to think that legislatures cannot move quickly, or that the vast executive branch can turn on a dime to fight a war. America's experience with the 9/11 crisis, and especially with the barriers to the passage of information within the government and the departmental jealousies it revealed, would appear to have put the lie to the idea that a 535-person Congress must necessarily move more slowly than an executive branch composed of millions of bureaucrats.

Some crises might require a response before an executive can obtain legislative approval. Arguably, one such case was Pierre Trudeau's invocation of Canada's War Measures Act in October 1970 to quell what he described as an "apprehended insurrection" by Quebec separatists, who had murdered Quebec's vice-premier. The statute, passed during the First World War, permitted the government to suspend the writ of habeas corpus; and with its new powers, Trudeau's government arrested about five hundred separatists (of whom nearly all were released within a few months). Trudeau's actions were immensely popular throughout Canada, even in Quebec, and were supported by the Opposition party in Parliament, which continued sitting during the crisis. The War Measures Act was subsequently repealed, replaced by a statute that requires a government, within seven days after declaring an emergency, to ask Parliament to sanction its action.[118] Even before this, Parliament could have fettered the exercise of emergency powers during the October Crisis by amending the War Measures Act. Where the legislature can be brought in to approve or reject exceptional measures, then, emergencies cannot be said to require Schmitt's sovereign—"he who decides on the exception." If the legislature recognizes the exception, it and not the executive is Schmitt's sovereign.

Nevertheless, when legislatures authorize emergency action, they must stand back and hand the ball to the executive. Legislatures (and courts) lack the informational resources to conduct wars or manage the response to an emergency. That responsibility must lie with the executive, who is held accountable for mismanagement. For example, George W. Bush took the political heat for FEMA's dismal response to the 2005 Katrina disaster. While the legislature cannot micromanage a crisis *ex ante*, there is an *ex post* settling of accounts, and this gives the executive an incentive to manage the crisis competently, as Bush discovered in the 2006 congressional elections.

The demand for a more legalistic response to Schmitt's challenge assumes that *ex post* political constraints of the executive are necessarily insufficient. The political metaphysician is apt to have similar qualms about the doctrine of parliamentary sovereignty. After all, if an executive may turn into a Schmittian dictator, what can one say about a Parliament that, as Jean-Louis de Lolme observed, can do everything but turn a woman into a man? Legalistic Americans sometimes assume that, logically, Britons must be less than free, since they lack a bill of rights. Indeed, as A. V. Dicey noted, parliamentary laws are binding, even if immoral and contrary to what one takes as natural law.[119] And yet Britons may rightly feel themselves as free as Americans, with a political culture that effectively fetters an overreaching government. Though Parliament's sovereignty is unbounded, it is nevertheless restricted by what Dicey called the external limits of what British voters will accept. The same might be said of American voters, who have reposed greater authority in presidents in wartime, authority that was retracted when the crisis was over. Even the courts treat the Constitution as elastic, and refrain from second-guessing a president during a crisis, while subjecting him to greater scrutiny once the immediate crisis has passed.[120]

In one respect, parliamentary governments are better able to deal with a crisis than the United States' constitutional one. After the defeat of a parliamentary government, whether in a general election or by a nonconfidence motion, a new government generally is installed the next day. In America, however, a ten-week period elapses between an election and the swearing-in of a new president (and prior to the Twentieth Amendment in 1933, the waiting period was a full four months). During this period, his predecessor continues to serve, with all the constitutional powers he exercised the day before the election. In constitutional law, there is no such thing as a lame-duck president. The delay exacerbated the banking crisis of 1932–33, as uncertainty mounted about the new administration's plans while FDR waited to be inaugurated.

Presidentialism and Crown Government. We have seen four explanations for the growth of Crown government: the weakness of a dispersed legislature in the face of a unitary executive, the expansion of the regulatory state, the role of the media in election campaigns, and the need to respond to emergencies. The first three explanations seem plausible; the fourth, not. In America there are three other explanations, which we'll see in Part II: Presidentialism fosters the rise of Crown government because it makes the head of government the head of state (chapter 7), because it makes it harder to remove a president and insulates him from accountability (chapter 8), and because it encourages a president to surmount the gridlock resulting from the separation of powers and rule personally (chapter 9).

In both the United States and Canada, executive powers have greatly expanded, while those of the legislature have shrunk. This can be seen as a return to the Crown government of 250 years ago, with the difference that we now have George Mason's "elective monarchy," with voters choosing the executive and clothing him with powers not unlike those of George III. To some extent there is no going back, since the rise of Crown government can be attributed to nonreversible economic and technological changes common to all three countries. But the more interesting questions are how each system—presidential and parliamentary—might respond to the dangers of Crown government, and which system is better able to do so. To those questions I now turn in Part II.

Assembly Room, Independence Hall, Philadelphia (Antoine Taveneaux). See page 26. *Source:* Wikipedia Commons.

James Wilson, 1742–98. The president will be "the man of the people." See pages 41–42. *Source:* TeachingAmerican History.org.

Gouverneur Morris, 1752–1816, (after a drawing by Pierre Eugène Du Simitière). "Come, Gentlemen, let us sit down again, and converse further on this subject." See page 57. *Source:* Library of Congress via Wikipedia Commons.

GOVERNEER MORRIS ESQ.ᴿ

Member of Congress.

Pub.ᵈ 15ᵗʰ May 1783, by R. Wilkinson Nº 58 Cornhill, London.

Let us Dance & Sing . — God bless the King . — For he has made us merry Men all."

Charles James Fox (in the center) takes Lord North and the crypto-Catholic Edmund Burke by the hand (James Gillray). See page 70. *Source:* National Portrait Gallery, London, via Wikipedia Commons.

Sir Francis Bond Head, 1793–1875, Lieutenant Governor of Upper Canada 1836–38 (from a painting by Nelson Cook). See page 96. *Source:* Archives of Ontario via Wikipedia Commons.

"Radical Jack" Lambton, 1st Earl of Durham 1792–1840 (Thomas Phillips). "I saw two nations warring within the bosom of a single state." See page 99. *Source:* National Portrait Gallery, London, via Wikipedia Commons.

Walter Bagehot, 1826–77. See pages 84 and 118. *Source: Popular Science Monthly* via Wikipedia Commons.

Charlottetown Conference, September 1864 (George P. Roberts). John A. Macdonald, rather the worse for wear, sits on the steps of Government House, with a seemingly more sober George-Étienne Cartier, hat in hand, standing to the immediate left. Between them, the startlingly ugly Thomas D'Arcy McGee squarely faces the camera. See page 110. *Source:* Library and Archives Canada via Wikipedia Commons.

A PERTINENT QUESTION.
Mrs. Britannia—"Is it possible, my dear, that you have ever given your cousin Jonathan any encouragement?"
Miss Canada—"Encouragement! Certainly not, mama. I have told him we can *never* be united."
(J. W. A. Bengough, *The Diogenes*, June 18, 1869.) *Source: A Caricature History of Canadian Politics*, by J. W. A. Bengough, Toronto: The Grip Printing & Publishing Co., 1886.

-II-

The Pitfalls of Presidentialism

-6-

AMERICAN EXCEPTIONALISM

*I believe in American exceptionalism, just as I suspect
that the Brits believe in British exceptionalism
and the Greeks believe in Greek exceptionalism.*

—BARACK OBAMA

Most Americans subscribe to the idea of "America exceptionalism." When polled, 80 percent of respondents said that, because of its history and Constitution, America "has a unique character that makes it the greatest country in the world."[1] For this, our thanks go to the Framers, who gave the country a presidential system that secured the blessings of liberty.

While that's a nice story, it lacks the added advantage of accuracy. As I explain in chapter 2, our modern presidential system, with its separation of powers, was an unexpected consequence of the democratization of American politics, and not a prominent feature of the Framers' Constitution. Nor is America the freest country in the world, at least as reported by the Index of Economic Freedom put out by the Heritage Foundation. In its 2013 rankings, Heritage lists the United States as "partly free"—tenth in the world, and well behind countries such as Australia and Canada.[2] Even this might be generous. In the 2010 economic freedom rankings produced by the Cato and Fraser institutes, the United States comes in at eighteenth, behind Britain and Chile as well.[3] *The Economist* also places the United States well down in the pack, as the nineteenth most democratic country, behind a group of mostly parliamentary countries, and not very far ahead of the "flawed democracies."[4]

These findings will come as no surprise to anyone who has examined the empirical literature on liberty and constitutional design. Parliamentary governments, which lack a separation of powers, rank significantly higher on measures of political freedom. That's not to deny that America is one of the freest countries in the world. It's simply to assert that it isn't the presidential system that makes the difference. What makes America exceptional is that, for more than two hundred years, it has remained free while yet presidential.

DEFINING LIBERTY

Reading the confederation debates, one is struck by how the Fathers insisted that Canadians had real liberty, more so even than Americans. D'Arcy McGee said that "there is not on the face of the earth a freer people than the inhabitants of [the Canadian] colonies."[5] He had lived in the United States, and didn't care for what he saw of liberty there. In part, that was an Irish Catholic's reaction to what he would have seen as a Protestant country; but there was more to the story. McGee simply had a different, more modern conception of liberty than that of classic American republicanism.

Benjamin Constant explained the difference between the two ideas of liberty in an 1819 essay, contrasting the "Liberty of the Ancients" with the "Liberty of the Moderns."[6] In the ancient world, he explained, liberty meant the right to participate in government in the public assembly, a right that the citizens of small Greek city-states might exercise, though not the subjects of a larger state. Transposed to America and to Madison's extended republic, the liberty of the ancients was a call to duty as well as a right, a duty of civic virtue and personal responsibility, by which citizens were summoned to deliberate about the public interest.

By contrast, the liberty of the moderns was the right to do what one wanted, without injuring others, free from government interference. Constant's ancients had had self-government, but could pass laws that imposed the broadest restrictions on the most private of personal decisions—one's religion and way of life. Constant's moderns recognized that they weren't going to be able to participate effectively in government in a large state. Their representatives would do that for them. That wouldn't matter so much, however, if the state left them alone. What they wanted was what years later Patrick Moynihan would call "benign neglect."

That was the kind of liberty that Canada provided, the Confederation Fathers thought—better than America. The Loyalists had a similar understanding when they spoke of "British liberty" at the time of the Revolution. Britain might appoint the royal governors, they said; but the important point was that, for the most part, they didn't bother the colonists with silly laws. Similarly, Britain retained a measure of control over Canadians after the grant of self-government in 1849, and even after confederation in 1867, but generally left them alone. Benign neglect, after all, was a form of freedom.

That was why McGee and the other Fathers thought Canada the freest country in the world. When they looked south, they saw a country with more of Constant's liberty of the ancients, but with less (so it seemed to them) of the liberty of the moderns. Moreover, of the former, the right of self-government had been corrupted by political machines and trivialized by elections for dogcatchers. The high ideals of the American Founders had been forgotten, and McGee thought that their republican virtue, in the era of Boss Tweed and Tammany Hall, was now little more than American braggadocio. As for the liberty of the moderns, there was that little matter of slavery and its aftermath. There was also what Europeans were fond of decrying as the tyranny of American public opinion, which Stendhal thought as small-minded and as unforgiving as that of the provincial Verrières in his *The Red and the Black*. The social norms enforced by shaming and shunning can seem almost as repressive as the most restrictive set of laws.

Personal liberty, the liberty of the moderns, is evidently a highly subjective concept. Whatever was the case in 1867, one couldn't easily say which country more generously tolerates personal idiosyncrasies today. Americans might think themselves more willing to embrace diversity, but the United States imprisons four times more people per capita than Canada does.

To escape the messiness of private intuitions about liberty, two things might be done. First, countries might more easily be ranked according to their political, rather than their personal, liberty—the liberty of the ancients, rather than of the moderns. Second, one can turn to organizations or scholars who rank countries according to their political liberty. The most widely used such rankings are Freedom House's index of liberal democracy, the Polity IV measure of constitutional democracy, Tatu Vanhanen's assessment of participatory democracy, and the measure of contested democracy provided by Adam Przeworski and his colleagues. While all four measures are strongly correlated with each other,[7] the Freedom House ranking is the best known and most authoritative.[8] Freedom House has the deepest bench of experts across the world, and each year ranks 195 countries according to their political rights, relying on a process of analysis and evaluation by regional experts and scholars. The rankings are based on a series of questions about free and fair elections, competitive political parties, and minority-group inclusion in the political process.

ARE PRESIDENTS HARMFUL TO POLITICAL FREEDOM?

There are three reasons why presidential government might be thought to threaten political freedom, which I examine in the following three chapters.

First, as heads of state, presidents enjoy a prestige and status denied prime ministers in a parliamentary system, and might exploit this to assume greater powers.

Second, presidents hold office for a fixed period of time, during which it is extremely difficult to remove them; while prime ministers may be removed at any time when Parliament is in session through a nonconfidence motion. Presidents are also free from daily accountability for their administration before an opposition party in a House of Commons.

Third, the checks and balances of the separation of powers in a presidential regime require both bodies to agree on legislation, and result in a deadlock when they fail to do so. George Tsebelis modeled the problem as one of "veto players," defined as players whose assent is required before any change is made to the status quo. As the number of veto players increases, so does the probability of deadlock.[9] In a parliamentary system with a majority government, only one party has a veto power: the prime minister's party. In a presidential system with a bicameral legislature, however, at least three players have veto powers: the president, and the majority party in each of the upper and lower houses. The increased likelihood of deadlock in a presidential system might invite dictators to step in and cure the problem by ruling extralegally, or at a minimum, by extending the scope of executive power.

I take up these subjects in chapters 7 through 9, and in this chapter report on the significant correlation between presidentialism and the denial of political liberty. Notwithstanding the proud boasts made about the American Constitution and system of government, it has not traveled well in other parts of the world. Parliamentary governments are significantly freer.

I am particularly interested in what has happened to political freedom in recent years. The democratic wave that began after the fall of communism has receded, and the world has slipped into what the Hoover Institution's Larry Diamond calls a "democratic recession."[10] Summarizing recent trends, the Economist Intelligence Unit reports:

> *A political malaise in east-central Europe has led to disappointment and questioning of the strength of the region's democratic transition. Media freedoms have been eroded across Latin America and populist forces with dubious democratic credentials have come to the fore in a few countries in the region. In the developed West, a precipitous decline in political participation, weaknesses in the functioning of government and security-related curbs on civil liberties are having a corrosive effect on some long-established democracies.*[11]

A fresh look at democratic trends is obviously timely.

What Counts as a Presidential System? I list presidential and parliamentary regimes by country in table 6.1. Not every country with a president counts as presidential, but only those whose president is the head of government as well as the head of state. This excludes countries such as Germany that have a merely ceremonial president. Where a country has a president as head of state, but a prime minister as head of government, I classify it as parliamentary.[12]

Among presidential countries there are a variety of constitutional forms. French sociologist Maurice Duverger proposed that "semi-presidential" regimes be distinguished from purely presidential ones.[13] In France, for example, the legislative chamber can dismiss the presidential cabinet, and thus has more power than an American Congress. The distinction between the various kinds of presidential regimes is blurred,[14] however, and I categorize all of them as simply presidential.

In her empirical study of presidentialism, Pippa Norris distinguished between parliamentary and presidential regimes on a formal basis, according to how they define themselves in their constitutions. As such, she classified Putin's Russia as a "mixed" regime, neither presidential nor parliamentary. By contrast, I categorize regimes according to where power really resides, and list Russia as a presidential country. Putin is the effective ruler of Russia, and I see his recent interlude as prime minister as a transparent device to sidestep term limits. While Norris classified

43 countries as presidential and 31 as parliamentary in 2003, my study lists 82 as presidential and 47 as parliamentary (with some countries switching from one classification to the other between 1972 and 2010).

Juan Linz was the first scholar to argue that presidentialism leads to dictatorship, and he placed the blame on the potential for conflict between the branches of government under the separation of powers.[15] This, he said, would lead to gridlock and instability, and would invite a dictator

---

TABLE 6.1 *Presidential and Parliamentary Governments*

Government	Countries
Presidential	Albania, Algeria, Angola, Argentina, Armenia, Azerbaijan, Bangladesh (1974–90), Belarus, Benin, Bolivia, Botswana, Brazil, Burma (prior to 1974), Burundi, Cameroon, Central African Republic, Chad, Chile, Colombia, Congo (Brazzaville), Congo (Kinshasa), Costa Rica, Croatia, Djibouti, Dominican Republic, Ecuador, Egypt, El Salvador, Equatorial Guinea, Eritrea, France, Gabon, The Gambia, Georgia, Ghana, Guatemala, Guinea, Guinea-Bissau, Guyana (1980–present), Haiti, Honduras, Indonesia, Côte d'Ivoire, Kazakhstan, Kenya, Kyrgyzstan, Latvia (before 1993), Liberia, Lithuania, Madagascar, Malawi, Maldives, Mali, Mexico, Moldova (before 2000), Mozambique, Nicaragua, Niger, Nigeria (after 1978), Pakistan (1972, 1978–87, 2002–10), Panama, Paraguay, Peru, Philippines, Romania, Russia, Rwanda, Senegal, Somalia, South Africa, South Korea, Sri Lanka (after 1977), Sudan, Suriname, Taiwan (after 1977), Tajikistan, Tanzania, Togo, Tunisia, Turkmenistan, Uganda, Ukraine, United States, Uruguay, Uzbekistan, Venezuela, Zambia, Zimbabwe (after 1986)
Parliamentary	Antigua and Barbuda, Australia, Austria, The Bahamas, Bangladesh (1972–73, 1991–2010), Barbados, Belgium, Belize, Bulgaria, Burma (after 1973), Canada, Czech Republic, Denmark, Dominica, Finland, Germany, Greece, Grenada, Guyana (pre–1980), Hungary, Iceland, India, Ireland, Italy, Jamaica, Japan, Latvia (after 1992), Luxembourg, Macedonia, Moldova (after 1999), Netherlands, New Zealand, Nigeria (before 1979), Norway, Pakistan (1973–77, 1988–2001), Poland, Portugal, Singapore, Slovakia, Slovenia, Spain, Sri Lanka (before 1978), Sweden, Switzerland, Taiwan (before 1978), Thailand, Trinidad and Tobago, Turkey, United Kingdom, Zimbabwe (before 1987)

Sources: Arthur S. Banks, Cross-National Time-Series Data Archive: User's Manual (2011); author (Macedonia, Poland, Switzerland)

to step in. But parliamentary regimes are often unstable themselves. While some parliamentary countries are effectively unicameral (e.g., Britain and Canada), with upper houses that lack real power, others are bicameral, with an elected and politically effective senate. This can result in a deadlock between the two houses of the legislature, as happened in Australia in 1975. Again, while some parliamentary governments (e.g., Britain and Canada) feature first-past-the-post plurality, single-member districts, others elect representatives by proportional representation (e.g., Denmark, Germany). Italy has a parliamentary form of government, but its system of proportional representation has notoriously led to political instability, with sixty-one different governments since 1945, the shortest of which lasted only nine days. Even in first-past-the-post systems, some countries (e.g., Canada) have for historical reasons had significant third parties, and nearly half the Canadian general elections since 1957 have returned minority governments. The minority Clark government lasted only two months from the time it first met Parliament in 1979.

If deadlock is not unknown in parliamentary systems, it is often absent in presidential systems. While it might seem a permanent feature of the separation of powers, it might not happen when one party scores a hat trick and takes the presidency and both branches of Congress. This has occurred more often than one might think (40 percent of the time since the Second World War in the United States). Moreover, even when different parties hold different branches, political parties often compromise on legislation. Until recently, as many bills were passed in periods of American divided government as in periods when one party controlled all three branches of government.[16] Similarly, when the executive and the legislature in other countries are controlled by different parties, both sides not infrequently work things out with a coalition government ("cohabitation" in France).

Deadlock can arise in both systems, then, and both systems have ways of dealing with it. In an empirical study, University of Illinois professor José Cheibub reported that presidential systems were no more vulnerable to breakdown than parliamentary ones.[17] He also found, however, that presidential democracies have shorter life spans than parliamentary ones. In his sample of the period between 1946 and 2002, he determined that the expected life of a parliamentary democracy was fifty-eight years, while that of a presidential democracy was only twenty-four years. Moreover, as reported in appendix B's empirical study, I found that presidential systems were significantly correlated with less political freedom, and if it wasn't deadlock that made the difference, then something else did.

What Other Factors Matter? The form of government isn't the only thing that might affect a country's political freedom. Other variables, which I list in the appendix's table B.1, might also make a difference.

Wealth is one of them. Adam Przeworski concluded that no country that became a democracy ever fell back into dictatorship if it had a per capita income higher than that of Argentina in 1975 ($6,055 in 1975 dollars).[18] Increased wealth grows a middle class that demands democracy and freedom, the example being Chile's evolution from military rule in the 1980s. Surprisingly, Przeworski and his colleagues did not find that increased wealth by itself leads to democratization, the example here being the Chinese model of relative economic liberty and political repression.[19] Wealth makes democracies stable, but doesn't seem to make dictatorships unstable.

Greater income inequality would be expected to lead to calls for redistributionist measures of the kind associated with populist strongmen and dictators (Argentina's Peróns and Venezuela's Chávez). Income inequality is measured by the Gini coefficient, expressed as a ratio from zero to one, where zero means perfect equality and one means perfect inequality. Clear data on income inequality is hard to come by, and there are significant measurement issues,[20] but the Gini coefficient nevertheless permits one to identify the states most susceptible to populist revolutions. With a higher Gini ratio, then, one would expect less political freedom.[21]

Newly independent countries, whose memories of political freedom are recent, can be expected to be more likely to relapse into dictatorship. Torsten Persson and Guido Tabellini reported that countries with greater experience with democracy have "democratic capital," and that this makes them less likely to fall into dictatorship and more likely to emerge from it.[22]

Labor unrest, demonstrations, and political protest are common in politically free countries. However, one would expect more severe forms of unrest, such as an illegal change in the country's leaders or an armed rebellion, to be associated with less political freedom.

Cultural differences importantly explain differences in economic growth. Ghana and South Korea had very similar economies and per capita GDP in the 1960s. Thirty years later, the South Korean per capita GDP was fifteen times that of Ghana. What explained the difference, said Samuel Huntington, was each country's culture.[23] One might similarly expect cultural differences to explain differences in political freedom. In part, this might result from the positive contribution of culture to wealth, but quite apart from this, cultural differences might explain the willingness to tolerate political oppression and departures from the rule of law.

Seymour Martin Lipset and Jason Lakin argued that Latin American countries were more ready to fall into dictatorship because they had been colonies of countries which were themselves undemocratic.[24] A preference for strongmen as leaders was part of their colonial inheritance. Similarly, many African countries enjoyed only a brief experience with political freedom after achieving independence. A British heritage might be correlated with greater political freedom, since the British colonial system is thought to have fostered self-government to a greater degree than other colonial empires like Spain's and Portugal's.[25] Finally, higher literacy rates have been found to be linked to greater political freedom.[26]

Results. Since Freedom House rankings are affected by more than one explanatory variable, what we want to know is what happens when one of these changes while the others are held fixed. In this way, we can see how the difference between presidential and parliamentary forms of government affects political freedom, shorn of the effects of the other explanatory variables. This I do through the multiple regression estimation techniques of appendix B, where I look at what variables were associated with a country's Freedom House ranking, using panel (cross-section time-series) data for 135 countries between 1972 and 2010. The basic unit of analysis is the country-year, with one observation for each country for each year, for a total of 4,387 observations.

In the appendix's table B.2, I find that presidentialism is significantly and strongly correlated with less political freedom. The difference between presidential and parliamentary systems was associated with a one- or two-point gain on the Freedom House scale. In 2012, a one-point differential was the difference between the United States and Cristina Kirchner's Argentina; a two-point differential was the difference between the United States and Evo Morales's Bolivia.

Wealthy countries were more likely to be free, as were older countries. The longer a country has been independent, the more likely it is to be free. Countries with a British heritage were also more likely to be free, as were countries with a higher literacy rate (although here the explanatory power was weak).

In sum, presidential systems have not proven hospitable to political liberty. Among presidential countries, America stands out as exceptional in its freedom. For every year in which Freedom House ranked countries, the United States (along with Britain, Canada, and most other first-world countries) received top marks. In an effort to understand just why America is exceptional, I compared it to other presidential regimes in table B.3, this time dropping parliamentary regimes from the mix. What explained the difference between American and other presidential regimes is that the United States is a wealthy, older country with a British heritage. This had made America a free country, in spite of its Constitution.

PRESIDENTS AND MILITARISM

Cheibub recognized that presidential democracies are more likely to turn into dictatorships than parliamentary ones, but sought to account for this by positing a relationship between presidentialism and militarism.

Scholars such as Linz, who think presidential government less stable, have the causal relationship backward, he argued. It's not that presidential regimes lead to undemocratic, militaristic governments; it's that when they become democratic, militaristic governments become presidential, and subsequently more easily flip back into a militaristic dictatorship.

I discount Cheibub's attempt to rescue presidentialism, since I found a significant correlation between presidential government and the absence of political freedom, even when I employed an explanatory variable for Latin America. In addition, Cheibub's failure to offer a satisfactory explanation for the military-presidentialism nexus weakens his argument. He rejected the suggestion that, on emerging from a military dictatorship, a country opts for presidentialism because the departing military dictators insist on presidential government as a condition for giving up power. The departing colonels seldom have much of a choice in the matter.[27] What Cheibub was left with, by way of explanation, is a historical accident particular to Latin America. Such a nexus does exist, however; and in what follows I offer an explanation that is consistent with the view that presidentialism is dangerous for democracy.

If the departing colonels don't pick presidents to succeed them, the most plausible explanation for the nexus is that causation works in the other direction: Presidents like colonels, and presidential regimes feature bigger militaries. Presidents can embark on a war without the need for congressional approval, and continue it once it has begun. Congress might vote to deny supplies to the troops in the field, but the political cost of doing so is too great to make this a serious option. In theory, a prime minister possesses the same unfettered ability to take his country into war. Nevertheless, the advantage lies with presidents, for prime ministers lack a president's ability to act unilaterally. The absence of the separation of powers in parliamentary regimes, plus the government's day-to-day accountability in the House of Commons, makes it far more difficult for a prime minister to disregard Parliament's wishes. A presidential government that can readily go to war is a government more likely to go to war, and a government with a greater military budget.

More than two thousand years ago Polybius noted the relation between militarism and constitutional design, in comparing the constitutions of Sparta and the Roman Republic. Sparta had something like a parliamentary government, in which the kings shared power with the ephors (or political leaders), senate, and assembly. Rome also had a mixed form of government, but when it came to war, the consuls' powers were almost uncontrolled. In Sparta, the "legislation of Lycurgus" served its purpose in defensive wars, when all branches of government were united against an external enemy, but proved less satisfactory in an offensive and less popular campaign.

> For the purpose of remaining in secure possession of their own territory and maintaining their freedom the legislation of Lycurgus is amply sufficient . . . but if anyone is ambitious of greater things, and esteems it finer and more glorious than that to be the leader of many men and to rule and lord it over many and have the eyes of all the world turned to him, it must be admitted that from this point of view the Laconiàn constitution is defective, while that of Rome is superior and better framed for the attainment of power, as is indeed evident from the actual course of events. For when the Lacedaemonians endeavoured to obtain supremacy in Greece, they very soon ran the risk of losing their own liberty; whereas the Romans, who had aimed merely at the subjection of Italy, in a short time brought the whole world under their sway.[28]

The lesson from Polybius is that, if one really wants a militaristic government and imperialism, presidential regimes are the way to go.

To test this, I estimated a country's military budget as a percentage of GDP in the regression equation in appendix table B.4. I posited that the size of the budget would depend principally on three things: the form of government (presidential vs. parliamentary); whether the country was threatened by foreign enemies; and whether it faced the threat of an internal revolution. The enemy variable is dichotomous (with 1 and 0 dummy variables) and takes the value of 1 if I thought it faced an external enemy, but not if it simply threatened another country itself.[29] To this I added two additional explanatory variables: first (following Cheibub), for Latin America; and second, for the United States. The United States provides 41 percent of the world's total military spending; the next country on my list (Russia) spends only a tenth of that. For an American president, this is a wonderful toy, which he can safely use in a series of splendid little wars (if not a costly and protracted land war in Asia). Unsurprisingly, there is evidence to support the "diversionary hypothesis" that presidents use military force strategically to distract the attention of voters from domestic messes, as mentioned in chapter 5.

As expected, I found that the presidential variable was associated with an increased military budget, with a switch from a parliamentary to a presidential regime associated with a 50 percent increase in military spending. While the equation explains only a small amount of the variance, the presidential coefficient was significant at the .001 level. Presidents like bigger militaries. The Latin America and U.S. variables were also positive, and significant at the .001 level. Latin American countries are indeed more militaristic, as Cheibub argued.

Conservative scholars including John Yoo have persuasively argued that presidents are better at waging war when their hands are not tied by Congress, and in this respect, presidential governments might enjoy an advantage over parliamentary ones.[30] The presidential power to embark on a war without the need for congressional approval, or to continue a war once it has begun, makes America a more dangerous foe. Yoo might thus be correct that presidential countries are better at fighting wars than parliamentary ones. The reverse of the coin, however, is that America may have gotten a bigger military—and more wars—in the bargain.

America is clearly exceptional in the size of its military budget. In other respects it is less than exceptional. It is not the only free country around, and not even in the top tier of economic freedom. What is exceptional about America, among presidential countries, is its political freedom.

Jack Sprat's Law

*A nation is an association of reasonable beings united in
a peaceful sharing of things they cherish; therefore to determine
the quality of a nation you must consider what those things are.*
—ST. AUGUSTINE, CITY OF GOD

If presidential governments are less free than parliamentary ones, the
simplest explanation may be found in a president's double role as head
of state as well as head of government. These functions are divided in
parliamentary governments, between prime ministers as heads of government and monarchs as heads of state. While Bagehot is remembered for
his celebration of the efficient power of Commons and prime ministers,
two chapters of his *The English Constitution* were devoted to the role of
the monarch. Queen Victoria was—merely, one is tempted to say—the
ceremonial head of the country, but Bagehot was astute enough to
recognize that ceremonies and the special role of the Queen in the life
of the British people were a matter of profound importance. Western
monarchies are not republics with a bit of fluff thrown in. They are different in kind from presidential republics, wealthier, more stable, and
more likely to be strong democracies.

THE BRITISH AND CANADIAN MONARCH

Once, during a service at Windsor Chapel, writer Graham Greene found himself seated beside Queen Elizabeth.

> *The officiating clergyman preached an absurd sermon and I found myself in danger of laughing. So, I could see, was the Queen, and she held the Order of Service in front of my mouth to hide my smile. Then Prince Philip entered. I was not surprised at all that he was wearing a scoutmaster's uniform, but I resented having to surrender my chair to him. As I moved away the Queen confided in me, "I can't bear the way he smiles."*[1]

This didn't really happen, at least not in what Greene called the "common world." Instead he dreamed it, and recorded it in his *Dream Diary*. It wasn't such an odd dream, either. Dreams about the Queen are not uncommon in Britain and throughout the Commonwealth.

Greene had a vivid dream life, in which he also encountered British prime ministers. That is most unusual; Britons seem not to chat with David Cameron in their dreams, nor do Canadians meet John Diefenbaker, in or out of a scoutmaster's uniform, in theirs. Prime ministers tend not to be idolized or revered. They are more likely to be figures of fun, like the Honourable Walter Outrage in Evelyn Waugh's *Vile Bodies* ("last week's Prime Minister"), or the butt of slanging matches during Question Period in the House of Commons. The difference can also be observed in official residences: Buckingham Palace for the Queen versus an unobtrusive 10 Downing Street in London for the British prime minister. For the Canadian prime minister, 24 Sussex Drive in Ottawa would have been a very suitable home for a lumber baron, which is not surprising since the house was built for the owner of a saw mill across the river in Hull, Quebec.

As the head of government, a prime minister wields at least as much power in his country as a president does in his. In one respect, however, a prime minister lacks the authority that a president enjoys; for presidents, but not prime ministers, are heads of state. As a matter of form, British monarchs, and not prime ministers, summon, prorogue, and dissolve Parliament; greet foreign heads of state; present honors and awards; sign commissions; receive ambassadors; sign bills into law; and take precedence before any of their subjects.

In all of this, the British monarch represents what Bagehot called the dignified (as opposed to the efficient) element of the British constitution. The efficient part is that which gives us laws, while the dignified part may be seen in the ceremonies associated with their enactment. Bagehot had recognized that the eighteenth-century British constitution, in which the House of Commons shared political power with the monarch and House of Lords, was no more; and that of the efficient part of the constitution, only the House of Commons remained. When it came to the dignified or ceremonial part of the constitution, however, the vestiges of the separation of powers could still be observed in the person of the sovereign and in the hereditary House of Lords, whose consent as a matter of form was required before a bill became law.

What Bagehot described was Jack Sprat's law, applied to the constitution, in which real power and ceremony, lean and fat, were cleaved off from each other. That was how, he thought, a republic had "insinuated itself beneath the folds of a Monarchy."[2] Yet Britain was not a republic either, and Bagehot would not have wished it to become one. The ceremonies served useful purposes, he thought, and one wouldn't want to get rid of them. Nor would one want to see the efficient and ceremonial parts commingled, with the power and the glory united in a single person. That would amount to a return to the personal rule of George III, when Lord North served as his puppet, or to a Bonapartist republic with an efficient ruler who assumes the trappings of royalty. Bagehot's British constitution of 1865, of Lord Palmerston and Queen Victoria, might have seemed quirky, but it satisfied the human need for pageantry and served to protect liberty.

The English Constitution has acquired the status of a canonical text for politicians and monarchs, for whom, observed Ferdinand Mount,

Bagehot's book had described a new career.[3] J. R. Tanner, an Oxford don, was employed to instruct George V (then the Duke of York) in constitutional law, and assigned Bagehot's book as the text. The duke read it carefully, then prepared a précis in a school notebook, which his official biographer, Harold Nicolson, was permitted to read. "Though it would be possible to construct a system of political machinery in which there was no monarchy," the duke generously observed, "yet in a State where a monarchy of the British type already exists, it is still a great political force & offers a splendid career to an able monarch,"[4] a sentiment with which it would be difficult to disagree. Nicolson noted that the duke recorded Tanner's visits less frequently than those of the philatelist J. A. Tilleard, for the future George V spent three afternoons a week on his extensive stamp collection. Whether this came down to nothing more than a hobby (taken perhaps to excess) or revealed a deeper family piety is unclear; for the stamps were from the British Empire and bore images of his relatives ("Look, there's grandmamma again!").

The distinction between the efficient and dignified parts of the constitution may also be observed in those members of the British Commonwealth that, while independent, retain the monarch as their sovereign. The Commonwealth has fifty-four members with a combined population of 2.3 billion, nearly a third of the world's total population. Of its members, twenty-one are monarchies, five with indigenous sovereigns (e.g., Lesotho, Tonga), and sixteen with the Queen as head of state. Among the latter is Canada, which has been a monarchy ever since Jacques Cartier claimed the country for the king of France in 1534. Only Japan and Sweden have had longer records of continuous monarchical governance (since Britain had a republican interregnum from 1649 to 1660).

The Canadian Constitution Act formally describes an absolute monarchy in which executive power is vested in the British monarch. A governor general serves as the Queen's representative, exercising all her powers, including those of the commander in chief of the armed forces. The prime minister is not even mentioned. This is Bagehot's dignified constitution, however. The efficient constitution is unwritten, and is a matter of conventions that had consolidated power in an elected lower house well before confederation in 1867, when Lord Elgin recognized the principle of responsible government in 1849. As recounted in chapter 4, responsible government also meant that Canada was self-governing in its internal affairs. After confederation, Canada gradually assumed the right to dictate its own foreign policies, and the country's entire independence from Britain was recognized in the 1926 Imperial Conference, which declared that the self-governing dominions were:

> *autonomous communities within the British Empire, equal in status,*
> *in no way subordinate to another in respect of their domestic or*
> *internal affairs, though united by a common allegiance to the Crown,*
> *and freely associated as members of the British Commonwealth of*
> *Nations.*[5]

This formula was adopted in the preamble to the 1931 Statute of Westminster, an act of the British Parliament that declared that Canada and the other self-governing dominions enjoyed full independence, and that British laws would not apply to them without their consent.[6]

The governor general serves as the Queen's agent. He does not, however, seek her advice when called upon to exercise her authority, nor is he in any sense the representative of the British government. Nevertheless, as an agent he is wholly supplanted when the Queen visits one of her Dominions—as Queen of Canada, for example. This has the appearance of a paradox, for she is both Queen of England and Queen of the Dominion, the sovereign of two independent countries. Before the American Revolution, it had been thought that dividing sovereignty was like dividing divinity, and not to be done without a St. Athanasius to solve the mystery of the Trinity. This was the riddle Kipling invoked when he wrote, in *Our Lady of the Snows*, of how the Queen in Right of Canada might (or might not) sign a trade bill favorable to Britain.

A Nation spoke to a Nation,
A Queen sent word to a Throne:
"Daughter am I in my mother's house,
But mistress in my own."

Whatever the theoretical difficulties, in practice divided sovereignty has not proven a problem for the Commonwealth, with the Queen serving as a unifying symbol for both the realms for which she serves as Head of State and the republics for which she serves as Head of the Commonwealth. The bond is necessarily weaker among the republics than the realms. As republics, India and Pakistan have gone to war with each other on four occasions, even though both were and are members of the Commonwealth. One can't easily imagine this happening between two realms that share the same sovereign. The sovereign might nevertheless be at war with one realm and at peace with another. In the Second World War, Australia and New Zealand took the position that they were automatically at war when Britain declared war on Germany on September 3, 1939. To make a point, however, Prime Minister Mackenzie King insisted on a separate Canadian Declaration of War, to which George VI assented on September 10, 1939. For a week, therefore, the King in Right of Britain was at war, while the King in Right of Canada was at peace.

Since Britain shares its monarchy with the dominions, it cannot alter the position of the sovereign unilaterally. During the 1936 abdication crisis, British Prime Minister Stanley Baldwin found it necessary to seek the advice of the prime ministers of Canada, Australia, South Africa, Newfoundland, the Irish Free State, and New Zealand about whether Edward VIII should be permitted to reign. (They all thought not, save Ireland's Eamon de Valera, who said, "What do I care!") The same need for consensus is now required over plans to permit a monarch to marry a Catholic, and to alter the line of succession in favor of first-born heirs, whether male or female.[7]

Even if political power reposes with the prime minister and the House of Commons, in Bagehot's efficient constitution the ceremonial or dignified part of the constitution continues to serve four purposes:

1. By preserving the monarchy, Commonwealth realms signal that they are not republics, and this may serve to protect national independence.
2. The monarch has the right to offer independent and nonpartisan advice to his prime minister.
3. The monarch retains a residual political power.
4. Monarchical ceremonies respond to a human need for color and drama in government, without imposing the costs that might arise when a president employs the pageantry of office to bolster his political power.

First, a monarchical form of government provides a form of product differentiation. As a republic, thought Prime Minister Macdonald, Canada might be unable to resist annexationist pressures to merge with its southern neighbor. If the form of government were the same for both countries, Canadians might have little to lose and far broader economic markets to gain were they to unite with the United States. As a monarchy, however, Canada would be inadmissible to the Union, because of the guarantee of a republican form of government for each state under the Constitution's Article IV.

Second, the Queen has the right to advise the prime minister, who is bound to meet with her every week when both are near London. Bagehot described this as the power "to be consulted, to encourage and to warn,"[8] and these are rights for which lobbyists would pay dearly. The advice is not always sound. When Chamberlain resigned, George VI expressed a preference for the pro-appeasement Viscount Halifax over Churchill as prime minister, and did not want to see the efficient Lord Beaverbrook in the cabinet.[9] However, when a long-serving monarch is paired with a less than prudent prime minister, the advice might well be worth taking, and on occasion *has* been taken. In one case, this might have spared Britain a wholly unnecessary war and Canada an American invasion. In the 1861 Trent Affair, an American warship stopped a British mail-packet ship on the high seas and seized two Confederate agents, James Mason and John Slidell. The aggressively pro-Southern prime minister, Lord Palmerston, thought this meant war, and asked the foreign secretary, Lord John Russell, to prepare a stern note to the Americans, giving them seven days to comply with British demands for apologies and the release of the Confederates—this at a time when the American secretary of state, William Seward, was boasting of his desire to seize Canada. The note was sent to the Queen for her approval, but Prince Albert, on his deathbed, proposed a softening of tone that avoided war. The peremptory demand was withdrawn; a revised note expressed the hope that the American captain had acted without instructions. Mason and Slidel were released, and the affair was permitted to fade away.[10] While what is said during these royal audiences is to be kept confidential, Margaret Thatcher reported that "anyone who imagines that they are a mere formality or confined to social niceties is quite wrong; they are quite businesslike and Her Majesty brings to bear a formidable grasp of current issues and breadth of experience."[11]

There is less consultation between prime ministers and governors general in the dominions. The latter are eminent people of sound judgment, and almost the only nonpartisan voices that a prime minister will hear. The first Canadian to hold the office was Vincent Massey (the actor Raymond's brother), of whom Harold Nicolson complained that he tended to make one feel inferior. Massey reported that his advice was often sought by prime ministers, "and not infrequently offered."[12] Even Pierre Trudeau, the least monarchical of any Canadian prime minister, praised the advice he received from governor general Roland Michener.[13] More recently, prime ministers do not appear to have met regularly with their governors general, who have sometimes come from the prime minister's cabinet.[14] They typically serve for only five years, and cannot hope to match the prestige of a reigning monarch.

Third, today's sovereign or her representative may exercise a "residual" political power, in which she shares a vestigial role in Bagehot's efficient constitution. In very limited circumstances, she might have a measure of discretion about whom to appoint as prime minister. This power will seldom be exercised, though. The Queen cannot dismiss a prime minister who enjoys the support of Parliament, as George III did in 1783 when he dismissed the Fox-North coalition and appointed Pitt prime minister. Nor will the Queen have a say in who will be prime minister when one party in a two-party system enjoys a clear majority after an election. Further, when he steps down, a prime minister will time his resignation to take effect after his party selects a successor, depriving the Queen of a choice.[15] Nevertheless, when a prime minister becomes incapacitated or · dies in office, the monarch or governor general is put on the spot, and might have to decide, after consulting with party leaders, on a successor. In 1923, when Prime Minister Bonar Law was diagnosed with throat cancer and unable to speak in Parliament, George V elected to replace him with Stanley Baldwin, and not with the ambitious Lord Curzon.

The sovereign has a greater opportunity to exercise his residual power in a multiparty parliamentary system when no party commands a majority, and it is less than clear who can command the support of the House of Commons. The monarch or governor general might then have to decide whether to dissolve Parliament, and might even choose who is to serve as prime minister, an issue that arose in the "King-Byng" controversy. Prime Minister Mackenzie King was the grandson of Sir Francis Bond Head's "tiny creature," William Lyon Mackenzie, and in the 1925 Canadian election King's Liberal Party won 101 seats, 22 short of a majority in the 245-man House. With 116 seats, Arthur Meighen's Conservatives had more seats, but King remained in office, believing he had the support of several smaller parties that held the balance of power. Eight months later, faced with a corruption scandal and an impending nonconfidence vote that his government was likely to lose, King asked the governor general, Lord Byng, to dissolve Parliament and call an election. King's relations with Byng, never easy, had not improved when Lady Byng's lady-in-waiting accused King of pinching her thigh while at a formal dinner.[16] Lady Byng, who gave her name to the National Hockey League trophy for "gentlemanly conduct," never forgave King, and Lord Byng had little better opinion of him. When King asked for dissolution, then, Byng decided that it was too soon for another election, and instead told King that Meighen should be given a chance to form a government, whereupon King resigned. A few months later, Meighen's government was defeated in a nonconfidence motion, and in the ensuing general election King was returned to power with 116 seats to Meighen's 91, in a campaign fought over the governor general's decision to appoint Meighen as prime minister without calling an election.[17]

The King-Byng precedent suggests there is a strong presumption that a governor general should defer to the prime minister in decisions about whether he might remain in office or call an election. The presumption, however, is not absolute. Otherwise a prime minister who is defeated in an election might simply continue to call new elections until he wins his majority. Similarly, a prime minister who fears losing an election might decide to dispense with elections and extend the life of a Parliament indefinitely. The most authoritative study of the governor general's residual power therefore concluded that Byng had acted properly, and that prime ministers are not always entitled to get their way.[18] King felt differently, of course, and recorded that years later Byng had asked him for forgiveness. Byng was dead at the time, but that was no impediment for King, who relied on a Ouija board for messages from the "Great Beyond."[19]

The governor general's residual power was last an issue in 2008, when Canadian Prime Minister Stephen Harper asked for and received a prorogation (or suspension) of Parliament when he was about to lose a vote of confidence.[20] Harper's Tories had first come to power in 2006, forming a minority government with 124 out of the 308 seats in Parliament. Two years later, complaining that Parliament had become dysfunctional, Harper asked the governor general to dissolve Parliament. In the ensuing general election, the Tories received 143 seats, 12 short of a majority. The Liberal leader, Stéphane Dion, announced that he would step down, and the emboldened Tories proposed a budget that would have defunded political parties, and that, in the middle of the 2008 financial meltdown, failed to contain a stimulus package. The minority parties were outraged. They depended upon public financing, and thought that the financial panic called for public spending. The minority parties controlled a majority of seats in Parliament, and together entered into a pact to support a Liberal government under Dion for a year and a half. Harper then sought, and received, a prorogation from the governor general, a decision that was criticized, but that has come to be recognized as a not unreasonable exercise of discretion.[21]

One remnant of the residual power that has almost entirely fallen into desuetude is the right to veto general legislation. In Bagehot's dignified constitution, the sovereign's consent is required as a matter of form before any bill becomes law. Were the sovereign to refuse assent to a bill, the clerk at the House of Lords would announce not the accustomed "*Le Roy le veult,*" but "*Le Roy s'avisera.*" The last time a monarch vetoed a public bill was in 1708,[22] however, and before one could imagine this happening today one would have to imagine a government that made the royal veto legitimate through legislation that would subvert the democratic basis of the constitution. In that case, constitutional law scholar Sir Ivor Jennings argued, the royal veto would be the last defense against dictatorship.[23]

Neither such antidemocratic legislation nor the revival of the royal veto is easily foreseeable, any more than the decision of an American president to suspend presidential elections. Against wholly unconstitutional actions, constitutions can do little but proscribe them, and this has not prevented other presidential regimes from falling into dictatorships. If an American dictatorship is exceedingly unlikely, so too is the probability that an antidemocratic autocrat will seek to seize power in Britain or Canada. In a parliamentary system, however, there is a final stopgap against dictatorship, and that is the monarch's veto.

Suppose that a government with a large majority proposed a deeply divisive measure that would fundamentally change the constitution and invite a civil war. That was the prospect facing George V when the Liberal Asquith ministry introduced the Parliament Act of 1911, which would have granted home rule to Ireland. The bill would have addressed Catholic discontent with direct rule from Westminster and given Ireland the same self-governing status as Canada. In the Protestant north, however, home rule was deeply unpopular, and civil war, of the kind that engulfed Ireland a decade later, seemed about to erupt. Irish paramilitary troops began to train, with those in the Protestant north encouraged by Conservative MP F. E. Smith: "Ulster will fight and Ulster will be right!" In these circumstances, the Tory leader Bonar Law told the King that, as sovereign, he must now enter the struggle, and that he might either give his assent to the bill or dismiss the government, but that in either case, half the country would think he had acted against them. In the end, George V decided that the home-rule crisis was not so great as to require his veto, and events in Ireland were soon overtaken by the outbreak of the First World War. Writing in 1959, Jennings concluded that a king could not refuse assent simply because he thought a bill wrong-headed, but that "there is something to be said for a power to dismiss an unconstitutional Ministry or to dissolve a corrupt Parliament."[24]

Queen Elizabeth II defended her power to disallow antidemocratic legislation in a 1964 royal tour of Canada, saying, "The role of a constitutional monarch is to personify the democratic state, to sanction legitimate authority, to ensure the legality of its methods, and to guarantee the execution of the popular will. In accomplishing this task it protects the people against disorder."[25] This was not an idle boast, for in other monarchies a king has played just such a role. In 1981, Juan Carlos I's support for democracy in Spain was crucially important in crushing a military coup, and during the Second World War, King Haakon VII of Norway and Queen Wilhelmina of the Netherlands helped preserve their governments in exile when they fled to England and Canada, respectively.

In the dominions, a governor general might be the last line of defense against a coup d'état or dictatorship. In 1983, the prime minister of Grenada and several of his cabinet members were executed in a Cuban-backed putsch, and the governor general, Sir Paul Scoon, was placed under house arrest. The new military government was quickly deposed by American forces invited by the governor general.[26] The freed Scoon appointed a new government and called for elections. Since then, Grenada has remained a democracy, as have the other fifteen dominions that retain the Queen as Head of State: Antigua and Barbuda, Australia, the Bahamas, Barbados, Belize, Canada, Jamaica, Mauritius, New Zealand, Papua New Guinea, Saint Kitts and Nevis, Saint Lucia, Saint Vincent and the Grenadines, the Solomon Islands, and Tuvalu. By contrast, what republicanism has meant for those members of the Commonwealth that chose to replace the monarch as head of state (including Bangladesh, Botswana, Cyprus, The Gambia, Ghana, Guyana, Kenya, Malawi, Nigeria, Pakistan, Sri Lanka, Tanzania, Uganda, and Zambia) is a sorry record of political repression. As for Hendrik Verwoerd's South Africa and Ian Smith's Rhodesia, white-only regimes found republicanism more to their liking.[27]

The residual power of the Queen (or her representative), which is really part of Bagehot's efficient constitution, serves to legitimize her ceremonial role. Were it all a matter of ceremony, one might perhaps ask why the monarchy survives. And yet ceremony matters, as Bagehot recognized. It provides a welcome diversion into a playful world of ritual, channeling emotional wants that otherwise make celebrities of Hollywood stars or Latin American dictators. "One half of the human race," observed Bagehot, "care fifty times more for a marriage than a ministry," and this is never more true than with a royal wedding. An estimated 750 million people watched the wedding ceremony of Charles and Diana in 1981, the largest TV audience in history, but this was topped in 2011 when the wedding of Prince William and Kate Middleton was viewed by an estimated 2.5 billion worldwide.[28]

Of ceremonies, nothing surpasses the grandeur of a British coronation. It begins with the "recognition," in which the Archbishop of Canterbury brings the monarch-to-be to each of the four corners of Westminster Abbey and demands attention: "Sirs, I here present unto you King [or Queen] ____, your undoubted King: wherefore all you who are come this day to do your homage and service, are you willing to do the same?" At which the trumpets sound, and the congregation murmurs "God save the King." The monarch then takes the coronation oath, promising to maintain the laws of God and the Church of England. This is followed by a communion service during which the choir sings Handel's coronation anthem: "Zadok the Priest and Nathan the Prophet anointed Solomon King, and all the people rejoiced." The monarch then assumes the Robe Royal or Pall of cloth of gold and ascends the coronation throne, known as King Edward's Chair. This thirteenth-century oak throne contains the ancient coronation stone of Scotland, the Stone of Scone, which Edward I brought to England and which, according to legend, is the stone upon which the patriarch Jacob rested his head when he dreamed that he saw a ladder ascending to Heaven. A canopy of cloth of gold, held aloft by four Knights of the Garter, is placed over the King, and the archbishop anoints the King's head, breast, and hands with consecrated oil. Next, the King is presented with the Great Sword of State, the crown jewels, the Sovereign's Orb, and two scepters, and at last is crowned with St. Edward's Crown and brought to the throne. The congregation cries "God save the King," the peers place their coronets on their heads, and peers and clergy both pay homage to their Sovereign.

With royal weddings and coronations, we enter into a world of play and theatricality, where things are not entirely what they seem. We are offered a respite from the serious business of life, of sound prescriptions, uplifting speeches, and moralizing politicians. We are brought instead into a world of politeness and grace, like the French court of novelist George Meredith's "vociferous quacks and snapping dupes, hypocrites, posturers, extravagants, pedants, rose-pink ladies and mad grammarians, sonneteering marquises, high-flying mistresses, plain-minded maids, inter-threading as in a loom, noisy as at a fair."[29] We seek diversions from the sober business of public policy, and are delighted to learn that Canadian governors general have the privilege, inherited from the royal governors of New France, of waiving the rule of silence in Trappist monasteries and of granting nuns the holiday of a *congé royal de trois jours*.[30] Man does not live by bread alone, observed Lionel Trilling. He also needs strawberry jam.

Rituals must be customs, ceremonies that are repeated. They cannot be one-shots. And as they are repeated, they offer conservatives the promise of order and continuity. There will be, following royal weddings, the promise of royal births, followed in time by royal funerals and succeeding coronations in an endless line, like the vision of Banquo's descendants in *Macbeth*. Looking backward, a Charles Maurras might see his nation defined by the *"quarante rois qui, en mille ans, firent la France."*[31] One is led to hope in the existence of permanent things, in the innocence and beauty that Yeats thought proceeded from custom and ceremony. At the same time, truly radical changes, such as those brought about by the 1832 Reform Act, are veiled and made to seem unthreatening by the continuity of a royal house.

While ceremonial, the rituals of a monarchy are nevertheless the symbols and affirmations of political allegiance. The oaths of loyalty at a coronation are acts of homage by peers who historically held real political power. And yet the ceremony is playful, and the element of frivolity, of peers without power affirming their loyalty to a monarch without power, is protective of liberty. Threats to freedom come from stuffy politicians and angry demagogues, not from jug-eared princes. Where the king, and not the politician or demagogue, commands our affection and loyalty, where the monarch reigns over all his subjects without regard to party or faction, where we are encouraged to laugh at prime ministers, we will see less of political oppression and tyranny. That, at least, is the evidence to be taken from the members of the Commonwealth that retained, and those that dispensed with, the monarchy.

THE AMERICAN PRESIDENT

Of Étienne de La Boétie we remember at most two things. First, he was the friend of Michel de Montaigne. When La Boétie died, Montaigne wrote "if you ask me why I loved him, all I can say is, because it was him, because it was I." La Boétie is less well known for his principal work, a rambling essay on political allegiance entitled *Discours de la servitude volontaire, ou le Contr'un*: the *Discourse on Voluntary Servitude, or the Anti-One*. The "One" was the sovereign, tyrant, or dictator who ruled the many; and why the many permitted that to happen was the puzzle La Boétie set out to answer, in a foundational, if neglected, work of political theory.

What La Boétie wanted to know was why people agree to be oppressed by their rulers. "I should like merely to understand," he wrote:

> *how it happens that so many men, so many villages, so many cities, so many nations, sometimes suffer under a single tyrant who has no other power than the power they give him; who is able to harm them only to the extent to which they have the willingness to bear with him; who could do them absolutely no injury unless they preferred to put up with him rather than contradict him.*

Why do we obey rulers anyway?

Max Weber offered an answer in a lecture on "The Profession and Vocation of Politics." The lecture was addressed not to La Boétie's submissive subjects, but to future rulers. You're going to govern people, Weber told his audience. Learn therefore why they might obey you. What is it that legitimizes a ruler and gives him a presumptive right to our submission? What is the source of the inner justification of a ruler's authority, which subjects feel without being instructed in obedience or threatened with sanctions for disobedience? That's the glue needed to hold a political state together.

Weber offered three possible sources of political obligation: custom, charisma, and constitutional governance. Those who draft a constitution must ask whether people will accept it as binding; and at their Convention in Philadelphia, the Framers considered these same three sources. They rejected the first, feared the second, and in their place offered the third, with a constitution that they hoped would appeal to Americans because of its intrinsic excellence.

Weber's *custom* (or tradition) was the authority of the "eternal past": We owe a debt of allegiance to those who came before us, and as we reverence them, we inherit their legal obligations. That might help to explain legal authority in a traditional society such as Britain or Weber's Wilhelmine Germany. It was not, however, something upon which the Framers could rely, after breaking America's bonds with the old country. The Framers had lived under a very traditional constitution, that of the British Empire; and that is just what they wanted to extinguish. Those most disposed to Weber's eternal past—the royal governors, the Anglican divines, the Loyalists—were forced to flee after the Revolution, and those who remained had very different ideas about political legitimacy.

Weber's second source of political authority was the *charismatic leader* who inspires personal trust and loyalty in his followers. The Framers had just such a leader in George Washington, but that wasn't the kind of government they had in mind. They knew that Washington wouldn't abuse his powers, but they didn't know who would come after him. What alarmed them was the possibility of a demagogue who would pander to an easily led populace, as state politicians had done during the period of the Articles of Confederation. James Madison, you will recall, complained that in a democracy people too often become "the dupe of a favorite leader, veiling his selfish views under the professions of public good, and varnishing his sophistical arguments with the glowing colours of popular eloquence."[32]

Most of the Framers were opposed to a strong central government and didn't care for democracy, and they thought that when you put the two together, in the form of a popularly elected president, you got what Edmund Randolph called "the fetus of monarchy." George Mason went him one better, saying that such a government would be "a more dangerous monarchy, an elective one," its president Weber's charismatic leader.

In place of the charismatic leader, the Framers designed a government they believed would rest on Weber's third explanation for political authority, that of legality, or *constitutional governance*. One might follow a rule because one thinks it valid in the sense that it was enacted or adopted by legal procedures which themselves are acknowledged to be valid. I do not have to know that a rule is benign to have a reason to follow it, if I know that it was properly enacted by a legislature whose legitimacy I recognize because it is founded upon and ruled according to principles that I approve. That was the constitution the Framers wished to give us; and that was the one that, until recently, was the principal icon of American identity.

"The American Constitution is unlike any other," wrote historian Hans Kohn. "It represents the lifeblood of the American nation, its supreme symbol and manifestation."[33] Other countries had their common cultures or religions. What America had was something else, said Robert Penn Warren. "To be American is not . . . a matter of blood; it is a matter of an idea."[34] And just what was the idea? Not simply liberty, or liberty under law, for those were also English ideas. The special American contribution, which defines the nation itself, is the idea of a constitutional order that, until recently, prominently included the separation of powers.

That constitution now is folding into a new constitution of strong presidential governance. The Framers would have found this troubling. They didn't want a popularly elected president, and their Constitution was one under which the people wouldn't do the choosing, except through intermediaries who would filter away the impurities of democracy. The Framers worried that a directly elected president would become Weber's charismatic hero, and supplant the Constitution as the source of political authority. They wanted their politics, like their churches, to be unadorned, and thought they could dispense with pomp and ritual through an appeal to abstract ideas of peace, reason, and morality.

That is not how it turned out, of course. By Andrew Jackson's time, republican chastity and simplicity began to be replaced with regal pomp and ceremony. "Ironically, but predictably," observed Michael Novak, "the more egalitarian the base of participation, the more deeply felt was the tug of royalty."[35] Sober forms of worship gave way to religious revivals and enthusiasm, and daring Episcopalians began to experiment with incense and candlesticks. That would have bothered Jefferson, who famously thought that most Americans would shortly become Unitarians. What would have distressed him, however, is the adulation given to presidents and their role in American consciousness.

In *The American Presidency*, Clinton Rossiter offered a mythic account of American government, in which the presidents portrayed on Mount Rushmore serve the need for mystery and theatrics in national life. Who, he asked, "are the most satisfying of our folk heroes? With whom is associated a wonderful web of slogans and shrines and heroics? The answer, plainly, is the . . . Presidents I have pointed to most proudly. Each is an authentic folk hero, each a symbol of some virtue or dream especially dear to Americans."[36] Like Rossiter, the public identifies with a president, and is raised up by a successful one and shamed by a lying one, sharing in the glory and the ignominy.

Republican ceremonies in the United States, centered around the president, mimic those of royalty in a monarchy. In place of a coronation there is a presidential inauguration, the departing president accompanying the new president from the White House to the Capitol, followed by the oath of office, the departure of the former president by helicopter from the Capitol's East Front, the inaugural address from the West Front, the parade down Pennsylvania Avenue, the prayer services and balls. In place of the Royal Family there is the First Family. In place of "God Save the Queen" there is "Hail to the Chief." A distinguished career merits a presidential medal; a national tragedy requires a presidential speech.

None of this comes cheap. The royal family costs Britain about $60 million a year. For his part, Obama quickly blew past that figure in a single 2010 presidential vacation to Mumbai. The president and his retinue booked eight hundred luxury hotel rooms, including all 570 rooms of the exclusive Taj Mahal Hotel. He arrived with two jumbo jets and Air Force One, flanked by security jets, and engaged a convoy of forty-five cars to carry his staff and the forty Secret Service agents who arrived before him. Indian journalists reported that the total cost of the visit was $200 million per day.[37] The White House disputes that figure (while declining to reveal the cost of the visit), but Britain's royal family seems positively frugal by comparison.

Perhaps all this was to be expected. Bagehot thought it natural that a state should make use of ceremonies and ritual. "The elements which attract the most easy reverence will be the theatrical elements; those which appeal to the senses."[38] Unsurprisingly, then, ceremonies have become an important element in American political and constitutional contests.[39] Those who imagine that rituals are simply the ephemera of political life, and count for little in the real world of power politics, might recall the role played in recent history by sit-in demonstrations in the 1960s, marches on Washington, and signing ceremonies. A group gathers at the Lincoln Memorial to hear a speech by a clergyman. Whyever might that be of interest? Breast cancer research requires funding, and so some people go jogging. What's up with that? These are rituals through which we express our deepest concerns, and they are immensely powerful in effecting and consolidating policy changes. It is not surprising, then, that politicians, and especially presidents, have made use of them. Rite makes might.

As national icons, however, the Constitution is in tension with its creature, the American president; and Weber's charismatic leader begins to displace constitutional governance as the ground of political obligation. The Constitution is not the same symbol of American identity that it was fifty years ago, when Hans Kohn and Robert Penn Warren wrote. Possibly conservatives have a point when they complain that schools no longer seek to inculcate pride in American institutions such as the Constitution.[40] As well, executive powers have expanded at the expense of the legislative branch, as we saw in chapter 5. Now, more than ever before, when one asks Washington to act, one is asking the president to do so. At the same time, the idea that the Constitution prescribes limits to power has been muted by the expansion of the federal government into areas formerly reserved for the states, or for individuals themselves. A stark example of this was provided with the clumsy response to the Katrina disaster in New Orleans, when a less-than-competent president took the blame while an egregiously incompetent mayor and governor were given a pass. In all these ways, the Constitution begins to take a back seat to the president, and specifically to a mythic, charismatic leader.

Just what would Weber's charismatic president—La Boétie's "The One"—look like? He must first be seen to possess more-than-human qualities, and must offer a transformation, long on emotion and short on facts, that transcends everyday policy questions. Every successful politician must appeal at an emotional level, and this was especially true of the 2008 Obama campaign. The man who told us that "we are the ones we've been waiting for" and that "this was the moment when the rise of the oceans began to slow and our planet began to heal" was not speaking the usual language of politics. Ordinary politicians don't talk that way—or at least, American politicians haven't in the past.

Second, the charismatic leader must ask voters to identify with him, to see his triumph as their triumph. Faoud Ajami noticed this phenomenon shortly before the 2008 election, observing that the crowds attending Obama rallies were reminiscent of third-world crowds he had seen at the feet of their demagogic leaders. "There is something odd—and dare I say novel," he wrote:

> in American politics about the crowds that have been greeting Barack Obama on his campaign trail. Hitherto, crowds have not been a prominent feature of American politics. We associate them with the temper of Third World societies. We think of places like Argentina and Egypt and Iran, of multitudes brought together by their zeal for a Peron or a Nasser or a Khomeini. In these kinds of societies, the crowd comes forth to affirm its faith in a redeemer: a man who would set the world right.[41]

Third, the charismatic leader cannot brook rivals. There can only be The One. Every other source of authority is suspect, both individuals and institutions. His charisma trumps them all. Sadly, Congress has been given a role of some kind under the Constitution. "What's frustrating people," Obama complained, "is that I haven't been able to force Congress to implement every aspect of what I said in 2008."[42] When the charismatic leader's promise of transformational change falls short, as it must, he turns bitterly against his opponents, against anything that would fetter his unbounded will.

Obama's unwillingness to brook criticism has not made him easy to work with. "It's almost as if someone cannot have another opinion that it different from his," recalled Eric Cantor, admittedly a not unbiased observer. "He becomes visibly agitated. . . . He does not like to be challenged on policy grounds."[43] His opponents are "enemies," against whom he seeks "revenge." As I write, there are fears of a new recession if the president and Congress fail to reach a grand bargain about reducing the public debt. But the real issue, argued Obama, *is* Obama. What it's all about is Republican personal animus toward himself. "It is very hard for them to say yes to me. But . . . at some point they've got to take me out of it."[44]

Turning the presidency into the icon of American identity brings to the fore a different kind of leader, a Weberian charismatic hero with a dangerously exaggerated sense of self. In part, this is a consequence of the rigors of the modern campaign cycle. The democratization of politics, in the form of primary elections, has meant that challengers must raise enormous amounts of money even before the nominee is chosen. Thereafter, the regular campaign burns through hundreds of millions more, with a total cost for each candidate of over a billion dollars in 2012. The hypomanic candidate, who runs for office against seemingly impossible odds, has an edge in the competition. His campaign begins as soon as the last election is over, and continues for four years of fund-raisers, Iowa breakfasts, and meet-and-greets in New Hampshire diners. The process winnows out those who lack the royal jelly of inflated self-regard and belief in their special "gift." It leaves voters with candidates who are superbly qualified to run for office, but less able to govern once elected. The president becomes the charismatic leader who surrounds himself with a bubble of admirers, and who, once in office, finds it difficult to conceal his contempt for members of the other party.[45]

Making the president a symbol of Americanism might weaken the sense of what it means to *be* an American. The core principles of the Constitution are unifying symbols when everyone subscribes to them, without regard to political differences. In politics there are winners and losers, and there is no great shame in being a loser. It is different, however, when policies are embodied in the Constitution. An American who thinks that the First Amendment was a mistake, and that a particular national church should be established, is on the wrong side of a constitutional issue, and to that extent is "un-American." When the charismatic leader becomes the symbol of Americanism, the bonds of a common identity might then be similarly frayed. Not everyone will support the Weberian hero, and those who don't might find themselves called unpatriotic.[46]

This might not be considered troubling, since Americans are in little danger of becoming insufficiently patriotic. Nevertheless, the quality of American patriotism might be degraded if the Constitution no longer serves as the icon of national identity. Modern American nationalism is liberal nationalism, built around adherence to universal ideals of human rights that, it is fondly thought, are uniquely promoted in the United States. In some other countries, a nationalism built on race or religion has proven highly dangerous for minority groups; and in its treatment of native and non-Americans who were viewed as obstacles to the country's "manifest destiny," American nationalism has also had a checkered past. But where the national icon is found in the Constitution, where the freedoms promised in the Declaration of Independence and guaranteed in the Bill of Rights have assumed the status of what historian Pauline Maier called "American Scripture,"[47] it would be self-defeating for a nationalist to oppress a minority. Were this sense of what it means to be an American lost, replaced by an identification with a Weberian hero, American nationalism might cease to be self-policing. After all, charismatic leaders in other countries have not been conspicuous in their defense of liberal values, and have often picked fights with the inconvenient institutions interposed between the people and their president.

In America, it is unlikely that the Constitution could be crowded out so effectively. What is of greater concern is the possibility that, by draping himself in the symbols of nationhood, a charismatic leader might amass an excessive degree of political power. That might help explain how third-world presidents become presidents-for-life; and if that is not on the cards in America, then it might at least help one understand the rise of Crown government in America.

-8-

TAMING THE KING

*The Strongest poison ever known /
Came from Caesar's Laurel Crown*
—WILLIAM BLAKE, AUGURIES OF INNOCENCE

One of the goals of a well-designed constitutional regime is to deter the country's leaders from misbehaving, a task that parliamentary systems perform better than presidential ones. As we saw in the last chapter, combining the offices of head of state and head of government tends to make criticism of a president seem like *lèse-majesté*, and that can't help. In addition, there are two other reasons why parliamentary regimes might more effectively rein in a wayward leader. First, presidents serve for a fixed term, while prime ministers can be dismissed on any day when Parliament is in session. Companies don't appoint their CEOs for a fixed four-year term, and a concern for misbehavior is the reason why. Second, the separation of powers immunizes presidents from the daily monitoring prime ministers receive from the House of Commons. For both of these reasons, presidents are less accountable than prime ministers, and this helps to explain the relative lack of political freedom in presidential regimes that we saw in chapter 5. It also helps explain the greater political corruption in presidential governments.

PRESIDENTIAL MISBEHAVIOR

Presidential misbehavior takes three forms.[1] First, there is the president, described in chapter five, who turns himself into a dictator and curbs political freedom. Then there is the slackard or incompetent, the person who doesn't give the job the attention it deserves, or who is simply not up to it. This is George W. Bush (in the eyes of many Democrats) or Jimmy Carter (in the eyes of many Republicans). Third, there is the president who is personally corrupt, or who tolerates corruption in his administration. He might be formidably able, but nevertheless be given to low tricks and skullduggery, like a Nixon. Or he might, like a Grant, be personally honorable, but nevertheless preside over a government of crooks. The different kinds of misbehavior may blur into each other. The personally honest but careless executive—pure of heart and empty of head—may lead an administration that is incompetent and fails to police corruption.

In theory, presidential systems might seem better able to respond to political corruption, because of the check that the separation of powers places on presidential power, and because presidents are elected by voters across the country (as compared to parliamentary systems, in which the prime minister is elected only in his riding). So Torsten Persson and Guido Tabellini have argued;[2] and similarly, Matthew Shugart and John M. Carey note that the separation of powers gives voters the opportunity to hold politicians in different branches of government to account for different things, and suggest that this argues for the superiority of presidential government.[3]

Which system is more effective in curbing corruption is an empirical question, however, and in appendix C, I present evidence of the superiority of parliamentary systems. I do so using the measures of political corruption provided by Transparency International,[4] a nongovernmental organization that compiles survey data about the misuse of power in the public sector by politicians and regulators. This includes such things as bribes and kickbacks for or embezzlement by public officials, as well as the effectiveness of anticorruption efforts.[5]

Corrupt countries, where the rule of law is weak and political pilfering is common, are poor countries.[6] More corruption means less wealth, as illustrated in figure 8.1, which plots the relation between Transparency International's Corruption Perceptions Index (which measures the perceived level of public-sector corruption around the world) and the logged value of the per capita GDP growth rate. The trend line predicts that a 10-point increase on the CPI scale (from 1 to 100; a higher score means less corruption) results in a 26 percent increase in GDP per capita. The message is that entrepreneurs and investors cannot safely start or finance businesses in corrupt states that don't respect property rights and honor contracts.

Public-sector corruption is thus an enormously important matter, and the appendix's table C.1 reports on a regression equation that estimates the determinants of the Corruption Perceptions Index, with the explanatory

FIGURE 8.1 *Transparency International's Corruption Perceptions Index 2011 results plotted against LogGDP 2011*

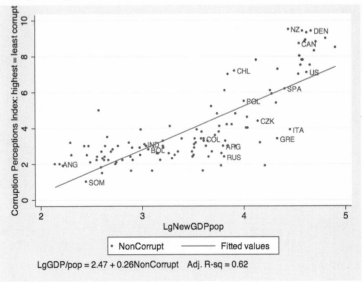

LgGDP/pop = 2.47 + 0.26NonCorrupt   Adj. R-sq = 0.62

variables defined in table C.2. As expected, presidential regimes are shown to be significantly more corrupt.

An American might ask, "What is this to me? My country is exceptional, and is not to be compared to Russia or Mexico." Indeed not, but then it's not quite a pristine pure New Zealand either. In the 2011 CPI rankings of table 8.1, the United States comes in last, at number 24.[7] Leaving Hong Kong and Qatar out of the mix, moreover, every country ahead of the United States on the list save for Chile has a parliamentary government.

The evidence points to the superiority of parliamentary systems in addressing the problem of public corruption, as well as in guaranteeing political freedom. This chapter explains why this might be so, comparing the United States to the country it most closely resembles: Canada. When two societies are as similar, the differences in political institutions stand out more starkly.

In comparing the two countries, one should distinguish between two methods of policing ministerial misbehavior.[8] Through *termination*

TABLE 8.1 *From Transparency International's Corruption Perceptions Index 2011*

	Rank	Score		Rank	Score
New Zealand	1	9.5	Iceland	13	8.3
Denmark	2	9.4	Germany	14	8.0
Finland	2	9.4	Japan	14	8.0
Sweden	4	9.3	Austria	16	7.8
Singapore	5	9.2	Barbados	16	7.8
Norway	6	9.0	United Kingdom	16	7.8
Netherlands	7	8.9	Belgium	19	7.5
Australia	8	8.8	Ireland	19	7.5
Switzerland	8	8.8	Bahamas	21	7.3
Canada	10	8.7	Chile	22	7.2
Luxembourg	11	8.5	Qatar	22	7.2
Hong Kong	12	8.4	**United States**	**24**	**7.1**

rights, a misbehaving executive might be dismissed from office. Alternatively, the constitution might appoint a body to examine and report upon the executive's misbehavior, or to veto his decisions, and this I call a *monitoring* strategy.

TERMINATION

The strong tenure granted an American executive, when compared with the relative ease with which a prime minister may be cashiered in a parliamentary system, makes it easier for presidents to assume dictatorial power. It also increases the problem of presidential misbehavior, by weakening his incentives to act in the interests of his citizens. For this one might blame the Framers, but for the fact that the constitution they proposed was one that they thought provided for something more closely resembling congressional government, with an executive subordinate to the legislature.

The Framers gave the president a fixed term, rejected term limits, and adopted the stringent standards of Article II, Section 4 for impeachment ("Treason, Bribery, or other high Crimes and Misdemeanors"). Surprisingly, they had considered giving the president a lifetime appointment. Hamilton had first proposed this,[9] and on July 17, 1787, Virginia's James McClurg moved that the president serve during "good behavior" without a specified term. When this was voted on, the motion was supported by Gouverneur Morris's Pennsylvania, Madison's Virginia, Dickinson's Delaware, and New Jersey,[10] but nevertheless failed, six states to four. What this would have meant, argued George Mason, was a lifetime appointment. "He considered an Executive during good behavior," Madison heard Mason say, "as a softer name only for an Executive for life. And that the next would be an easy step to hereditary monarchy."[11] If guilty of bad behavior, McClurg's president could be removed by Congress; but bad behavior, said Mason, would be difficult to prove. Standards of good behavior are less exacting than the test of impeachment outlined in Article II, Section 4, but removal would still require a showing of wrongdoing. Tenure during good behavior is different from tenure "during pleasure," in which a person might be dismissed for no reason at all, as in a contract for employment at will.[12]

In a note that appeared when the records of the debates were published more than thirty years later, an embarrassed Madison described his support for McClurg's motion as strategic.[13] After the Convention, Madison's thoughts on government had become considerably less Hamiltonian and more Jeffersonian, and a lifetime appointment would have seemed like heresy to his new political allies. But that wasn't really what Madison had wanted in 1787, he afterward claimed. Instead, he had supported McClurg in order to signal his opposition to a congressionally appointed president, by showing the lengths to which it would be necessary to preserve the president's independence if he were not popularly elected. The explanation rings hollow, since Madison and the other delegates had previously voted unanimously for a congressionally appointed president.[14] A little before that, the Convention had voted down a proposal for a popularly elected president, 9 states to 1, with only Pennsylvania in dissent, and Madison's Virginia voting with the majority.[15] The most plausible explanation for the voting patterns is that Madison and the other nationalist delegates wanted a lifetime appointment in order to empower the president and strengthen the central government.

The two Virginians, Mason and Madison, both agreed that tenure during good behavior would make it most difficult to remove a president. For Mason, this was regrettable; for Madison, it was necessary, if the executive were not to become subservient to the legislative. Had McClurg proposed not tenure during good behavior but tenure during pleasure, Mason might well have supported the resolution, as this would have come down to the form of congressional government that he desired. It would also have resulted in a parliamentary government almost identical to that of Britain and Canada, with an executive appointed without term, and removable at will.

Mason feared a powerful president, and at the end of the Convention proposed a broad definition of impeachment that would have brought American government somewhat closer to parliamentarism. The Committee on Unfinished Parts had proposed a "treason or bribery" standard,[16] and Mason suggested that presidents also be impeachable for "maladministration." This was McClurg's standard of tenure during good behavior, which Mason had thought too difficult to prove when it was coupled with a lifetime appointment, but which now seemed to him more appropriate for a president with a fixed four-year term. Madison objected that, on a maladministration standard, presidents could be removed for any reason, and that this would amount to tenure at pleasure. Mason knew the game was lost, and in place of maladministration proposed the "high crimes and misdemeanors" test now found in Article II, Section 4.[17] The Framers did not anticipate the way in which the presidency would emerge as the dominant branch of the government, and did not think that a broad impeachment power would be necessary to keep the executive branch in check.

During the Clinton impeachment, the president's supporters correctly asserted that he had not committed high crimes and misdemeanors. His low and tawdry crime earned him a suspension of his law license in his home state of Arkansas, but it was anything but high; moreover, it was not committed "against the United States," which was the standard to which the delegates had agreed, before Gouverneur Morris dropped the reference to the country in cleaning up their language. Should that have mattered, however? High crimes are whatever the Senate says they are, inasmuch as there is no appeal from its verdict. That was then House minority leader Gerald Ford's point, in proposing to impeach Justice William O. Douglas.

> *What, then, is an impeachable offense? The only honest answer is that an impeachable offense is whatever a majority of the House of Representatives considers it to be at a given moment in history; conviction results from whatever offense or offenses two-thirds of the other body considers to be sufficiently serious to require removal of the accused from office.*[18]

In that sense, it would have been perfectly proper for the Senate to have convicted Clinton, and Andrew Johnson too, and any other president it had a mind to remove from office. That it has always failed to do so in part reflects the political costs senators would bear if they voted to convict the country's head of state. In addition, the high crimes standard has assumed the status of a legal convention, one that the Senate has seen as binding upon itself.

While spectacularly bad presidents will face a threat of impeachment, in 225 years no president has ever been removed in that way (although Nixon may have saved himself from this fate only by resigning from office). Impeachment, observed Jefferson in his old age, was not even a scarecrow—a judgment seconded by Henry Adams.[19] By contrast, a prime minister may be removed at any time, once he loses the confidence of the House.

The fateful precedent was the unfortunate acquittal of Andrew Johnson in 1868. Johnson had refused to comply with the constitutionally dubious 1867 Tenure of Office Act, which had passed despite his veto. The act provided that all federal officials whose appointment required Senate confirmation could not be removed without the consent of the Senate. Secretary of War Edwin Stanton had taken a harder line than Johnson over reconstruction of the South, and when the president fired him, over the Senate's objection, impeachment proceedings were immediately begun.

Nearly fifty years later, the Supreme Court held the Tenure of Office Act an unconstitutional restriction on the executive power,[20] but that would not have mattered had Johnson been removed. Today Congress is unable to prevent a president from firing a cabinet secretary, but the threat to fire the president would be enough to keep him in line. And that's just what impeachment manager Benjamin Butler wanted, telling his fellow senators that they could remove Johnson for any reason whatever. "You are bound by no law . . . you are a law unto your selves."[21] Not surprisingly, the trial, though judicialized with formal pleadings and rules of evidence, was a highly politicized battle fought over Reconstruction policies.[22] In the end, Johnson won by a single vote. Thirty-five senators voted to convict and nineteen to acquit, one short of the requisite two-thirds needed to remove the president. Had the vote gone the other way, Congress would have set a precedent for its power to fire a president, without the need for a Tenure of Office Act. The government would have become less presidential, and more parliamentarian.

The opposition party in a parliamentary regime need not prove misconduct in voting nonconfidence in a government. That said, prime ministers have two advantages over presidents. First, they have no term limit. They must stand for election at least once every five years, but if their party is reelected they may continue in office until removed by death or illness. Second, their ability to determine when to call an election amounts to an important strategic advantage over their opponents.

In America, elections are held every four years, and one knows today when the election will be held twenty years hence. It is sometimes said that, were the United States a parliamentary democracy, the government would have fallen in 1994, as indeed it would have, had the president been required to "go to the people" that year. As prime minister, however, Clinton would not have wanted to risk a general election two years into his first term after his heath-care proposal had foundered and the Republicans had launched their Contract with America. Instead, he went on to win reelection in 1996. Similarly, the Democratic revival in 2006 and the Republican resurgence in 2010 did not bring down the respective Republican and Democratic administrations.

In a parliamentary system, by contrast, elections are held when called by the prime minister. General elections must in theory be held at least once every five years, and even this may be waived.[23] The Queen or governor general might refuse an election writ, and this happened in 1925, when Lord Byng turned down Mackenzie King's request for an election. Before doing so, however, the governor general would have to be confident that the request was abusive. It so seemed to Byng, because the Opposition party had more seats than King's Liberals, and the country had had a general election within the prior twelve months, but that is not a precedent many governors general will choose to follow unless a prime minister's attempt to cling to power seems a perversion of democracy. As a consequence, a prime minister will usually wait for a favorable headwind and launch his campaign at the most opportune moment.[24]

This advantages prime ministers, and the American system of regular elections has been thought fairer to opposition parties. Accordingly, in Canada the Harper government amended the Elections Act in 2006 to require a general election every four years, in October (Novembers being colder in Canada than the United States).[25] In 2008, however, Harper disregarded the statute and called an election two years before the four-year period had elapsed. An advocacy group, Democracy Watch, challenged this, but the Federal Court held that, as elections are formally called by the governor general, questions about their timing are matters of Crown prerogative, and cannot be restricted without a constitutional amendment.[26] Notwithstanding the amendment to the Elections Act, the prime minister could always choose to call an election before the four-year period had expired.

Differences in the tenure of presidents and prime ministers might therefore matter less than one might think. Since 1951, presidents and prime ministers in America, Britain, and Canada (excluding John F. Kennedy and current leaders) have on average all served for about the same five-year length of time. Only two British prime ministers—Thatcher and Blair—served for longer than eight years, and then only by a few years. Since 1951, five other British prime ministers and four Canadian prime ministers served for less than a single four-year presidential term. In the modern era, parliamentary careers have become shorter, and the long runs of Robert Walpole (twenty years) and Pitt the Younger (eighteen years) are things of the past. For political leaders, time has seemingly accelerated, with a burnout rate coming more quickly today than in the time of "Old Tomorrow," Sir John A. Macdonald (nineteen years). "The trouble," said Harold Wilson (eight years) in 1974, "is that when old problems recur, I reach for the old solutions. I've nothing to offer any more."[27]

Still, presidents do enjoy greater security of tenure, and there is perhaps something to be said for this. Even if prime ministers might also enjoy a lengthy period in office, a president's promises and threats are more credible, especially when he exercises his powers as commander-in-chief. In a parliamentary regime, a war might be abandoned on the fall of a ministry, as happened in 1782 when the Rockingham Whigs came to power and sought peace with the Americans, or in 1710 when the Harley ministry broke faith with its allies in the War of Spanish Succession (giving us the expression "perfidious Albion").

Economists refer to this as a "credible commitment problem."[28] A bare promise might be dismissed as cheap talk, unless backed by a sanction for a breach of promise. Seventeenth-century philosopher Thomas Hobbes first identified the problem, and said no one should rely on a promise unless it is legally enforceable.[29] This overstates the problem; the promise of good government by a country with a long reputation for honesty may become self-enforcing even without a formal sanction for breach.[30] Nevertheless, executive promises are more credible when made by fixed-term presidents than by prime ministers.

We saw one example of this with presidential threats of war. The president's power to embark on a war without the need for congressional approval, or to continue a war once begun, makes America a more dangerous foe.[31] It raises the costs of attacking the United States, while at the same time reducing the fetters on the country going to war. In negotiating an end to the Vietnam war, for example, Nixon could tell the Soviet ambassador, "I want you to understand that the Soviet Union is going to be stuck with me for the next three years . . . and during all that time I will keep in mind what is being done right now."[32] For an enemy, such as Robert E. Lee, who knows that he will face an implacable opponent in the White House, it might dictate a risky offensive strategy, like Lee's invasion of Pennsylvania.[33]

The president's power to conduct a war has not escaped criticism, and the 1973 War Powers Resolution, mentioned in chapter 5, represented an effort to subject presidents to the fetters of congressional government.

The resolution, which requires legislative approval for wars of more than sixty days in duration, sought to reduce the number of wars in which the country engages. As John Hart Ely put it, "the point was not to exclude the executive from the decision—if the president's not on board we're not going to have much of a war—but rather to 'clog' the road to combat by requiring the concurrence of a number of people of various points of view."[34]

Credible commitment theories would provide a powerful argument for the superiority of presidential systems, if one thought that presidential wars were always a good thing. But if, like Ely, one worries about a president's unchecked war power, one might prefer that the checks be provided by parliamentary government. Again, as noted in chapter 5, there is empirical support for the proposition that American presidents wage war to boost their popularity, and one is permitted to be agnostic about the value of an unfettered presidential war power. Presidential promises and threats are superior to prime ministerial ones—but only if one assumes that they are always benign. Where a president might for strategic reasons commit to payoffs to cronies or to punishments for enemies, a parliamentary system, with the accountability of a nonconfidence motion, is plausibly better able to commit to good government

MONITORING

A government might bond itself to good behavior through monitoring strategies, subjecting itself to oversight by groups that review and report on its performance or that can veto decisions of which they disapprove. The separation of powers in the American presidential system is such a monitoring strategy, since it forces presidents to seek the consent of Congress to enact their legislative agenda. The First Amendment is also an implicit monitoring strategy, since it permits the media to report on presidential misbehavior. Nobel laureate economist Amartya Sen famously noted that no substantial famine has ever occurred in any country with a relatively free press.[35]

In parliamentary systems, in the absence of a separation of powers, monitoring strategies are less formal. Implicit monitoring techniques—notably, a free and active press—are, if anything, more apt to identify a government's failings than the highly partisan American media, which seems too ready to take sides and excuse a favored president's lapses. Most importantly, while Parliament is in session, the discipline of daily accountability in the House of Commons by the prime minister and his cabinet provides a much stronger opportunity for on-the-spot monitoring than a presidential system can.

Accountability before Parliament and Congress. Daily accountability before a house of commons makes government more transparent, and polices abuses. Decisions about what issues are brought to Parliament lie importantly with the opposition, which can decide to prolong debate over perceived government weaknesses. "No better method," observed Harold Laski, "has ever been devised for keeping administration up to the mark."[36]

While the opposition might choose to attack the government on broad principles, it might also choose to focus on narrower issues, such as a minister's corruption or a bureaucrat's abuse of power. Ultimately, the government is answerable for every act by every public servant, down to the expulsion of a thirteen-year-old cadet, George Archer-Shee, from a naval academy, for the purported theft of a five-shilling postal order. The Archer-Shee case, which formed the basis for playwright Terence Rattigan's *The Winslow Boy*, took up half a day of debate in the British House of Commons, when the government was pressed to reimburse the wrongly accused cadet.[37] Ultimately the government did so, after listening to lengthy tirades by F. E. Smith and Sir Edward Carson, who had represented the family before the Crown. Some MPs objected, with justice, that the issue was trivial in itself; but when every minister and bureaucrat knows that oppressive decisions may be ventilated before the House, there are bound to be fewer of them. He who is faithful in small things is faithful also in great.

Those kinds of debates are not to be heard in Congress. The Senate has been called "the world's greatest deliberative body," but it does not really deliberate. Like the House of Representatives, it takes votes, but it is principally the venue for speeches made for television, before an empty chamber. There might on occasion be a major war or bill to consider, when congressmen self-consciously speak to the C-SPAN cameras, but the speeches and votes count for little, even for the speaker. The murder of U.S. diplomats on Benghazi, Libya, on September 11, 2012, would have occasioned a lengthy debate in any parliament, but a speech in the House of Representatives decrying the attack was followed by a resolution honoring the Petaluma National Little League All-Stars.[38] A congressional committee eventually held hearings on Benghazi, but only after a lapse of eight months, and after the presidential election.

This is unsurprising, for it follows directly from the separation of powers. A president need not answer to Congress, as a prime minister must answer to Parliament during Question Period. An American administration cannot be defeated by a vote in Congress, while governments may fall in Parliament through nonconfidence motions. The stakes are higher in parliamentary debates than they are in congressional ones, and the difference shows.

That's not to say that Parliament is a deliberative body. The deliberations take place offstage, where the government plans its agenda and the opposition crafts its response. What Parliament is more than anything is a debating society, where the government must face an opposition similarly anxious to score points before the television cameras. It is also a venue for interrogatories from the opposition, through which the government may be called to account. Unsurprisingly, opposition MPs seldom give the government notice of their questions, so there is always an element of surprise in the proceedings. Although there are fewer opportunities for follow-up questions than in an American congressional committee hearing, a parliamentary government's front bench is regularly in attendance to respond to its critics.

In place of this, a well-staffed American congressional committee might use oversight or investigative hearings to call cabinet secretaries and bureaucrats to account. Recalcitrant witnesses may be summoned by subpoena to testify, and failure to appear (or to answer questions truthfully) could invite contempt proceedings. But this doesn't compare with an opposition party's ability to keep an issue on the front burner in Parliament for as long as it likes. As well, a presidential administration charged with incompetence may drag its feet in responding to a committee's request for information, and might assert the executive privilege doctrine to shield documents from Congress.

Matters of national security may be kept from the public in both presidential and parliamentary regimes, as can background discussions about policy matters.[39] In Parliament, however, everything else is fair game; and the opposition's ability to keep an issue alive as long as it wants makes it politically difficult for a government to bury a scandal. By contrast, the American executive privilege doctrine offers presidents far greater protection, since they may invoke the doctrine of separation of powers. That's not to say that the assertion of executive privilege is always successful, as Richard Nixon discovered in the wake of the Watergate scandal. In *United States v. Nixon*,[40] the Supreme Court unanimously rejected the president's claim of an absolute executive privilege, requiring him to turn over the White House tapes that were reasonably thought to contain evidence of criminal conduct, and this precipitated his resignation. The privilege does shield the president, however, since it raises the debate to a higher constitutional level. (Watergate wasn't about himself, said Nixon; it was about a loftier institution called "the presidency.") The privilege can also tie a congressional committee in knots, delaying an investigation until it fades from public view. A leading study of the executive privilege doctrine concluded that its use by Bill Clinton in the Lewinsky scandal gave his administration time to blame things on Independent Counsel Kenneth Starr, and thus save Clinton's presidency.[41]

Quite apart from executive privilege, an American president has an enormous discretion about the information he might reveal (or chose not to reveal). When U.S. Navy SEALs killed Osama bin Laden, the White House released pictures of a worried president and his staff huddled around a desk, and subsequently used the event in campaign commercials. However, when Ambassador J. Christopher Stevens and three other Americans were killed in Benghazi, the administration sat on the news, successfully distracting attention with a story that falsely blamed an American filmmaker for the attack—this shortly before the 2012 election. Presidents have an ability to control the message that, while never perfect, is nevertheless much more effective than anything prime ministers can muster, with their daily oversight.

The differences in constitutional regimes are mirrored in different attitudes to corruption in the United States and Canada, as evidenced by Transparency International's rankings. There is a demand for public accountability in Canada that is at times lacking in the United States. Government spending in Canada is vetted by an auditor general, who is a public figure, unlike his U.S. counterpart, the comptroller general of the Government Accountability Office. After one particular auditor general's report, in a 2006 election Canadian voters ousted a government that had engaged in a questionable and obscure payoff, the "sponsorship scandal." Funds meant to promote Canadian unity in Quebec before a referendum on secession went instead to political cronies, some of whom did no work. The amount in question was less than $2 million, chump change in America, but enough to turn voters away from the Liberal Party. The scandal came to light because then auditor general Sheila Fraser had a nose for corruption and a taste for digging up government shenanigans. She became a media figure in her own right, and in a 2004 CBC poll was ranked sixty-sixth in a list of the 100 "greatest Canadians" (behind *Baywatch*'s Pamela Anderson, but ahead of Joni Mitchell).

In the United States, Congress monitors the executive branch through inspectors general (or IGs), who are confirmed by the Senate, and who report semiannually to Congress. They are charged with uncovering fraud, waste, and abuse, and have full audit and investigative powers. In exceptional cases, their reports can put an end to the careers of mid-level civil servants, as happened when the Department of Justice IG released his 2012 report on the ATF's questionable "Fast and Furious" "gunwalking" operation.[42] Some IGs have been particularly active in uncovering wrongdoing. For example, the CIA's John Helgerson helped end the "enhanced interrogation techniques" (i.e., torture) employed during the George W. Bush administration,[43] and the Tea Party scandal came to light because the IRS IG, J. Russell George, was about to issue a report on the matter. Other IGs seem to go native, though, and serve more as their department's representative to Congress than the other way around.[44] American IGs seldom become media figures, like Sheila Fraser. When Obama fired the inspector general for the Corporation for National and Community Service, Gerald Walpin, after he had blown the whistle on an Obama supporter for financial misdealings, there was barely a ripple of protest.[45]

Appointments. Congress is formally given more power than Parliament through the Constitution's Appointments Clause (Article II, Section 2, clause 2), under which presidential appointments of ambassadors, Article III federal judges, and "all other officers of the United States" require the Senate's "advice and consent." Prime ministers are not hampered in this way. In Canada, the prime minister appoints ambassadors, federal judges, cabinet members, and even senators without the formal need to consult anyone else. As a matter of form, the governor general does the appointing;[46] but this is Bagehot's dignified constitution, and the real appointment power, in Bagehot's efficient constitution, vests in the prime minister, who instructs the governor general on whom to appoint. While this would seem to clothe prime ministers with much more power than presidents, the difference is less than meets the eye. Though Senate confirmation is required for cabinet members and ambassadors, Congress generally defers to the executive (as illustrated by the 2013 confirmations of Treasury Secretary Jack Lew and Defense Secretary Chuck Hagel). The convention is that a president is entitled to the cabinet he wants,[47] and the Senate rarely will refuse to confirm a nominee, even when the president is of a different party. Since 1900, only two cabinet nominees have been rejected by the Senate, and seven nominations withdrawn. Of the latter, nearly all were for peccadillos revealed during the confirmation process, such as attorney general nominee Zoë Baird's use of undocumented nannies. Ambassadors, many of whom are political donors and bundlers,[48] might receive greater scrutiny; some nominations are withdrawn because they never reach a hearing. The Senate's hand is strengthened by the custom of "senatorial courtesy," by which nominations for federal positions within a given state are not confirmed unless they have received the approval of the senators of the president's party from that state.[49]

The Senate exercises more oversight over judicial nominations. Of the 160 nominations made to the Supreme Court since 1789, 36 were not confirmed.[50] In recent years the stakes have become higher, as courts have been seen as more ideological. Nominations have become famously contentious, with nominees quietly dispatched by being denied a hearing, or by the Judiciary Committee's "blue slip" procedure, which gives both home-state senators veto rights over the nomination.[51]

While there is nothing like this in parliamentary regimes, once again the difference matters less than one might think, since prime ministers are constrained by political conventions about whom they appoint. British and Canadian ambassadors are career foreign service officers, who (if British) might receive a KCMG ("Kindly Call Me God") knighthood or a posting to Paris at the summit of their careers, and not as a payoff for political contributions. The prime minister's discretion is also circumscribed when it come to judges, for by convention, they are not chosen on an ideological basis. As for the cabinet, political consideration may leave a prime minister with relatively little choice about who will serve, since nearly all members must be MPs in his party (with due consideration paid for regional, sex, or linguistic quotas). A politically astute prime minister will also want to ensure that, after a leadership convention, his rivals have honored places in the cabinet. In theory, prime ministers have more leeway on appointments; but in practice, presidents might exercise more real power.

A president may sidestep Senate confirmation hearings through "recess appointments." Article II, Section 2 of the Constitution provides that "the President shall have power to fill up all Vacancies that may happen during the Recess of the Senate, by granting Commissions which shall expire at the End of their next Session." In the past, such appointments were generally made between sessions. Such recesses often lasted as long as seven months during the Republic's early days, and now are generally two months long. Giving the president the power to make a temporary appointment during such a gap might not seem to derogate meaningfully from the powers of Congress. The same might be said of appointments made in the middle of a session while Congress is in recess, when such recesses might last as long as a month.

Remarkably, however, presidents began to make recess appointments when Congress had asserted it was *not* in recess. In 2007, the Democratic Senate leadership moved to block these recess appointments by adjourning for holidays without formally going into recess; a Democratic senator showed up every three days to bang the gavel, keeping the Senate in "pro forma" session. During the remainder of Bush's Republican administration the tactic worked, for he did not make any further recess appointments. The tables were turned after the Obama victory in 2008; Senate Republicans—despite being a minority—continued to keep the chamber in session in this way. When Republicans took control of the House of Representatives in January 2011, they continued to block recess appointments by relying on Article 1, Section 5, which provides that "Neither House . . . shall, without the Consent of the other, adjourn for more than three days." But while the Senate was in pro forma session in January 2012, Obama appointed three members to the National Labor Relations Board, and made Richard Cordray director of the new and contentious Consumer Financial Protection Bureau.

Sending in a single senator to bang a gavel before an empty chamber would seem to elevate form over substance, but the tactic nevertheless serves to vindicate the principle that underlies Article II, Section 2: that presidents should be permitted to make recess appointments only when these are urgently needed, and the Senate is unable to consider them. The Framers adopted the provision without discussion, and could not have intended that it should be used to avoid confirmation hearings for controversial nominations that the Senate could consider expeditiously. The Office of Legal Counsel defended the appointment by impugning pro forma legislative sessions as an unconstitutional restriction on the president's recess appointment power.[52] However, the District of Columbia Court of Appeals found that the practice violated the principle of separation of powers,[53] and the Supreme Court will likely consider the question during its 2014 term (unless it finds that the subsequent confirmation of the recess appointees has made the issue moot).

The presidential appointment power has also expanded through the president's use of czars, the high-level officials who are charged with oversight of specific policy areas, a development that parallels the way power has shifted from Canadian cabinet members to the Prime Minister's Office. Czars report directly to the president, as members of his staff, and ensure White House supervision and control of government operations. They have been appointed to manage programs that Congress has declined to approve (such as George W. Bush's "faith-based" initiative) or that the president was too hurried to run by Congress (such as Bush's Office of Homeland Security).[54] The Obama administration is especially reliant on czars, having appointed more than forty of them.[55]

Czars' powers are often enormous. As Homeland Security czar, Tom Ridge oversaw the administration's response to the threat of internal terrorism after the 9/11 attacks. As Obama's car czar, Steve Rattner supervised the 2009 auto bailout, deciding on the payouts to creditors and employees and firing the head of General Motors. And while they might have more say in government policies than a cabinet member, czars can be appointed without Senate approval. This has raised concern when questionable people are appointed as czars without being vetted. For example, had a Senate committee been able to question Obama's "green jobs" czar, Van Jones, it might have asked him to explain why he had signed a 911Truth.org petition suggesting that George W. Bush had masterminded the 9/11 attacks.

The Character of the Leader. Presidential and parliamentary regimes bring different kinds of leaders to the fore. The imperious leader who might flourish as president, and who might hope for extraconstitutional powers, would fare poorly in Parliament, where his pretensions may more easily be mocked, and where his shortcomings are more clearly on view.

It is amusing to speculate on the prime ministers who would have risen to power had America adopted a parliamentary form of government. We might then remember the nineteenth century as the era of Daniel Webster and Henry Clay, and the twentieth as the time of Robert Taft and Sam Rayburn. More recently, a Gingrich government might have defeated that of Prime Minister Daniel Patrick Moynihan (for a fondness for liquor seems not to disqualify parliamentary leaders). What one would not have seen are the ill-informed (Eisenhower), inarticulate (George W. Bush), thin-skinned (Nixon), and grandiose (Obama) leaders.

American presidents are often outsiders, state governors who run "against Washington" in their campaigns, and who come to the office less than well informed about foreign, and even national, concerns. Thereafter, they live in a bubble, protected from daily scrutiny by their supporters and chosen friends in the media. By contrast, a prime minister must always have a detailed and up-to-the-moment understanding of the range of issues before his government. On October 24, 2012 (to take a date at random), British Prime Minister Cameron took questions about a breaking scandal involving an alleged pedophile, overcharges by energy companies, the number of neighborhood police officers, the state of the Northern Irish economy, expenditures on criminal rehabilitation, favoritism shown to a political donor, the taxation of multilateral companies, the crisis in the Euro, modern-day slavery, Scottish independence, and an energy-from-waste incinerator on the edge of King's Lynn, among many others. Prime ministers must be able to do this without the aid of a teleprompter, or fawning reporters from *People* magazine or *Entertainment Tonight*.[56]

A prime minster must be quick on his feet, as well as knowledgeable. A stumbling, extemporaneous speech would expose him to ridicule. Some prime ministers are masters of repartee, and all can provide serviceable answers to the questions that come their way in Parliament. Among Canadian prime ministers, one of the weakest debaters was Lester Pearson, a former diplomat who had won the Nobel Peace Prize, but who seemed ill at ease in the rough-and-tumble of the House of Commons.[57] Yet even he could rise to the occasion. Summoned from a diplomatic reception, he arrived at the House in full evening dress to defend the Liberal government on the last night of the month-long 1956 pipeline debate. The government, dominated by C. D. Howe, had promised TransCanada PipeLines (then an American company) that it would approve plans to build a line from Alberta before a July deadline, and had invoked cloture to terminate debate.

Hon. L. B. Pearson (Secretary of State for External Affairs): Mr. Speaker, this afternoon the hon. member for Eglington (Mr. Fleming), in a speech part of which at least I hope he will regret, suggested that we on this side, and especially we in the government, were putty in the hands of the Minister of Trade and Commerce (Mr. Howe).

Mr. Lennard: Aren't you?

Mr. Pearson: He went on to say, with that fine disregard for accuracy which he so often displays—.

Mr. Nowlan: He studied under you.

Mr. Pearson: The hon. member was a disgrace to my teaching. "Where are all those members of the government? There is not one of them who has stood up here"—I am proud to be the eighth member of the government to speak on this bill.

We are now, Mr. Speaker, ending a debate which began, and we often forget this, on May 14th.

Mr. Fulton: It began on May 17th, and you know it. Why persist in falsifying the record?

Mr. Pearson: In the immortal words of the hon. member for Prince Albert (Mr. Diefenbaker), I ask the hon. member for Kamloops (Mr. Fulton) to maintain silence and listen to the truth. We occasionally forget also that this is a debate on a pipeline. The opposition to this bill has been long and vigorous.

Some hon. Members: Hear, hear.

Mr. Pearson: At times it has been frenzied. It was forecast many years ago, the tactics that should be followed by a Conservative opposition in such a discussion.

Mr. Nolan: That was when you were a Tory.

Mr. Pearson: I can stand heckling, but I do not like to be insulted in that way. A great Canadian, Mr. Speaker, the late John W. Dafoe, in his book "Clifford Sifton in Relation to his Times", had this to say in describing the tactics of the opposition of 1897 to a railway bill introduced by Mr. Sifton. From his book I quote the following paragraphs which have a peculiar relationship to the debate we have been having in this house. He said: "If any Canadian satirist wishes to write an oration for the use of an opposition resisting a government proposition to build or assist in building a railway"—or, if you like, a pipeline—"he can readily find his material in that vast repository of talk, the Canadian *Hansard*. The lines of the attack are defined by usage and sanctified by tradition." This was written many years ago. "First it must be urged that the building of the road is too early or too late . . . then the route is all wrong; it either starts at the wrong place or follows the wrong course. The parties to whom the building of the road"—or the pipeline—"is given are not the right parties."

Then, Mr. Dafoe put in quotes some of his own reflections on this. "Is not the government aware, Mr. Speaker, that the bankers of London, New York, Paris and Kalamazoo, in alliance with the engineers of Great Britain, the United States, Germany and Kamschatka are eager to build this railway, and given the opportunity are prepared to make a proposition which will save this country millions and rescue the people from the hands of the exploiters whom the government delight to honour?" Then Mr.

Dafoe went on. "Since the government cannot tear up the contract, any alternative offer can be put in the most attractive light; while conversely, the arrangement to which the government is committed is to be painted in the darkest colours. Flagitious, corrupt, improvident, perfidious, knavish, faithless are words very suitable to be used. Any member of the opposition can be trusted to say that the treasury of the country is being robbed in order that means may be obtained for the debauching of the electors;—

Mr. Nowlan: That is obvious.

Mr. Pearson: I continue the quotation:—"but only those most skilful in the art of innuendo should be permitted to hint that there is a private and sinister explanation of the favouritism displayed by the minister. By the use of some such formula an opposition running to interminable length can be offered."

Well, Mr. Speaker, the opposition has undoubtedly run to an interminable length, but there has not been as much discussion on the bill during this interminable length as on things external to the bill. This is probably a good reason why the Minister of External Affairs should take part. The opposition, of course, claim, and they claim very often, to be gagged. If that is true, Mr. Speaker, they are the noisiest group of gagged men in history. They have talked, gag or no gag, endlessly on the bill, around the bill, above the bill and below the bill. They have ranged far and wide from Alcibiades, through Shakespeare down to poor old Guy Fawkes and then on to Hitler. They have raised endless points of order, questions of privilege, especially from one or two members.

A charge, and it is a serious one, has been levelled that what we are witnessing in this debate is the end of our parliamentary freedom.

Some hon. Members: Hear, hear.

Mr. Pearson: Well, that is the charge, Mr. Speaker.

Mrs. Fairclough: Absolutely right.

Mr. Pearson: What in reality are exaggerated and excitable statements cannot destroy the facts any more than carefully contrived scenes in the House of Commons can obscure them. Parliamentary government is in danger when the government elected in a democratic way is prevented from carrying on the business of government by a minority using and exploiting the rules of the house. To prevent that, Mr. Speaker—

An hon. Member: What about closure?

Mr. Pearson: I wonder if some of the apostles of free speech would allow me to continue my speech. To prevent this, there are rules of closure recognized in every deliberative assembly, and in most of them the rules are far stricter than they are in this assembly. That rule has been applied here, not to stop debate but to limit it. In that connection, reference has been made very often to the use of closure in the mother of parliaments, about which we have heard so much in the discussion. Let us see what happens in the parliament at Westminster. From 1945 to 1951, which was the period when the Socialist government was in power in the United Kingdom, the maximum time actually devoted to the consideration of any government money bill by the House of Commons during that period of six years was 21 hours and 25 minutes.

Mr. Dufresne: It was defeated since.

Mr. Pearson: And of that total time, including 44 minutes on the resolution preceding the bill, 7 hours and 18 minutes were given to second reading, 10 hours in committee, 22 minutes on the report and 2 hours and 35 minutes on third reading.

In the six Socialist sessions covered by this period, 55 money bills became law in the United Kingdom. Altogether, they took up 260 hours, 9 minutes, of parliamentary time, which would suggest—

Mr. Knowles: Good legislation.

Mr. Pearson: —that the average time spent in debate on a bill over there during that parliament was 4 hours and 44 minutes. That country, Mr. Speaker, the home of parliamentary freedom, also understands the necessities of parliamentary government, the responsibilities and rights of the government as well as of the opposition.

There is going on tonight in Paris, Mr. Speaker, a debate on which the government of that country has staked its existence. Before that debate began a period of three days was allowed for it. Is that the end of democracy in France?

Some hon. Members: Pretty much.

Mr. Pearson: Or is the real danger to democracy in France from the extremists in that country, right or left, who delay, obstruct, provoke scenes, shout down the presiding officer, or walk out? Extremists in those countries know, Mr. Speaker, that the best way to destroy democratic government—and in some of them they have succeeded—is to prevent it from governing; that the way to destroy freedom is to promote licence and confusion, and the best way to destroy democratic authority is to bring it into ridicule.

Mr. Hees: Is this your pitch for the leadership?

Mr. Lennard: No, it is his swan song before leaving.

Mr. Pearson: The hon. member for Broadview (George Hees), whose interruptions in this debate are as vociferous as they are vacuous, must remember that all members are not consumed with the political ambition that seems to consume him.

Mr. Sinclair: Back to the bush leagues.

Mr. Pearson: The people of this country are not going to believe that a Liberal government headed by the present Prime Minister is going to destroy the liberties of parliament.

Some hon. Members: Oh, oh.

Mr. Pearson: There is no one in this country who is also going to believe that the Minister of Trade and Commerce (Mr. Howe), who has done so much for Canada in peace and war is—to use, Mr. Speaker, the shameful phrase that came from the other side—the tool of United States interests.

Mr. Hees: Do you think you can catch Walter (Harris, the Minister of Finance and a possible leadership candidate)?

Mr. Pearson: The hon. member for Broadview (Mr. Hees) is a physical heavyweight but a mental featherweight.

Mr. Hees: You were ahead last year but not this year.

Mr. Pearson: If we could have a little free speech for once I would appreciate it. I now come to a very important aspect of this discussion which has been referred to by a good many speakers, and that is the international side of the question. It has been suggested in the debate that our relations over this bill with the United States have been humiliating; that this bill represents a sell-out to United States interests.

Some hon. Members: Hear, hear.

Mr. Pearson: Mr. Speaker, there is no reason for not speaking very frankly on our relations with the United States of America on any subject. I have done it in the past and I hope to do it in the future. But it is no service to our country or to the United States to indulge in unfair references to Americans, to make destructive and insulting comments on United States investment; to use coarse epithets and charge that our resources are falling into the hands of United States buccaneers.

Mr. Nowlan: What does the *New York Times* say today?

Mr. Pearson: It is humiliating and degrading to suggest that we are becoming hewers of wood, drawers of water and diggers of holes for our United States neighbours.

Mr. Hees. That is your Montreal speech.

Mr. Pearson: That is a defeatist attitude. It is as defeatist as some of the references on the other side to 54-40 or fight, or to suggest that we are becoming a banana republic. I know the members of the opposition get quite violent in denying that they are unfriendly to United States investments in Canada. Well, if they are so friendly to United States investments in Canada why scare them away with this kind of talk?

Mr. Lennard: Oh, rot.

Mr. Fleming: Hand it to them on a platter.

Mr. Deputy Speaker: Order.

Mr. Hees: Where else would they invest it?

Mr. Pearson: Their attitude, Mr. Speaker, reminds me of the old English music hall ballad: "I forgive you, my dear, for dissembling your love, but why did you kick me downstairs?" There is no danger of our losing control in Canada of any investment in Canada in connection with any project under Canadian control, federal and provincial as this one is.

A good deal of talk has occurred in this debate about the analogy of the Canadian Pacific Railway. There was a case of a Canadian enterprise being controlled, not in theory, but in fact, out of Canada, in London, and at a time when Canada was not a self-governing, free country as she is now, but at a time when Canada was a colony ruled from Downing street. Did it stop our growth, politically and economically? It did not. Who says, then, that this trans-Canada pipeline project will stop our growth politically or economically, or sell us to any outside country?

Mrs. Fairclough: Now I have heard everything.

Mr. Pearson: It is just as well that we should stop talking, even the hon. lady from Hamilton, if it is not too much to ask, in a way which is going to disturb the inflow of needed capital into this country.

Mr. Hees: You were ahead last year.

Mr. Pearson: I take the hon. gentleman's interruption as a tribute to the fact that I am getting under their skin. Next year, $750 million will be invested, capital investment, in Canada, 23.5 per cent of our gross national product. We shall not be able to find all that money in Canada. We must get some of it from outside, especially from the United States, if we are to maintain, the development which we have begun—

Mrs. Fairclough: Let us get the $80 million, too.

Mr. Pearson: —unless we want to slowdown the development; but let there be no suggestion, because we have had this $600 million worth of capital come into this country last year and maybe more next year, that that makes us a satellite.

This country, Mr. Speaker, Canada, in the councils of the world has won a reputation for frankness, for independence, above all, for courage in facing the problems of development and for energy to conquer them: Therefore, let us get ahead and pass this bill and take one more step in national development.[58]

Pearson had hit back hard, but had only given as good as he had got; and by his performance had amused the House, and won its respect. Nevertheless, the Liberals were seen to have overplayed their hand in invoking cloture, and the government fell in the 1957 general election, after twenty-two uninterrupted years in power. When criticized, they had seemed touchy and petulant, almost begging to be taken down a notch; and the voters obliged.

The thin-skinned and grandiose fare better in presidential than in parliamentary regimes. The fall of the Chamberlain ministry in May 1940 was not inevitable, despite the failure of the Allies' Norwegian expedition. Leo Amery had delivered his ferocious "In the name of God, go!" speech on May 7, but the government had a majority of 213, and had seemingly neutralized Churchill by bringing him into the cabinet. What sealed Neville Chamberlain's fate, according to Harold Nicolson, then a National Labour MP, was the prime minister's response to his critics the next day. When attacked by the Labour front bench over the fall of Norway, Chamberlain responded that the situation was grave, and that the attack upon the government "and upon me in particular" had made it graver still. "This really horrifies the House," wrote Nicolson in his diary, "since it shows that he always takes the personal point of view. He goes on to say that he accepts the challenge of a [nonconfidence motion], since it will show who is with him and who is against him. 'I have,' he says with a leer of triumph, 'friends in this House'."[59] But when the vote was taken, forty-one of Chamberlain's supporters voted against the government, and about sixty abstained. Two days later, on the day that German forces invaded Denmark and Norway, the prime minister resigned.

In America, by contrast, the imperial style wears better. Presidents do not appear before Congress to face the brickbats thrown at prime ministers in Parliament. Instead, they appear once a year to deliver the quasi-regal State of the Union address, and were they to receive the kinds of abuse to which Lester Pearson was subjected, American sensibilities would be shocked to the core. When Justice Samuel Alito seemed to mouth the words "not true" in response to Obama's criticism of the court, he was himself criticized for "flamboyantly insinuating himself into a pure political event, in a highly politicized manner."[60]

In sum, the executive enjoys greater independence from scrutiny and accountability in presidential than in parliamentary regimes, in spite of the mechanisms of congressional oversight found under the separation of powers. This plausibly explains why corruption levels are higher in presidential regimes, and may also help account for the tendency of presidential governments to degenerate into dictatorships. There are, moreover, other inconveniences associated with the separation of powers, and to them we now turn.

-9-

MADISONIAN INFIRMITIES

*When Congress refuses to act, and as a result, hurts our
economy and puts our people at risk, then I have an obligation
as President to do what I can without them.*

—BARACK OBAMA

Presidential regimes are more likely than parliamentary ones to turn into
dictatorships, and to rank lower on measures of public corruption. Thus
far we have examined two explanations for this: The president is the
head of state and symbol of the nation; and he is relatively immunized
from accountability to the legislature. We now turn to a third possible
explanation: The separation of powers creates inefficiencies in government that invite the president to step in and correct, and in so doing,
to augment his powers and independence from congressional oversight.

There are worse things than inefficiency in government. Supreme
Court Justice Louis Brandeis put it bluntly. "The doctrine of the separation of powers was adopted by the Convention of 1787 not to promote
efficiency but to preclude the exercise of arbitrary power."[1] But what if,
as we have seen, presidential regimes are more likely than parliamentary
ones to install a dictator in power? In that case, the inefficiencies of

separationism would be a deadweight loss. Further, they may contribute to the threat of one-man rule by encouraging a president to take charge when the legislature is deadlocked. Obama's "We Can't Wait" initiative, launched after the battle over raising the debt ceiling in July 2011 and the downgrade of public debt, sought to sidestep Congress through executive orders. "We can't wait for an increasingly dysfunctional Congress to do its job," he announced. "Where they won't act, I will."[2]

As was shown in chapter 6, deadlocks are not unknown in parliamentary regimes during periods of minority government, and in presidential regimes, parties can bargain away their differences. Recently, however, politics have become much more ideological. The Dixiecrats and Liberal Republicans of years past are now no more, and Blue Dog Democrats are a dying species. The smoke-filled back rooms of American politics have been replaced by the energized grass roots of democratized parties, and divided government is even more likely to result in gridlock today.[3] This, in turn, has led to an expansion of presidential power. Those who object to this might regret the weakening of the separation of powers. But since separationism imposes its own costs, what I regret is the absence of the kind of congressional government the Framers had wanted. Parliamentary regimes have preserved the political freedom that Brandeis prized, without the attendant costs imposed by the separation of powers.

DEADLOCK AND REVERSIBILITY

It is generally conceded that America's tax system is broken. Here's *Time's* Fareed Zakaria on the tax code:

> *The American tax code is a monstrosity, cumbersome and inefficient. It is 16,000 pages long and riddled with exemptions and loopholes, specific favors to special interests. As such, it represents the deep, institutionalized corruption at the heart of the American political process, in which it is now considered routine to buy a member of Congress's*

support for a particular, narrow provision that will be advantageous for your business.[4]

Corporate tax rates are an especial source of concern. While America's corporate tax rates are among the highest in the first world, that's far from the whole picture. In 1952 corporate taxes generated 32.1 percent of all federal tax revenues, but this had fallen to 8.9 percent in 2010.[5] What brought the figure down were "tax expenditures," the scores of special tax breaks for activities the government wishes to promote: rapid depreciation allowances, oil and gas extraction, green energy, state and local government, housing, and so on. All told, they add up to the same amount as total corporate tax revenues, and took the effective tax rate down to 13 percent in the last quarter of 2012, a far cry from the 35 percent federal rate before the tax breaks.[6]

An object lesson is provided by General Electric, the country's largest company, which earned profits of $14.2 billion in 2010 but nevertheless paid no taxes. In part this was because the tax code gave the company the incentive to keep the earnings of foreign subsidiaries offshore, but it also sheltered $5 billion in U.S. earnings through tax breaks for investments in property depreciation, low-income housing, green energy, and research and development, with a tax return that came to fifty-seven thousand pages.[7] In the past, making money was all about making a good product that consumers wanted, but now tax planning and lobbying lawmakers can be just as important.

Commentators who have looked at the problem see the makings of a reform bargain that would lower too-high corporate tax rates, eliminate loopholes, bring jobs back to America, and increase tax revenues.[8] One might think that, for legislators, this should be a no-brainer. But with the deadlock in Washington, just when might we expect no-brainer reforms to be adopted?

Reforming the tax code would require changing an existing law, and it's always harder to reverse course than to start afresh. It's easier to launch a new program than to close an existing one; it's easier to hire a public servant than to fire him. In the case of the tax code, the special breaks and loopholes have created constituencies that will fight tooth and nail to retain them.[9] The tax breaks may be inefficient, imposing more costs than the benefits they confer, but when the costs are dispersed among the entire population and the benefits are concentrated, the winners can more easily form interest groups and hire lobbyists to oppose the repeal of laws that favor them. This will happen in both presidential and parliamentary systems, but there are special reasons why reversibility is particularly difficult in the former case.

Getting legislation passed or repealed in America is like waiting for three cherries to line up in a Las Vegas slot machine. Absent a supermajority in Congress to override a presidential veto, one needs the simultaneous concurrence of the president, Senate, and House. The possibility of deadlock is magnified by the Senate filibuster, which since 1975 has permitted forty-one senators to limit debate. Since 1979, no party has controlled all three branches and enjoyed a sixty-person majority in the Senate, but for a nine-month period in 2009. Obviously, the filibuster is strongly antidemocratic, and there are signs that it has weakened of late. In the face of Democratic threats to employ the "nuclear option" and override the filibuster, Republican senators in 2013 agreed to abandon their opposition to the appointments of Richard Cordray to head the Consumer Financial Protection Bureau and of two members of the National Labor Relations Board. It is too early to say whether the threat of an override will become routine when the filibuster is employed to block presidential appointments.[10] What is less likely is that the threat of the nuclear option might be extended to every use of the filibuster. Sadly, conservatives have defended filibusters on the grounds that they enhance the doctrine of separation of powers at the core of the U.S. Constitution.[11]

By contrast, in a parliamentary system, one needs only one cherry from the one-armed bandit.[12] In Canada, neither the governor general nor the Senate has a veto power. All that matters is the House of Commons, dominated by the prime minister's party. While his party commands a majority in the House (and he enjoys his party's support), the prime minister is immune from the infirmities of divided government.

There is nevertheless a downside to the dominance of the prime minister in a parliamentary system. In a presidential system, bills require the concurrence of different branches of government, and so they might be vetted more closely. This was Hamilton's argument for the separation of powers in Federalist No. 73: "The oftener [a] measure is brought under examination, the greater the diversity in the situations of those who are to examine it, the less must be the danger of those errors which flow from want of due deliberation, or of those missteps which proceed from the contagion of some common passion or interest." If the government legislates less under the separation of powers, then, that is no bad thing, if good laws survive and bad laws don't. On the other hand, it is harder to repeal a bad law in a presidential system, which raises the question of whether pre-enactment screening is more desirable than reversibility.

That question will always give rise to partisan feelings. In the past, conservatives thought that *ex ante* screening was more important.[13] If fewer laws were passed, that was just fine with them. Progressives, on the other hand, lamented the brake that the separation of powers places on new legislation. They looked back fondly to the first one hundred days of the Roosevelt administration in 1933, when the executive drafted bills that Congress rubber-stamped without debate. That was how government should work, progressives thought.[14] Today, however, after much of their agenda has been adopted, it is the progressives who might prefer separationism's ability to block new laws, and conservatives who might value reversibility.

There are four reasons, generally free from the partisanship of the moment, why reversibility trumps pre-enactment screening. First, and most obviously, bad laws passed free from separationist screening can more easily be reversed in a parliamentary system—easier passed, easier mended. Second, it is easier to identify bad laws with the benefit of hindsight. Bad laws, based on bad ideas, with what are conceded as bad consequences, are enacted everywhere. In dictatorships, bad laws are often bad from the start. In democratic regimes, bad ideas are typically recognized only after the fact. When one parliament reverses a prior parliament, it does so with more information than the prior enacting parliament. It will know better what works, and what doesn't. That's how hindsight works.

Reversibility is particularly important for what might be called "experience laws." The economist's "experience goods" are goods whose quality cannot be evaluated until after they are sold. Many a used car looks good on the lot, only to fall apart after three months. Similarly, legislation that looks good on paper sometimes results in unintended consequences that are more costly than the problem it was meant to remedy. The 1965 Immigration and Nationality Act is a useful example of experience laws, since no one at the time seemed able to foresee how it would work out. The bill's chief sponsor, Massachusetts Senator Edward Kennedy, testified that it would not really change things very much at all. In truth, it effected a revolution in immigration flows, and over time profoundly advantaged the Democratic Party. Kennedy could never have expected that he would subsequently have to sponsor a visa lottery to admit in Irishmen excluded by the 1965 act.[15] To some extent, all laws are experience laws, whose effects can only be seen with hindsight. We can't always foresee how people will bargain around legislation, or what interest groups will arise to protect it. What separationism has given us, then, is a one-way ratchet; bad ideas are adopted and inexorably turned into the laws of the Medes and the Persians.

Third, such pre-enactment screening as might occur does not seem greater in the United States than in parliamentary systems. If anything, there is less legislative oversight in America; major amendments are quietly inserted at the last moment, escaping the scrutiny of regulators charged with overseeing the bill. For example, the housing crash's cost to the federal government was greatly increased by an obscure amendment inserted into legislation by Connecticut Democratic Senator Chris Dodd that made FDIC emergency financing available to insurance companies, most of whom were located in the senator's state.[16]

The "fiscal cliff" bill passed in January 2013 illustrates just how messy and hurried the American legislative process can be. Congress had had many months to prepare legislation to restore the Bush-era tax cuts, and for three months avoided the sequester of funds that the August 2011 budget deal would have mandated. Instead of negotiating a compromise, Congress and the president remained at loggerheads until the Bush tax cuts expired on the last day of 2012. The hasty legislation they ended up with, reported the *Washington Post*, was a bill "written only the day before by Washington insiders working in the dark of night. It was crammed with giveaways and legislative spare parts: tax breaks for wind farms and racetracks . . . government payments for cheese."[17] The Senate had voted on the 154-page bill at 1:39 a.m. on January 1, after receiving it at 1:36 a.m., a mere three minutes before.[18] Only in America.

Since they are packed with interest-group goodies, bills passed in Congress are significantly longer than their counterparts in a parliamentary system. At the extreme, a statute might be so lengthy as to greatly reduce any possibility of meaningful pre-enactment screening. One might have expected the chairman of the House Judiciary Committee to have had something to say about Obamacare, whose constitutionality took up six hours of argument before the Supreme Court.[19] Congressman John Conyers's difficulty was that it's a little hard to have an opinion about a bill one has not read. One can't be unsympathetic, though. "What good is reading the bill if it's a thousand pages," said Conyers, "and you don't have two days and two lawyers to find out what it means after you've read the bill?"[20]

Fourth, and finally, reversibility matters more than pre-enactment screening in the ongoing fiscal crisis. The structural problems of American government were prominently on display in the political gridlock over the debt crisis in the summer of 2011. Portugal's 2011 gross public debt was 111 percent of that country's GDP; that country is an economic basket case. America is at 101 percent, 5 percent more than the fifteen countries of Europe.[21] Some people think that *net* public debt (all financial liabilities less financial assets) is a better measure of a country's solvency; if that's the criterion, America looks shakier still. At 75 percent of GDP, the United States is tied with Portugal, with debt 15 percent higher than European Union countries.[22] None of this includes unfunded future payouts for Medicare and Social Security. Add that to the hopper, and the American debt problem exceeds that of either Portugal or Greece.[23] When Obama said that America was exceptional in the same way that Greece is exceptional, we didn't know what that meant. Now perhaps we do.

U.S. public debt levels increased significantly from 2008 to 2011, as the Bush and Obama administrations employed bailouts and stimulus programs to avert a market crash and restart the economy. The economy remained in the doldrums, however, and the sense that government spending was out of control, and that Democrats were in denial about the problem, accounts for the Republican resurgence in November 2010. Thereafter, Republicans in Congress, strengthened by new members who owed their election to Tea Party support, opposed an increase in the debt ceiling without a budget deal that addressed the debt crisis. The threat was a serious one; for unless the debt ceiling were raised, the government would not be able to borrow, and would be forced to shut down its programs. After months of wrangling, Republicans and Democrats finally agreed to a budget plan and to an increase in the debt ceiling on August 2, 2011—but three days later, Standard & Poor's nevertheless downgraded America's public debt. The budget deal merely kicked the can down the road, and the problem would only get worse with time. The obstacle, said the credit-rating agency, was the American system of separation of powers between branches of government under the Constitution, and the gridlock that results from divided government and polarized political parties.

Because of this, many have begun to question the value of separationism. President Obama blamed the tortured negotiations and the risk that Congress would fail to raise the debt ceiling on the gridlock produced by the American political system. "We did not have a AAA political system to match our AAA credit rating," he said. Presumably

Standard & Poor's has corrected the imbalance, with a downgraded fiscal system to match a second-rate political system.

The comparison with Canada is instructive. In 1994 that country had a federal-debt-to-GDP ratio of 67 percent (about where America is today). The *Wall Street Journal* labeled it an honorary member of the third world. Over the next sixteen years, Canada's federal debt fell to 29 percent of GDP, almost entirely from spending cuts. Economist David Henderson explained why it would be difficult for America to duplicate the Canadian experience.

> *There is . . . one important political factor that would make reform more difficult in the United States than in Canada: the structure of the U.S. political system. In Canada, once the Prime Minister has decided on the budget, the members of his or her Party almost always vote for it. Moreover, under Canada's Constitution, the government, meaning the ruling party, has sole power to initiate expenditure proposals. Parliament's only power on spending is to approve the government's proposals in full, approve them at a reduced level, or reject them. In the United States, by contrast, there are three important players or sets of players: the president, the House of Representatives, and the Senate.*[24]

Formerly, American economic conservatives could take heart in the relatively smaller size of government in their country. In 1960, American government spending expressed as a percent of GDP was roughly the same as that of comparable first-world countries. By 1990, after several decades of Keynesian spending in other countries, the American government was 10 percent smaller than its first-world rivals. An economic study of government spending as a percent of GDP over that decade found that presidential regimes were significantly smaller in size than parliamentary ones. Since then, the gap has narrowed considerably, as seen in table 9.1, which compares government spending in presidential America and comparable parliamentary countries. The size of the U.S. government is now about the same as those of Australia, Canada, and

New Zealand—and this is before the bill for Obamacare comes due.[25] In the future, what will be crucially important is whether a country can reverse course—and the current deadlock in Congress gives little reason for optimism about America's chances for a turnaround.

DEADLOCK AND TRUST

Trust is crucially important in fostering a climate where people are ready to deal with each other. When I trust people, I don't expect them to cheat or wiggle out of promises, and am more willing to enter into agreements with them. Sadly, America seems to be experiencing a trust deficit. In *Bowling Alone*, Robert Putnam reported on survey data that revealed a growing sense of mistrust in this country. The percentage of people who agreed that "most people can be trusted" fell from 55 in 1960 to 34 in 1998.[26] Similarly, the University of Chicago's General Social Survey found that, between 1976 to 2006, there was a 10-point decline in the percentage of Americans who believed other people can generally be trusted. Trust in the federal government has also fallen off a cliff since 1960, particularly during the Johnson, Nixon, and George W. Bush administrations. When asked "how much of the time do you trust the government in Washington," 26 percent of respondents said "just about always" or "most of the time" in 2013, down from 73 percent in 1958.[27]

There has also been a breakdown in trust within government in the United States, with legislative deals that don't get made because politicians no longer trust each other. In part, this reflects the disappearance of middle-of-the-road congressmen, and it might perhaps also be linked to a general breakdown in trust in society. There's something else going on, however, and that's the special contribution of divided government and the rise of Crown government. As we saw in chapter 5, presidents increasingly assert the right to ignore legislation with which they disagree, leading some politicians to ask, why bother? As I write, Congress is struggling with proposals for immigration reform, and one

TABLE 9.1 *Size of Government: Government Spending as a Percent of GDP*

	Government Spending/GDP (1960)	Government Spending/GDP (1990)	Government Spending/GDP (2012)
Australia	21.2	34.9	34.8
Austria	35.7	38.6	51.7
Canada	28.6	46	42
Germany	32.4	45.1	44.4
Italy	30.1	53.4	49.4
Ireland	28.0	41.2	43.2
Japan	17.5	31.3	41.2
New Zealand	26.9	41.3	43
Norway	29.9	54.9	43.3
Sweden	31	59.1	50.8
Switzerland	17.2	33.5	32.1
U.K.	32.2	39.9	48.8
Average	27.6	43.3	43.7
U.S.	**28.0**	**32.8**	**40.4**

Sources: Vito Tanzi and Ludger Schuknecht, *Public Spending in the 20th Century* 6, at table 1.1 (2000); OECD Economic Outlook No 89 (June 2011), *Total disbursements, general government, as a percentage of GDP*

thing that's holding it up are Republican fears that the president cannot be trusted to fortify the U.S.-Mexico border to prevent further illegal immigration. After Obama decided to ignore Obamacare's employer mandate in the face of clear legislative language, Arkansas Congressman Tom Cotton wrote, "what's to stop President Obama from refusing to enforce this law? After all, he just announced he won't enforce Obama-Care's employer mandate."[28] More pithily, Kansas Congressman Tim Huelskamp tweeted, "trusting Obama w/ border security is like trusting Bill Clinton w/ your daughter."[29]

Under the separation of powers, legislation is a bargain between the branches in which the president is charged with seeing the laws faithfully executed. When he no longer feels obliged to do so, deals won't be made and legislation won't get enacted. This in turn will encourage presidents to step in and rule by decree, and accelerate the move to Crown government.

IRRESPONSIBILITY

To the extent that the separation of powers constrains the president, it also absolves him from responsibility for useful laws that don't get enacted. The same is true for Congress, which can point its collective finger at the president who vetoes its bills. With both sides blaming the other, no one bears the burden of things that don't get done, and politicians are encouraged to behave irresponsibly, as they did in Canada before the advent of responsible government in 1849. James Bryce, an astute nineteenth-century observer of American government, noted the difference between parliamentary and presidential systems in *The American Commonwealth.*

> *In England, if a bad Act is passed or a good one rejected, the blame falls primarily upon the ministry in power .... But in the United States the ministry cannot be blamed for the cabinet officers do not sit in Congress; the House cannot be blamed because it has only followed the decision of its committee; the committee may be an obscure body, whose members are too insignificant to be worth blaming.*[30]

By way of example, in the current debt crisis, neither side took responsibility for the budgetary impasse. Obama blamed Republicans in the House of Representatives, and in his August 20, 2011, radio address, told listeners that "the only thing preventing us from passing these bills is the refusal by some disloyal souls in Congress to put country ahead of party."[31] Meanwhile, his proposed 2012 and 2013 budgets were thought so profligate that they were defeated by votes of 97 to 0 and 99 to 0 in the Senate.[32] For its part, the Democratically controlled Senate failed to pass a budget in each of 2010, 2011, and 2012. The freedom from responsibility gives both sides an inadequate incentive to take needed measures, and makes American government seem deeply unserious to people in other countries.

By contrast, in a parliamentary system, there is always someone to blame. Even during periods of minority government, the coalition of parties backing the government will bear the political costs of inaction, while the opposition can campaign on the issue. Problems are not as easily ducked as in the United States.

THE COMMON POOL PROBLEM

In his essay *Vices of the Political System of the United States*, Madison identified a problem of majoritarian misbehavior and minoritarian oppression. In a small republic, a dominant faction with more than half the votes might oppress a minority. For this reason, he argued, an extended republic that comprised many different factions would better protect liberty. No one faction would command a majority, and each would check the other in the competition for power.

What this ignores is the common pool problem of minoritarian misbehavior and majoritarian oppression. In a common pool, people behave in ways that are individually rational, but collectively irrational. Suppose that thirty people live around a lake stocked with trout. If they all overfish, the fish stocks will be depleted, and the lake will soon be without trout. It is therefore collectively rational for everyone to agree to observe fishing quotas that keep the lake replenished. However, if one of the thirty overfishes, he gains 100 percent of the benefits of his overfishing, yet bears only one thirtieth of the cost; and so he will overfish. What is individually rational for him is individually rational for all of them, and so all will overfish, leaving the lake depleted.

The common pool problem (which is the prisoners' dilemma problem in another guise) may be observed in congressional earmarks: in bridges to nowhere; in the John Murtha airport in Johnstown, Pennsylvania; and, in West Virginia, the Robert Byrd Center for this, that, and the other thing.[33] Let us stipulate that all of these are wasteful, with costs that exceed any possible benefits. Their costs are borne by American taxpayers in general, however, while their benefits are concentrated in the congressman's state or district. Here the minority oppresses the majority. Could we write a grand bargain to ban overfishing or wasteful earmarks, we should all want to do so. But where this cannot be done, we must expect the problem of minoritarian oppression to continue.

This, by the way, explains the paradoxical polling figures about Congress and congressmen. We all hate Congress, pollsters tell us, but love our individual congressman. We love his ability to bring home the bacon, even if we recognize that the system that permits him to do so is corrupt. Congressional earmarks have been defended as a relatively small outlay—less than 2 percent of federal government spending—but that understates the nature of the problem. A congress composed of members primarily concerned with directing spending to their districts is not one that is likely to show much discipline in curbing total government spending. The Robert Byrds and John Murthas didn't become masters of pork by worrying overmuch about financial deficits. This magnifies the obstacles to budget reform that separationism imposes, and makes it all the more unlikely that Congress will rein in spending.

To reverse the common pool problem, what is needed is a grand coalition—a coalition of the whole of the voters—that will vote for the general welfare, rather than the narrow interest of individual congressional districts. Economist Mancur Olson called this a "superencompassing majority,"[34] one that treats minorities as well as it treats itself, and which stands in proxy for the nation as a whole. Discovering and empowering such a majority might then be thought the very goal of constitution making. It was the idea behind Lord Bolingbroke's idealized Patriot King, who governs "like the common father of his people . . . where the head and all the members are united by one common interest."[35]

That might not seem like a desirable goal to some. Some Americans identify less with the nation as a whole, and more with the interests of a particular group within the nation. For them, questions of social justice turn primarily on how members of a particular class, defined by race, sex, or sexual preference, might fare. They might not be willing to sacrifice the interests of their identity group, or might take the national interest to be nothing more than the sum of the interests of similar progressive groups. Those who take a broader view of the national interest might fear that majoritarian coalitions will not be superencompassing, that they will treat minorities unfairly; and that was precisely the problem that separationism's checks and balances was meant to address. Even if one takes the national interest as the primary good, one might view the threat of a majority that oppresses a minority as a greater evil than the minoritarian misbehavior of interest groups that prey off the public purse.

If it's a trade-off between the two kinds of oppression, however, minoritarian misbehavior seems the greater concern. Otherwise we would expect to find that minorities—Afro-Britons, Native Canadians—have fared worse in parliamentary countries of similar culture that lack America's separation of powers. But without putting too fine a point on it, that has not been the experience. The rights of minorities are to be judged by how they have fared as a matter of history, and not by rights on paper.

As for the minoritarian misbehavior of wasteful rules adopted at the behest of narrow interest groups, these seem less of a problem in a parliamentary regime. In a presidential system, where national parties are weaker,[36] one votes for the congressman who brings home the bacon to one's district. In parliamentary systems, national parties are stronger; and with a two-party system and a diverse electorate, a party requires broad, national support to be elected. It will therefore have a greater incentive to acquire a reputation that puts what it understands as the common, national good ahead of wasteful local projects. There are few legislative earmarks in Pierre Trudeau's Parliament of Nobodies.

Take member of Parliament Ruth Ellen Brosseau. In the 2011 Canadian general election, the voters of Berthier-Maskinongé in Quebec elected the comely Brosseau, a 27-year-old barmaid. Ms. Brosseau did not visit her riding during the election campaign because she does not speak the language, and instead holidayed in Las Vegas. Her party's website noted that "one of her passions is rescuing and rehabilitating injured animals. For many years Ruth Ellen has committed her time and energy to finding homes for stray animals in her community." Did I mention she was comely?

When MPs are "nobodies," voters don't expect them to bring any pork back to the riding. Instead, any pork comes from the national party, which has broader incentives than, say, a John Murtha does. Brosseau might not possess Murtha's legislative skills, but a Parliament of Ruth Ellens more closely resembles the idealized assembly described by Edmund Burke in his address to the electors of Bristol: an assembly "of *one* nation, with *one* interest, that of the whole; where, not local purposes, not local prejudices, ought to guide."

The person most likely to represent the majority of voters in the United States is the president, as he alone is elected by the country as a whole. Like the winning party in a parliamentary regime, he might claim to represent Olson's superencompassing majority.[37] We might then expect presidents to oppose the minoritarian misbehavior of congressional pork; and that was the thinking behind the 1996 Line Item Veto Act, passed by a Republican Congress to permit the president to zero out wasteful spending projects earmarked by Congress in an appropriations bill.[38] The law was immediately challenged by a master of the art, West Virginia's Senator Byrd, and was ultimately found unconstitutional by the Supreme Court in *Clinton v. City of New York*.[39] The line-item veto might have been a salutary way to address problems of overspending and corruption in congressional earmarks, but the court held that it violated the Constitution's Presentment Clause of Article I, Section 7:

> *Every Order, Resolution, or Vote to which the Concurrence of the Senate and House of Representatives may be necessary . . . shall be presented to the President of the United States; and before the Same shall take Effect, shall be approved by him, or being disapproved by him, shall be repassed*

by two thirds of the Senate and House of Representatives, according to the Rules and Limitations prescribed in the Case of a Bill.

Did this mean that the president's only option is to sign or veto a bill in its entirety? While the clause is less than clear, the ambiguity was unfortunately resolved against the line-item veto, to vindicate the principle of separationism. "Separation of powers was designed to implement a fundamental insight: concentration of power in the hands of a single branch is a threat to liberty."[40]

There are nevertheless two reasons why an American president is less likely to serve as a proxy for a superencompassing majority than a winning political party in a parliamentary regime. First, the separation of powers makes Congress a player; and the problem of minoritarian misbehavior is largely one of congressional excesses. When Obama sought to enact his health-care package, for example, he had to swallow the special payoffs that individual congressmen demanded as the price of supporting the bill. Second, a president's incentives to act on behalf of the nation as a whole are weakened by term limits, and by the immunity from accountability described in the previous chapter. Presidential candidates have an incentive to campaign for the votes of a superencompassing majority, but once elected, have a weaker incentive to govern on its behalf.

This is not to say that pork-barrel spending is unknown in parliamentary regimes. A study of Canadian electoral districts between 1988 and 2001 found that spending was targeted towards swing districts and districts represented by members of the government party.[41] Similarly, a president might seek to direct pork to battleground states, and to the districts of his supporters in Congress.[42] The common pool problem of majoritarian oppression never goes away, but nevertheless, appears smaller in parliamentary systems. What pork there was in Canada was understandably directed at Quebec, which was threatening to secede, and yet even then governments thought to favor that province unduly fared poorly in subsequent general elections.

"PRESIDENTIALIZED" POLITICAL PARTIES

Political parties are structured differently in presidential and parliamentary regimes. In a parliamentary system, the prime minister is the leader of the majority party in the House, and may determine who runs under the party's banner. He is also accountable to the MPs in his party, however, and serves as their agent in an election. A weak leader, like John Diefenbaker in 1963, might thus be dumped by his party when he seems likely to lead it to defeat. By contrast, in presidential systems there is a greater degree of independence between a president and individual congressmen, as a consequence of the separation of powers. One reason for this is the separate power base congressmen have, because of their ability to direct pork-barrel spending to their districts. The other reason is the option voters are given to split their ticket by casting separate ballots for president and legislators. That isn't possible in a parliamentary regime, where one can't vote for the party and against the prime minister.

David Samuels and Matthew Shugart argue that the separation of powers creates a competition between the president and congressmen of the same party.[43] In 1996, for example, Clinton successfully "triangulated" between the Democratic left and Republican right to win reelection. You don't have to put all your eggs in one basket, he told voters. Similarly, when Obama rails against "Congress," he seldom makes much of a distinction between Republican and Democratic legislators. Instead, he is picking a constitutional battle, asserting that he stands above party, and uniquely acts for the country as a whole. The intraparty competition gives rise to a "presidentialized" party, built around the president (or one who seeks the job), and distinct from congressional parties of the same name. None of this is possible in a parliamentary system.

Presidentialized parties have different sets of activists and donors than the regular political party. For example, "Obama for America," the 2008 network of two million Obama volunteers, was not part of the Democratic Party, and the primary allegiance of its members was to Obama, and not to the Democratic Party. Obama for America subsequently merged with the party, but for the 2012 presidential election it was relaunched as "Organizing for America," again separate from the party. It doesn't take much imagination to see how that kind of power could be abused by a charismatic president.

It also doesn't take much imagination to see how an American presidential party might come to dwarf congressional parties. If a president can make laws by diktat and unmake them at will, and if spending decisions require his approval, as we saw in chapter 5, then donors are going to start asking themselves why they're putting their money into congressional races, and lobbyists are going to start asking themselves why they care about some furbelow on a piece of legislation. Increasingly, that's not where action is. Power feeds on itself, and the recent transfer of political power to the executive branch will hasten the growth of presidentialized parties and Crown government.

MICROMANAGING AND BUBBLE LAWS

When Madison thought that ambition would counteract ambition, he took little account of the abuses to which this might give rise. Presidential ambitions are expressed through the kind of executive lawmaking outlined in chapter five. As for the legislative branch, an ambitious Congress would seek to clip the president's wings through overlong statutes that leave little room for the exercise of discretion.[44] While Congress often delegates the broadest rule-making authority to federal agencies, as it did with the Dodd-Frank act, it sometime veers in the opposite direction, with legislation that micromanages the regulators.

There is a trade-off between inadequate and excessive specificity in statutory draftsmanship. Too little specificity gives the executive insufficient information about the legislature's intention, permitting a president to make of a law whatever he will. Contrariwise, excessive specificity might prevent the executive from adjusting to new circumstances not foreseen by the legislature on a law's passage. It could also prevent the executive from recognizing exceptions, or expanding the scope of a rule, where this is warranted.

One would expect a parliamentary regime to be more likely than a presidential one to strike the right balance between terseness and prolixity in statutory draftsmanship. Where the executive and legislative branches are united, as in a parliamentary government, the competition between branches is absent, as is the incentive to prolixity. One can test this by comparing the length of statutes in Britain and Canada on the one hand, and the United States on the other. Almost without exception, major pieces of legislation are longer—far longer—in the United States. In part, this is due to the interest-group bargains that are enshrined in American legislative earmarks, so as to prevent the executive or the courts from undoing them. In addition, sometimes congressional legislation micromanages the executive to a degree that British and Canadian draftsmen would find extraordinary. There has never been anything like a thousand-page Obamacare statute in a parliamentary regime. Canada's medicare legislation is twelve pages long—and it's bilingual. One can sympathize with John Conyers's refusal to read the American statute. Almost certainly, it will be found full of unpleasant surprises, of wrinkles that, with the benefit of hindsight, will seem regrettable.

A secondary problem is the grandstanding laws enacted in a presidential regime. In a parliamentary system, all major legislation is introduced by the ruling party, and no one MP is formally identified as its sponsor. With a separation of powers, the most wretched of bills typically bear the name of boastful congressmen: Davis-Bacon, Smoot-Hawley, Sarbanes-Oxley, Dodd-Frank. Such bills are the triumphal arches of a career in Congress, and give their sponsors a form of legislative immortality. For presidential aspirants, they are a credential that raises them from the mass of congressmen.[45]

Grandstanding of this kind gives us what Stephen Bainbridge has decried as "bubble laws," laws passed in the heat of a crisis, sponsored by congressmen who want to claim credit for solving a problem.[46] Such laws are prepared hastily, with little thought given to long-term consequences. They fight the last war, and lose the next. The Sarbanes-Oxley act, passed in response to the Enron and WorldCom financial scandals, greatly increased the financial reporting duties of U.S. public companies, and appears to have driven securities firms offshore. A decade ago, the New York Stock Exchange launched half the world's new public companies. By 2006 this had dropped to one in twelve, as firms moved to the London Stock Exchange and other venues. Photos of Paul Sarbanes and Michael Oxley are prominently displayed in the offices of London brokers.[47] They know whom to thank.

What, then, is to be done? Nothing, some might think, if the costs of the separation of powers are exceeded by the benefits of greater political freedom. The pathologies of divided government, while not observed in parliamentary systems, might seem a necessary evil if, as Brandeis claimed, separationism precludes the exercise of arbitrary power. As it turns out, Brandeis was wrong; trading efficiency in government for freedom was a bad bargain. Parliamentary regimes are freer than presidential ones, and the United States cannot meaningfully be said to have either more efficiency or political freedom than the parliamentary countries it most resembles.

One way to address the costs of separationism would be to confer greater power on the executive branch. This indeed has been the recent history of American government. Taking it to the next level would entirely eliminate the costs of divided government, which were not to be found in Hugo Chávez's Venezuela. Were this to happen, however, the threat to political liberty identified by Brandeis would be all too real, and even the present concentration of power in the American presidency is regrettable. As in John Dunning's day during the personal rule of George III, the power of the executive has increased, is increasing, and ought to be diminished.

What remains is the possibility of expanded congressional power. How feasible this is I do not know, but it is the least dangerous response to the inefficiencies of divided government. In its posturing, earmarks, and bubble laws, Congress has governed irresponsibly. But the conferral of greater authority might change this; and with more responsibility, legislative parties might govern more responsibly. They might pass budgets, police the minoritarian misbehavior of earmarks, and govern more effectively on behalf of the country as a whole. Moreover, an expansion of congressional power would be faithful to the vision of the Framers, as we saw in chapter 2. They did not foresee the inefficiencies of divided government, as nearly all imagined they had given the country something resembling congressional government. When the Philadelphia Convention was over, however, Madison became the principal apologist for separationism, and it is not unfair to label its inconveniences as Madisonian infirmities.

–10–

Tyrannophilia

*The accumulation of all powers, legislative, executive,
and judiciary, in the same hands, whether of one, a few, or
many, and whether hereditary, self-appointed, or elective, may
justly be pronounced the very definition of tyranny.*
—JAMES MADISON, FEDERALIST NO. 47

Tyrants have gotten a bum rap. Oedipus τ ραννος wasn't a bad ruler. Marrying his mother and killing his father was simply bad luck. (*Really* bad luck.) In Greece's classical period, a tyrant was often a benign ruler who had risen to power with the support of the middle and lower classes, whom he thereafter protected against the aristocracy. Under Peisistratus, for example, Athenian trade expanded, the economy improved, and temples were built. Afterward, his rule was remembered as a golden age. What made one a tyrant was not misrule, but the violent way in which one seized power.

Polybius saw it a little differently. Peisistratus wasn't the problem. It was the kids. Peisistratus was in effect a king, applauded by everyone for his wise rule, but his children were something else. It was like a family firm the founder had built up, only to see his children fritter it away. The founder might have had dirt under his fingernails, but he was a tough old geezer, with a soft spot for those less well off. As for the kids with their fancy MBAs, not to mention the grandchildren on Ritalin, they simply weren't up to the job. In this way, said Polybius, a monarchy would degenerate into a tyranny, with succeeding generations that lacked the skill to command the affection of their subjects, and whose rule would become oppresive.[1] That's what happened to the Peisistratids, and (if Livy does not lie) to the Tarquins of Rome as well.

Jefferson saw the same pattern of decline in the British royal family, and in the Declaration of Independence he called George III a tyrant. That overstates it, however, for even during the period of his personal rule, before the fall of the North ministry in 1782, George III did not hold all the cards. He could not ignore Parliament, and over time power shifted from him to the House of Commons, and to Bagehot's cabinet government. More recently, this has been overtaken by what I have labeled Crown government, with a much more powerful prime minister. So too, the former American Constitution, of a balanced separation of powers, has been overtaken by a Constitution of strong executive power, which I also see as a form of Crown government.

That doesn't make a modern president a tyrant, and the concern that he might be so described has been mocked as tyrannophobia.[2] America has had a successful run as a democracy for 225 years, and with its never-ending campaign cycles, initiatives, and referenda, might be thought excessively democratic. That said, one is permitted to wonder whether it will be quite so democratic in twenty to forty years. The assumption that the future will resemble the past is always heroic, and particularly so after a sharp discontinuty. In 1865, one would not have looked to antebellum history to predict the future of American federalism. So too, one might not unreasonably wonder whether the recent, remarkable concentration of power in the American executive might be followed by a further expansion of presidential power. The vectors that have pointed towards Crown government—the regulatory state, the role of the media—will remain unchanged, in magnitude and direction; and the very powers that presidents have amassed might just possibly be employed to deepen their hold over the government and to restrict political freedom, even as this has happened in most other presidential regimes.

In what follows, I look at four ways in which presidential power might be strengthened in undemocratic ways. New technologies for data mining and evesdropping might be employed to gather information about political enemies. The president's control over the machinery of criminal justice and regulatory enforcement is an invitation for abuse by a power-seeking president and his party. The president's power to nominate judges to the Supreme Court, and the deference given to his nominees by the Senate, also empowers him to reshape the structure of government and constitutional liberties, particularly the liberties enjoyed by intermediate organizations, such as religious groups that serve as focal points for opposition to dictatorial government. Finally, immigration policies have resulted in demographic changes that many have welcomed, but that at the same time may result in an electorate less committed to democratic government.

TECHNOLOGY AND CORRUPTION

Whether technology will strengthen or weaken the hands of tyrants over the next twenty to forty years is an open question. In repressive states it has strengthened the opposition. Thirty years ago, a George Soros who sought to promote democracy in the Soviet Bloc could do little more than buy books and donate Xerox copiers to universities. Nowadays, with Meetups organized on Facebook, Twitter and cell phones, viral YouTube videos, and the informational resources of the Internet, old techniques of censorship and coercion have proven less potent, with four dictators swept from office in the Arab Spring. More recently, Egypt's Mohamed Morsi has the dubious distinction of being the first leader to be elected *and* deposed through revolutions inspired by new communication technologies.

In democratic states, however, technology has given governments much more information about their citizens, as seen in Edward Snowden's revelations about the National Security Agency's monitoring of electronic communications. That doesn't make the United States a police state, concluded Pentagon Papers leaker Daniel Ellsberg. "But given the extent of this invasion of people's privacy, we do have the full electronic and legislative infrastructure of such a state."[3]

Before such information could be used for political purposes, someone would have to seriously misbehave. That said, there's been a fair bit of serious misbehavior of late: lies about Benghazi, illegally hidden email accounts, the Justice Department's secret seizure of Associated Press phone records. If IRS employees could blacklist Tea Party groups seeking 501(c)(4) status before the 2012 election and reveal sensitive donor information to left-wing groups, it's not beyond imagining that partisan data miners will find their jobs made easier with leaked phone calls and emails. That's speculative, of course, but those who discount the possibility of bureaucratic corruption and partisanship always seem to think they're living in Nirvana—or New Zealand.

CRIMINALIZING POLITICAL DIFFERENCES

More than other countries, the United States relies on criminal law to deal with its citizens' behavioral problems, and this has led to concerns across the political spectrum about overcriminalization.[4] America has the largest per capita incarcerated population on earth, and even in absolute numbers, it puts more people in prison than any other country (with the possible exception of China).[5] A noted American criminal law scholar has complained that "with 5 percent of the world's population, we hold nearly 25 percent of its prisoners. That is embarrassing."[6] In addition to America's 2.3 million incarcerated, an additional 5 million are under "criminal justice supervision," i.e., parole, probation, or supervised release. The combined total of 7.2 million people (excluding most juvenile detentions) represents about 3 percent of American adults.

The overcriminalization problem is exacerbated by the number of crimes on the statute books, particularly under federal law. One commentator described federal criminal code as "simply an incomprehensible, random and incoherent, duplicative, incomplete, and organizationally nonsensical mass of federal legislation."[7] The number of federal criminal offenses is literally unknowable. The result, according to a leading criminal law academic, the late William Stuntz, is that we are moving closer to a world in which the law on the books makes every American a felon.[8]

In times past, a person might have protected himself against a criminal prosecution simply by being honest. That's not enough today. Crimes once required a guilty mind—what the lawyer calls *mens rea*—but this has been abandoned in a wide range of "public welfare crimes." Consider, for example, the plight of Krister Evertson:

> *Evertson never had so much as a parking ticket prior to his arrest....*
> *An Eagle Scout, National Honor Society member, science whiz, clean*
> *energy inventor, and small business entrepreneur, Krister is now a felon.*
> *The nightmare that took two years of his freedom and hundreds of*
> *thousands of dollars . . . began when he made a simple error: he failed*
> *to put a "ground" sticker on a package that he shipped. Despite his clear*
> *intention to ship by ground—as evidenced by his selection of "ground"*
> *on the shipment form and payment for "ground" shipping—the govern-*
> *ment prosecuted him for his error anyways.*
>
> *When the jury acquitted Krister, the government turned around*
> *and charged him again, this time for alleged abandonment of toxic*
> *materials. Krister had securely and safely stored his valuable research*
> *materials in stainless steel drums, at a storage facility, while he fought*
> *for his freedom in trial over the missing shipping sticker. He ultimately*
> *spent two years in a federal prison for his mistake.*[9]

The *mens rea* requirement was imported into common law by medieval canonists, who argued that criminal wrongdoing, like sin, assumed moral guilt. "God considers not the action, but the spirit of the action,"[10] said Peter Abelard, which meant that he thought we should move on from Anglo-Saxon strict liability criminal offenses. This was a signal advance in personal liberty—Constant's liberty of the moderns—since it limited the possibility of jail time. Nowadays, however, *mens rea* standards are "just a few ideas that have ceased to be modern," as Evelyn Waugh's Basil Seal remarked. Their abandonment, inspired by the most progressive political thought of the day, puts everyone at risk of the most severe restrictions on liberty available to the state.

What makes it especially dangerous is that American criminal procedure gives ambitious prosecutors enormous powers, with little accountability when they overreach. In federal grand juries, which operate in secret and can go on for years, prosecutors are virtually immune from judicial supervision. They can call witnesses (including the target of the investigation) without revealing the nature of the case, and can introduce hearsay evidence. Not surprisingly, they seldom fail to win an indictment. Since a firm suffers an enormous reputational loss on indictment, the mere threat of grand jury proceedings is often enough to bring it to its knees.

The Department of Justice increasingly employs its bargaining leverage to obtain convictions of company executives. Under the "Holder memorandum" (named after then deputy attorney general Eric Holder), the Department of Justice encourages prosecutors to base their prosecutorial decisions on the degree to which the target firm cooperates with the investigation. This includes hanging a company's executives out to dry by inducing their employer to breach its contractual duties to pay for its employees' legal fees.

Prosecutors are given a leg up with their ability to bring multiple charges, under multiple theories of criminal liability. The prosecutor need win a conviction on only one count, while the defense must win them all. A jury, minded to split the difference, might easily acquit on ninety-nine counts, and convict on one. For sentencing purposes, there is generally no difference between conviction on one count or many. If the principal charge fails, a lesser charge will often do just as well, in a system seemingly designed for the purpose of convicting Al Capone for tax evasion.

As well, when federal prosecutors bring a case, they have all the financial and investigative resources of the Department of Justice at their disposal. They can buy favorable testimony by selectively granting or threatening to deny immunity from prosecution, and can coerce a guilty plea to a lesser charge by threatening to indict on a more serious one. The inequality in bargaining power is magnified by the "trial penalty" courts impose, in the harsher sentences they hand defendants who, refusing to plead, go to trial and are convicted.[11] As a consequence, nearly everyone caught in the meshes of the federal criminal system pleads guilty. Of the cases federal prosecutors most recently pursued, they secured guilty pleas from 96 percent of defendants, and won convictions at trial for 3 of the remaining 4 percent. Fewer than 1 percent of defendants were acquitted.[12]

The expansion of criminal law obviously restricts personal liberty, Constant's liberty of the moderns. It might also threaten political liberty, Constant's liberty of the ancients. Anton Chekhov said that, when the audience sees a loaded pistol on the wall in act 1, it must go off by act 3. The potential for political misuse in federal criminal law is a loaded pistol, and the mystery is why it hasn't gone off yet. It has obviously gone off in other countries, such as Russia, where oligarch Mikhail Khodorkovsky was sent to prison after a series of show trials, ostensibly for fraud, but in reality for having the temerity to oppose Vladimir Putin.

If an American president sought to strengthen his hand, a first step might be to employ the federal criminal justice system for political ends. District attorneys are political appointees, and though George W. Bush was severely criticized when he fired seven of them in 2006, there was little comment from the media over Clinton's decision after taking office in 1993 to fire nearly all of them, including a district attorney investigating Clinton's involvement in the Whitewater affair. Thus an incoming president might easily replace all incumbent district attorneys. The new appointments would require Senate confirmation, and individual senators have by tradition had a strong say in the choice of who will serve, but it cannot be beyond the wit of a president to place several partisan allies in office, and then let nature take its course.

One saw a hint of what this might mean in the 2012 election campaign, when Obama's deputy campaign manager, Stephanie Cutter, suggested that the Republican nominee had committed a felony under federal securities law. "Either Mitt Romney, through his own words and his own signature, was misrepresenting his position at Bain to the SEC, which is a felony," she said, "or he was misrepresenting his position at Bain to the American people to avoid responsibility for some of the consequences of his investments."[13] The charge went nowhere, except as one more element in an ugly campaign. What was remarkable, however, was that no one noted that the campaign had flirted with a descent into Khodorkovsky territory. Whether Romney had committed a felony became a political issue,[14] but not the degradation of American political discourse.

America isn't Russia, of course, not by a very, very long shot. But one has the strong sense that it isn't a democratically pristine New Zealand, either. It has a greater tolerance for corruption than most other first-world countries, and a taste for populism in its criminal justice system. Criminal prosecutions of the likes of Conrad Black, Dennis Kozlowski, Michael Milken, Martha Stewart, and other Enemies of the People have little parallel in the rest of the first world. When the stock market crashes, one doesn't hear a British call to jail financial executives, as one does here,[15] or calls to arrest speculators, if gas prices soar.[16] That's simply the media, of course. The criminal justice system has itself remained very largely above politics. As for act 3, it is less than clear that the separation between criminal law and politics will be maintained in quite the same way twenty to forty years hence.

That's not to say that presidents will throw opposition leaders into jail, as they do in the Ukraine. But it is not beyond the realm of possibility that investigative magazines, right-wing press lords, and major opposition donors will find themselves under criminal investigation, or that IRS tax audits, EPA decisions, and Labor Department investigations will be shaped by political considerations—if only because all that seems to happen now.[17] During the Clinton administration, conservative groups thought it more than a little curious that Juanita Broaddrick, Gennifer

Flowers, and Paula Jones were all audited after their sexual harassment and assault charges against the president were reported (to say nothing of audits of opposition groups such as the Heritage Foundation, the National Rifle Association, and *National Review* magazine). A senior IRS official is reported to have said, "What do you expect when you sue the president?"[18]

THE SUPREME COURT

American constitutional *history* is a fascinating subject, full of the fine reasoning and scholarly erudition of brilliant judges. American constitutional *law* is another matter. A cynic might think it included in law school curricula solely to prove that lawyers have a sense of humor. In such courses one studies what courts in the past have said about the structure of government, but that may reveal little about what the law is—the law made by the Supreme Court—for that depends much more on the court's present and future membership than on its prior decisions, and never more so than in recent years.

The American federal bench is perhaps the strongest in the world—except at the very top. District and circuit court judges are a national treasure. They are wise and learned public servants who, for the most part, carefully adhere to the binding precedents of higher courts, and in this way promote the rule of law. But the Supreme Court does not consider itself bound to follow its prior decisions under the doctrine of *stare decisis*. For its members, *stare decisis* is at most a rule of prudence, one that permits a justice to depart from prior cases, provided he can reasonably assert that doing so vindicates fundamental constitutional principles, or corrects a prior error.[19] Even that overstates it. The reality is that past precedents do not seem to constrain the court very much. From Obamacare to affirmative action to same sex marriage, experts have found themselves unable to predict just how Supreme Court decisions will come out. In one sense that's not surprising, since it's precisely the case that might go either way that gets appealed. However, the experts couldn't even predict the grounds on which the case would be decided. Who expected, for example, that Chief Justice Roberts would find that Obamacare could be upheld under the federal government's taxing power?[20] As for same-sex marriage, would that turn on the Fifth Amendment's promise of equal protection or on principles of federalism? Or would the problem just go away because of a lack of standing?

The reality is that past precedents do not seem very much to constrain the Supreme Court. The uncertainty is compounded, moreover, when one factors in changes in the court's composition. Suppose, for example, that section 4(b) of the Voting Rights Act, which the court struck down in *Shelby County v. Holder*,[21] comes up again before the court, but that before then conservative Justice Scalia falls under a bus. Given the partisan nature of the court, and the president's broad ability to place a supporter on the court, one would not be entirely surprised were the ruling undone by a new court. American constitutional law is a lottery, where the winner is the president who is lucky enough to be in office at a time when members of the court are unlucky enough to become ill or die in office.

There is a further way in which a Supreme Court packed by an ambitious president might empower the executive. A power-seeking president would find the subsidiary institutions interposed between himself and his people a troubling obstacle. Such institutions, most especially religious ones, give people the diversity of a range of choices and information about how to live that the state cannot provide alone. For the tyrant, they simply get in the way. If they provide social services, schools, hospitals, and adoption agencies, they are doing what government should be doing, and often with a dangerously illiberal agenda.[22] When every other barrier to oppression is removed, in a Soviet-era Poland or in China, what remains are churches faithful to their mission.

The Supreme Court's jurisprudence on church-state relations is replete with messy compromises over such issues as religious symbols in public places and state aid for religious schools. For example, the federal government may not directly subsidize religion, but nevertheless can do so indirectly, through grants for nonreligious purposes to religious colleges and financial aid for the students who attend them. As for the states, it remains unclear whether they may provide vouchers that subsidize education at religious schools, and new members on the court might resolve these ambiguities in one direction or the other. The expanding scope of federal mandates over such issues as health care and abortion can also collide with religious sensibilities. For example, the recent Health and Human Services mandates that would force religious believers to offer health insurance that includes coverage for contraceptive and abortifacient drugs to their employees can be expected to come before the Supreme Court. After taking some flak, the administration came out with an "accommodation," an accounting sleight-of-hand that requires insurance companies to provide the drugs for free, a tactic that stripped away many of the rule's critics. If the prior rule was offensive, however, the "accommodation" might seem even more so, because without relaxing the requirement, it insulted one's intelligence. Only the economically illiterate would believe that insurers will offer a costly service without passing on the cost to those insured. The administration had, from one corner of its mouth, complained of the financial burden imposed on women who must pay for contraception out of their own pockets, while telling voters, out of the other side of its mouth, that the cost is so trivial that the insurer will assume it. By adopting the change, the administration had signaled a willingness to enter into the cultural wars that separate the groups that support abortion from a religion that doesn't, and that is something one might see more of in the future.

Same-sex marriage is on the front lines of the culture wars today, a controversy that the recent Supreme Court decisions on the subject did nothing to quell. Section 3 of the Defense of Marriage Act had provided that federal statutes should not be interpreted to recognize same-sex marriages, and in *United States v. Windsor* the court held that this violated the Equal Protection Clause of the Fifth Amendment.[23] Then, in *Hollingsworth v. Perry*, decided on the same day, the court declined to rule on whether the initiative (Proposition 8) that banned same-sex marriages in California could be upheld;[24] and this had the effect of reinstating the trial court decision that found the ban unconstitutional. The logic of the *Windsor* case seems to suggest that, when faced with the issue again, the court will require all states to recognize same-sex marriage—but that depends, of course, on just who shows up on the bench that day. One can also expect plaintiffs to argue that, in order to keep their jobs or carry on business, religious institutions must accommodate same-sex couples, even if this violates the institution's religious principles. Again, this might be thought to follow from the *Windsor* decision, which held that a ban on same-sex marriage impermissibly demeans homosexuals. The decision elevated the need for respect to the level of a constitutional principle, and if this is employed to restrict religious freedoms it will be an example of what conservative cultural historian Robert Nisbet labeled "the ingenious camouflaging of power with the rhetoric of freedom."[25]

The First Amendment guarantees the free exercise of religion, and bans the establishment of a state church. The Founders did not see these provisions in tension with each other, but they have become so, and the secularist's strong disestablishmentarianism may take precedence over weak free-exercise rights. Many secularists view churches as dangerous quasi-governments that inculcate regressive values that are at odds with the progressive moral code of the state. For them, the right to freedom from religion might trump freedom of religion. These views (which in the past were not entirely free from an anti-Catholic bias) seem poised for a revival.[26] Ironically, this would go some way to the establishment of religion, by privileging the mainline religions that espouse approved, socially liberal views over the more conservative religions against which this administration picks fights for political reasons.[27]

DEMOGRAPHY AND DEMOCRACY

With the legislative, expanded veto, spending, and war powers described in chapter 5, American presidents might already be described as George Mason's "elective monarchs." Looming on the horizon is the possibility of an Argentinian solution to term limits, in which one spouse succeeds another, for a "third" term. This would not constitute a tyranny, since presidents would ascend to office through democratic means. However much power might be concentrated in the executive branch, it is fanciful to suppose that the requirement of a quadrennial election might be waived.

Any curb on presidential power must ultimately be supplied by the voters, then, through an election that disciplines an overreaching executive. The demand for democracy transformed the Framers' Constitution, and brought us the rule of strong presidentialism. Might democracy in turn correct the abuses of an excessive concentration of power in the executive branch, if this is seen as undemocratic?

If recent history is any guide, the voters would not be much assisted by a hyper-partisan media. During the George W. Bush administration, the mainstream media possessed antennae that bristled at the slightest suggestion of presidential abuses. They were sharply critical of the prison at Guantanamo, renditions of prisoners to unsavory allies, the surveillance programs under the Patriot Act, military tribunals, and interrogation methods such as waterboarding. What this all came down to, reported the prescient Elizabeth Drew in the *New York Review of Books*, was tyranny.[28]

Since then, the question of the president's war powers has receded from view, this in spite of the fact that few of the Bush-era military policies have been abandoned. When Obama took office, the media celebrated the end of the "war on terror";[29] but nevertheless, Guantanamo remains open, renditions continue, domestic surveillance has increased, military tribunals still try terrorist prisoners, and the inconvenient interrogation techniques have been replaced by a take-no-prisoners policy of drone execution, with the president personally selecting the targets from "baseball cards" of terrorists. Some of the targets are American citizens, in countries with which America is not at war. Civilian casualties—CIVCAS, in the dehumanizing argot of the U.S. military—are kept artificially low through a policy of counting all male casualties over the age of 16 as terrorists, though even then women and children are killed by drones.[30] The very term "war on terror" has been abandoned;[31] but when the secret Justice

Department legal opinion on the use of drones was released, it revealed that the administration asserts the right to kill any al-Qaeda member, even U.S. citizens, and even if they are not engaged in an active plot to harm America.[32] If that's not a war on terror, nothing is.

One might think that, given the choice, a terrorist might prefer waterboarding to death, particularly if his wife and children might be killed along with him. Nevertheless, there has been little show of concern about the kill list and the continuation of Bush-era policies.[33] The media quietly supports the president, and the legion of lawyers who defended Guantanamo prisoners pro bono are back servicing their paying Fortune 500 clients. The IRS scandals raised some eyebrows here and there, but it was really only the Justice Department's secret subpoena of private phone records of several Associated Press reporters and editors that resonated with most members of the media. The takeaway is that the press cares terribly about its freedoms, less so about those of the rest of us. A generous interpretation of the lack of interest is the Nixon-to-China notion that, even as conservatives can be trusted when they make nice to Communists, liberals can be trusted to deal with national security issues (and kill the right people). More plausibly, the concern over national security abuses during the Bush administration, voiced in hysterical tones, was simply an example of partisan bias.

The willingness of media elites to tolerate the expansion of presidential power during a Democratic administration was remarkably on display during a June 15, 2012, presidential press conference. The president had announced a constitutionally questionable executive order that gave legal status to "illegal" immigrants. Obama refused to take questions (and has given few press conferences), and so one reporter interrupted him to ask a question. That wouldn't have raised any eyebrows in Britain or Canada, but things are ordered differently in America. The president flashed with anger, and the reporter was strongly taken to task by his media colleagues,[34] who criticized the interruption, but not the expansion of presidential power. And that is how their stories are written, on the front page, in the metro, style, business, and food sections, on the religion and health pages. As Martin Peretz said of his former magazine, the *New Republic*, one doesn't need editorials any more, given the articles themselves.[35]

La Boétie's puzzle about why people agree to be oppressed by their rulers isn't really so difficult to understand. It's simply the common pool problem. We mice might all be better off could we agree on belling the cat, but which mouse is going to do it? That partly explains the fawning media, too, since the president can play off reporters by trading access in return for favorable stories. Media friends who can be trusted to ask softball questions are given a one-on-one interview; real reporters are frozen out. In an era of declining circulation, the incentive to reveal that the emperor wears no clothes is weak. The White House Press Corp might be more respected were it less biased; but what is rational for the group as a whole might not be rational for the individual reporter. Part of the answer is ideological, too. The media was quite prepared to take a run at George W. Bush (does the name Dan Rather ring a bell?), but gives an ideological soul mate (Obama) a pass. Just how partisan the traditional media has become became clear when postings on the journalist List-serv JournoList (or J-List) were made public. For several years, until the forum was shut down in 2010, prominent journalists discussed privately among themselves how they might advance a progressive agenda, support Obama, and demonize his opponents. Media members have permitted themselves to be used as a conduit by the White House to spread dirt about its opponents, and at times appear to mimic the bootlickers of a third-world dictator, without the need for bayonets to prod them.

Was that a little harsh, just now? If you think so, consider John Dickerson, the political director of once-revered CBS News. If nothing else, one should expect members of the media to support the two-party system of American democracy. Yet there was Dickerson, arguing for a one-party state. "The president who came into office speaking in lofty terms about bipartisanship and cooperation can only cement his legacy if he destroys the GOP. If he wants to transform American politics, he must go for the throat."[36] What the president should do, urged Dickerson, is "pulverize" and "delegitimize" the opposition party. That's not the kind of language one hears in the rest of the first world.

The American media have seemingly become two solitudes, reporting on alternative universes; major stories carried by one side (Fast and Furious, Benghazi) emerge slowly (or not at all) as news items on the other side, and then only with excuses from "fact-checkers" explaining why they really aren't newsworthy at all. *Newsweek* editor Evan Thomas notoriously said that "in a way Obama's standing above the country, above—above the world, he's sort of God." For their part, conservative media outlets are equally sharp in their attacks on the president's ideology, friends, and motives. This level of partisanship does not so much inform as cater to the prior beliefs of its readers, viewers, and listeners. It might reinforce their views, but is not designed to change their minds.

That leaves the voters, who can pick and choose where to get their news, and who in quadrennial elections provide the principal check on presidents. Unlike media elites and academics, the American electorate seems able to change *its* mind. The Bush victory in 2004 was followed by the Democratic takeover of the House in 2006, over dissatisfaction with the Iraq war; and the Obama victory in 2008 was followed by a sharp turn to the right in the 2010 congressional election, over concerns about government spending. This, in turn, was followed by Obama's reelection in 2012.

Will this prevent a descent into Mason's elective monarchy? Eric Posner and Adrian Vermeule argue that, because of their educational levels, income mobility, and wealth, American voters are not about to tolerate a grant of excessive power to a president.[37] On closer examination, however, none of these would seem to insulate America against a substantial increase in presidential power. There are other reasons—notably, the country's immigration intake—why one-man rule may prove attractive to future voters.

Education. The relationship between educational levels and political freedom appears tenuous at best. In table B.2 of the appendix, the literacy variable was significantly associated with more freedom, but the magnitude of the sign was exceedingly small. Dictators do not seem much impeded by the reading ability of their subjects.

In any event, it requires a certain hubris to boast of the average American's educational attainments. The best cross-country measure of what ordinary people know is provided by the OECD's Program for International Student Assessment (PISA) rankings. These provide a snapshot of a 15-year-old's knowledge and skills in math, science, and reading in 65 countries, and in the most recent report, the United States placed thirtieth in math, and twenty-third in science. In reading it placed fifteenth, well below most other first-world nations.

In economic terms, the differences are startling. By one estimate, increasing the percentage of proficient students to the levels attained in Canada would increase the annual U.S. growth rate by 0.9 percentage points, or about 30 percent. Translated into dollars, that amounts to about a trillion dollars a year, in a fifteen-trillion-dollar economy.[38]

TABLE 10.1 *PISA Scores 2009*

	Math	Science	Reading
Australia	514	527	515
Canada	527	529	524
France	497	498	496
Germany	513	520	497
Italy	483	489	486
Japan	529	539	520
Netherlands	526	522	508
Norway	498	500	503
Singapore	562	542	526
Sweden	494	495	497
U.K.	492	514	494
U.S.	**487**	**502**	**500**

Source: OECD Program for International Student Assessment

Some have offered demographic explanations for the poor U.S. performance. Immigrant children represent a special challenge for teachers; but Australia and Canada have much higher immigrant populations. When African-Americans and Latinos are taken out of the mix, the remaining two-thirds of U.S. students are reported to perform at Canadian levels. But the suggestion that one-third of American students, segregated by race or background, count less than other Americans is more than a little distasteful.

Can American voters be trusted to oppose Crown government, then? When questioned, they don't appear very knowledgeable. Television comics can always raise a laugh with man-in-the-street interviews in which ordinary people are shown to be startlingly dumb about things everyone is supposed to know. There is a scholarly literature on the self-defeating preferences of voters who, for example, oppose free trade or blame profit-seeking oil companies for gas prices at the pump, ideas nearly all economists would think ill-informed.[39] The lack of knowledge is understandable, however. Economists tell us that voters are rationally ignorant about policies that they personally can't change. The probability that they will cast a deciding vote that determines the outcome of an election is effectively nil, and it is not surprising that they know a good deal more about Fergie than Fast and Furious, about Snooki than Solyndra. Given the choice between two candidates for president, they might struggle to identify the policies of each.

On the other hand, people don't require a great deal of information to make complicated decisions. Psychologist Gerd Gigerenzer explains how a few simple cues can adequately substitute for a mass of information. His "fast" heuristics (problem-solving hunches and mental shortcuts) economize on time spent on calculation, while his "frugal" heuristics do not need much information. When asked whether San Diego or San Antonio had the greater population, German students got the right answer (San Diego) every time. They recognized San Diego as an American city, but had never heard of San Antonio. By contrast, only 62 percent of Americans got the right answer—they knew more about both cities, and the additional information just got in the way.[40] Similarly, we don't need to wade through a ton of speeches to recognize basic differences between political parties. We can disregard extraneous information—Mitt Romney's fifty-nine economic policies, whatever they were—and bring to mind only the relevant information.

In the political realm, fast and frugal rules permit voters to make inferences about candidates based on very limited information. For example, we might always vote for the businessman over the community organizer (or vice versa). A voter might also employ nonsubstantive, symbolic cues that seem coded with substantive information. To take a much-derided example, suppose that some voters decide whom to support on the basis of whether a candidate embraces the symbols of republican government. They might worry about a president who bows to foreign heads of state, or a candidate who fails to hold his hand to his breast during the Pledge of Allegiance. While such acts might seem trivial in themselves, they might provide a useful guide for voters if they are correlated with the candidate's stands on other, more substantive issues. Indeed, no one better understands how symbolic gestures signal broader information than the politicians themselves, who ordinarily are careful to employ them.

Political parties also make it easier for voters to get information about candidates. As Anthony Downs noted,[41] political parties are brand names that incorporate broadly understood public policies and ease the informational burden voters face. If I want lower taxes, I don't have to pay overmuch attention to fifty-nine-point plans: I simply vote Republican. I will understand that the party has an interest in maintaining its brand name; that it will choose and vet candidates to ensure that they meet minimal levels of intelligence, and won't stray too far from the party line. If they do stray, as George H. W. Bush did in agreeing to a tax hike after promising "Read my Lips—No New Taxes!," the voters can be expected to turn on the party, as if to teach it a lesson.

Save for their role as informational arbitrageurs, there would be little reason for political parties to exist. Suppose that every voter had as much information about a candidate as the party did, about his record, and how he was likely to vote. In such a transparent world, there would be no reason for think tanks, advocacy groups, political action committees, campaign finance committees, or even political parties to exist. Every political organization is a creature of an impacted informational problem, and succeeds to the extent that it establishes a popular and reliable brand name.[42]

In a variety of ways, then, a voter might cast an intelligent vote without investing an inordinate amount of time in researching the candidates. He might look for useful cues about the candidate, rely on the signals politicians provide about their beliefs, and free-ride on the information provided by a candidate's party affiliation. While the voter might know little about market economics, he might nevertheless ask himself, "Am I better off than I was four years ago?"

One should not conclude that voters are ill-informed, then. When they elect a president who has enlarged executive power, as they did in 2012, they presumably believe that this will make them better off. They voted for Obamacare, entitlement protection, and free cell phones. They wanted a better safety net against illness, unemployment, and financial hardships, and all of that is understandable. What was seemingly not of great concern was the question of separation of powers or Crown government.

Income Mobility. Seymour Martin Lipset and Gary Marks argued that socialism never took hold in the United States because, more than other people, Americans did not believe that their place in the economic ladder was fixed.[43] They didn't want to impose confiscatory taxes upon the rich because they saw themselves becoming rich one day. Income mobility explained why "it didn't happen here," and Posner and Vermeule argue that it also explains why a descent into one-man rule is unlikely.

Such arguments have lost much of their purchase after the 2012 presidential election, fought over issues of class warfare, the 1 percent versus the 99 percent, or Romney's 47 percent of takers versus the 53 percent of taxpayers. In addition, the idea that America is a place where people can get ahead, no matter where they start, begins to look a little dated. There has always been more income inequality in the United States than in comparable countries,[44] and now there is less income mobility as well. In its 2011 report, the Pew Economic Mobility Project reported that the United States is one of the least mobile societies in the first world.[45]

The Pew study measures "intergenerational elasticity," defined as the relationship between a father and his son's rank on the income ladder. An elasticity of 0 denotes a highly mobile society, with no relationship between the income levels of parent and child. An elasticity of 1 describes a society with no mobility between the two generations.

Of the countries sampled, income mobility is greatest in the Nordic countries and least in the United Kingdom, where half the earnings advantage is passed on by parents to their children. That's not surprising, as one is apt to regard Britain as a class-ridden society; the surprise is that America is almost as immobile a society as Britain. By taxing income and not wealth, by erecting regulatory barriers that are stumbling blocks

TABLE 10.2 *Cross-Country Intergenerational Elasticity of Earnings*

Country	Elasticity
U.K.	0.5
Italy	0.48
U.S.	0.47
France	0.41
Spain	0.4
Germany	0.32
Sweden	0.27
Australia	0.26
Canada	0.19
Finland	0.18
Norway	0.17
Denmark	0.15

Source: Pew Economic Mobility Project 2011

for entrepreneurs, by immigration policies that admit maids but exclude professionals, by legacy admissions to elite colleges, the American aristocracy does a quietly efficient job in satisfying the very human, indeed noble, desire of parents to pass on their advantages to their children.

If it turns out that Americans are more class-ridden than Europeans, then a core understanding of what American exceptionalism means will have been lost. So too, a barrier to one-man rule will have been erased. Take mobility away, and income inequality presents an ambitious president with transformational opportunities. That's the story of Venezuela.

Wealth. As we saw in chapter 6, countries have not been found to tumble into dictatorships once they become wealthy. America is certainly wealthy. Expressed in GDP per capita, the United States is the thirteenth richest country in the world, tied with Ireland, and behind a group of Nordic and British Commonwealth countries.[46] A better measure might be net wealth (total assets minus personal indebtedness) per adult, where the United States comes in tenth of twenty-six mostly first-world countries in a list prepared by Credit Suisse.[47]

These numbers might nevertheless give one a sense of false comfort. What insulates a country from a slide into dictatorship is not a raw number, but rather the sense people in rich countries might have that one-man rule would threaten their acquired wealth. That sense of confidence in American government might, however, be threatened in two ways. First, China's remarkable growth in recent years has shown that material wealth may coexist with dictatorship, at least in the short run. The OECD reports that from 2001 to 2010, U.S. GDP grew at 1.69 percent a year.[48] Over that same period, China's growth rate was 10 percent. Were these trends to continue, the United States would be quickly overtaken, not only as an economic power, but also as a provider of social welfare. Indeed, the International Monetary Fund projects that in 2016, America's share of world GDP will fall to 17.7 percent, less than China's share.[49] This has led some intellectuals, notably Thomas Friedman, to question whether Americans might profitably adopt some features of the Chinese economic model.[50] The subjective sense that material wealth requires democratic government clearly has been weakened.

The second reason why present material prosperity might not guarantee democratic government is the possibility of future economic downturns. Before the Great Depression, most of the European countries that later became dictatorships had been prosperous. What did them in was an economic crisis, for which Fascism seemed to many clever minds of the day to provide an answer. Not a few people predict that America will face such an economic crisis in the future; and it is difficult to predict how voters will react, should that happen.

The report of the National Commission on Fiscal Responsibility and Reform (commonly referred to by the names of its co-chairs, "Simpson-Bowles") warned of what it saw as a coming debt crisis:

> *By 2025 revenue will be able to finance only interest payments, Medicare, Medicaid, and Social Security. Every other federal government activity—from national defense and homeland security to transportation and energy—will have to be paid for with borrowed money. Debt held by the public will outstrip the entire American economy, growing to as much as 185 percent of GDP by 2035. Interest on the debt could rise to nearly $1 trillion by 2020. These mandatory payments—which buy absolutely no goods or services—will squeeze out funding for all other priorities.*[51]

What the report predicted is a perfect economic storm, one in which longstanding deals about welfare benefits would be broken. Should that happen, the confidence that voters repose in democratic government may be shaken.

Immigration. Americans pride themselves on being a nation of immigrants. There is not a little puffery in that claim, since the percentage of foreign-born people in Australia is nearly twice that of the United States. Canada isn't that far behind Australia, either. Nevertheless, Americans make the most of their immigrant origins. In a 1998 address, Clinton remarked:

> More than any other nation on Earth, America has constantly drawn strength and spirit from wave after wave of immigrants. In each generation they have proved to be the most restless, the most adventurous, the most innovative, the most industrious of people. Bearing different memories, honoring different heritages, they have strengthened our economy, enriched our culture, renewed our promise of freedom and opportunity for all.[52]

In celebrating America's immigrants, Clinton's speech was not in any way remarkable. We are often told of how recent arrivals have made the country more tolerant, and expanded cultural horizons. To take but one example, America's dining habits have come a long way from the meat-and-potatoes dinners of the 1950s. At the same time, immigrants have also transformed American politics. An American electorate that resembled the America of 1960 would likely have elected Romney as president in 2012.[53] This can importantly be explained by the different views the candidates held about immigration (as seen in Romney's churlish invitation to nondocumented aliens to "self-deport"). However, other issues may divide new arrivals from native-born Americans, and among these is Crown government.

Refugees from dictatorships like Cuba are most likely to share George Mason's concerns about an elective monarchy. Similarly, those who arrived from czarist Russia in the nineteenth century might have objected to presidential czars. There was also an overlap between the views of immigrants and natives during the "closed-door" policy from the 1920s to 1965, when 70 percent of immigrants came from first-world countries. After the 1965 Immigration and Nationality Act, however, immigrants were less likely to "look like America." Today about 70 percent of immigrants arrive under "family preferences" guidelines, mostly from third-world countries. They might confer all of the economic benefits to the country that Clinton ascribed to them, and yet have different beliefs about the role of the president. They might have admirable cultural values and work habits, and still have different views about the proper role of government.[54] Presumably, many come simply to be with their families, and bring with them whatever thoughts about government they had before emigrating. In short, it wasn't that they had read the Federalist Papers. It should not be surprising, therefore, if they tend to nudge American politics further along the road to the strong presidential rule with which most were familiar in the countries they left. If America's undocumented immigrants are given a path to citizenship, moreover, the push to strong presidentialism can be expected to strengthen.

There is a way of measuring this, by looking at the Freedom House rankings of the emigration countries from which the immigrants leave. Immigrants to America in the 1950s came from freer countries than immigrants did fifty years later. For the 1950s, an emigration country's weighted Freedom House ranking was 1.58. For arrivals between 2000 and 2009, however, that number had risen to 3.26 (a higher score meaning less freedom).[55] The 1950s score was halfway between the freedom rankings of the United States and Brazil; fifty years later, the ranking was now somewhere between 3 (Mexico, Columbia) and 4 (Pakistan, Nigeria).

Again, some immigrants were drawn to the United States by its system of government; others came simply to join their families, and brought the politics of their country with them. Of course, after a time, immigrants tend to go native—though going native doesn't mean the same thing today as it did fifty years ago, since the country has changed since then, and one reason for this, everyone appears to agree, is the change in immigration patterns since 1965.

Bowling Alone. Immigrants account for just 13 percent of Americans. What about the other 87 percent, the people born in the United States? A chagrined Democrat, Congressman Barney Frank, thought they were nothing to write home about either, after the 1994 Republican landslide.

Specifically, one might wonder whether the decline in community organizations and civic participation reported by sociologist Robert Putnam and political scientist Charles Murray might weaken American democracy and its style of government.

Alexis de Tocqueville famously said that nineteenth-century Americans liked to form clubs. What Putnam reported in *Bowling Alone*, however, was a sharp decline in the place of civic associations in late twentieth-century America.[56] Putnam wrote in 2000; ten years later, Charles Murray presented an even darker view of the social pathologies of modernity in the United States. Among lower-class Americans, white and black, he found a startling decline in families, industriousness, honesty, and religiosity.[57]

The well-documented decline in civic associations plausibly weakens democratic institutions. Murray reported that the number of people voting in a presidential election declined by 22 percent from 1960 to 1996, and found a 35 percent decline in the number of people who attended a public meeting between 1973 and 1994.[58] When that happens, argued Putnam, one is left with the "politics at a distance" of plebiscitary democracy.[59] Those who continue to participate in civic life are not the ones who used to show up at town halls or school boards, but rather the more passionate voters at the ideological extremes. Voters do not engage with people of opposing views, but cluster around the spokesmen for their camp, on television and talk radio or in the White House.

As this has happened, presidential power has greatly expanded. The greatest of spokesmen for his followers is the charismatic president, who draws power from their support, and who chafes at constitutional barriers to executive power. Is this the future, then, an even greater reign of Crown government? While such suggestions are speculative, it is equally speculative to assume that the future will resemble the past, and that recent social changes (which Frank Fukuyama labeled *The Great Disruption*) will leave the institutions of American government untouched.[60]

IS CROWN GOVERNMENT REVERSIBLE?

Crown government is likely a permanent feature of American government. It arose in the United States, Britain, and Canada at the same time, as a consequence of broad forces not particular to a single country. In America, unlike in Britain and Canada, it cannot be reversed without changes to an extremely inflexible Constitution. Nor can the courts be counted on to correct the tilt towards excessive executive power. Where they have stepped in, to police the boundaries between the branches under the doctrine of separation of powers, they have as often as not gotten it wrong. In the rare case where executive power might reasonably be strengthened—to permit a president to root out congressional earmarks—the court struck down the line-item veto.[61] In the much more typical case, where Congress seeks to rein in the president, the court has invoked the separation of powers to limit the power of Congress, thereby strengthening Crown government, as we saw in chapter 5.

The Framers did not see separationism as the fundamental principle of American government, however; and they would plausibly have thought these cases wrongly decided. They were practical men, and cared more for the overall structure of government than for abstract principles such as the separation of powers. Where the executive branch has so greatly expanded, at the expense of the legislative branch, they would likely think it a mistake to apply separationist norms in a neutral fashion, as though both branches were evenly matched. They would have expected the courts to redress the balance of power, and vindicate their vision of a government in which the legislative branch would dominate. Sadly, Gouverneur Morris's separationist ploy at the Convention, and Madison's defense of divided government, has beguiled the courts and generations of legal scholars.

That said, there are ways in which, short of amending the Constitution (or waiting for a revolution in Supreme Court jurisprudence), the growth of executive power might be arrested. It is a bit late in the day to adopt the parliamentary form of government the Framers had wanted, and which better protects liberty. Nevertheless, some reforms might be suggested to help cure the problems that I have identified. That is really the subject of another book, but in what remains of this one, I briefly suggest three reforms.

1. National Referenda. One reason for the relative weakness of Congress is the want of a nationwide popular mandate when it bargains with the president. Members of Congress are elected by voters in their state or district, and cannot speak authoritatively for the country as a whole, as can a president elected by all Americans. When there is a conflict between the two branches, particularly when Congress employs the power of the purse to threaten a government shutdown, voters blame Congress more than the president, as seen in Clinton's reelection after the 1995–96 shutdown.

Congress might address this imbalance through a national referendum in which citizens vote directly on a measure. These are regular events in other countries. They are held frequently in Switzerland, whose constitution recognizes them as a means of effecting legislative change. Even where there is no explicit constitutional recognition of referenda, they have been employed to resolve fundamental political problems. In Canada, the government has gone to the people on three occasions in nonbinding plebiscites, most recently in 1992, on the Charlottetown Accord to amend the Constitution. As for the effect of a referendum, the Canadian Supreme Court held, in *Reference re Secession of Quebec*,[62] that while a vote to secede in a Quebec referendum would not suffice to make the province independent, the referendum would not be without legal effect. The federal government would be required to pursue negotiations with the province to define the terms of Quebec's independence, in a manner faithful to such fundamental values as democracy, the rule of law, and the protection of minorities.

In the United States, twenty-three states permit laws to be enacted through referenda and initiatives, and forty-nine states require that amendments to the state constitution be approved by referendum. Most such laws were passed during the Progressive Era, when there were also proposals for national referenda. That these went nowhere is curious, since it is odd that a country founded on the Lockean principle that government derives its just powers from the consent of the governed should be less ready to rely on referenda than parliamentary regimes. The direct democracy of state initiatives has been found to promote policies more attuned to the wishes of voters than the indirect democracy of representative government,[63] and there is little reason to think that the same would not be true of national referenda. In this way, Congress might also break a logjam of legislative inaction, or a stalemate caused by divided government.

2. Congressional Reform. My second suggestion is that Congress clean up its act. If congressional power has in recent years declined, much of this is deserved. Congressional approval levels are in the teens, always much less than the approval ratings of unpopular presidents, and lower still than root canals from your dentist. One reason for this is the common pool problem, where voters rationally reelect a congressman who brings home the bacon to their district, while decrying a system in which inefficient earmarks flourish, and scorning a Congress that tolerates them. Another reason is the lack of responsibility legislators have shown in a Congress that, like the Canadian Parliament prior to 1849, lacks the badges of responsible government. Because of the separation of powers, congressmen can avoid responsibility for inaction by pointing their fingers elsewhere. They can be for a war before they are against it; they can make speeches about their local Little League teams after a devastating attack on their country; they can espouse impossible, wasteful schemes. They can do all that knowing that it simply doesn't matter, that they will not be held responsible.

As a second reform, therefore, I suggest ways in which Congress might correct its infirmities, which were conspicuously on display when Obamacare was passed, in a frenzied atmosphere of deal making and last-minute earmarks, with a bill so long that no one seemed to know its contents. Speaker Nancy Pelosi notoriously said, "we have to pass this bill so you can find out what's in it."[64] At one thousand pages, people are still finding out what's in it.

In 2008 the Democrats were elected in a landside. The party won the White House, the House of Representatives, and (with two independents who caucused with their party) fifty-eight votes in the Senate. The Republicans had forty senators, just enough for a filibuster. Soon after the election, however, Republican Senator Arlen Specter crossed the aisle, leaving his former party with only thirty-nine senators; and with this, Republicans lost their ability to block legislation by filibuster. Now nothing seemed in the way of the Democrats' ambitious progressive agenda, of which health-care reform was a signature priority.

After a futile search for Republican support, Democrats in Congress passed dueling health-care reform measures in the fall of 2009. In November, the House of Representatives voted, 219 to 212, for a bill that included a "public option" offering Americans a voluntary government-sponsored insurance program to compete with private insurers. The Senate balked at the public option, and passed a competing bill the next month. While virtually all members of the Democratic caucus in the Senate wanted a public option, they needed the support of Connecticut Independent Joe Lieberman, and he was opposed to it. Since all thirty-nine Senate Republicans were opposed to the bill, Lieberman's support was essential to avoid a Republican filibuster. And so the public option was dropped from the Senate bill.

Senator Lieberman wasn't the only holdout with whom Senate Majority Leader Harry Reid had to bargain. He also had to deal with the many members of his caucus who demanded earmarks. Among these, the "Louisiana Purchase" gave one hundred million dollars in extra Medicaid funds to the Bayou State, to help get Senator Mary Landrieu reelected. Then came the "Cornhusker Kickback" for Nebraska Senator Ben Nelson: a permanent exemption from his state's share of Medicaid expansion, which would cost taxpayers an additional $45 million in the first decade. Next came "Gator Aid" for Florida Senator Bill Nelson, a grandfather clause that would allow Floridians to preserve their pricey Medicare Advantage program. The list went on and on.[65]

Reid was unapologetic about the last-minute deals. "You'll find a number of states that are treated differently than other states. That's what legislating is all about. It's compromise," he explained. The president agreed. "As with any legislation, compromise is part of the process," Obama said.[66] Compromise doesn't begin to describe what happened, however. "I don't know if there is a senator that doesn't have something in this bill that was important to them," Reid said. "And if they don't have something in it important to them, then it doesn't speak well of them."[67]

Even that wasn't quite enough to ensure passage. Senator Edward Kennedy had died in August 2009, and was replaced by Paul Kirk, who was appointed by Massachusetts's Democratic governor, Deval Patrick. Kirk became part of the Democratic majority that passed Obamacare; but in the special election to fill Kennedy's seat in January 2010, Republican Scott Brown won, and the Democrats lost their filibuster-proof majority. Many thought that health-care reform was dead, since the House and Senate bills were so dissimilar, and new legislation was required to eliminate the differences. To avoid this, the House was asked to hold its nose and vote on the Senate bill, with all its earmarks. Now, however, opposition to the bill was stronger than ever. Scott Brown had won a Senate seat in the bluest of blue states, in what was taken as a referendum on health-care reform. The Tea Party movement had begun; congressional elections were only eight months away. Democratic members of the House from conservative districts reasonably wondered if voters would forgive them for supporting an increasingly unpopular health-care bill. Evidently, they needed persuading by the House leadership. And they were persuaded.

Speaker Nancy Pelosi had to scramble for the 216 votes needed for passage of the bill, and West Virginia Democrat Alan Mollohan reportedly was undecided.[68] Mollohan had been listed as one of the most corrupt members of Congress by nonpartisan group Citizens for Responsibility and Ethics in Washington, for steering earmarks to family, friends, and former employees in exchange for campaign contributions. Just before the vote, the Justice Department announced that it was dropping an FBI investigation into Mollohan, who ended up supporting the bill. As well, two California congressmen, formerly opposed to the health-care bill, switched their opposition when the water allocation for their parched districts was increased two weeks before the vote.[69] Then there were allegations of payback against congressmen who voted against the bill. Michigan Representative Bart Stupak led the fight against abortion funding in the bill, and was attacked by MSNBC host Rachel Maddow, who questioned the legality of the low rent that a conservative Christian group charged Stupak for his D.C. apartment: "Bottom line here, as Bart Stupak tries to shut down health reform for an antiabortion stunt that won't succeed but will make him famous, who's been paying Bart Stupak's rent in Washington all these years?"[70]

To get the bill enacted, one final device was employed. The Senate and House bills were still not identical, and a Senate vote was required for passage of the final bill. There was majority support for a revised bill in the House, but after the Massachusetts election, the Democrats no longer had the requisite sixty-member supermajority needed to avoid a Senate filibuster. By wrapping the amendments into a "reconciliation" bill, however, the Democrats found they could sidestep a Republican filibuster. The reconciliation measure stripped off the "Cornhusker kickback," but the other earmarks were retained. Since reconciliation had never been used in the past for substantive policy bills, its use poisoned relations in Congress, and animated conservative protest groups. Nine months later, voters gave the Republicans control of the House of Representatives.

Passage of the bill was a shocking display of corrupt bargaining and Chicago-style power politics at its crudest. None of this would seem exceptional, were it to happen in Borat's Kazakhstan; for other democracies, however, the methods employed to enact American health-care reform will seem foreign indeed. A landslide election like that of November 2008 would give an English-style parliamentary government free rein to pass its favored legislation. There would be no need to have a supermajority on one's side to overcome a filibuster. Or to undo the bill, once Americans had taken a closer look at it.

Worse still is the practice of senatorial "holds." An individual senator may block consideration of a bill or presidential nomination until he gets something he wants, often in the form of an earmark for his constituents. In 2010, Alabama Senator Richard Shelby put a hold on seventy presidential nominations for executive positions until his state got billions of dollars of pork-barrel spending, this at a time when Republicans were ostensibly concerned about government spending.[71]

Filibusters and holds are wonderful devices for extracting special payouts to one's constituents, and no one concerned with promoting integrity in government should mourn their passage. Apart from that, a party might adopt self-denying strategies to forswear reliance on wasteful earmarks, as Republicans did after their takeover of the House in 2010. A self-denying statute might also introduce special parliamentary procedures that, if not followed, would invalidate a subsequent earmark.[72] Such legislation, and the procedures it mandates, could be overridden by subsequent legislation, but would still increase the political costs borne when earmarks are attached to a bill.

Congress might also enact electoral reforms to ban gerrymandering, and give an independent commission the power to reset electoral boundaries. Because of gerrymandering, only about a fifth of House seats are in play in any congressional election, and the resultant immunity from the voters reduces a member's accountability. In other countries, independent commissions that set electoral boundaries have placed more seats in play; there is no reason why this could not be done in America, as well.

3. Impeachment. My third suggestion is simplicity itself. Congress should impeach and remove presidents often: when their policies fail, when they are touched with scandal, or for no reason—just for the spirit of the thing.

But how likely is that? Not very, for reasons that the Framers could scarcely have surmised. The first is the rise of political parties. Granted, that happened very quickly after the Convention, but they were still in the future. With political parties, one is not apt to see a successful impeachment and removal unless one party holds the presidency and the other party holds the Senate and House of Representatives. That's not a great obstacle; it has happened half the time since 1969. What makes it almost impossible to secure a conviction is the further requirement in Article I, Section 3, that two-thirds of the senators present must vote to remove the president. For that to happen, one needs either misbehavior on the level of a Nixon, or else an administration where a majority of the House and two-thirds or the Senate are held by the opposition party; and that has happened only once in American history, during the Fortieth Congress, which impeached Andrew Johnson.

Until the very end of the Philadelphia Convention, the delegates had agreed that presidents might be removed by a simple majority of votes, either by the House or the Senate. The decisive move to a supermajoritarian requirement came at the very end, from the Committee on Unfinished Parts, in its draft on September 4. Thereafter, the delegates spent only five days debating the draft. They knew they were almost finished, and were impatient for the Convention to end. In the time that remained, they devoted nearly all of their attention to what seemed the more important questions of how a president was to be chosen, what his powers might be, and how the Constitution might be amended. George Mason managed to broaden the impeachment standard, from treason and bribery to "other high Crimes and Misdemeanors," but the new requirement of a Senate supermajority passed without comment, seemingly unnoticed. And yet it was as fundamental a change as any in the new draft. But for the requirement of a supermajority, Reagan might have been removed by a Democratic Congress over the Iran-Contra scandal, and Clinton would have come perilously close to removal when fifty senators voted to convict him for obstruction of justice.

There is a further reason, which few of the Framers would not have anticipated, why impeachments are unlikely: the almost religious regard that Americans have for their presidents, and the myths that surround them. Some of us may remember John Kennedy's *Profiles in Courage* and its celebration of Republican Senator Edmund Ross, who broke with his party and provided a key vote against the conviction of Andrew Johnson. Had Ross voted otherwise, Johnson would have been removed from office, and the office of the presidency would have been diminished. That, said Kennedy, was a principled and heroic decision, one that "may well have preserved . . . constitutional government in the United States."[73] Those are the myths. The reality is that Kennedy's constitution is not our Constitution, that he didn't write the book himself, and that Ross was likely bribed to vote as he did.[74]

None of that matters today, since Kennedy's high regard for the presidency is shared by nearly all Americans. Crown government would seem to be here to stay, unless, through a reassertion of congressional power, the Framers' Constitution can somehow be recovered. Even if that cannot be done, the modest steps I propose might usefully prevent a further centralization of power in the Once and Future King.

-Appendix A-

The Framers

The delegates debated the method of selecting the president on twenty-one different days, and took more than thirty votes on the subject. In sixteen roll calls they voted on how to select the president. In six of these (once unanimously), they voted for a president appointed by Congress, which would have resembled a parliamentary regime. Once, they voted 8 to 2 for a president appointed by state legislatures. When asked whether they wanted a president elected by the people, they voted no each time.

To understand how the delegates arrived at their final compromise, I examined the coalitions that emerged over the first three months of the Convention. I hypothesized that a nationalist would want a popularly elected president, as this would increase his political authority in his dealings with states; and that is what I found. Delegates were also more likely to support a popularly elected president if they were wealthy. On the other hand, they were less likely to do so if they wanted to weaken presidents by limiting them to a single term of office, as country party members would seek to do.

I employed two different kinds of estimation procedures. The first measured the intensity of delegate preferences by seeing how often they voted for a popularly elected president in roll calls 11 and 355. Here, I employed an ordered logistic regression procedure,[1] which permitted an

TABLE A.1 *The Delegates Vote for a President Appointed by the States*

Roll Call Date Page	Resolution (Movers)	Outcome	Aye	No	Divided
36 **June 9** **I.175**	State governors appoint (Gerry)	0-10-1 (NH absent)		MA, CT, NY, NJ, PA, MD, VA, NC, SC, GA	DE
166 **July 17** **II.24**	State legislatures appoint (Ellsworth, Broom)	2-8 (NH, NY absent)	DE, MD	MA, CT, NJ, PA, VA, NC, SC, GA	
182 **July 19** **II.51**	Substituting an election by electors in place of a congressional appointment (Ellsworth)	6-3-1 (NH, NY absent)	CT, NJ, PA, DE, MD, VA	NC, SC, GA	MA
183 **July 19** **II.51**	State legislatures appoint (Ellsworth)	8-2 (NH, NY absent)	MA, CT, NJ, PA, DE, MD, NC, GA	VA, SC	

overall look at delegate preferences, on the assumption that they were stable over the course of the entire Convention. Delegates most strongly in favor of a popularly elected president would have voted yes in both roll calls, while those least in favor of an elected president would have voted no both times.

In addition, I wanted to see how delegate preferences evolved over the course of the Convention, and therefore looked at how the delegates voted on the selection of the president on three significant roll calls, once in each month from June to August 1787. During these votes, different coalitions of delegates assembled and split apart. For these three votes I

TABLE A.2 *The Delegates Vote for a President Appointed by Congress*

Roll Call Date Page	Resolution (Movers)	Outcome	Aye	No	Divided
12 **June 2** **I.79**	For an appointment by Congress	8-2 (NH absent)	MA, CT, NY, DE, VA, NC, SC, GA	PA, MD	
45 **June 11** **I.195**	For the Virginia Plan (Randolph)	6-5 (NH absent)	MA, PA, VA, NC, SC, GA	CT, NY, NJ, DE, MD	
46 **June 12** **I.213-14**	For the Virginia Plan (Randolph)	6-3-2 (NH absent)	MA, PA, VA, NC, SC, GA	CT, NY, NJ	DE, MD
167 **July 17** **II.24**	For an appointment by Congress	10-0 (NH, NY absent)	MA, CT, NJ, PA, DE, MD, VA, NC, SC, GA		
215 **July 24** **II.98**	For an appointment by Congress (Houstoun, Spaight)	7-4 (NY absent)	NH, MA, NJ, DE, NC, SC, GA	CT, PA, MD, VA	
218 **July 25** **II.108**	Congress appoints for the first term, state legislatures appoint for subsequent terms (Ellsworth)	4-7 (NY absent)	NH, CT, PA, MD	MA, NJ, DE, VA, NC, SC, GA	
225 **July 26** **II.118**	Congress appoints, seven-year term, term limits, impeachable on malpractice (Mason)	6-3-1 (MA, NY absent)	NH, CT, NJ, NC, SC, GA	PA, DE, MD	VA

TABLE A.3 *The Delegates Vote Against a Popularly-Elected President*

Roll Call Date Page	Resolution (Movers)	Outcome	Aye	No	Divided
11 **June 2** **I.79**	Election by electors elected by the people (Wilson)	2-7-1 (NH, NJ absent)	PA, MD	MA, CT, DE, VA, NC, SC, GA	NY
165 **July 17** **II.24**	Election by the people	1-9 (NH, NY absent)	PA	MA, CT, NJ, DE, MD, VA, NC, SC, GA	
355 **August 24** **II.399**	Election by the people (Carroll, Wilson)	2-9 (NY absent)	PA, DE	NH, MA, CT, NJ, MD, VA, NC, SC, GA	
359 **August 24** **II.399**	Election by electors elected by the people (G. Morris, Carroll)	5-6 (NY absent)	CT, NJ, PA, DE, VA	NH, MA, MD, NC, SC, GA	

employed an ordinary least squares (OLS) regression procedure, which permits one to dispense with a marginal effects table. I also employed a binary logistic regression procedure (logit) and arrived at very similar results, which I do not report.

A disadvantage of OLS, when the dependent variable is dichotomous, is that the model necessarily suffers from heteroskedasticity, and I sought to correct for this by clustering the standard errors by state.[2] An OLS model makes the unrealistic assumption that the model is correctly specified, and that the residual of each observation is independent of the others. By clustering, one can identify and adjust for relationships among the standard errors, eliminating within-group dependence in a cluster. Even though delegates within a state often disagreed with each other, the state level is the most intuitively likely place for there to be such dependence, since the delegates were appointed, and voted, by state.

THE DEPENDENT VARIABLES

The dependent variables measure the preferences and votes of the delegates on the choice of executive, and permit us to examine two different coalitions among the delegates: those who favored the election of the president by popular ballot, and those who favored the appointment of the president by Congress.

The President dependent variable, employed in the ordered logistic regression equation, measures the intensity of a delegate's preference for a popularly elected president. President takes the value 3 if the delegate voted yes on both James Wilson's June 2 motion that the president be elected by electors elected by popular ballot, on roll call 11; and on Daniel Carroll's August 24 motion that the president be elected by the people, in roll call 355. It takes the value 2 if the delegate voted yes only once on the two motions, and 1 if he voted no both times.

For the OLS estimations, I examine delegate preferences and votes for each of roll call 11 and 355, and also for roll call 215 on July 24, on William Houstoun's motion that the president be appointed by Congress. A delegate who wanted a popularly elected president would have voted yes on roll calls 11 and 355, and no on roll call 215. After roll call 355, the coalitions of delegates began to break down; and twelve days later, the delegates agreed to the compromise found in Article II, Section 2, with a president chosen by electors who themselves would be selected by a method to be determined by state legislators.

THE EXPLANATORY VARIABLES

I hypothesized that nationalists at the Convention would want a popularly elected president, as this would increase his political authority in his dealings with states. As a proxy for nationalist sentiment, I looked at how delegates voted on June 8, on roll call 34, on a motion by Charles Pinckney and James Madison on whether Congress could veto any state legislation it thought improper.[3] This was an acid test of nationalist sentiment, and indeed the proposal drove states'-rights supporters up a wall.

I boiled down the delegates' economic interests to a simple dichotomous distinction between rich versus not-rich delegates, since the records as to property ownership are sketchy. At the time the country was suffering from a credit crisis, caused by pro-debtor policies that states had adopted; and one would expect that wealthier delegates would be most sensible of this, and would support a powerful national presidency.[4]

The suggestion that the delegates were motivated by economic considerations was first made by Charles A. Beard's pioneering work nearly a century ago, which Gordon Wood called the most influential history book ever written in America.[5] Beard saw the Constitution as the product of a class struggle won by a rising capitalist class of bondholders, who were displacing an agrarian class of indebted landowners.

Beard's marxisant view of the Framers, which reduced high theory and republican virtue to self-seeking economic motives, was popular with contemporary Progressives, who chafed at the barriers to social welfare legislation imposed by the separation of powers, and sought to debunk the Framers. Since then, however, the Beard thesis is considered to have been refuted, by Robert Brown in 1956 and Forrest McDonald in 1958.[6] Beard had claimed that the Federalists who supported the Constitution were creditors who held public and private debt, and who had a personal stake in the revival of credit;[7] but Brown and McDonald reported that Beard had misrepresented the property holdings and voting records of the delegates. Together, the two authors lay waste to the Beard thesis, plowed it underground, and sowed salt in the earth.

That didn't amount to a refutation of the thesis that economic motives played a role, however. What Brown and McDonald concluded was not that the delegates were unmoved by economic interests, but only that Beard had failed to find evidence of this. The delegates did not appear to be influenced by their holdings of public debt, as Beard had claimed; but where he failed, others might yet succeed in providing an economic interpretation of the Constitution. Moreover, as Beard noted, the delegates to the Philadelphia Convention had expostulated frequently, passionately, and at length on the sad decline of credit during the Articles of Confederation period, and the need to remedy this and protect creditor rights. Anyone reading the records of the deliberations would be surprised to be told that the delegates were unmoved by economic concerns, particularly when it came to slavery. When Robert McGuire brought more sophisticated empirical tools to the task, he was able to find that private economic interests (slaves, public and private debt, wealth in land) were correlated with votes on certain key roll calls.[8] McGuire did not, however, examine the roll calls on the method of selecting the president, as I do.

Any attempt to reduce the delegates' motives solely to economics is crude, and mistaken. There was more going on, and most (if not all) delegates shared the disinterested concern for the country's welfare so transparent in a Washington or Mason. At the same time, a concern for America's welfare obviously included a concern for its economic well-being. Not merely could the two motives overlap; they might at times come down to the selfsame patriotic motive. Further, if wealthier delegates wanted a stronger presidency, this does not prove that they were motivated by the prospect of a personal payoff. Instead, and more plausibly, the wealthier delegates were simply those who had a better understanding of the financial crisis, and a greater desire to fix it.

The delegates voted on several proposals that would have curbed the president's authority. Some delegates wanted a triumvirate instead of a single president; others wanted the president to share his veto power with judges; and still others wanted the president limited to a single term in office. I selected the last of these—a vote for term limits—as the proxy for the desire for a weak president, and rejected the first two. Several delegates who wanted a weak central government rejected a plural executive because a three-man presidency simply made little sense; and motions for a single executive passed unanimously on July 17 and August 24.[9]

Similarly, some states'-rights delegates did not think that judges were competent to share in the presidential veto power, while others did not want any kind of a presidential veto power.

That leaves term limits as a proxy for the desire to limit presidential power. On June 2, the delegates voted 7 to 2 for term limits, in roll call 15.[10] This was the first of five roll calls on term limits. The delegates voted 6 to 4 against term limits in roll call 168; 8 to 2 against term limits in roll call 184; 6 to 5 against term limits in roll call 220; and 7 to 3 for term limits in roll call 224.

I rely primarily on delegate preferences in roll call 15, when it was thought that the president would be appointed by Congress. Subsequently, the delegates considered the possibility of an appointment by state legislatures, and indeed voted for this in roll call 183. Several states'-rights supporters (notably Elbridge Gerry and the New Jersey delegates) who had previously supported term limits voted against them in roll call 184, when they thought the states would do the appointing. Because of this, the continuing support for term limits by other delegates in roll call 184 stands out in sharper relief.

The Officer variable was included because the officer corps of the Revolutionary Army was thought to be aristocratic and antidemocratic.[11] As such, its members might be expected to be opposed to the popular election of the president.

On several issues before the delegates, there was a split between delegates from large and small states. Because of this, I employ a variable measuring what the delegates saw as the population of each state in 1787, as estimated by Charles Pinckney.[12] This understates the actual figures, but what matters is what the delegates *thought* was the population of each state.

Six of the twelve states at the Convention were slave states. Of these, Delaware had relatively few slaves, but the remaining five states had very large slave populations, particularly Virginia.[13] One might expect

TABLE A.4 *Variables*

Dependent Variables

President	Equals 1 if the delegate did not vote for a popularly elected president in either roll call 11 or 355; 2 if the delegate voted yes once only in roll calls 11 and 355; and 3 if the delegate voted yes in both roll calls
Pop11	Equals 1 if the delegate favored the election of the president by popular suffrage, as expressed in their speeches prior to July 19, or in roll call 11; 0 otherwise
Leg215	Equals 1 if the delegate favored the appointment of the president by the national legislature, as expressed in their speeches on or prior to July 24, or in roll call 215; 0 otherwise
Pop355	Equals 1 if the delegate favored the election of the president by popular suffrage, as expressed in their speeches on or prior to August 24, or in roll call 355; 0 otherwise

Explanatory Variables

Veto	Equals 1 if the delegate voted to give the national legislature an absolute veto power over state legislation in roll call 163 on June 8; 0 otherwise
Term Limits15	Equals 1 if the delegate expressed a preference or voted to restrict the president to a single term of office on roll call 15 on June 2; 0 otherwise
Term Limits184	Equals 1 if the delegate expressed a preference or voted to restrict the president to a single term of office on roll call 184; 0 otherwise
Officer	Equals 1 if the delegate served as an officer during the American Revolution; 0 otherwise
Rich	Equals 1 if the delegate was wealthy; 0 otherwise
Pop1787	Estimated population in 1787
%Slave	Estimated percent slave population
Fixed State	Taking a separate number for each state

delegates from slave states to want a weak national government and a congressionally appointed president, lest a federal government seek to limit or abolish slavery.

DELEGATE PREFERENCES

A total of fifty-five delegates attended the Convention, but two dropped out after a week (Virginia's George Wythe and New Jersey's William Houston), leaving a sample of fifty-three delegates.

For the purpose of determining the delegates' preferences as to the method of choosing a president and term limits, I relied on the speeches of the delegates and state voting records, as well as the analysis of factional allegiances and personal backgrounds by McDonald and Rossiter (1966), as well as the close analysis of delegate voting patterns by Riker.[14] I took attendance records from Farrand and Hutson, and was assisted by Rossiter and the TeachingAmericanHistory.org website.

There are at least three obstacles to identifying the preferences of the delegates.

1. The delegates might have hidden their true sentiment in their votes, and even in their speeches. They might have engaged in log-rolling, trading off votes on one issue for votes in another. They might also have voiced their sentiments strategically, so as to frame the debate in a manner that ultimately favored them.

2. The delegates changed their minds on issues over the course of the Convention. In some cases they abandoned positions they initially favored, but which they knew could never command the support of a majority of states. In other cases, they might have been persuaded by what they took to be the superior arguments of the other side.

3. Finally, attendance was not taken each day of the Convention, and we cannot always be certain who voted on a particular roll call.[15] If a delegate was absent for a vote, I nevertheless took him

to have expressed his preference one way or the other, based on his speeches and political allegiances.

Identifying delegate preferences therefore requires a close reading of the delegate speeches and attendance data, an understanding of their background, and a careful analysis of state voting patterns. I provide my analysis of delegate votes on my website at buckleysmix.com.

RESULTS

The voting patterns at the Philadelphia Convention of 1787 were significantly correlated with the personal ideologies and economic interests of the delegates. A coalition of nationalist delegates supported a popularly

TABLE A.5 *Estimated Coefficients for President in an Ordered Logistic Regression*

Veto	1.52**	1.24*		1.34*
	(.62)	(.66)		(.73)
Rich		1.70**		2.07**
		(.67)		(.76)
Term Limits15	-1.46**	-1.64**		-1.24
	(.69)	(.77)		(.86)
Officer		-.42		-.56
		(.66)		(.71)
Pop1787			.007**	-.0002
			(.003)	(.004)
%Slave			-2.26*	-1.46
			(1.20)	(1.59)
Fixed State	-.05	-.05	.15	.07
	(.10)	(.11)	(.15)	(.18)
Number of Observations	53	53	53	53
Pseudo R^2	0.13	0.20	0.06	0.22

Notes: Standard errors in parentheses.
* significant at the .10 level
** significant at the .05 level
*** significant at the .01 level

TABLE A.6 *OLS Estimated Coefficients for Pop11*

Veto	.27	.18		.13
	(.19)	(.17)		(.14)
Rich		.37**		.43**
		(.15)		(.16)
Term Limits15	-.30	-.30**		-.22**
	(.19)	(.12)		(.09)
Officer		-.10		-.08
		(.14)		(.14)
Pop1787			.001	.0002
			(.0006)	(.0005)
%Slave			-.40*	-.35**
			(.19)	(.15)
Constant	34	.25	.042	.22
	(.21)	(.16)	(.11)	(.13)
Number of Observations	53	53	53	53
F	2.27	13.01	0.10	13.64
R²	0.22	0.41	0.18	0.48

Notes: Standard errors in parentheses. Clustered for state effects. To assess the extent to which multicollinearity is a problem for each independent variable, I tested for the variance inflation factor, using STATA's estat vif command, with the following results: NatVeto (1.42), Term15 (1.12), Officer (1.15), Rich (1.25), Pop1787 (1.83), %Slave (1.38), Mean VIF (1.36); these results are not suggestive of a problem.
* significant at the .10 level
** significant at the .05 level
*** significant at the .01 level

elected president, presumably because they believed this would strengthen the office, and that a powerful president would serve as a counterweight to the states. Wealthier delegates also favored a popularly elected president, likely for the same reason, as they more than most delegates would have recognized the need to protect credit markets against pro-debtor state laws. Delegates who supported term limits and worried about excessive presidential power were more likely to vote against a popularly elected president in the three roll calls.

TABLE A.7 *OLS Estimated Coefficients for Leg215*

Veto	-.49**	-.42**	-.42**		-.46**	-.45**
	(.17)	(.15)	(.14)		(.19)	(.17)
Rich		-.26*	-.26**		-.27	-.23
		(.12)	(.10)		(.16)	(.14)
Term Limits15	.10	.10			.12	
	(.15)	(.09)			(.10)	
Term Limits184			.24*			.27*
			(.12)			(.14)
Officer		.11	.07		.13	.07
		(.13)	(.13)		(.14)	(.13)
Pop1787				-.001*	.0003	.0001
				(.0006)	(.0007)	(.0006)
%Slave				.10	-.07	-.14
				(.14)	(.09)	(.11)
Constant	.79**	.83**	.84**	93**	.79**	.83**
	(.17)	(.14)	(.12)	(.14)	(.14)	(.09)
Number of Observations	53	53	53	53	53	53
F	5.36	6.58	6.11	2.53	12.63	23.60
R²	0.29	0.40	0.42	0.10	0.37	0.42

Notes: Standard errors in parentheses. Clustered for state effects.
* significant at the .10 level
** significant at the .05 level
*** significant at the .01 level

As expected, the Veto coefficient, for the federal government's right to "negative" state laws, is significant in table A.5's ordered logistic regression. Overall, the nationalist delegates who wanted such a veto also wanted a popularly elected president. This didn't happen at once. In table A.6, the Veto coefficient is not significant on June 2's roll call 11, as the nationalist Virginia delegates continued to back the congressionally appointed president of the Virginia Plan. By July 24, however, the nationalists had gotten their act together, and united to oppose a congressionally appointed president in roll call 215, as seen in table A.7. This coalition weakened, but remained in place on August 24 for

TABLE A.8 *OLS Estimated Coefficients for Pop355*

Veto	.31*	.26*	.27*		.29	.28*
	(.15)	(.14)	(.14)		(.17)	(.14)
Rich		.21	.19		.25	.19
		(.15)	(.12)		(.14)	(.12)
Term Limits15	-.25	-.25			-.23	
	(.19)	(.15)			(.16)	
Term Limits184			-.44**			.44**
			(.15)			(.16)
Officer		-.05	.030		-.06	.030
		(.14)	(.13)		(.12)	(.11)
Pop1787				.0009	-.0003	-.00002
				(.001)	(.001)	(.001)
%Slave				-.20	-.06	.04
				(.20)	(.21)	(.19)
Constant	.40	.34	.29	.20	.39	.29
	(.22)	(.22)	(.20)	(.33)	(.36)	(.29)
Number of Observations	53	53	53	53	53	53
F	4.26	3.86	17.58	0.52	3.98	13.43
R^2	0.18	0.23	0.37	0.05	0.23	0.37

Notes: Standard errors in parentheses. Clustered for state effects.
* significant at the .10 level
** significant at the .05 level
*** significant at the .01 level

roll call 355, as seen in table A.8. The magnitudes of the coefficient are large, and a nationalist was almost 50 percent more likely to oppose a congressionally appointed president in roll call 215.

Wealthier delegates were significantly more likely to support a popularly elected president in the ordered logistic regression and in roll call 11, and to oppose a congressionally appointed president in roll call 215. On roll call 11, wealthier delegates were about 40 percent more likely to prefer a popular election of the president.

Delegates who wanted to term-limit the president were more likely to want a congressionally appointed president, as that method of appointment would also tend to fetter his discretion.

The Officer variable had no significant explanatory power. Delegates who served as officers during the American Revolution, and who were seen as an aristocratic element in American society, appeared to split their votes on the appointment of the president. As an aristocratic class, one might have expected them to oppose a popular election. However, some of them, such as Hamilton, were nationalists who were close to the likely first president, George Washington.

There was no evidence of a small-state coalition when it came to the method of choosing a president. The coalition of small-state delegates, who were so powerful on the questions of the state appointment of senators and congressional veto powers over state laws, broke apart on the question of the appointment of the president. The coefficients were not significant, and the magnitudes of the marginal effects vanishingly small.

There was also no evidence of a slave-state effect when it came to the method of choosing a president. Slave-state delegates opposed a popularly elected president in roll call 11, but this was because the nationalist Virginia delegates were still supporting the Virginia Plan. By roll calls 215 and 355, they had switched sides, and the slave-state effect had disappeared.

The findings support the view that, from the beginning of the Convention until roll call 355 on August 24, the delegates were divided into two factions. One faction, composed of the more nationalistic and wealthier delegates, preferred a strong presidential system; a second faction, composed of less wealthy delegates who favored states' rights, preferred a parliamentary (Congress appoints the president) regime.

After roll call 355, the delegates compromised their differences to arrive at the language of Article II, Section 2, of the Constitution, and in doing so, the factions I have identified dissolved.

-Appendix B-

Presidentialism and Liberty

In what follows, I estimate Freedom House rankings through an ordinary least squares (OLS) linear regression with panel-corrected standard errors (PCSE).

OLS regression assumes that errors (variations around the regression line) are uniform across different levels of democracy. This assumption is likely to be violated with panel data, where the variances of the errors can be expected to differ for each country; this would inflate the significance level of the coefficients. Following an influential article by Nathaniel Beck and Jonathan Katz, it is now conventional to correct for this with PCSE estimation procedures,[1] which are most appropriate where, as here, the number of countries (136) is far greater than the number of years (39).

Nevertheless, the PCSE assumption that the errors are free of serial correlation is unwarranted in time-series cross-sectional data. Political transitions are rare, and the regime in time t can be expected to be correlated with the regime in t-1. I therefore employ a Prais-Winsten regression to correct the standard errors for autocorrelation, which generally has the effect of reducing both the R^2 and size of the coefficients.

The explanatory (independent) variable of greatest interest is Presidential, which takes the value of 1 for presidential regimes and 0 for parliamentary ones. Had I primarily sought to show the relationship

TABLE B.1 *Variables and Sources*	
Dependent Variables	
Freedom House	Freedom House ranking of freedom, with 1 = most free and 7 = least free *Source*: http://www.freedomhouse.org/report-types/freedom-world
Military	Average of Military Expenditure/GDP in 1988 and 2010. *Source*: Stockholm International Peace Research Initiative (SIPRI) at http://www.sipri.org/
Explanatory Variables	
Presidential	Equals 1 if a presidential regime; 0 if a parliamentary regime *Source*: Banks Cross-National Time-Series Data Archive ("Banks"), at http://www.databanksinternational.com/71.html
U.S. Presidential	Equals 1 if the United States, 0 if a presidential regime other than the United States
LogGDP	Log of GDP per capita *Source*: World Bank, United Nations, at http://unstats.un.org/unsd/snaama/dnllist.asp
Gini	Gini measure of statistical dispersion of income, where 0 represents perfect equality and 1 perfect inequality *Source*: CIA Fact Book
Age	Number of years the country has been independent/210 (on the assumption that the oldest country achieved independence in 1800) *Source*: Democracy Cross-National Codebook compiled by Pippa Norris, at http://www.hks.harvard.edu/fs/pnorris/Data/Democracy%20CrossNational%20Data/Democracy%20Crossnational%20Codebook%20March%202009.pdf
Revolution	Equals 1 if there was any illegal or forced change in the top government elite, any attempt at such a change, or any successful or unsuccessful armed rebellion whose aim was independence from the central government; 0 otherwise *Source*: Banks Domestic7
British	Equals 1 if the country is Britain or was once a British colony; 0 otherwise
Latin	Equals 1 if the country is a Spanish- or Portuguese-speaking country in South or Central America; 0 otherwise
African	Equals 1 if the country is in Africa; 0 otherwise
Literacy	Percent literate, 15 years of age and over. *Source*: Banks school12 (.001)
Enemy	Equals 1 if the country is threatened by an external enemy; 0 otherwise *Source*: Author
U.S.	Equals 1 if the United States; 0 otherwise

TABLE B.2 *Political Systems and Freedom House's Measure of Political Freedom, 1972–2010*

	Economic	Political	Cultural	All
Presidential	.89***	1.52***	.94***	.74***
	(.15)	(.15)	(.16)	(.16)
LogGDP	-1.18***			-.49***
	(.12)			(13)
Gini	.008			.02
	(.009)			(.01)
Age		-2.31***		-1.51***
		(.25)		(20)
Revolution		.09***		.11***
		(.02)		(.03)
British			-.34*	-.61***
			(.17)	(.24)
Latin			-.27	.10
			(.28)	(.34)
African			.89***	.37
			(.28)	(.33)
Literacy			-.003***	-.002***
			(.0004)	(.0004)
Constant	6.33***	3.55***	4.83***	6.02***
	(.61)	(.15)	(.16)	(.61)
Number of Observations	3492	4277	3805	3092
Number of Countries	108	133	135	105
R^2	.23	.23	.25	.28

Notes: The dependent variable is the Freedom House ranking of political freedom, where higher scores indicate less freedom. Entries are OLS linear Prais-Winsten regression coefficients on pooled, time-series cross-national data, with panel-corrected standard errors, using the Stata xtpcse y x_1 x_2 x_3, pairwise corr (ar1) command, after encoding the data by country with the encode Country, gen (country1), and xtset country1 Year commands. For a list of countries by type of government, see table 6.1. Standard errors in parentheses.
* significant at the .05 level
** significant at the .01 level
*** significant at the .001 level

TABLE B.3 *Political Systems and Freedom House's Measure of Political Freedom, 1972–2010: U.S. vs. Other Presidential Regimes*

	Economic	Political	Cultural	All
U.S. Presidential	-2.01***	-2.01***	-2.77***	-.13
	(.24)	(.26)	(.27)	(.46)
LogGDP	-.99***			-.38*
	(.15)			(.19)
Gini	-.03**			-.005
	(.01)			(.01)
Age		-2.66***		-2.30***
		(.41)		(.46)
Revolution		.07**		.09**
		(.02)		(.03)
British			-.39	-.72*
			(.28)	(.36)
Latin			-1.29***	.38
			(.30)	(.40)
African			.17	.16
			(.27)	(.32)
Literacy			-.002***	-.002***
			(.0004)	(.0005)
Constant	8.58***	5.67***	6.12***	7.84***
	(.67)	(.22)	(.37)	(.65)
Number of Observations	2285	2801	2552	2022
Number of Countries	74	91	92	73
R^2	.21	.24	.25	.27

Notes: The dependent variable is the Freedom House ranking of political freedom. Entries are OLS linear Prais-Winsten regression coefficients on pooled, time-series cross-national data, with panel-corrected standard errors, using the Stata xtpcse y x_1 x_2 x_3, pairwise corr (ar1) command, after encoding the data by country with the encode Country, gen (country1), and xtset country1 Year commands. For a list of countries by type of government, see table 6.1. Standard errors in parentheses.
* significant at the .05 level
** significant at the .01 level
*** significant at the .001 level

TABLE B.4 *Political Systems and Military Expenditures per GDP*

Presidential	.87***	.61***	.52***
	(.04)	(.04)	(.05)
Enemy	.59***	.72***	.58***
	(.06)	(.06)	(.05)
Revolution	.22	.24	.26*
	(.13)	(.13)	(.13)
Latin		1.08***	1.12***
		(.04)	(.04)
U.S.			2.59***
			(.06)
Constant	1.72***	1.67***	1.72***
	(.04)	(.04)	(.03)
Number of Observations	3966	3966	3966
Number of Countries	123	123	123
R^2	.01	.03	.03

Notes: The dependent variable is the average of military expenditure/GDP in 1988 and 2010. Entries are xtpcse regressions, using the Stata xtpcse y x_1 x_2 x_3, pairwise command. For a list of countries by type of government, see table 6.1. Standard errors in parentheses.
* significant at the .05 level
** significant at the .01 level
*** significant at the .001 level

between per capita GDP (sometimes called modernization) and transitions to democracy, where the outcome is binary, I would have employed the now canonical Markov estimation procedure employed by Adam Przeworski et al. and David Epstein et al.[2]

As expected, the Presidential variable is significantly and strongly correlated with Freedom House rankings, with presidential regimes less free than parliamentary ones. I replicated these findings in an ordered logistic regression procedure, clustered by country to absorb the effects particular to each country, with similar results. I also replicated these findings in a regression on Polity IV, which ranks countries on a scale of -10 to +10, with higher scores indicating greater political freedom (unlike Freedom House, which gives higher scores to countries with less freedom). The

Polity IV and Freedom House rankings are closely correlated (Pearson's r = -0.90); and again, presidential regimes were significantly correlated with less political freedom.

-Appendix C-

Presidents and Corruption

For the following regression equations, I employ the explanatory variables defined in table C.1, to estimate the determinants of public corruption. Public corruption is thought to be greater in countries that suffer from an "oil curse," in which government leaders are able to pocket a portion of the country's oil revenues sold abroad. The oil curse is likely to be greatest when (1) the volume of oil sales is enormous, (2) strongmen control the government, (3) the oil industry has been nationalized (as it is in most countries), and (4) oil revenues are not disclosed by the government. In these circumstances, oil exports invite corruption, as defined by Robert Klitgaard: corruption equals monopoly plus discretion, minus accountability.[1]

The strongmen can most easily cash in through foreign oil sales, and most studies use as a measure of the oil curse the value of a country's petroleum exports, rather than its total oil production.[2] Because some countries export little or no oil, while others export vast quantities of it, the distribution of values is highly skewed, and I use a log of oil exports in the regressions. Following Ross, I then divide this by the country's population, rather than by its GDP.[3] Dividing oil exports by GDP introduces an endogeneity problem, as higher oil exports will result in a higher GDP. The oil curse appears to be particularly severe in countries that

TABLE C.1 *Variables and Sources*

Dependent Variable

| Corrupt | Transparency International Corruption Perceptions Index 2011 *Source*: http://cpi.transparency.org/cpi2011/ |

Explanatory Variables

Presidential	Equals 1 if a presidential regime; 0 if a parliamentary regime *Source*: Banks Cross-National Time-Series Data Archive ("Banks"), at http://www.databanksinternational.com/71.html
LogOil/Pop	Log of Country's Oil Exports in bbl. per day/Pop *Source*: CIA World Factbook
LogOil/Pop*New	Log of New*(Oil/Pop)
Pop	Country's Population *Source*: Banks
New	1/Age
Age	Number of years the country has been independent/210 (on the assumption that the oldest country achieved independence in 1800) *Source*: Democracy Cross-National Codebook compiled by Pippa Norris, at http://www.hks.harvard.edu/fs/pnorris/Data/Democracy%20CrossNational%20Data/Democracy%20Crossnational%20Codebook%20March%202009.pdf
British	Equals 1 if the country is Britain or was once a British colony; 0 otherwise
Latin	Equals 1 if the country is a Spanish- or Portuguese-speaking country in South or Central America; 0 otherwise
Catholic	Percent Catholic *Source*: http://www.catholic-hierarchy.org
Freedom House	Freedom House ranking of freedom, with 1 = most free and 7 = least free *Source*: http://www.freedomhouse.org/report-types/freedom-world

TABLE C.2 *Determinants of Transparency International's Corruption Perceptions Index 2011*

Presidential	-3.25*** (.06)	-2.51*** (.04)	-1.65*** (.05)
LogOil/Pop	892.91*** (22.92)	576.74*** (13.42)	565.0*** (11.3)
LogOil/Pop*New	-190.62*** (4.74)	-105.65*** (3.18)	-102.3*** (2.78)
Age		3.25*** (.04)	2.71*** (.06)
British		.21*** (.02)	.09*** (.02)
Latin		-1.49*** (.04)	-1.58*** (.04)
Catholic		-.005*** (.0006)	-.007*** (.0005)
Freedom House			-.31*** (.02)
Constant	6.31*** (.04)	-4.69*** (.04)	5.55*** (.09)
Number of Observations	4087	3950	3950
Number of Countries	126	121	121
R^2	.53	.62	.66

Notes: The dependent variable is Transparency International's Corruption Perceptions Index 2011. Entries are OLS linear regression coefficients, with panel-corrected standard errors for pooled, time-series cross-national data, using the Stata xtpcse, pairwise command. For a list of countries by type of government, see table 6.1.
* significant at the .05 level
** significant at the .01 level
*** significant at the .001 level

have emerged relatively recently from colonialism,[4] and I therefore add an interactor term, in which the log of oil revenues divided by population is multiplied by the reciprocal of the Age variable. This has the effect of separating the effect of the oil curse between older and newer countries.

One might expect to see less corruption in countries with a British inheritance. Catholic countries have traditionally been seen as more corrupt.

My data set includes presidential and parliamentary countries, whether democratic or not. Nondemocratic countries can be expected to be more corrupt, and if they were excluded, this would bias the findings.[5] However, I do include the Freedom House ranking of political freedom as an explanatory variable, to capture the effect of democratic government.

As expected, the Presidential coefficient is strongly and significantly negative. Parliamentary regimes are relatively free from corruption, compared with presidential ones. This result is consistent with the findings of Blume et al. that government corruption, as measured by the CPI index, was significantly higher in presidential countries (but not in an extended data set comprising some smaller countries omitted from my study, such as Saint Kitts and Nevis).[6] It is also consistent with the findings of Daniel Lederman et al., who reported that presidential systems increased corruption by 0.8 points on the International Country Risk Guide corruption index (0 to 6), which measures the likelihood that government officials would demand or accept bribes, based on surveys of experts.[7] Similarly, Jana Kunicova and Susan Rose-Ackerman found that presidential systems interact with proportional representation voting rules to produce governments that are particularly susceptible to corruption.[8] And John Gerring and Strom Thacker found that parliamentary systems were associated with less corruption, when employing a federalism/unitary government explanatory variable.[9] Gerring, Thacker, and Carola Moreno subsequently found that parliamentarism was correlated with the World Bank measure of corruption control, but only in a reduced-form model that eliminated most insignificant explanatory variables.[10]

The outlier is from Persson and Tabellini; it found that presidential systems were significantly correlated with less corruption, as measured by the World Bank, when worse and younger democracies were excluded from the mix, or when an interactor explanatory variable was added which multiplied the presidential dummy variable by a measure of the quality of democracy.[11] Excluding the inconveniently bad presidential systems comes rather close to cherry-picking, however, since one would expect more corruption in undemocratic countries; and when these techniques were dropped, the authors were unable to find that presidential governments were correlated with less corruption, whether measured by Transparency International or by the World Bank, on normal standards of statistical significance.

Older countries with a British heritage are less likely to experience political corruption, as are wealthy countries. The oil curse appears absent in older oil-exporting countries, such as Britain and Canada, even when the age of the country is taken into account. The oil curse is particularly a problem in countries in which democracy is less well established.

Notes

The records of the Framers' deliberations were edited by Max Farrand, and issued in a four-volume set originally published in 1911. They comprise the sketchy notes of the Convention's secretary, as well as notes made by the delegates, principally James Madison: *The Records of the Federal Convention of 1787*, rev. ed. (New Haven: Yale University Press, 1937) [hereafter cited by volume number and page]. On the accuracy of the records, see James H. Hutson, "Introduction," in IV.xv ff. We would know little of the minds of the delegates had Dolly Madison not rescued her husband's notes when the British burned the White House in the War of 1812.

Among the best recent books on the Convention are Richard Beeman, *Plain, Honest Men: The Making of the American Constitution* (New York: Random House, 2009); David O. Stewart, *The Summer of 1787: The Men Who Invented the Constitution* (New York: Simon & Schuster, 2007); and Carol Berkin, *A Brilliant Solution: Inventing the American Constitution* (Boston: Mariner Books, 2003). The best-known earlier popular accounts are Catherine Drinker Bowen, *Miracle at Philadelphia* (Boston: Little, Brown, 1966); and Clinton Rossiter, *1787: The Grand Convention* (New York: Macmillan, 1966). The idea that the work of the Framers might be studied from an economic perspective has been ably revived by Robert A. McGuire in *To Form a More Perfect Union: A New Economic Interpretation of the United States Constitution* (Oxford: Oxford University Press, 2003).

The leading biography of Madison remains that of Irving Brant, whose *James Madison: The Nationalist 1780–1787* (Indianapolis: Bobbs-Merrill, 1948) deals with Madison's role at the Convention. More recent, useful studies include Jack N. Rakove, *James Madison and the Creation of the American Republic* (New York: Pearson Longman, 2007); Samuel Kernell, ed., *James Madison: The Theory and Practice of Republican Government* (Stanford: Stanford University Press, 2003); Lance Banning, *The Sacred Fire of Liberty: James Madison and the Founding of the Federal Republic* (Ithaca: Cornell University Press, 1995); Richard K. Matthews, *If Men Were Angels: James Madison and the Heartless Empire of Reason* (Lawrence: University Press of Kansas, 1995); and William Lee Miller, *The Business of May Next: James Madison and the Founding* (Charlottesville: University of Virginia Press, 1992). For Madison's papers, see Robert A. Rutland et al., eds., *The Papers of James Madison* (Chicago: University of Chicago Press, 1962–1977; Charlottesville: University of Virginia Press, 1977–1991). [hereafter "PJM"].

The story of Canadian confederation is little known outside Canada, and is best told by Donald Creighton in *The Road to Confederation: The Emergence of Canada, 1863–1867* (Boston: Houghton Mifflin, 1965). Creighton hit on the device of using Arthur Hamilton Gordon to launch his narrative, and noted the presence of the circus in Charlottetown. A shorter and highly readable account of confederation is provided in Christopher Moore's *1867: How the Fathers Made a Deal* (Toronto: McClelland and Stewart, 1997). The first Canadian prime minister, Sir John A. Macdonald, has been the subject of two remarkable biographies. The first of these was Donald Creighton's two-volume *John A. Macdonald: The Young Politician* and *The Old Chieftan* (Toronto: Macmillan, 1952 and 1955). Creighton was a Tory and a Canadian nationalist who rescued Macdonald from a dismissive Whig interpretation of Canadian history. More recently, Richard Gwyn has written another two-volume biography of Macdonald, more objective than Creighton's but equally readable: *John A.: The Man Who Made Us* and *Nation Maker: Sir John A. Macdonald: His Life, Our Times* (Toronto: Random House Canada, 2007 and 2011). For the background debates in the provincial assemblies on confederation, see Janet Ajzenstat et al., eds., *Canada's Founding Debates* (Toronto: University of Toronto Press, 2003) 179–80.

Scholars in both the United States and in parliamentary systems have noted the rise of strong executive government. American writers have sometimes celebrated an expanded presidential power when their man was in office—see Richard E. Neustadt, *Presidential Power and the Modern Presidents* (New York: Macmillan, 1990)—and decried it when he was not—see Arthur M. Schlesinger Jr., *The Imperial Presidency* (Boston: Houghton Mifflin, 2004). For a more balanced analysis of what he called the "plebiscitary presidency," see Theodore J. Lowi, *The Personal President: Power Invested, Promise Unfulfilled* (Ithaca: Cornell University Press, 1985). One of the best recent studies of excessive presidential power is Gene Healy's *The Cult of the Presidency: America's Dangerous Devotion to Executive Power* (Washington: Cato Institute, 2008). For Crown government in Canada, see Donald J. Savoie, *Court Government and the Collapse of Accountability in Canada and the United Kingdom* (Toronto: University of Toronto Press, 2008).

For chapter 6's regressions, I rely on data provided by the Arthur S. Banks Cross-National Time-Series Data Archive 2011, courtesy of Banner Software, Inc., Binghamton, NY 13905. The literature on the lack of political freedom in presidential regimes was sparked by a seminal article by Juan J. Linz, "Presidential or Parliamentary Democracy: Does It Make a Difference?," in *The Failure of Presidential Democracy: The Case of Latin America*, eds. Juan J. Linz and Arturo Valenzuela (Baltimore: Johns Hopkins University Press, 1994). See also Pippa Norris, *Driving Democracy: Do Power-Sharing Institutions Work?* (Cambridge: Cambridge University Press, 2008), ch. 6; Alicia Adserà and Carles Boix, "Constitutions and Democratic Breakdowns," in *Controlling Governments: Voters, Institutions, and Accountability*, eds. José María Maravall and Ignacio

Sánchez-Cuenca (Cambridge: Cambridge University Press, 2008) 247; Arend Lijphart, "Constitutional Design for Divided Societies," *Journal of Democracy* 15, no. 2 (2004): 96; Matthew Shugart and Stephan Haggard, "Institutions and Public Policy in Presidential Systems," in *Presidents, Parliaments, and Policy*, eds. Stephan Haggard and Matthew McCubbins (Cambridge: Cambridge University Press, 2001); Alfred Stepan and Cindy Skach, "Constitutional Frameworks and Democratic Consolidation: Parliamentarism versus Presidentialism," *World Politics* 46, no. 1 (1993): 82.

The inefficiencies of the separation of powers has spawned a lengthy literature, beginning with Woodrow Wilson, *Congressional Government: A Study in American Politics* (Mineola: Dover, 2006), 206. More recently, the rise of gridlock has drawn a great deal of critical attention. Three of the best of these books are Daniel Lazare's *The Frozen Republic: How the Constitution Is Paralyzing Democracy* (New York: Harcourt Brace, 1996); Jonathan Rauch's *Demosclerosis: The Silent Killer of American Government* (New York: Random House, 1994), 131–42; and *Government's End: Why Washington Stopped Working* (New York: Public Affairs, 1994).

Reforming American government would be easier could one fiddle with the Constitution. For two highly readable and scholarly (if somewhat quixotic) takes on constitutional reform, see Lawrence Lessig, *Republic, Lost: How Money Corrupts Congress—and a Plan to Stop It* (New York: Twelve, 2011); and Sanford Levinson, *Our Undemocratic Constitution: Where the Constitution Goes Wrong (And How We the People Can Correct It)* (Oxford: Oxford University Press, 2006).

CHAPTER 1: REX QUONDAM, REX FUTURUS

1. For examples, see Eric Posner and Adrian Vermeule, The Executive Unbound: After the Madisonian Republic (Oxford U.P., 2011); George Thomas, The Madisonian Constitution (Johns Hopkins U.P., 2008).

2. Walter Bagehot, The English Constitution 11–13 (Oxford World's Classics, 2001).

3. I.101.

4. John Stuart Mill, On Liberty 36 (New York: W. W. Norton, 1975).

5. Montesquieu, The Spirit of the Laws 157 at XI.6 (Cambridge U.P., 1989).

6. Bagehot at 11.

7. Stephen Leacock, Sunshine Sketches of a Little Town 132 (London: Prion, 2000).

8. Federalist 47, in The Federalist 249 (George W. Carey and James McClellan, eds., Indianapolis: Liberty Fund, 2001).

9. Woodrow Wilson, Congressional Government: A Study in American Politics 206 (Mineola: Dover, 2006) [1885].

10. See, e.g., Bernard Bailyn, Atlantic History: Concept and Contours (Harvard U.P., 2005); Exclusionary Empire: English Liberty Overseas 1600–1900 (Jack P. Greene, ed., Cambridge U.P., 2010).

CHAPTER 2: THE AMERICAN PRESIDENT

1. An "original intent" originalism of this kind must be distinguished from an "original meaning" originalism. The former looks only to the writings of the Framers for guidance, while the latter would interpret the Constitution as the intelligent reader of 1787 would have done. I argue elsewhere that the former kind of originalism is more compelling. The Efficient Secret: How America Nearly Adopted a Parliamentary System, and Why It Should Have Done So, 1 British Journal of American Legal Studies 349, 351 (2012).

2. William Ewart Gladstone: Life and Public Services 323 (Thomas W. Handford, ed., Chicago: Dominion, 1899).

3. II. 501. Madison recalled "tedious and reiterated discussions" about the presidency in a letter to Thomas Jefferson dated October 24, 1787, 10 PJM 208.

4. I.291.

5. I.451–52.

6. III.423 (Autobiography of William Few).

7. III.391.

8. To R. H. Lee, July 7, 1785, 8 PJM 315.

9. For more upbeat views about the American economy of the 1780s, see Merrill Jensen, The New Nation: A History of the United States During the Confederation, 1781–1789 384–88 (Northeastern U.P., 1981); E. James Ferguson, The Power of the Purse: A History of American Public Finance, 1776–1790 (UNC P., 1961).

10. Gordon S. Wood, The Radicalism of the American Revolution 250 (New York: Vintage, 1991).

11. I.11.

12. III.86–87.

13. August 30, 1787, Thomas Jefferson, Writings 909 (New York: Library of America, 1984).

14. Robert A. McGuire, To Form a More Perfect Union: A New Economic Interpretation of the United States Constitution 52–53 (Oxford U.P., 2003).

15. Rossiter, 1787 at 146–47.

16. Rufus Griswold, The Republican Court: Or, American Society in the Days of Washington 98–99 note (D. Appleton: New York, 1867).

17. I.301.

18. Forrest McDonald, E Pluribus Unum: The Formation of the American Republic 1776–1790 267–68 (Indianapolis: Liberty Fund, 1979).

19. IV.295 (Hugh Williamson to John Gray Blount, June 3, 1788). Mason was repaid in kind by Oliver Ellsworth, writing as the "Landholder." See Landholder VI, December 10, 1787, at http://www.infoplease.com/t/hist /federalist/landholder06.html. The acerbic Mason had a profound influence on the contours of the Constitution, which paradoxically he did not sign for reasons that have puzzled historians. Jeff Broadwater, George Mason: Forgotten Founder 206–08 (UNC P., 2006).

20. IV.111.

21. Beeman at 92. Jefferson, thankfully, was in Paris.

22. James M. Varnum to George Washington at III.47.

23. I The Founders' Constitution 187 (Philip B. Kurland and Ralph Lerner, eds., U. Chicago P., 1987).

THE ONCE AND FUTURE KING

24. James Madison, Origin of the Constitutional Convention, in II The Writings of James Madison, comprising his Public Papers and his Private Correspondence, including his numerous letters and documents now for the first time printed (New York: G.P. Putnam's Sons, 1900) at http://oll.libertyfund.org/title/1934/118600.

25. III.23.

26. At http://avalon.law.yale.edu/18th_century/const04.asp, quoted in Winton Solberg, The Federal Convention and the Formation of the Union 64 (Indianapolis: Bobbs-Merrill, 1958).

27. 9 PJM 348. Madison arrived at his views on the presidency sometime between an April 8, 1787 letter he sent to Edmund Randolph and an April 16 letter he sent to George Washington. 9 PJM 368; 9 PJM 382.

28. David Hume, "Idea of a Perfect Commonwealth," in Hume, Political Essays at 221 (Cambridge U.P., 1994). Douglas Adair is credited as the person who first identified Hume as the source of Madison's thoughts on government. See Douglas Adair, That Politics May Be Reduced to a Science: David Hume, James Madison, and the Tenth Federalist, in Fame and the Founding Fathers: Essays by Douglas Adair 132 (Trevor Colbourrn, ed., Indianapolis: Liberty Fund, 1998); Douglas Adair, The Intellectual Origins of Jeffersonian Democracy: Republicanism, the Class Struggle, and the Virtuous Farmer 130–39 (Lanham: Lexington Books); Mark G. Spencer, Hume and Madison on Faction, 59 Wm. & and Mary Q. (third series) 869 (2002).

29. David Hume, That Politics May Be Reduced to a Science, Political Essays at 4.

30. I.50. Other delegates subscribed to the filtration theory: I.133 (Wilson); I.136 (Dickinson); I.152 (Gerry); II.54 (G. Morris). Hamilton subsequently endorsed it in the New York ratifying debates. June 21, 1788, 5 The Papers of Alexander Hamilton 41 (Harold C. Syrett and Jacob E. Cooke, eds., Columbia U.P., 1962).

31. Montesquieu, The Spirit of the Laws 124 at VIII.16 (Cambridge U.P., 1989).

32. Idea of a Perfect Commonwealth.

33. Hume had argued elsewhere for the need for a constitution in which private interests check each other in his essay "Of the Independence of Parliament."

34. I.136. Martin Diamond argued that this speech converted the other delegates to Madison's theory of extended republics. However, the theory was not mentioned elsewhere in the Convention, and there is little evidence to support Diamond's claim. Martin Diamond, The Founding of the Democratic Republic 37 (Boston: Wadsworth, 1981). See Christopher Wolfe, On Understanding the Constitutional Convention of 1787, 39 J. Pol. 103 (1977); James H. Hutson, Riddles of the Federal Constitutional Convention, 44 Wm. & Mary Q. (third series) 411, 421–22 (1987).

35. E. E. Schattschneider, Party Government 9 (New Brunswick: Transaction, 2004).

36. After responding to Sherman on June 6, Madison must have voted in favor of a congressionally appointed president in roll calls 45, 46 and 167, on 11, 12 and 17 June, respectively. Madison continued to support a filtration theory of government on June 26 (the people and many representatives "were liable to err . . . from fickleness and passion"). I.422. While the filtration theory had been nearly swallowed up in Federalist 10 by the manner in which the defects of democracy would be cured in an extensive republic, Madison continued to insist on the need for "auxiliary precautions" in Federalist 63, the last of the papers he authored.

37. I.48.

38. I.21.

39. Id. Randolph presented the Virginia Plan on May 29. On the same day, South Carolina's Charles Pinckney tabled his own plan of government. A record of its contents was not kept, but New York's Robert Yates reported that Pinckney stated that it was grounded on the same principles as the Virginia Plan. A draft of the plan that Pinckney subsequently provided featured a congressionally appointed president. See III.604–09. Pinckney is a less than reliable witness about his role in the Convention, but there is no reason to suppose that he differed from Randolph on how the president was to be chosen.

40. A Council of Revision was nevertheless adopted in the New York Constitution of 1771, and abolished only in the state constitutional convention of 1821. See Democracy, Liberty, and Property: The State Constitutional Conventions of the 1820s 116, 133–48 (Merrill D. Peterson, ed., Indianapolis: Liberty Fund, 2010).

41. II.74.

42. II.76.

43. Veto Message to Congress. James Madison, Writings 718 (New York: Library of America, 1999).

44. Veto Message, February 16, 1887, at http://www.presidency.ucsb.edu/ws/index.php?pid=71489#axzz1TzmvIGZj.

45. I.66.

46. Forrest McDonald, Novus Ordo Seclorum: The Intellectual Origins of the Constitution 240–41 (U.P. Kansas, 1985).

47. I: 299 (Hamilton), I.86–87 (Dickinson), I.398 (Pinckney).

48. I.83.

49. I.66.

50. II.101.

51. See Louise Dunbar, A Study of "Monarchical" Tendencies in the United States from 1776 to 1801 60, 91 (U. Illinois P., 1922).

52. II.191–92.

53. Gordon S. Wood, Revolutionary Characters: What Made the Founders Different 50 (New York: Penguin, 2006).

54. A procedure recommended in 1776 by John Adams, Thoughts on Government, The Revolutionary Writings of John Adams 290 (Indianapolis: Liberty Fund, 2000).

55. II.35. See Charles C. Thach, The Creation of the Presidency, 1775–1789: A Study in Constitutional History ch. 2 (Indianapolis: Liberty Fund, 2007); Bernard Bailyn, The Origins of American Politics 78–79 (New York: Vintage, 1967).

56. Letter to Thomas Jefferson, August 12, 1786, 9 PJM 95.

57. II.29.

58. See Daniel Walker Howe, What Hath God Wrought: The Transformation of America, 1815–1848 (Oxford U.P., 2007), on how new technologies in travel and communication helped shape the movement toward popular sovereignty.

59. I.48 (Gerry), I.301 (Hamilton).

60. I.51 (Randolph).

61. I.132.

62. I.48.

63. II.31.

64. I.422–23.

65. Gordon S. Wood, A Note on Mobs in the American Revolution, 23 Wm. & Mary Q. 635 (1966); Arthur M. Schlesinger, Political Mobs and the American Revolution, 1765–76, 99 Am. Phil. Soc. 244 (1955).

66. I.318.

67. Beeman, Plain, Honest Men at 77, 226–27.

68. II.24.

69. Pauline Maier, Popular Uprisings, 27 Wm. & Mary Q. (third series) 29, 33–34 (1970); John K. Alexander, The Fort Wilson Incident of 1779: A Case Study of the Revolutionary Crowd, 31 Wm. & Mary Q. (third series) 589 (1974).

70. I.68.

71. I.113.

72. I.101. Mason was echoing Thomas Jefferson. "An *elective despotism* was not the government we fought for." Thomas Jefferson, Notes on the State of Virginia, Query 13, in Writings at 245.

73. Sherman proposed other measures to curtail the president's power. He would have permitted Congress to remove the president at its pleasure (I.85). He also wanted Congress to appoint a council of advice that, like the executive councils of state governments, could veto the president's decisions (I.97). He opposed a presidential veto over the legislature (I.99), and would even have approved a multiple presidency with the number of co-presidents left blank, so that Congress might appoint additional co-presidents should it want to overrule a president to whom it objected (I.65).

74. Even John Adams, in his 1776 Thoughts on Government, wanted a governor who was elected annually by the legislature and who was "stripped of most of those badges of domination called prerogatives."

75. John Locke, Second Treatise on Government ch. xiv, § 159.

76. The revival of interest in a country party ideology of republican virtue began with the work of a brilliant set of historians in the mid-1960s, notably Bernard Bailyn and Gordon Wood. See Bernard Bailyn, The Ideological Origins of the American Revolution (Harvard U.P., 1967); Gordon S. Wood, The Creation of the American Republic 1776–1787 (U.N.C. P., 1969).

77. Luxury was also an enemy, since it made citizens focus on their self-interest and wealth, and as a member of the country party Mason proposed that Congress be given the power to enact sumptuary laws against luxury goods. "No Government can be maintained unless the manners be made consonant to it," he argued (II.344). Let those who seek distinction be channeled into ways more conducive to the public welfare. The motion failed (roll call 319 at II.340), but received support from Delaware, Maryland, and Georgia.

78. Idea of a Perfect Commonwealth.

79. A list that overlaps somewhat with that of McDonald, Novus Ordo Seclorum at 200. Many of the delegates do not fall neatly on one side or other of the country-court divide. For example, John Dickinson seemed in some respects a country party member, but he also admired Hume and believed that all history proved "that trade and freedom are nearly related to one another" (Letter V from a Farmer).

80. II.364

81. In Washington, country party ideals could coexist with a realistic understanding of human shortcomings. While no one better represented republican virtue, he had had his nose rubbed in it when he sought to persuade his soldiers to re-enlist or requested supplies for his troops from Congress. From his experiences in the field he concluded that "the few . . . who act upon Principles of disinterestedness are, comparatively speaking, no more than a drop in the Ocean." Washington to John Hancock, September 24, 1776, in John C. Fitzpatrick (ed.), VI Writings of Washington at http://etext.virginia.edu/toc /modeng/public/WasFi06.html.

82. I.288.

83. See Selected Political Essays of James Wilson 180 (Randolph G. Adams, ed., New York: Knopf, 1930) (speech at the Pennsylvania Ratifying Convention, November 24, 1787). Yet it was more than a legal fiction to Wilson, who employed his theory to impugn the doctrine of sovereign immunity that the state of Georgia had invoked when sued by a private citizen from another state. Chisholm v. Georgia, 2 U.S. (2 Dall.) 419 (1793). The ruling in the case was subsequently reversed by the Eleventh Amendment, which removed such cases from federal courts. On the difficulties of current attempts to give life to Wilson's theory, see Henry Paul Monaghan, We the Peoples, Original Understanding, and Constitutional Amendment, 96 Colum. L. Rev. 121 (1996), responding to Akhil R. Amar, The Consent of the Governed: Constitutional Amendment Outside Article V, 94 Colum. L. Rev. 457 (1994); Akhil R. Amar, Philadelphia Revisited: Amending the Constitution Outside Article V, 55 U. Chi. L. Rev. 1043 (1988).

84. Albeit one recognized as such only in recent years. See William Ewald, James Wilson and the Drafting of the Constitution, 10 U. Pa. J. Const. L. 901 (2008). Like Robert Morris, Wilson speculated wildly in land development schemes and ended up in a debtor's prison. His leading role in the Convention remained hidden from view until Madison's notes were published in 1840, and by then the country had moved on.

85. II The Documentary History of the Ratifying Conventions 452 (Merrill Jensen, John P. Kaminski, et al., eds., Madison: Wisconsin Historical Society, 1976 ff.) [hereafter DHRC].

86. I.79.

87. Roll call 12 at I.79. Wilson's subsequent motion for a Senate elected by the people fared even worse. Only his state supported the motion, and it was voted down 10 to 1. Roll call 31 at I.149.

88. Thach at 67–68. It is sometimes suggested that Washington's presence at the Convention helped persuade the delegates to support a popularly elected president, since everyone expected that he would also be the first president. If it were thought that a popularly elected president might abuse his powers, he must have seemed a reassuring figure. South Carolina's Pierce Butler thought

that the delegates would not have been so willing to repose their confidence in the executive "had not many of the members cast their eyes toward General Washington as President; and shaped their Ideas of the Powers to be given to a President, by their opinions of his Virtue." Letter to Weedon Butler, May 5, 1788, at III.302. And yet the delegates voted down a popularly elected president again and again.

89. I.80 (Gerry). See also I.154 (Sherman). The split between nationalists and states'-rights supporters was the dominant cleavage at the Convention. See Keith L. Dougherty and Jac C. Heckelman, A Spatial Analysis of Delegate Voting at the Constitutional Convention at http://papers.ssrn.com/sol3/papers .cfm?abstract_id=1953436.

90. I.175–76. See also I.152, where Gerry argued for state-appointed senators for this reason.

91. Roll call 32 at I.149.

92. Jay S. Bybee, Ulysses at the Mast: Democracy, Federalism, and the Sirens' Song of the Seventeenth Amendment, 91 Nw. U. L. Rev. 500 (1997). Even before 1913, voters had begun to view state legislators as proxies for the more important position of senator. That was what the 1858 Illinois state elections and the Lincoln-Douglas debates were all about. See William H. Riker, The Senate and American Federalism, 49 Am. Pol. Sc. Rev. 452 (1955).

93. Paterson had seemingly subscribed to Madison's filtration argument, but turned it around to argue for senators filtered by state legislatures. I.251.

94. I.242.

95. Roll call 120 at I.549.

96. Roll call 156 at II.15. In an extraordinarily short time the delegates in Philadelphia and in Congress at New York arrived at two of the most momentous decisions in American history. Sixteen of the Philadelphia delegates had left for New York at the end of June to represent their states in Congress, which on 13 July passed the Northwest Ordinance, which abolished slavery north of the Ohio River and prepared the way for the admission of six new states.

97. "The time was wasted in vague conversation," wrote Madison. II.19–20.

98. Roll call 34 at I.163. Madison had wanted to grant the federal government the power to veto any state law, whether or not it was constitutional. Letter to George Washington, April 16, 1787, 9 PJM 382. After the Convention was over, he continued to regret the absence of a federal veto over state legislation. Letter to Thomas Jefferson, October 24, 1787, 10 PJM 206.

99. Roll call 34 at I.163.

100. Roll call 163 at II.24.

101. I.244 (Resolution 4).

102. Roll call 165 at II.24.

103. Roll call 166 at II.24.

104. Roll call 167 at II.24.

105. IV.172.

106. Hamilton too was no democrat, but as a nationalist saw that a popularly elected president would change the balance of power between the states and federal government. Before anyone else, he recognized that the day would come "when every vital interest of the state will be merged in the all-absorbing question of *who shall be the next* PRESIDENT." Letter to Governor Lewis at III.410.

107. II.29–31.

108. I.80.

109. I.517.

110. I.584.

111. James J. Kirschke, Gouverneur Morris: Author, Statesman, and Man of the World 345 at n. 47 (New York: St. Martin's Press, 2005).

112. I The Diary and Letters of Gouverneur Morris 91 (Anne Cary Morris, ed.) (New York: Scribner's, 1888).

113. III.236.

114. III.92.

115. III.94–95.

116. I.242.

117. Letter to Jared Sparks, April 8, 1831, at III.500.

118. April 8, 1787, 9 PJM 368.

119. It is not easy to reconcile the Madison of 1787, with his congressional veto of state legislation, with the Madison of 1798, with his Virginia Resolution which argued that states had the right, when confronted with "dangerous" and unconstitutional federal laws, "to interpose for arresting the progress of the evil, and for maintaining within their respective limits, the authorities, rights and liberties of the states." Years later an embarrassed Madison sought to distinguish this from Calhoun's nullification doctrine. "Notes on Nullification," in The Mind of the Founder: Sources of the Political Thought of James Madison 417 (Marvin Meyers, ed., Brandeis U.P., 1973).

120. II.34. In a note he wrote afterward Madison said that this speech was meant to defend Dr. McClurg's suggestion of a president appointed without a fixed term during good behavior. Id. In making the suggestion, McClurg had invoked the separation of powers. However, it is much more likely that, in adopting separationism, Madison was influenced by Gouverneur Morris than he was by Dr. McClurg, who had been picked from obscurity to come to Philadelphia. He was a naïf who very likely did mean his motion seriously, adopting it from a similar suggestion Hamilton had made at I.292. Other delegates also seemed to take McClurg seriously, as four states supported his motion on roll call 169 at II.24. Madison continued to think well of McClurg's proposal for an unlimited presidential term in an October 24, 1787 letter to Thomas Jefferson. 10 PJM 208. William Riker's reliance on McClurg's motion as a peg from which to hang an account of strategic voting therefore seems considerably overdrawn. William H. Riker, The Heresthetics of Constitution-Making: The Presidency in 1787, with Comments on Determinism and Rational Choice, 78 Am. Pol. Sc. Rev. 1 (1984).

121. Roll call 11 at I.79.

122. I.80 and II.57.

123. Roll call 166 at II.24.

124. Roll call 182 at II.51.

125. Roll call 183 at II.51.

126. II.98.

127. Roll call 218 at II.109.

128. Roll call 225 at II.118.

129. I.66 (Randolph); I.68 (Sherman); I.113 (Mason); I.101, I.113; II.30 (Pinckney).

130. I.48, I.132 (Gerry); I.154, II.29 (Sherman); II.30 (Pinckney).

131. II.171, II.185.

132. II.399.

133. Id.

134. Roll call 361 at III.399. William Riker mischaracterized this as a vote for the popular election of the president. Riker, id. at 6.

135. II.55–56 (King). Williamson was opposed to a president elected by the people on July 17, but also saw objections to a congressional appointment on July 25. His state voted consistently for a congressional appointment. He remained a strong state supporter on September 6, proposing an election by the House voting by state, if the electors failed to elect a president by majority vote. II.527.

136. James Madison to George Hay, August 23, 1823, The Writings of James Madison: Comprising his Public Papers and his Private Correspondence, including Numerous Letters and Documents now for the first time Printed 147 (New York: G.P. Putnam, 1910).

137. That was not quite the end of the matter. On September 5 John Rutledge moved that the committee's vote be postponed and that the delegates take up the original proposal for a president appointed by the legislature. This failed, 8 to 2, in roll call 445, and thereafter the Virginia Plan's idea of a president appointed by Congress was never again raised.

138. II.500.

139. II.501.

140. X DHRC 1377; 11 PJM 154.

141. II.57 (Madison).

142. As Hamilton emphasized in Federalist 68.

143. II.500. See also II.512. Mason raised the figure to 98 percent on June 18, 1788, in the Virginia ratifying convention.

144. II.500, X DHRC 1377 (Madison); II.522 (Wilson); II.524–25, II.530 (Hamilton); II.513 (Dickinson); II.513 (Randolph); II.501 (Pinckney); II.511 (Rutledge); II.499 (Sherman). See also II.524 (Clymer); II.501 (Williamson).

This was not what Madison had wanted, see II.513, but his motion to let the electors choose the president if only a third of them settled on a candidate was defeated 9 to 2 in roll call 448 at II.508. The majority of delegates wanted Congress to play a role in presidential elections. By the end of the Convention, however, Madison described Article II as providing for a president "elected by the people." II.587.

145. II.512. For an example of the floor manager at work, see Morris's anxious demand that Wilson get with the program, II.523. Baldwin was the only other delegate who expressed the view that a majority of electors would agree on a candidate. II.501.

146. II.527.

147. III.461.

148. IV.300.

149. IV.301.

150. I.101. See also I.215 (Gerry); II.201 (Ellsworth).

151. II.278.

152. While this is a nice story, it's not the only one that can be told. Pierce Butler, another member of the Committee on Unfinished Parts, took credit for proposing the method of presidential elections in a May 1788 letter to an English kinsman. III.302. This seems an exaggeration, however. In the same letter Butler wrote that he thought the powers of the president excessive, and in an earlier letter to the same relative, written less than a month after the Convention ended, he wrote that "a Copy of our deliberations . . . is not worth the expense of postage, or I wou'd now enclose it to You." Quoted in S. Sidney Ulmer, The Role of Pierce Butler in the Constitutional Convention, 72 Rev. of Politics 361, 374 (1960). On the whole, Dickinson seems a considerably more reliable witness than the foppish Butler, who was given to boasting and whom the delegates took much less seriously than Dickinson.

153. IV.301.

154. John Dickinson, The Letters of Fabius, Letter II, in Pamphlets on the Constitution of the United States, published during its Discussion by the People, 1787–1788 (Paul Leicester Ford, ed., Brooklyn, N.Y., 1888).

155. Id.

156. II DHRC 449, 497; The Works of James Wilson 77 (Robert G. McCloskey, ed., Harvard U.P., 1967). See generally Jennifer Nedelsky, Private Property and the Limits of American Constitutionalism ch. 4 (U. Chicago Press, 1990).

157. II DHRC 349, 363. Bernard Bailyn notes that this speech attracted far more attention from contemporaries than did the Federalist Papers. Bernard Bailyn, Faces of Revolution: Personalities and Themes in the Struggle for American Independence 230 (New York: Vintage, 1990).

158. II DHRC 567.

159. I.512.

160. II.542. A year later Madison had swung back to supporting a strong form of independence for the executive against the legislature, in his comments on Jefferson's draft for a new Virginia constitution. 11 PJM 289.

161. II.524.

162. III.77 (italics in original).

163. The essays were seldom published outside of New York. Pauline Maier, Ratification: The People Debate the Constitution, 1787–88 84 (New York: Simon & Schuster, 2010). Credit for the rediscovery of Madison's Federalist 10 goes not to a conservative or public-choice theorist, but to the brilliant, marxisant Charles Beard. See further Larry D. Kramer, Madison's Audience, 112 Harv. L. Rev. 611 (1999).

164. "It was hard to see how any President could be more Federalist than Jefferson himself," observed Henry Adams. History of the United States during the Administrations of Thomas Jefferson 354 (New York: Library of America, 1986).

CHAPTER 3: THE BRITISH PRIME MINISTER

1. Almost all the way back, it seems. See Alan Macfarlane, The Origins of English Individualism: The Family Property and Social Transition (Oxford: Blackwell, 1978) (examining social and geographic mobility in the England of the later Middle Ages).

2. Sir Lewis Namier, England in the Age of the American Revolution 6 (London: Macmillan, 1963).

3. To Barbeu-Dubourg, October 2, 1770, 5 The Life and Writings of Benjamin Franklin 280 (A. H. Smyth, ed., London: Macmillan, 1906). See generally Jack P. Greene, The Constitutional Origins of the American Revolution (Cambridge U.P., 2011).

4. Sir William Blackstone, 1 Commentaries on the Law of England ch. 2 (1765).

5. 7 & 8 Wm. III c. 22. See R. L. Schuyler, Parliament and the British Empire: Some Constitutional Controversies Concerning Imperial Legislative Jurisdiction 33 (Columbia U.P., 1929).

6. 18 Cobbett's Parliamentary History of England 771 (October 26, 1775) [hereafter "Parl. Hist."].

7. 1 Wraxall's Historical and Posthumous Memoirs 369 (London: Bickers, 1884).

8. 18 Parl. Hist. 769 (October 26, 1775).

9. Quoted in Herbert Butterfield, George III, Lord North, and the People 1779–80 131 (New York: Russell & Russell, 1968)

10. 20 Parl. Hist. 1225 (November 26, 1779).

11. 21 Parl. Hist. 367 (April 6, 1780).

12. Alan Valentine, Lord North 274 (U. Oklahoma P., 1967).

13. 2 The Correspondence of King George the Third with Lord North 393 (W. Bodham Donne, ed., London: John Murray, 1867).

14. 22 Parl. Hist. 1048.

15. 2 Correspondence of King George the Third with Lord North at 414.

16. 22 Parl. Hist. 1214 (March 20, 1782).

17. Lord John Russell, 1 Memorials and Correspondence of Charles James Fox 295–96 (London: Richard Bentley, 1853).

18. Sir David Lindsay Keir, The Constitutional History of Modern Britain 299 (London: Adam & Charles Black, 1969).

19. Sir Lewis Namier, The Structure of Politics at the Accession of George III (London: Macmillan, 1965). Namier disputed the views of Whig historians such as Erskine May who saw George III as an ambitious innovator who had

increased the power of the crown. Thomas Erskine May, 1 The Constitutional History of England since the Accession of George the Third, 1760–1860 1–17 (London, 1896). A more nuanced view of the debate, closer in spirit to Namier than to the Whig historians, was taken by Richard Pares, King George III and the Politicians (Oxford U.P., 1953).

20. 11 Parl. Hist. 1302–03 (February 13, 1741).

21. In 1770 there were thought to be nearly two hundred such place-holders. George Veitch, The Genesis of Parliamentary Reform 21 (Hamden: Archon, 1965).

22. 2 Memorials and Correspondence of Charles James Fox 51–52 (Lord John Russell, ed., Philadelphia: Blanshard, 1853).

23. Stanley Ayling, George the Third 299 (New York: Knopf, 1972).

24. Henry Grattan, 4 Speeches 157 (London: Longman, Hurst, 1822).

25. Edward Gibbon, Memoirs of the Life of Edward Gibbon 190 (New York: Funk & Wagnalls, 1966).

26. 2 The Last Journals of Horace Walpole 496 (A. Francis Steuart, ed., London: Bodley Head, 1910).

27. John Heneage Jesse, 2 George Selwyn and his Contemporaries 227 (London: Richard Bentley, 1843).

28. Russell, 2 Memorials and Correspondence of Charles James Fox 220.

29. Letter to Lord North (December18, 1782), 6 The Correspondence of King George III from 1760 to December 1783 476 (Sir John Fortescue, ed., London: Macmillan, 1928).

30. 3 Nathaniel Wraxall, Historical and Posthumous Memoirs 636 (London: Cadell, 1819).

31. Amanda Foreman, Georgiana, Duchess of Devonshire ch. 9 (New York: Random House, 1998).

32. 24 Parl. Hist. 597 (February 18, 1784).

33. II.104.

34. Keir, supra n. 18 at 297.

35. The exchange of correspondence between Pitt and the King is in Earl Stanhope, 2 Life of the Right Honourable William Pitt, appendix at 457–64

(London: John Murray, 1879). See Donald Grove Barnes, George III and William Pitt, 1788–1806 368–81 (Stanford U.P., 1939).

36. William Cobbett, Rural Rides 102–03 (London: Penguin, 1985); see also Veitch at 3–4.

37. John Morley, 2 The Life of William Ewart Gladstone 88–92 (Toronto: Morang, 1903).

38. 18 Parl. Hist. 1287 (March 21, 1776).

39. Id. at 1293.

40. Id. at 1297.

41. George W. E. Russell, Sydney Smith 137 (London: Macmillan, 1905).

42. 25 Parl. Hist. 475 (April 18, 1785).

43. 28 Parl. Hist. 467.

44. 29 Parl. Hist. 1299 (April 30, 1792).

45 1 The Creevey Papers 287 (Sir Herbert Maxwell, ed., London: John Murray, 1903).

46. G. M. Trevelyan, Lord Grey and the Reform Bill 169 (New York: Longman, Green, 1920).

47. 60 Geo. III & 1 Geo. IV c. 6.

48. The Greville Memoirs: A Journal of the Reigns of King George IV and King William IV 219 (Henry Reeve, ed., London: Longmans, Green, 1875).

49. 1 John Morley, The Life of William Ewart Gladstone 72 (London: Macmillan, 1908).

50. Hansard, House of Lords, November 2, 1830, § 53.

51. 1 Morley 69.

52. Hansard, House of Commons, March 1, 1831 § 1077.

53. Trevelyan, supra n. 46 at 281–82. Cf. 1 Croker Papers 504 (Lewis Jennings, ed., New York: Scribner's, 1884).

54. The Life and Letters of Lord Macaulay 146–47 (G. O. Trevelyan, ed., London: Longmans, Green, 1881).

55. Trevelyan at 291.

56. Hansard, House of Lords, April 21, 1831, § 1741.

57. 2 Creevey Papers at 229.

58. Hansard, April 22, 1831 § 1831.

59. Id. at § 1832.

60. Trevelyan at 296.

61. Hansard, House of Lords, October 5, 1831, § 1307.

62. Hansard, House of Lords, October 4, 1831, § 1203.

63. Hansard, House of Lords, October 7, 1831 § 340.

64. Walter Bagehot, The English Constitution 80 (Oxford U.P., 2001); Edward Pearce, Reform! The Fight for the 1832 Reform Act 300 (London: Jonathan Cape, 2003).

65. Hansard, House of Lords, October 7, 1831 §§ 251–52.

66. Keir at 414, n. 5.

67. J. R. M. Butler, The Passing of the Great Reform Bill 228–29 (London: Longmans, Green, 1914).

68. Bagehot at 11.

69. Bagehot at 20.

CHAPTER 4: EXPORTING WESTMINSTER

1. 1867, 30–31 Vict., c. 3 (U.K.). In 1982, the BNA Act was amended and renamed the Constitution Act by the Constitution Act 1982, c. 11 (U.K.). The latter statute adopted a Charter of Rights and Freedoms and "patriated" the Canadian constitution through an amending formula that permitted constitutional change without recourse to the British Parliament.

2. This quickly became a matter of Canadian acquiescence rather than submission. Canada refused to participate in the 1885 relief of Khartoum, but sent two thousand volunteers to fight in the second Boer War. It alone decided the extent of its contribution to Britain's war effort in 1914. Formal independence came with the 1931 Statute of Westminster, which repealed the veto power over Canadian legislation that Westminster had retained under the 1865 Colonial Laws Validity Act. In practice, the veto power had been lost long before.

3. W. E. Gladstone, Kin Beyond the Sea, 127 North American Rev. 179, 185 (1878).

4. And yet something did come of it. In Art. III, § 2, cl. 1, the Constitution gave federal courts jurisdiction in cases between foreign subjects and

an American state *or* its citizens. That ousted Virginia's state courts in claims by British creditors against individual Virginia debtors, and as Virginians owed two-thirds of the new country's private debts, mostly to British creditors, and as Virginian state courts had done everything to prevent British creditors from recovering their debts, the provision sparked much of the antifederalist opposition to the Constitution in the Virginia ratifying debates. See Isaac Samuel Harrell, Loyalism in Virginia (Duke U.P., 1926). The provision was inserted at the last minute by the Committee on Unfinished Parts, which reported its draft on September 4, and seems to have slipped by the normally perspicacious George Mason at the Convention. On August 27 he had written in his notes that federal courts would have jurisdiction in cases between foreign subjects and "a State *and* the citizens thereof." The subsequent change from conjunctive to disjunctive made all the difference.

5. 23 Parl. Hist. 468, February 17, 1783.

6. To speak of a Second British Empire risks being misleading, since Britain's interest in its colonies waned during the thirty-year period beginning with the repeal of the Corn Laws, and since the Empire of Joseph Chamberlain bore little resemblance to that of Lord Durham. See Bernard Semmel, The Rise of Free Trade Imperialism: Classical Political Economy, the Empire of Free Trade and Imperialism 1750–1850 (Cambridge U.P., 1970).

7. 28 Parl. Hist. 1378, March 1, 1791.

8. Alan Taylor, The Civil War of 1812 37 (New York: Knopf, 2010).

9. J. Steven Watson, The Reign of George III 1760–1815 302 (Oxford U.P., 1960).

10. Constance MacRae-Buchanan, "American Influence on Canadian Constitutionalism," in Canadian Constitutionalism 1791–1991 145 (Jane Ajzenstat, ed., Ottawa: Canadian Study of Parliament Group, 1991).

11. 29 Parl. Hist. 112, April 8, 1791

12. 29 Parl. Hist. 107, April 1, 1791.

13. 29 Parl. Hist. 249, April 15, 1791.

14. 29 Parl. Hist. 387–88, May 6, 1791.

15. 29 Parl. Hist. 110, April 8, 1791).

16. Frederick Jackson Turner, The Frontier in American History (New York: Holt, 1921).

17. The best biography of Dorchester remains A. G. Bradley, Sir Guy Carleton (Toronto: University of Toronto, 1966).

18. Letter to the Duke of Portland, January 22, 1795, 3 The Correspondence of Lt. Gov. John Graves Simcoe 265 (E. A. Cruikshank, ed., Toronto: Ontario Historical Society, 1925) [hereafter "Simcoe Papers"].

19. Letter to the Duke of Portland, December 21, 1794, 3 Simcoe Papers at 235. See also Letter to Sir Joseph Banks, January 8, 1791, 1 Simcoe Papers at 17.

20. Letter to Evan Nepean, December 3, 1789, 1 Simcoe Papers at 7.

21. Duc de la Rochefoucauld-Liancourt, Travels through the United States of North America, the Country of the Iroquois, and Upper Canada 208 (London: Philips, 1799).

22. The Letters of Charles Dickens 236, May 12, 1842 (Oxford U.P., 1974).

23. On Mackenzie, see William Kilbourn, The Firebrand: William Lyon Mackenzie and the Rebellion in Upper Canada (Toronto: Clarke, Irwin, 1956); John Sewell, Mackenzie: A Political Biography of William Lyon Mackenzie (Toronto: Lorimer, 2002).

24. Francis Bond Head, A Narrative 34–35 (London: Clowe, 1839).

25. Id. at 31.

26. Patrick Brode, Sir John Beverley Robinson: Bone and Sinew of the Compact 195 (U. Toronto P., 1984).

27. The Seventh Report from the Select Committee of the House of Assembly of Upper Canada on Grievances iii (Toronto: Reynolds, 1832).

28. Sydney W. Jackman, Galloping Head: A Biography of Sir Francis Bond Head 1793–1875 118 (London: Phoenix House, 1958); David Cecil, Melbourne 306 (London: Reprint Society, 1955).

29. While Durham was ably assisted by two remarkable aides, Charles Buller and Edward Gibbon Wakefield, both leading colonial reformers, he is nevertheless taken to be the author of the report. Stuart J. Reid, 2 Life and

Letters of the First Earl of Durham 1792–1840 338–41 (London: Longmans, Green, 1906).

30. Michael S. Cross, Robert Baldwin: The Morning Star of Memory 36 (Don Mills: Oxford U.P., 2012).

31. G. M. Trevelyan, British History in the Nineteenth Century (1782–1901) 260 (London: Longmans, Green, 1922).

32. Thomas Storrow Brown, Brief Sketch of the Life and Times of the Hon. Louis Joseph Papineau, Dominion Monthly, January 1872, at 11.

33. Lord Durham's Report 50 (G. M. Craig, ed., McGill-Queens U.P., 2007). Did this mean Bagehot's efficient secret, with a figurehead governor general and an executive composed of a prime minister and his cabinet? That was the result, as soon as responsible government became a reality, but was this what Durham intended? In his report, he spoke of the need for "an executive sufficiently powerful to curb popular excesses," id. at 80, and Janet Ajzenstat suggests that what Durham wanted was something closer to Pitt's constitution than that of Bagehot. The Political Thought of Lord Durham 60–66 (McGill-Queen's U.P., 1988). However, Durham knew that in Britain the reins of power were held by the prime minister, and not the Queen; and as the country's leading reformer, whose hero was Fox, he would not have wanted it otherwise. If the Canadian constitution was to be modeled on that of Britain, then, it is likely that Durham expected that the executive power in Canada would be exercised by a Canadian prime minister. The "popular excesses" Durham feared were likely those of a French-Canadian electorate, for which he had a different solution.

34. Lord Durham's Report at 137.

35. Id. at 149.

36. Id. at 13.

37. The Whig tradition in Canada, which sees responsible government and the BNA Act as the work of Canadian radicals who wrested self-government from hidebound British imperialists, is a misleading caricature. See Ged Martin, Britain and the Origins of Canadian Confederation, 1837–67 (Vancouver: U.B.C.P., 1995). On the movement for responsible government, see W. L. Morton, The Kingdom of Canada: A General History from Earliest Times 241–45, 252–68 (Toronto: McClelland and Stewart, 1963).

38. 105 Hansard §§ 566–67, May 16, 1849.

39. "Self-government would be utterly annihilated if the views of the Imperial Government were to be preferred to those of the people of Canada. It is, therefore, the duty of the present Government distinctly to affirm the right of the Canadian Legislature to adjust the taxation of the people in the way they deem best, even if it should unfortunately happen to meet with the disapproval of the Imperial Ministry." Report of the [Canadian] Minister of Finance, Sir Alexander Galt, October 25, 1859, in 2 Selected Speeches and Documents on British Colonial Policy 1763–1917 60 (A. B. Keith, ed., Oxford U.P., 1918).

40. Earl of Malmesbury, Memoirs of an Ex-Minister 260–61 (London: Longmans, Green, 1885) (letter to Lord Malmesbury, August 13, 1852).

41. 1 The Elgin-Grey Papers 351–52 (Sir Arthur Doughty, ed., May 18, 1849, Ottawa: Patenaude, 1937).

42. Quoted in H. E. Egerton and W. L. Grant, Canadian Constitutional Development 300 (London: John Murray, 1907).

43. 1 The Elgin-Grey Papers at 378 (July 5, 1849).

44. Charlottetown Vindicator, September 7, 1864, in Confederation, 1854–1867 80 (P. B. Waite, ed., Toronto: Holt, Rinehart, 1972).

45. J. K. Chapman, The Career of Arthur Hamilton Gordon, First Lord Stanmore 1829–1912 4 (U. Toronto P., 1964).

46. Id. at 6.

47. Id. at 9.

48. See W. L. Morton, The Critical Years: The Union of British North America 1857–1873 113 (Toronto: McClelland and Stewart, 1964).

49. Goldwin Smith, Canada and the Canadian Question 143 (London: Macmillan, 1891).

50. When the Quebec Conference concluded, Brown excitedly wrote to his wife "All right!!! . . . French Canadianism entirely extinguished!" J. M. S. Careless, Brown of the Globe: Statesman of Confederation 171 (Toronto: Macmillan, 1963).

51. Goldwin Smith, Reminiscences 433 (New York: Macmillan, 1910).

52. Id. at 430.

53. 2 Joseph Pope, I Memoirs of Sir John Alexander Macdonald 276 (London: Edward Arnold, 1894).

54. Gwyn, 1 John A. at 267.

55. Macdonald was nevertheless an early supporter of extending the franchise to women. 2 Pope at 247 note.

56. Emerson Bristol Biggar, Anecdotal Life of Sir John Macdonald 191 (Montreal: John Lovell, 1891).

57. Edward Whelan, The Union of the British Provinces 9 (Charlottetown: Haszard, 1865).

58. P. B. Waite, The Life and Times of Confederation 1864–67 86–87 (Toronto: Robin Brass, 2001).

59. P. B. Waite, Edward Whelan Reports from the Quebec Conference, 42 Canadian Hist. Rev. 23, 36 (1961).

60. Id. at 41.

61. Parliamentary Debates of the Subject of Confederation of the British North American Provinces 34 (Quebec: Hunter, Rose, 1865) [hereafter "Confederation Debates"].

62. The Economist, 23 February 1867, at 203.

63. Confederation, being a series of hitherto unpublished documents bearing upon the British North America Act 55–56 (Joseph Pope, ed., Toronto: Carswell, 1895) [hereafter "Confederation Documents"].

64. Confederation Debates at 44.

65. Confederation Documents at 39.

66. Pope at 318–19.

67. Confederation Documents at 77.

68. Confederation Debates at 32.

69. Id. at 89.

70. John Mercer Johnson, New Brunswick House of Assembly, July 2, 1866, in Canada's Founding Debates 179–80 (Janet Ajzenstat et al., eds., U. Toronto P., 2003).

71. Confederation Debates at 132.

72. W. Stewart Wallace, The United Empire Loyalists 58 (Toronto: Glasgow, Brook, 1914).

73. While they were opposed to slavery, many Canadians were pro-Southern (or at least anti-Northern) in their sympathies. Before the Civil War, Southern senators had supported free trade with Canada and opposed its annexation into the United States. By 1864, with the South on its knees before an enormous Union army, the Canadians could not help but wonder what plans a stronger and aggressive America had for Canada. See Robin W. Winks, Canada and the United States: The Civil War Years 207–10 (McGill-Queen's U.P., 1998); John Boyko, Blood and Daring: How Canada Fought the American Civil War and Forged a Nation (Toronto: Knopf Canada, 2013).

74. Confederation Debates at 33.

75. Id. at 37.

76. Id. at 270–71. Macdonald cited Bagehot in a letter to the Nova Scotia lieutenant governor as a sure guide regarding his duties. Correspondence of Sir John Macdonald, July 29, 1884, at 316 (Sir Joseph Pope, ed., Toronto: Doubleday, Page, 1921).

77. The Economist, 23 February 1867, at 204. As a free trader, noted Christopher Moore, Bagehot would naturally have welcomed competition. Moore at 215.

78. For the letters to Arthur Hamilton Gordon, see Documents on the Confederation of British North America 174, 178 (G. P. Browne, ed., McGill-Queen's U.P., 2009).

79. Letter to Baron Knutsford, July18, 1889, Macdonald Correspondence at 451.

80. 185 House of Commons Debates, February 28, 1867, c. 1196.

81. Waite at 125.

CHAPTER FIVE: THE RISE OF CROWN GOVERNMENT

1. "Crown" is an ambiguous term. Used by John Dunning, it referred to George III. More generally, it refers to the state as a whole. For example, Canadian criminal prosecutions are styled R. (or Regina) v. _____ and are argued for the state by Crown attorneys. See Geoffrey Marshall, Constitutional Theory

17–27 (Oxford U.P., 1971). As I use the term, it refers to the executive, be he president or prime minister.

2. Theodore J. Lowi. The Personal President: Power Invested, Promise Unfulfilled xi (Cornell U.P., 1985).

3. Arthur M. Schlesinger Jr., The Imperial Presidency. Not to be outdone, conservative writers at the Heritage Foundation detected an even more serious threat than the imperial presidency of the Reagan administration. See The Imperial Congress: Crisis in the Separation of Powers (Gordon S. Jones and John A. Mariani, eds., New York: Pharos, 1988). For the most partisan of writers, the Michael Savages and Bruce Ackermans, the contest is always between the forces of light and darkness, between the moral heroes on Our Side ("anything but imperial") and the criminals on Their Side (with their "scandalous," "flagrant abuses" and "shocking outbreak of presidential illegality"). Bruce Ackerman, The Decline and Fall of the American Republic 5, 115, 143 (Harvard U.P., 2010).

4. Richard E. Neustadt, Presidential Power and the Modern Presidents xvi (New York: Free Press, 1990). James MacGregor Burns had also argued for expanded presidential power when the Democrats were comfortably in power. The Deadlock of Democracy: Four-Party Politics in America (Englewood Cliffs: Prentice Hall, 1963).

5. Susan R. Johnson, Ronald E. Neumann, and Thomas R. Pickering, Bring back professional diplomacy, Washington Post, April 12, 2013, at A13.

6. The Obama administration is heavily reliant on czars, and Judicial Watch lists more than forty of them. President Obama's Czars, Judicial Watch, September 15, 2011.

7. John Hicks, At House Hearing, Treasury IG Defends Audit of IRS Practices, Washington Post, July 19, 2013, at A16.

8. Dodd-Frank Wall Street Reform and Consumer Protection Act, Pub. L. 111–203, 124 Stat. 1376 (2010).

9. A federal court dismissed the lawsuit brought by the AIG minority shareholder, which was owned by the former AIG CEO, "Hank" Greenberg. Starr International Co. v. Federal Reserve Bank of New York, ___ F.3d ___ (E.D.N.Y., November 19, 2012). A subsequent action, based on the Takings Clause of the Constitution, is proceeding through the courts. See Editorial, That

AIG Lawsuit, Wall Street Journal, January 10, 2013. Hank Greenberg tells his side of the story in Maurice R. Greenberg and Lawrence A. Cunningham, The AIG Story 243–60 (Hoboken: John Wiley & Sons, 2013).

10. At http://bigthink.com/ideas/17844. See John A. Allison, The Financial Crisis and the Free Market Cure: How Destructive Banking Reform Is Killing the Economy 170–73 (New York: McGraw Hill, 2013).

11. Id. at § 1031(b), 124 Stat. at 2006.

12. Id. at § 1403(c)(3).

13. Consumer Financial Protection Bureau, Consumer Financial Protection Bureau to pursue discriminatory lenders, April 18, 2012, at http://www.consumerfinance.gov/pressreleases/consumer-financial-protection-bureau-to-pursue-discriminatory-lenders/. See also John Carney, Obama Administration Pressuring Banks to Lower Standards, CNBC, July 15, 2011, at http://www.cnbc.com/id/43768290/Obama_Administration_Pressuring_Banks_to_Lower_Standards.

14. Rosalind S. Helderman, Democrats urge Obama to bypass GOP on debt, Washington Post, January 12, 2013, at A4.

15. Paul Krugman, Death Panels and Sales Taxes, New York Times, November 14, 2010.

16. 5 USC § 553(b)(3)(B)

17. General Accounting Office, Agencies Could Take Additional Steps to Respond to Public Comments, GAO 13-21 (December 2012).

18. John M. Broder, Powerful Shaper of U.S. Rules Quits, With Critics in Wake, New York Times, August 3, 2012.

19. On the two models, see Steven F. Hayward, The EPA is Politicized—So Make It Official, Wall Street Journal, January 9, 2013, at A11.

20. Massachusetts v. EPA, 549 U.S. 497 (2007).

21. Coalition for Responsible Regulation v. EPA, ___ F.3d ___ (D.C. Cir., June 26, 2012).

22. See Phillip J. Cooper, By Order of the President: The Use and Abuse of Executive Direct Action (U.P. Kansas, 2002); Peter M. Shane, Madison's Nightmare: How Executive Power Threatens American Democracy 153–55 (U. Chicago P., 2009); Elena Kagan, Presidential Administration, 114 Harv. L. Rev. 2245, 2251 (1991).

23. James Bennet, True to Form, Clinton Shifts Energies Back to U.S. Focus, New York Times, July 5, 1998. See Kenneth R. Mayer, With a Stroke of the Pen: Executive Orders and Presidential Power 132 (Princeton U.P., 2001).

24. See James Q. Wilson, Bureaucracy: What Government Agencies Do and Why They Do It 254–56 (New York: Basic Books, 1989) (reviewing the literature); Terry M. Moe, An Assessment of the Positive Theory of "Congressional Dominance," 12 Legis. Stud. Q. 475 (1987); Douglas Kreiner, Can Enhanced Oversight Repair the "Broken Branch," 89 B.U. L. Rev. 765 (2009).

25. 295 U.S. 495 (1935). See F. H. Buckley, The Morality of Laughter 134–27 (U. Michigan P., 2003).

26. For a rare such case, see South Dakota v. United States, 69 F.3d 878 (8th Cir. 1995), vacated on other grounds, 106 F.3d 247 (8th Cir. 1996). Such cases are very much the exception. See, e.g., Whitman v. American Trucking Associations, Inc., 531 U.S. 457 (2001) (reversing the D.C. Circuit on the nondelegation doctrine). The nondelegation doctrine has also been invoked as a rule of construction, to narrow the scope of Congress's grant of authority to an agency. See National Cable Television Ass'n v. United States, 415 U.S. 336 (1974).

27. There is an extensive legal literature on how the abandonment of the nondelegation doctrine has led to the decline of the separation of powers doctrine. See Larry Alexander and Saikrishna Prakash, Delegation Really Running Riot, 93 Va. L. Rev. 1035 (2007); Ken I. Kersch, Constructing Civil Liberties: Discontinuities in the Development of American Constitutional Law 112 (Cambridge U.P., 2004); Lowi at 143–44. See generally Ronald D. Rotunda and John E. Nowak, Constitutional Law §§ 2.7(c), 3.12(a), 4.7(a),(b), 4.8,(b),(c) (8th ed. Thomson-West, St. Paul, Minn. 2010).

28. 529 U.S. 120 (2000). A subsequent Congress reversed this decision and gave the FDA the authority to regulate the tobacco industry. Family Smoking Prevention and Tobacco Control Act, 123 Stat. 1776–1858 (2009).

29. Patricia Wald, The Contributions of the D.C. Court to Administrative Law, 40 Admin. L. Rev. 507, 528 (1988).

30. Chevron U.S.A. Inc. v. Natural Resources Defense Council, Inc., 467 U.S. 837 (1984).

31. Under the Administrative Procedure Act, 5 USC § 706(2)(a).

32. __ F.3d ___ (D.C. Cir., January 25, 2013). Before applying the Chevron standard, a court must determine whether Congress did indeed delegate to the agency the authority to make the rule in question. If, as in Brown & Williamson, it did not, the Chevron standard is ousted and courts are more willing to question the rule. See United States v. Mead Corp., 533 U.S. 218 (2001). This has been described as a "Chevron step zero enquiry." See Cass Sunstein, Chevron Step Zero, 92 Va. L. Rev. 187 (2001).

33. Eric A. Posner and Adrian Vermeule, The Executive Unbound: After the Madisonian Republic 98 (Oxford U.P., 2010). See, e.g., Balt. Gas & Electric Co. v. Natural Res. Def. Council, Inc., 462 U.S. 87 (1983).

34. 272 U.S. 52 (1926).

35. 478 U.S. 714 (1986).

36. In Bowsher, Chief Justice Burger adopted the warning a few of the Framers had made about the threat of legislative domination, as the court had earlier done in Buckley v. Valeo, 424 U.S. 1, 129 n. 166 (1976).

37. 295 U.S. 602 (1935). Humphrey's Executor was followed in the Independent Counsel case, Morrison v. Olson, 487 U.S. 654 (1988).

38. 130 S. Ct. 3138 (2010).

39. 462 U.S. 919 (1983). The court also invoked the presentment clause of Art. I, § 7, cl. 2 ("Every Bill which shall have passed the House of Representatives and the Senate, shall, before it becomes a law, be presented to the President of the United States . . .").

40. Sean D. Croston, Congress and the Courts Close Their Eyes: The Continuing Abdication of the Duty to Review Agencies' Noncompliance with the Congressional Review Act, 62 Admin. L. Rev. 907 (2010).

41. Morris at II.29 and II.76, Wilson at II.30 and II.501 and James Madison at II.34–35, II.52–53 and II.74.

42. I.292.

43. I.195, 200.

44. Roll call 510 at II.583.

45. Statement, June 24, 2009, at http://www.presidency.ucsb.edu/ws/index.php?pid=86345.

46. As argued by the Office of Legal Counsel, 18 Op. O.L.C. 199, 200–03 (1994).

47. Hamdi v. Rumsfeld, 542 U.S. 507 (2004) (U.S. citizens detained indefinitely may challenge their "enemy combatant" status before an impartial judge); Hamdan v. Rumsfeld, 548 U.S. 557 (2006) (impeaching procedures of military commissions set up to try terrorists). See generally James P. Pfiffner, Power Play: The Bush Presidency and the Constitution 194–228 (Washington: Brookings, 2008).

48. Development, Relief, and Education for Alien Minors Act of 2011, H.R. 1842.IH.

49. Steve Hendrix, Application Process Starts for Residency Hopefuls, Washington Post, August 15, 2012, at A3 (quoting Luis Gutierrez (D-Ill.).

50. Robert Rector and Kiki Bradley, Obama Guts Welfare Reform, Heritage Foundation (July 12, 2012) at http://blog.heritage.org/2012/07/12/obama-guts-welfare-reform/.

51. Sam Baker, Baucus warns of 'huge train wreck' enacting ObamaCare provisions, The Hill, April 17, 2013.

52. Raines v. Byrd, 521 U.S. 811 (1997).

53. Robert Pear, Health Law Waivers Draw Kudos, and Criticism, New York Times, March 19, 2011. See Richard Epstein, Government by Waiver, National Affairs, Spring 2011.

54. Joseph Story, 3 Commentaries on the Constitution § 1342 (Boston: Hilliard, Gray, 1833).

55. Pub. L. 93–344, 88 Stat. 297, 31 U. S. C. § 1301 et seq. (1970 ed., Supp. IV).

56. Train v. New York, 420 U.S. 35 (1975).

57. Mark Matthews, Bolden: NASA legit as it readies to end moon program, Orlando Sentinel, February 23, 2010.

58. Andy Sullivan, House bans some earmarks amid ethics concerns, Reuters, March 10, 2010.

59. The American Recovery and Reinvestment Act of 2009, Pub. L. No. 111–5, 123 Stat. 115.

60. The Solyndra Mess, New York Times, November 24, 2011.

61. Eric Lipton and Matthew L. Wald, E-Mails Reveal Early White House Worries Over Solyndra, New York Times, October 3, 2011.

62. David M. Herszenhorn and David E. Sanger, Senate Abandons Automaker Bailout Bid, New York Times, December 11, 2008.

63. See Gary Lawson, Burying the Constitution Under a TARP, 33 Harv. J. Law & Pub. Policy 55 (2010).

64. See Office of the Special Inspector General of the Troubled Asset Relief Program, Factors Affecting the Decisions of General Motors and Chrysler to Reduce their Dealership Networks, July 19, 2010, at 18, at http://www.sigtarp .gov/Audit%20Reports/Factors%20Affecting%20the%20Decisions%20of%20 General%20Motors%20and%20Chrysler%20to%20Reduce%20Their%20 Dealership%20Networks%207_19_2010.pdf.

65. James Sherk and Todd Zywicki, Obama's United Auto Workers Bailout, Wall Street Journal, June 13, 2012.

66. David Skeel, The New Financial Deal: Understanding the Dodd-Frank Act and Its (Unintended) Consequences 35 (Hoboken: John Wiley, 2011).

67. John R. Lott, At the Brink 117–22 (Washington: Regnery, 2013).

68. See I.65, II.318 (Charles Pinckney); III.250, Debates in the South Carolina Legislature, January 16, 1788 (Pierce Butler).

69. III.250.

70. Id.

71. I.300 (notes of Robert Yates).

72. I.363 (William Johnson).

73. William G. Howell and Jon C. Pevehouse, While Dangers Gather: Congressional Checks on Presidential War Powers ch. 3 (Princeton U.P., 2007). But see David Brulé, Congressional Opposition, the Economy, and U.S. Dispute Initiation 1946–2000, 50 J. Conflict Res. 463 (2006).

74. Elana Schor, Senate Democrats backtrack, opt not to tackle Iraq in 9/11 Commission bill, The Hill, February 28, 2007.

75. James W. Pindell and Rick Klein, Obama defends votes in favor of Iraq funding, Boston Globe, March 22, 2007.

76. 50 U.S.C. §§ 1541–48 (1973).

77. In Dellums v. Bush, 752 F. Supp. 1141 (D.C., 1990), the court stated that the first President Bush lacked the power to begin military operations against Iraq without congressional approval, but refused to grant relief because Congress as a whole had not sought the injunction.

78. http://clerk.house.gov/evs/1999/roll049.xml.

79. Howell and Pevehouse at 67–70.

80. The same agility in performing a volte-face can be observed in constitutional scholars who "voted for it before they voted against it." See, e.g., Harold H. Koh, Presidential War and Congressional Consent: The Law Professors' Memorandum in Dellums v. Bush, 27 Stan. J. Int'l L. 247 (1991); Eric Posner, Stop Complaining About Harold Koh's Interpretation of the War Powers Act, The New Republic, July 1, 2011.

81. Marc Lacey, Look at the Place! Sudan Says, 'Say Sorry,' but U.S. Won't, New York Times, October 20, 2005.

82. Charles W. Ostrom and Brian Job, The President and the Political Use of Force, 80 Am. Pol. Sc. Rev. 541 (1986); Patrick James and John R. Oneal, The Influence of Domestic and International Politics on the President's Use of Force, 35 J. Conflict Resolution 307 (1991); Gregory D. Hess and Athanasios Orphanides, War Politics: An Economic Rational-Voter Framework, 85 Am. Econ. Rev. 842 (1995).

83. See Howell and Pevehouse at 65–66, tables 3.2 and 3.3; Jong Hee Park, Structural Change in U.S. Presidents' Use of Force, 54 Am. J. Pol. Sc. 766 (2010).

84. Charlie Savage and Mark Landler, White House Defends Continuing U.S. Role in Libya Operation, New York Times, June 15, 2011.

85. On occasion, prime ministers have publicly announced major policy changes within a minister's department before the minister has been told of them. Eddie Goldenberg, How It Works 118–19 (Toronto: McClelland and Stewart, 2006).

86. Donald J. Savoie, Court Government and the Collapse of Accountability in Canada and the United Kingdom (U. Toronto P., 2008). Something like this has also happened in Britain. Strong prime ministers routinely dominate their cabinets and disregard its advice. Michael Heseltine once described

a cabinet meeting at which he lost a vote by 17 to 1, 17 ministers for him and only Margaret Thatcher against. Christopher Foster, British Government in Crisis 92 (Oxford: Hart, 2005). See Richard Heffernan and Paul Webb, "The British Prime Minister: Much More Than 'First Among Equals'," in Thomas Poguntke and Paul D. Webb, The Presidentialization of Politics: A Comparative Study of Modern Democracies 26 (Oxford U.P., 2005).

87. Gordon Robertson, Memoirs of a Very Civil Servant: Mackenzie King to Pierre Trudeau 256 (U. Toronto P., 2000). As the power of cabinet ministers declined, so too did the concept of ministerial responsibility, under which ministers bore strict responsibility for misbehavior in their department even if they had no knowledge of it and were not personally at fault. The last cabinet minister in Britain or Canada so to resign was Lord Carrington in 1982, over his department's failure to anticipate the Falklands crisis.

88. John Hart, The Presidential Branch 120 (Oxford: Pergamon, 1987); Charles O. Jones, The Presidency in a Separated System 100 (Washington: Brookings, 1994).

89. Id. at 257. Structural differences between the bureaucracy in Canada and the United States explain the importance of the PCO. The entire Canadian civil service is made up of permanent appointees. When a new administration is elected in Washington, however, four thousand political appointees lose their jobs.

90. Theodore J. Lowi, The End of Liberalism: Ideology, Policy, and the Crisis of Public Authority 2–3 (New York: W. W. Norton, 1969).

91. The trend began as early as 1945, when Gordon Robertson moved from the Department of External Affairs to the Prime Minister's Office. Robertson at 47. Later, Derek Burney left the Department of External Affairs to become Brian Mulroney's Chief of Staff at the PMO. Arnold Heeney and Jack Pickersgill made the reverse move, from the PMO to the PCO, in 1940 and 1952, respectively.

92. Gregory Tardi, "Departments and Other Institutions of Government," in The Handbook of Canadian Public Administration 25, 32 (Christopher Dunn, ed., Don Mills: Oxford U.P., 2010).

93. P.-E. Trudeau, Memoirs 115 (Toronto: McClelland and Stewart, 1993).

94. Paul Martin, Hell or High Water: My Life in and out of Politics 244–45 (Toronto: McClelland and Stewart, 2008).

95. Corinne Reilly, In congressional races, underdogs abound, but why?, Washington Post, October 2, 2012.

96. The Spirit of the Laws VIII.16.

97. Jean-Jacques Rousseau, Social Contract III.2 (Cambridge U.P., 1997).

98. Christopher DeMuth, The Regulatory State, 12 National Affairs 70 (2012).

99. David Lieberman, The Province of Legislation Determined: Legal Theory in Eighteenth Century Britain (Cambridge U.P., 1989).

100. Jeremy Bentham, A Comment on the Commentaries (with A Fragment on Government) 119–20 (J. H. Burns and H. L. A. Hart, eds., London: Athlone, 1977). See also Gerald J. Postema, Bentham and the Common Law Tradition (Oxford U.P., 1986).

101. Max Weber, 2 Economy and Society 956–58 (U. California P., 1968). That's not to say that Weber thought that bureaucrats would govern in so neutral a fashion, since their expertise would make them difficult to second-guess. Id. at 991–92. On the reception of scientific planning in government in America, chiefly through Herbert Croly and The New Republic, see Samuel Haber, Efficiency and Uplift: Scientific Management in the Progressive Era, 1890–1920 86–90 (U. Chicago P., 1964). Weber's scientific expert was also the hero of the most influential early work in the developing field of administrative law. See James M. Landis, The Administrative Process 23–24 (Yale U.P., 1938).

102. G. W. F. Hegel, Philosophy of Right §§ 225–27, 289–95 (T. M. Knox trans.) (Oxford U.P., 1952). See Carl K. Y. Shaw, Hegel's Theory of Modern Bureaucracy, 86 Am. Pol. Sc. Rev. 381 (1992). The same point was made earlier in Pascal's distinction between the *esprit de finesse* and the *esprit de géométrie*, and a century later by Henri Bergson, The Two Sources of Morality and Religion (Notre Dame U.P., 1979).

103. David A. Fahrenthold, Watch him pull a USDA-mandated rabbit disaster plan out of his hat, Washington Post, July16, 2013.

104. See, e.g., William A. Niskanen, Bureaucracy and Representative Government (Chicago: Aldine, Atherton, 1971).

105. Henry I. Miller and David R. Henderson, The FDA's Risky Risk-Aversion, Policy Review 5 (October-November 2007).

106. A process described by the then New Dealer, James Burnham, The Managerial Revolution (Indiana U.P., 1966).

107. Lord Hewart, The New Despotism 77 (London: Ernest Benn, 1929).

108. John G. Nicolay and John Hay, 2 Abraham Lincoln 286–87 (New York: Century, 1890).

109. Richard Nixon, RN: The Memoirs of Richard Nixon 219 (New York: Grosset & Dunlap, 1978).

110. Trudeau, Memoirs at 99.

111. Jim Vanderhei and Mike Allen, Obama, the Puppet Master, Politico, February 18, 2013.

112. Joseph Schumpeter, Capitalism, Socialism and Democracy 138 (New York: Harper & Row, 1950).

113. Carl Schmitt, Political Theology, Four Chapters on the Concept of Sovereignty 5 (George Schwab, trans., U. Chicago P., 2005). See John P. McCormick, "The Dilemmas of Dictatorship: Carl Schmitt and Constitutional Emergency Powers," in Law as Politics: Carl Schmitt's Critique of Liberalism 217, 231–34 (David Dyzenhaus, ed., Duke U.P., 1998).

114. Jan-Werner Müller, A Dangerous Mind: Carl Schmitt in Post-War European Thought 2 (Yale U.P., 2003).

115. Alan B. Krueger, At FEMA, Disasters and Politics Go Hand in Hand, New York Times, September 15, 2005.

116. Thomas A. Garret and Russell S. Sobel, The Political Economy of FEMA Disaster Payments, 46 Economic Inquiry 496 (2003); Thomas A. Garrett, Thomas L. Marsh, and Maria I. Marshall, Political Allocation of Agriculture Disaster Payments in the 1990s, 26 Int'l Rev. Law and Econ. 143 (2006).

117. See Arthur S. Miller, Constitutional Law: Crisis Government Becomes the Norm, 39 Ohio St. L.J. 736 (1978).

118. Emergencies Act, R.S.C., 1985, c. 22 (4th Supp.), § 58.

119. A. V. Dicey, Introduction to the Study of the Law of the Constitution 19 (Indianapolis: Liberty Fund, 1982).

120. Eric Posner and Adrian Vermeule label this the "deferential" view of constitutional governance during wartime. Eric A. Posner and Adrian Vermeule, Terror in the Balance: Security, Liberty, and the Courts (Oxford U.P., 2007).

CHAPTER SIX: AMERICAN EXCEPTIONALISM

1. Byron York, Poll: Americans Believe in American Exceptionalism, Not as Sure about Obama, Washington Examiner, December 22, 2010.

2. At http://www.heritage.org/index/.

3. At http://www.cato.org/pubs/efw/.

4. Economist Intelligence Unit Index of Democracy 2011: Democracy under Stress at https://www.eiu.com/.

5. Canada's Founding Debates 16 (Janet Ajzenstat et al., eds., Toronto: Stoddard, 2003).

6. Benjamin Constant, "The Liberty of the Ancients Compared with that of the Moderns," in Political Writings 307 (Cambridge U.P., 1988).

7. Pippa Norris, Driving Democracy: Do Power-Sharing Institutions Work? 56, 61–71, 152–53 (Cambridge U.P., 2008).

8. At http://www.freedomhouse.org/report-types/freedom-world.

9. George Tsebelis, Veto Players: How Political Institutions Work (Princeton U.P., 2002).

10. Larry Diamond, The Democratic Rollback: The Resurgence of the Predatory State, 87 Foreign Affairs 36 (2008).

11. Economist Intelligence Unit Index of Democracy 2011 at 3.

12. I used the data provided by Arthur S. Banks, User's Manual, Cross-National Time-Series Data Archive 2011. In categorizing countries by types of regime, however, I listed Macedonia, Poland, and Switzerland as parliamentary. If a country was once presidential (e.g., Nigeria) or parliamentary (e.g., Turkey) and thereafter became undemocratic, I list it by its former type of government, since that is precisely the relationship of interest.

13. Maurice Duverger, A New Political System Model: Semi-Presidential Government, 8 European J. Political Res. 165 (1980).

14. Alan Siaroff, Comparative Presidencies: The Inadequacy of the Presidential, Semi-presidential and Parliamentary Distinction, 42 European J. Political Res. 287 (2003); Steven D. Roper, Are all Semipresidential Regimes the Same? A Comparison of Premier-Presidential Regimes, 34 Comparative Politics 253 (2002).

15. Juan J. Linz, "Presidential or Parliamentary Democracy: Does It Make a Difference?," in The Failure of Presidential Democracy: The Case of Latin America (Juan J. Linz and Arturo Valenzuela, eds., Johns Hopkins U.P., 1994). See also Arend Lijphart, Constitutional Design for Divided Societies, 15 J. Democracy 96 (2004); Matthew Shugart and Stephan Haggard, "Institutions and Public Policy in Presidential Systems," in President, Parliaments, and Policy 82 (Stephan Haggard and Matthew McCubbins, eds., Cambridge U.P., 2001).

16. See David R. Mayhew, Divided We Govern: Party Control, Lawmaking, and Investigations, 1946–2002 76 (Yale U.P., 2005).

17. José Antonio Cheibub, Presidentialism, Parliamentarism, and Democracy (Cambridge U.P., 2007). But see Norris at 154–55.

18. Adam Przeworski, "Self-Enforcing Democracy," in Oxford Handbook of Political Economy 312 (Donald Wittman and Barry Weingast, eds., Oxford U.P., 2006).

19. Adam Przeworski et al., Democracy and Development: Political Institutions and Well-Being in the World, 1950–1990 98 (Cambridge U.P., 2000). The authors report that historical factors specific to each country crucially explain the relation between democracy and economic development, and that on a fixed-effects model there is no evidence that one causes the other. See also Daron Acemoğlu et al., Income and Democracy, 98 Am. Econ. Rev. 808 (2008). However, Epstein et al. challenge Przeworski et al.'s findings with a three-way rather than a dichotomous characterization of regimes. David L. Epstein, Robert Bates, Jack Goldstone, Ida Kristensen, and Sharyn O'Halloran, Democratic Transitions, 50 Am. J. Pol. Sc. 551 (2006).

20. The Gini data were compiled from the CIA World Fact Book, since other cross-country data sets are problematic. The World Bank data use both

income and consumption metrics as well as individual and household methodologies, without clarifying what metric and methodology is employed. By contrast, the CIA data are consistently based on family income. I averaged the data for each country and extrapolated through the entire period.

21. Daron Acemoğlu and James A. Robinson, Economic Origins of Dictatorship and Democracy 58–61, Figure 3.15 (Cambridge U.P., 2006). As the authors note, however, the empirical literature on the relationship between inequality and democracy is mixed.

22. Torsten Persson and Guido Tabellini, Democratic Capital: The Nexus of Political and Economic Change, 1 Am. Econ. Rev.: Macroeconomics 88 (2009).

23. Culture Matters: How Values Shape Human Progress xiii (Lawrence E. Harrison and Samuel Huntington, eds., New York: Basic Books, 2000).

24. Seymour Martin Lipset and Jason M. Lakin, The Democratic Century ch. 11 (U. Oklahoma P., 2004).

25. Among poor countries, ex-British colonies are more likely to be stable democracies. Christopher Clague, Suzanne Gleason, and Stephen Knack, Determinants of Lasting Democracy in Poor Countries: Culture, Development, and Institutions, 573 Annals of the Academy of Social Sc. 16 (2001). Less plausibly, "legal origins" explanations of economic development claim that the British common law system made the difference, when compared with the civil law systems of the Continent. Rafael La Porta et al., The Economic Consequences of Legal Origins, 46 J. Econ. Lit. 285 (2008). Apart from personal property-secured lending law, however, the differences between the two kinds of legal systems are largely theoretical.

26. Acemoğlu and Robinson at 54, Figure 3.7.

27. However, it has been suggested that presidential regimes were chosen in the former Soviet Union because Communist Party leaders sought to retain dictatorial control. Gerald M. Easter, Preference for Presidentialism: Postcommunist Regime Change in Russia and the NIS, 49 World Politics 184 (1997). That's not a compelling argument for presidential rule.

28. Polybius, III The Histories 383 at vi.50 (Cambridge: Loeb, 2011). Montesquieu had a different explanation for the warlike tendency of republics.

Secure in his tenure, a supine monarch might relax in comfortable idleness. A Roman consul, on the other hand, had only a limited time to make his mark, and "not being able to obtain the honor of a triumph, except by a conquest or a victory, made war with an extreme impetuosity." Les causes de la grandeur des Romains, in 2 Œuvres complètes 72–73 (Paris: Gallimard, 1951).

29. As such, I considered that NATO countries faced an enemy from the date they joined the alliance until the fall of communism, and from 2002–10 (since Article V of the Nato Treaty had been invoked after 9/11). Other countries that I considered to have enemies were Taiwan, Egypt, Georgia, India, South Korea, Pakistan, Poland, and the Ukraine. I did not list Russia as possessing an enemy.

30. John Yoo, The Powers of War and Peace: The Constitution and Foreign Affairs after 9/11 (U. Chicago P., 2006).

CHAPTER SEVEN: JACK SPRAT'S LAW

1. Graham Greene, A World of My Own: a Dream Diary 68 (New York: Viking, 1992).

2. The English Constitution at 48.

3. Ferdinand Mount, The British Constitution Now: Recovery or Decline 94 (London: Mandarin, 1992).

4. Harold Nicolson, George V 62–63 (New York: Doubleday, 1953).

5. Cmd. 2768 (1926)

6. 22 George V, c. 4 (U.K.).

7. George Trefgarne, The Succession to the Crown Bill Is a Constitutional Can of Worms, The Spectator, January 22, 2013.

8. Bagehot at 64.

9. Sarah Bradford, George VI 412–15 (London: Penguin, 1989). Both Churchill and Beaverbrook had been strong supporters of Edward VIII.

10. Amanda Foreman, A World on Fire: Britain's Crucial Role in the American Civil War 175–96 (New York, Random House, 2010).

11. Margaret Thatcher, The Downing Street Years 18 (London: Harper-Collins, 1995). See Vernon Bogdanor, The Monarchy and the Constitution 69–74 (Oxford U.P., 1995).

12. Vincent Massey, What's Past in Prologue 508 (New York: St. Martin's, 1964).

13. Frank Mackinnon, The Crown in Canada 103 (Calgary: McClelland and Steward, 1976).

14. Peter Boyce, The Queen's Other Realms: The Crown and Its Legacy in Australia, Canada and New Zealand 51 (Sydney: Federation Press, 2008).

15. Colin Turpin and Adam Tomkins, British Government and the Constitution 379 (Cambridge U.P., 2011).

16. Allan Levine, King: William Lyon Mackenzie King—A Life Guided by the Hand of Destiny 152 (Vancouver: Douglas & McIntyre, 2011).

17. A similar constitutional crisis arose in Australia, when the governor general, Sir John Kerr, replaced Gough Whitlam in 1975 with Malcolm Fraser because of gridlock between the Australian lower and upper houses, both of which are elected bodies. An election was immediately called, which Fraser's Liberal Party won.

18. Eugene Forsey, The Royal Power of Dissolution in the British Commonwealth (Oxford University Press, 1968). The same problems of democratic legitimacy arise in republics, where one looks to the courts for a resolution. In Bush v. Gore, 531 U.S. 98 (2000), for example, the Supreme Court held that a series of recounts initiated by the Democratic Party must cease and that George W. Bush had been elected president.

19. Levine at 165. On Mackenzie King's spiritualism, and his willingness to take counsel from his dead mother and dogs, see C. P. Stacey, A Very Double Life: The Private World of Mackenzie King (Toronto: Macmillan, 1976).

20. For an account, see Parliamentary Democracy in Crisis (Peter H. Russell and Loren Sossin, eds., U. Toronto P., 2009), particularly the essays by Michael Valpy and C. E. S. Franks.

21. First, her meeting with Harper was hardly pro forma. It took two and a half hours, during which she made clear that it was within her discretion to turn him down. Second, had she insisted on an election, it would have

been the fourth general election in four years. If, on the other hand, she had followed Byng's example and, without calling an election, had asked the leader of the Opposition to form a government, she would have had to turn to the lame duck Liberal leader, who had just been rejected by the electorate. Third, the delay Harper sought was only for seven weeks, at a time when the world was entering into a recession, and the government might reasonably ask for time to decide how to address an unfolding financial crisis. Fourth, Harper's request for prorogation met the test of success, for when Parliament returned in January 2009, the Liberal Party under its new leader, Michael Ignatieff, refused to join in a motion of nonconfidence. Harper's government survived a further two years until the May 2011 election, when the Tories won a clear majority in Parliament and the Liberals were reduced to thirty-four seats. The prorogation didn't bother the voters. Finally, the calls for the governor general to exercise her residual powers came from the parties of the left, unlike the King-Byng crisis of 1925. As such, the episode left the governor general's residual powers strengthened. Any doubts about the prerogative power were removed when four provincial premiers prorogued their legislatures in 2012.

22. The monarch retains the right to veto legislation that trenches upon her property rights as a landowner, or which would affect the royal prerogative. In 1998, for example, the Queen blocked a private member's bill that would have permitted the government to take the country to war without her formal consent. Rodney Brazier, Legislating about the Monarchy, [2007] Cambridge L.J. 86, 95 at n. 36. See Office of the Parliamentary Counsel, House of Commons, Queen's or Prince's Consent, December 19, 2012, at http://www.cabinetoffice .gov.uk/sites/default/files/resources/QC_PC_pamphlet_191212.pdf; Robert Booth, Secret papers show extent of senior royals' veto over bills, The Guardian, January 14, 2013.

23. Sir Ivor Jennings, Cabinet Government 412 (Cambridge U.P., 3d ed., 1959). See also Rodney Brazier, Constitutional Practice 190–92 (Oxford U.P., 2d ed. 1995).

24. Jennings at 400.

25. Quoted in MacKinnon at 27. See also Vernon Bogdanor, The Monarchy and the Constitution 74–75 (Oxford U.P., 1997).

26. John Norton Moore, Grenada and the International Double Standard, 78 Am. J. Int'l Law 145 (1984).

27. Both countries rejoined the Commonwealth when white-only rule ended. Rhodesia, now Zimbabwe, is a republic with a president for life, and left the Commonwealth after it was suspended.

28. Suzy Menkes, We're All Invited to the Wedding, New York Times, April 25, 2011.

29. George Meredith, An Essay on Comedy 24 (London: Archibald Constable, 1905).

30. Vincent Massey, What's Past Is Prologue 472–73 (New York: St. Martin's, 1964).

31. Charles Maurras, Le Tombeau du Prince at http://maurras.net /textes/42.html. The description, which was incorporated into the oath sworn by members of Action Française, was resurrected and employed by President Sarkozy in a tribute he paid to the orléaniste pretender.

32. Vices of the Political System of the United States, 9 PJM 348.

33. Hans Kohn, American Nationalism: An Interpretive Essay 8 (1957).

34. Robert Penn Warren, The Legacy of the Civil War: Meditations on the Centennial 78 (1961).

35. Michael Novak, Choosing Our King 22 (New York: Macmillan, 1974).

36. Clinton Rossiter, The American Presidency 110 (New York: Time, 1963).

37. Barack and Michelle's Mumbai darshan plans, Mumbai Mirror, October 23, 2010; US to spend $200 mn a day on Obama's Mumbai visit, Press Trust of India, November 30, 2010.

38. Bagehot at 9.

39. On the uses of ritual in politics, see David Kertzer, Ritual, Politics, and Power (New Haven: Yale U.P., 1988).

40. And not just conservatives. See Arthur M. Schlesinger Jr., The Disuniting of America: Reflections on a Multicultural Society 71–74 (New York: W. W. Norton, 1998).

41. Obama and the Politics of Crowds, Wall Street Journal, October 30, 2008.

42. At http://today.msnbc.msn.com/id/46279899/ns/today-today_news/t/obama-presidency-you-get-better-time-goes/#.UETsJbJlRlQ.

43. Editorial, Washington Times, October 27, 2011.

44. Dana Milbank, Obama in focus, all over the map, Washington Post, December 20, 2012, at A2.

45. Gene Healy labels the way in which the office transforms the candidate as "acquired situational narcissism," the learned narcissism that afflicts a person when he discovers that he is a celebrity. Gene Healy, The Cult of the Presidency 254–55 (Washington: Cato Institute, 2008).

46. See, e.g., Frank Rich, The State of the Union Is Comatose, New York Times, January 30, 2010.

47. Pauline Maier, American Scripture: Making the Declaration of Independence (1997). On the uniqueness of American nationalism's identification with constitutional ideals of liberty, see F. H. Buckley, Liberal Nationalism, 48 UCLA L. Rev. 221 (2000).

CHAPTER EIGHT: TAMING THE KING

1. Economists call the problem of presidential misbehavior one of agency costs. Political leaders can be seen as the agents of the citizens who, as principals, elect them to office, and who incur agency costs when the leaders misbehave. The canonical analysis of agency costs in the theory of the firm is Michael C. Jensen and William H. Meckling, Theory of the Firm: Managerial Behavior, Agency Costs and Ownership Structure, 3 J. Fin. Econ. 305 (1976).

2. Torsten Persson and Guido Tabellini, The Economic Effects of Constitutions 23–24 (MIT Press, 2003).

3. Matthew S. Shugart and John M. Carey, Presidents and Assemblies: Constitutional Design and Electoral Dynamics 44–45 (Cambridge U.P., 1992).

4. While CPI rankings are available for the last dozen years, they are not meant to be compared over time, since each year's ranking is a relative score in which one country is compared to other countries in that year. A country's rank

may therefore change if perceptions of its corruption are unchanged but those of other countries change, or countries are added or removed from the mix. See Michael Johnston, "Measuring the New Corruption Rankings: Implications for Analysis and Reform," in Arnold J. Heidenheimer and Michael Johnston, Political Corruption: Concepts & Contexts 865 (New Brunswick: Transaction, 2002).

5. To come up with its rankings, Transparency International rejects objective measures of corruption as unreliable. Relatively honest countries prosecute corruption, while wholly corrupt countries tolerate it; and one might thus expect to see more corrupt officials behind bars in the United States than in, say, Russia. Relying on objective measures of corruption might therefore turn the world upside down. That leaves the survey data on which TI relies. Various groups ask knowledgeable people in each country to assess public sector corruption, and TI aggregates this information on a scale of 1 to 10 in a Corruption Perceptions Index (CPI). The CPI has been criticized for its subjectivity, see John G. Peters and Susan Welch, "Gradients of Corruption in Perceptions of American Public Life," in Heidenheimer and Johnston at 155, but any similar ranking system must inevitably rely on judgment calls.

6. Andrei Shleifer and Robert W. Vishny, Corruption, 108 Q.J. Econ. 599 (1993); Stephen Knack and Philip Keefer, Institutions and Economic Performance: Cross-Country Tests Using Alternative Institutional Measures, 7 Econ. & Politics 207 (1995); Rafael La Porta, Florencio López-de-Silanes, Cristian Pop-Eleches and Andrei Shleifer, Judicial Checks and Balances, 112 J. Pol. Econ. 445 (2004); see generally Pranab Bardhan, Corruption and Development: A Review of Issues, 35 J. Econ. Lit. 1320 (1997).

7. Similarly, the United States ranks 29th out of 214 countries in the World Bank's 2011 Worldwide Governance Indicators (WGI) measure of public corruption. See http://info.worldbank.org/governance/wgi/index.asp. Next to the TI rankings of corruption, the WGI rankings, which aggregate thirty different data sources, are the most commonly accepted measure of public corruption.

8. A third device might in theory be adopted, one which gives the executive an incentive to govern well by tying his salary and benefits to the country's long-term performance, on the model of the compensation strategies firms

employ to incentivize firm managers. F. H. Buckley, The Uneasy Case for the Flat Tax, 11 Constitutional Political Economy 295 (2000) (with Eric Rasmusen); Mancur Olson, Power and Prosperity 9–11 (New York: Basic Books, 2000). After he leaves office, a successful president might thus be rewarded though speaking tours and book royalties, and in the ten years after he left the presidency, Clinton received $90 million in this way. "I never had any money until I got out of the White House, you know, but I've done reasonably well since then," he observed. Robert Yoon, Clinton surpasses $75 million in speech income after lucrative 2010, CNN Politics, July 11, 2011. The problem, however, is that a leader might as easily be bribed for questionable decisions. A $10 million gift by the Saudi royal family for the Clinton presidential library raised eyebrows, as did the pardon of the husband of a political donor on Clinton's last day in office. John Solomon and Jeffrey H. Birnbaum, Clinton Library Got Funds From Abroad, Washington Post, December 15, 2007.

    9. I.300.

   10. Roll call 169 at II. 24.

   11. II.35.

   12. On the difference between impeachment standards, tenure during good behavior, and tenure during pleasure, see Saikrishna Prakash and Steven D. Smith, How to Remove a Federal Judge, 116 Yale L.J. 72 (2006).

   13. Note at II.36.

   14. Roll call 167 at II.24.

   15. Roll call 165 at II.24.

   16. II.495, 499.

   17. II.550. This passed 7 to 4 in roll call 491 at II.546.

   18. 116 Cong. Rec. H. 3113–14 (April 15, 1970). Most scholars agree that high crimes need not, in fact, be crimes at all. Raoul Berger, Impeachment: The Constitutional Problems 52–102 (Harvard U.P., 1973); Charles L. Black Jr., Impeachment: A Handbook 35 (Yale U.P., 1974).

   19. Thomas Jefferson to Spencer Roane, 12 The Works of Thomas Jefferson 137 (September 6, 1819) (New York: Knickerbocker, 1905); Henry Adams, History of the United States during the Administrations of Thomas Jefferson 465 (New York: Library of America, 1986).

20. Myers v. U.S., 272 U.S. 52 (1926).

21. Quoted in Raoul Berger, Impeachment: The Constitutional Problems 275 (New York: Bantam, 1974).

22. Michael Les Benedict, The Impeachment and Trial of Andrew Johnson 61–75 (New York: W. W. Norton, 1973).

23. The requirement on a quinquennial election is a matter of statute law in Britain, and as such can be extended by amending the law. During the First and Second World Wars, British governments entered into coalitions with the Opposition and the life of Parliament was extended, but no other Commonwealth country found it necessary to postpone elections while at war, and in Britain, elections were held as soon as the war was over.

24. A prime minister might also lose office when abandoned by the members of his party, as happened to Neville Chamberlain in 1940. As Cheibub and Przeworski note, almost half of all prime ministerial turnovers in parliamentary systems result from factors other than elections, including deaths, illnesses, and backbencher revolts. José Antonio Cheibub and Adam Przeworski, "Democracy, Elections, and Accountability for Economic Outcomes," in Democracy, Accountability, and Representation 222, 232–33 (Adam Przeworski, Susan Stokes, and Bernard Manin, eds., Cambridge U.P., 1999).

25. Bill C-16, First Session, 39th Parliament (2006).

26. Conacher v. Canada (Prime Minister), 2009 F.C. 920.

27. Joe Haines, Glimmers of Twilight 110 (London: Politico, 2003).

28. See Douglass C. North and Barry R. Weingast, Constitutions and Commitment: The Evolution of Institutions Governing Public Choice in Seventeenth-Century England, 49 J. Econ. Hist. 803 (1989); Irfan Nooruddin, Coalition Politics and Economic Development: Credibility and the Strength of Weak Governments (Cambridge U.P., 2011).

29. "If a covenant be made wherein neither of the parties perform presently, but trust one another, in the condition of mere nature (which is a condition of war of every man against every man) upon any reasonable suspicion, it is void. . . . And therefore he which performeth first doth but betray himself to his enemy." Thomas Hobbes, Leviathan 14.18 (1651).

30. Lester Telser, A Theory of Self-Enforcing Agreements, 53 J. Bus. 27 (1980).

31. In theory, a prime minister possesses the same untrammeled ability to take his country into war. If anything, the prime minister's authority stands on firmer constitutional grounds, since the Queen or governor general may declare war, on the advice of the prime minister, under the Crown prerogative powers. Colin Turpin and Adam Tomkins, British Government and the Constitution 192 (Cambridge U.P., 2011). However, the absence of the separation of powers in parliamentary regimes and the government's day-to-day accountability before the House of Commons make it far more difficult for a prime minister to disregard Parliament's wishes.

32. Richard Nixon, RN: The Memoirs of Richard Nixon 407 (New York: Grosset & Dunlap, 1978).

33. I thank Allen C. Guelzo for this suggestion.

34. John Hart Ely, War and Responsibility: Constitutional Lessons of Vietnam and Its Aftermath 4 (Princeton U.P., 1993).

35. Amartya Sen, The Idea of Justice ch. 6 (Harvard U.P., 2011).

36. Harold Laski, Parliamentary Government in England 119 (New York: Viking, 1938).

37. House of Commons Debates, April 6, 1911, vol. 23 §§ 2437–93.

38. 158 Cong. Rec. 122 at H5684 (September 12, 2012).

39. Burmah Oil Co. v. Bank of England, [1979] 1 W.L.R. 473 (C.A.), rev'd on other grounds, [1979] 3 W.L.R. 722 (H.L.). To like effect, see Gravel v. United States, 408 U.S. 606 (1972); United States v. Nixon, 483 U.S. 683, 705–06 (1974) ("The valid need for protection of communications between high government officials and those who advise and assist them in the performance of their manifold duties . . . is too plain to require further discussion. Human experience teaches that those who expect public dissemination of their remarks may well temper candor with a concern for appearances and for their own interests to the detriment of the decision-making process").

40. 483 U.S. 683 (1974).

41. Mark J. Rozell, Executive Privilege: Presidential Power, Secrecy, and Accountability 144 (U.P. Kansas, 2010).

THE ONCE AND FUTURE KING

42. Department of Justice, Office of the Inspector General, A Review of ATF's Operation Fast and Furious and Related Matters 2012 at http://www .justice.gov/oig/reports/2012/s1209.pdf.

43. Jack Goldsmith, Power and Constraint: The Accountable President after 9/11 100–05 (New York: W. W. Norton, 2012).

44. See Neil Barofsky, Bailout: An Inside Account of How Washington Abandoned Main Street While Rescuing Wall Street (New York: Free Press, 2012).

45. The White House Fires a Watchdog, Wall Street Journal, June 17, 2009.

46. Constitution Act §§ 9–11, 24, 96.

47. Louis Fisher, Constitutional Conflicts between Congress and the President 35 (U.P. Kansas, 2007).

48. Paul Richter, Caroline Kennedy Nomination as Envoy to Japan Points to Larger Trend, Los Angeles Times, July 26, 2013 ("more than 56% of Obama's 41 second-term ambassadorial nominations have been political, compared with an average of about 30% for recent administrations").

49. Haynes, Senate of the United States, Its History and Precedent 740 (Boston: Houghton Mifflin, 1938).

50. Henry B. Hogue, Supreme Court Nominations Not Confirmed, 1789–2005, Congressional Research Service Report RL31171.

51. Jonathan Turley, Seeing Red on Blue Slips, Los Angeles Times, May 16, 2001, at B-13.

52. Charlie Savage, Obama Tempts Fight Over Recess Appointments, New York Times, January 4, 2012. The opinion of the Office of Legal Counsel is available at http://www.justice.gov/olc/2012/pro-forma-sessions-opinion.pdf.

53. Noel Canning v. NLRB, __ F.3d __ (January 25, 2013). The court also held that the president lacks the power to make intra-session recess appointments when Congress has been adjourned for a few days or weeks. As this power was upheld in Evans v. Stephens, 387 F.3d 1220 (11th Cir., 2004), the Supreme Court will likely be asked to resolve the conflict between the circuits (unless the issue is found to be moot).

54. Mitchel A. Sollenberger and Mark J. Rozell, The President's Czars: Undermining Congress and the Constitution 138–40 (U.P. Kansas, 2012).

55. Judicial Watch, President Obama's Czars, September 15, 2011.

56. Morgan Little, Obama campaign defends selective press availability, Los Angeles Times, August 19, 2012.

57. The considered judgment of his friend and adviser, Tom Kent, A Public Purpose 214 (McGill-Queen's U.P., 1988).

58. Hansard, June 5, 1956. Pearson's account of the circumstances of the speech can be found at Mike: The Memoirs of the Rt. Hon. Lester B. Pearson 7 (U. Toronto P., 1975).

59. Sir Harold Nicolson, The War Years 1939–1945: Diaries and Letters 78 (New York: Atheneum, 1967).

60. Glenn Greenwald, Justice Alito's Conduct and the Court's Credibility, Salon, January 28, 2010, at http://www.salon.com/2010/01/28/alito_2/.

CHAPTER NINE: MADISONIAN INFIRMITIES

1. Myers v. U.S., 272 U.S. 52, 242 (1926) (Brandeis J., dissenting). See Scott Mainwaring and Matthew S. Shugart, Juan Linz, Presidentialism, and Democracy: A Critical Appraisal, 29 Comparative Politics 449 (1997).

2. Mary Bruce, Obama Offers Mortgage-Relief Plan: 'We Can't Wait' for Congress, ABC News, October 24, 2011.

3. On the polarization of politics, see Alan I. Abramowitz, The Disappearing Center: Engaged Citizens, Polarization, and American Democracy 139–42 (Yale U.P., 2010); Thomas E. Mann and Norman J. Ornstein, It's Even Worse than It Looks: How the American Constitutional System Collided with the New Politics of Extremism 44–46 (New York: Basic Books, 2012).

4. Fareed Zakaria, "How to Restore the American Dream," Time Magazine, October 21, 2010.

5. Mark P. Keightley and Molly F. Sherlock, The Corporate Income Tax System: Overview and Options for Reform, Congressional Research Service 7-5700 (September 13, 2012), at http://www.fas.org/sgp/crs/misc/R42726.pdf.

6. Peter Orszag, As Foreign Profits Rise, Corporate Tax Rates Fall, Bloomberg View, January 22, 2013. See Information on Estimated Revenue Losses and Related Federal Spending Programs, Government Accounting Office, GAO 13-339 (March 2013), at http://www.gao.gov/assets/660/653120.pdf.

7. David Kocieniewski, G.E.'s Strategies Let It Avoid Taxes Altogether, New York Times, March 24, 2011; John McCormack, GE Filed 57,000-Page Tax Return, Paid No Taxes on $14 Billion in Profits, Weekly Standard, November 17, 2011, at http://www.weeklystandard.com/blogs/ge-filed-57000-page-tax-return-paid-no-taxes-14-billion-profits_609137.html.

8. See, e.g., Lawrence Summers, Tax reform can aid multinationals, cut deficit, Washington Post, July 7, 2013.

9. The canonical references are to Mancur Olson, The Logic of Collective Action: Public Goods and the Theory of Groups (Harvard U.P., 1965) and The Rise and Decline of Nations: Economic Growth, Stagflation, and Social Rigidities (Yale U.P., 1982).

10. See Republicans Get Filibustered, Wall Street Journal, July 17, 2013, at A14.

11. John O. McGinnis and Michael B. Rappaport, In Praise of Supreme Court Filibusters, 33 Harv. J. Law & Pub. Policy 39 (2010) (defending filibusters of judicial nominees); George F. Will, Why Filibusters Should Be Allowed, Washington Post, March 20, 2005.

12. For a simple model explaining why it is harder to enact legislation in a separation-of-powers presidential system than in a parliamentary system, see Robert D. Cooter, The Strategic Constitution 213–15 (Princeton U.P., 2000). For a more elaborate model, see George Tsebelis, Veto Players: How Political Institutions Work ch. 1 (Princeton U.P., 2002).

13. See, e.g., James Q. Wilson, Does the Separation of Powers Still Work?, 86 Public Interest 49 (1987).

14. See E. E. Schattschneider, Party Government (New Brunswick: Transaction, 2004); James MacGregor Burns, The Deadlock of Democracy: Four-Party Politics in America (Englewood Cliffs: Prentice Hall, 1963); James L. Sundquist, Constitutional Reform and Effective Government ch. 1 (Washington: Brookings, 1992).

15. U.S. Senate, Subcommittee on Immigration and Naturalization of the Committee on the Judiciary 1–3 Washington, D.C., February 10, 1965. See Anna Law, The Diversity Visa Lottery—A Cycle of Unintended Consequences in United States Immigration Policy, 21 J. Am. Ethnic Hist. 3 (2002). Immigration from Europe to America had declined from more than 50 to less than 12 percent from 1951–60 to 2010. Borjas at 42, Table 3-1; Department of Homeland Security, Yearbook of Immigration Statistics: 2011 53 at Table 21 (Washington: U.S. Department of Homeland Security, Office of Immigration Statistics, 2012).

16. Gretchen Morgenson and Joshua Rosner, Reckless Endangerment: How Outsized Ambition, Greed, and Corruption Led to Economic Armageddon 40–41 (New York: Times, 2011).

17. David A. Fahrenthold, Rosalind S. Helderman, and Ed O'Keefe, For the Tea Party, a Bill Full of Anathema, Washington Post, January 2, 2013, at A1.

18. Matt Cover, Senate Ok'd 154-Page Bill in 3 Minutes, Washington Times, January 2, 2013, at http://times247.com/articles/senators-got-cliff-bill-3-minutes-before-voting-on-it.

19. N.F.I.B. v. Sebelius, __ U.S. __ (2012).

20. Abby Schachter, Quick Fix for Congress: Speak English, N.Y. Post, December 15, 2010.

21. Gross public debt is a consolidation of accounts for the central, state, and local government. See OECD Economic Outlook no. 89 (June 2011) at http://stats.oecd.org/Index.aspx?QueryId=29868.

22. OECD Economic Outlook No. 89 Annex Tables, Annex Table 33 at http://www.oecd.org/document/3/0,3343,en_2649_34573_2483901_1_1_1_1,00.html.

23. Laurence J. Kotlikoff, America's Debt Woe Is Worse than Greece's, CNN Opinion, September 20, 2011.

24. David R. Henderson, Canada's Budget Triumph, Mercatus Working Paper 10–52 (2010).

25. Obamacare will increase the long-term federal deficit by $6.2 trillion, according to a General Accountability Office (GAO) report. See Patient Protec-

tion and Affordable Care Act, GAO 13-281 (January 2013) at http://www.gao
.gov/assets/660/651702.pdf.

26. Robert D. Putnam, Bowling Alone: The Collapse and Revival of
American Community 140 (New York: Simon & Schuster, 2000). See also
Pamela Paxton, Is Social Capital Declining in the United States? A Multiple
Indicator Assessment, 105 Am. J. Soc. 88 (1999).

27. Public Trust in Government: 1958-2013, Pew Research Center
for the People and the Press (January 31, 2013), at http://www.people-press
.org/2013/01/31/trust-in-government-interactive/.

28. Tom Cotton, It's the House Bill or Nothing on Immigration, Wall
Street Journal, July 11, 2013.

29. Ed O'Keefe, House GOP Struggles with Immigration Reform in
Meeting, Washington Post, July 11, 2013.

30. James Bryce, 1 The American Commonwealth 162–63 (New York:
Macmillan 1914).

31. Laura MacInnis, Obama accuses Congress of holding back U.S.
recovery, Reuters, August 20, 2011.

32. Erik Wasson and Daniel Strauss, Senate rejects Obama budget in
99–0 vote, The Hill, May 16, 2012.

33. For a list of the more than fifty centers or buildings names after Byrd,
see http://en.wikipedia.org/wiki/List_of_places_named_after_Robert_Byrd.

34. Mancur Olson, Power and Prosperity: Outgrowing Communist and
Capitalist Dictatorships 19–23 (New York: Basic Books, 2000).

35. Bolingbroke: Political Writings 257–58 (David Armitage, ed., Cambridge U.P., 1997).

36. On how stronger political parties reduce minoritarian misbehavior
costs, see Philip Keefer and Stuti Khemani, When Do Legislators Pass on Pork?
The Role of Political Parties in Determining Legislator Effort, 103 Am. Pol. Sc.
Rev. 99 (2009).

37. See Gary W. Cox and Mathew D. McCubbins, Legislative Leviathan:
Party Government in the House 121–22 (U. California P., 2d ed. 2007).

38. P.L. 104–130. This was subject to a congressional override, which the president could veto. Congress could again override this, subject to a two-thirds vote in both houses of Congress.

39. 524 U.S. 417 (1998).

40. Id. at 450 (concurring opinion of Kennedy J.). Whether a line-item veto would rein in excessive spending has been doubted, however. See, e.g., Louis Fisher, Constitutional Conflicts between Congress and the President 133–35 (5th ed., U. P. Kansas, 2007).

41. Kevin Milligan and Michael Smart, Regional Grants as Pork Barrel Politics at http://SSRN.com/abstract=710903.

42. Douglas L. Kriner and Andrew Reeves, The Influence of Federal Spending on Presidential Elections, 106 Am. Pol. Sc. Rev. 348 (2012).

43. David J. Samuels and Matthew S. Shugart, Presidents, Parties, and Prime Ministers: How the Separation of Powers Affects Party Organization and Behavior (Cambridge U.P., 2010).

44. See Terry M. Moe, "The Politics of Structural Choice: Toward a Theory of Public Bureaucracy," in Organization Theory: From Chester Barnard to the Present and Beyond 116, 136 (Oliver Williamson, ed., Oxford U.P., 1990).

45. David R. Mayhew, Divided We Govern: Party Control, Lawmaking, and Investigations 104–05 (Yale U.P., 2d ed., 2005).

46. Stephen M. Bainbridge, "How American Corporate and Securities Law Drives Business Offshore," in The American Illness: Essays on the Rule of Law 381 (F. H. Buckley, ed., Yale U.P., 2013).

47. L. Gordon Crovitz, Exporting Wall Street, Wall Street Journal, February 28, 2011, at A17.

CHAPTER TEN: TYRANNOPHILIA

1. Polybius, Histories VI.7.

2. Eric Posner and Adrian Vermeule, The Executive Unbound: After the Madisonian Republic (Oxford U.P., 2011).

3. Daniel Ellsberg, Edward Snowden: Saving us from the United Stasi of America, The Guardian, June 10, 2013.

4. Adam Liptak, Right and Left Join Forces on Criminal Justice, New York Times, November 23, 2009, at A1.

5. Roy Walmsley reports that, in absolute terms, China might have more people in jail than America if one counts some 850,000 people held in Chinese "administrative detention." But even so, China's total of 2.4 million (in a population of 1.3 billion) would exceed the U.S. total of 2.3 million by only 100,000. Walmsley, World Prison Population List—8th edition (data as of 2008) (King's College London: International Centre for Prison Studies), available at www.prisonstudies.org.

6. Jeffrey Parker, "Corporate Crime, Overcriminalization and the Failure of American Public Morality," in The American Illness: Essays on the Rule of Law 407, 420 (F. H. Buckley, ed., Yale L.J., 2013).

7. Julie R. O'Sullivan, The Federal Criminal "Code" Is a Disgrace: Obstruction Statutes as a Case Study, 96 J. Crim. L. & Criminology 643 (2006).

8. William Stuntz, The Pathological Politics of Criminal Law, 100 Mich. L. Rev. 506, 511 (2001). See also William Stuntz, The Collapse of American Criminal Justice (Harvard U.P., 2011); Harvey A. Silverglate, Three Felonies a Day: How the Feds Target the Innocent (New York: Encounter Books, 2009).

9. Statement of Jim E. Lavine before the House Committee on the Judiciary Subcommittee on Crime, Terrorism, and Homeland Security, September 28, 2010, at http://judiciary.house.gov/hearings/pdf/Lavine100928.pdf. United States v. Evertson, 320 Fed. Appx. 509; 2009 U.S. App. LEXIS 5936 (9th Cir. 2009, cert. den., 130 Sup. Ct. 460 (2009).

10. Abelard, "Intention and Sin," in Freedom and Responsibility: Readings in Philosophy and Law 170 (Herbert Morris, ed., 1964). See also Francis Sayre, Mens Rea, 45 Harv. L. Rev. 974 (1932).

11. Richard A. Oppel, Sentencing Shift Gives New Leverage to Prosecutors, New York Times, September 25, 2011.

12. U.S. Department of Justice, Federal Justice Statistics, 2009, 12 at Table 9 (December 2011).

13. Jennifer Epstein, Obama team: Romney committed a felony or lied to voters, Politico, July 12, 2012.

14. Andrew Sullivan, Yes, Romney Perjured Himself, The Daily Dish, July 16, 2012.

15. William Greider, How Wall Street Crooks Get Out of Jail Free, The Nation, March 23, 2011.

16. Jeremy Pelofsky and James Vicini, As gas prices soar, task force to explore energy fraud, Washington Post, April 21, 2011.

17. Byron York, The Life and Death of the American Spectator, The Atlantic, November 2001; Editorial: In Thrall to Sheldon Adelson, New York Times, August 16, 2012; Marilyn Young, Michael Reksulak and William F. Shughart, The Political Economy of the IRS, 13 Economics and Politics 201 (2001); Eric Lichtblau, Republicans See a Political Motive in I.R.S. Audits, New York Times, October 8, 2010; John Strassel: Obama's Enemies List—Part II, Wall Street Journal, July 19, 2012.

18. Tom Fitton, The Corruption Chronicles 17–18 (New York: Simon & Schuster, 2012).

19. That was the rationale Chief Justice Roberts gave in Citizens United for refusing to follow an earlier Supreme Court decision, though his explanation manifestly failed to persuade his critics, among them the president. Citizens United v. Federal Election Commission, 558 U.S. 310 (2010).

20. National Federation of Independent Business v. Sebelius, 567 U.S. ___ (2012).

21. 570 U.S. ___ (2013).

22. The same jealousy of rival institutions may be seen in the Obama administration's proposals to limit the tax deduction for charitable gifts, a move that would weaken religious charities and other nongovernmental organizations that compete with the state in providing social services. Jerry Markon and Peter Wallsten, White House, nonprofit groups battle over charitable deductions, Washington Post, December 13, 2012.

23. United States v. Windsor, ___ U.S. ___ (2013).

24. Hollingsworth v. Perry, ___ U.S. ___ (2013).

25. Robert Nisbet, The Quest for Community: A Study in the Ethics of Order & Freedom 141 (San Francisco: ICS Press, 1990). One might think that duties to respect religious beliefs and duties to respect practices condemned

by a religion, such as homosexuality, would cancel out, at least for the respect demanded for same-sex unions. But that, seemingly, is just what the secularist would deny, in rejecting an abstract right to respect religious beliefs. See Brian Leiter, Why Tolerate Religion? ch. 4 (Princeton U.P., 2012).

26. The taxonomy of weak and strong free exercise and disestablishment jurisprudence is proposed in Kathleen M. Sullivan, The New Religion and the Constitution, 116 Harv. L. Rev. 1397 (2003). The dominant scholarly literature favors strong restrictions on free exercise rights, in the name of disestablishment and the vindication of the state's moral code. For an example of how this may threaten free exercise rights, Ted G. Jelen argues that a Catholic bishop who would impose religious sanctions against dissident church members is guilty of "a religiously based threat to the prerogatives of democratic citizenship." Ted G. Jelen, "In Defense of Religious Minimalism," in Mary Segers and Ted G. Jelen, A Wall of Separation?: Debating the Public Role of Religion 3, 31 (Lanham: Rowman and Littlefield, 1998). For an analysis of the views of current members of the Supreme Court, see Kathleen M. Sullivan, Justice Scalia and the Religion Clauses, 22 Hawaii L. Rev. 449 (2000) On historical attitudes toward Catholicism as reflected in the law, see Philip Hamburger, Separation of Church and State (Harvard U.P., 2002).

27. William Galston, The Morning After: What a Narrow Win Would Mean for Obama's Second Term, The New Republic, November 1, 2012.

28. Elizabeth Drew, Power Grab, New York Review of Books, June 22, 2006.

29. Dana Priest, Bush's 'War' on Terror Comes to a Sudden End, Washington Post, January 23, 2009.

30. Jo Becker and Scott Shane, Secret 'Kill List' Proves a Test of Obama's Principles and Will, New York Times, May 29, 2012. See U.S. Department of Defense News Briefing with Lt. Gen. Scaparotti, June 11, 2012, at http://www .defense.gov/transcripts/transcript.aspx?transcriptid=5059.

31. Paul Richter, Obama administration ditches 'war on terror' phrase, Los Angeles Times, March 31, 2009.

32. Michael Isikoff, Justice Department memo reveals legal case for drone strikes on Americans, NBC News Open Channel, February 4, 2013.

33. Ari Melber, Do Liberals Support Obama's Kill List?, The Nation, June 18, 2012.

34. Byron Tau and Donovan Slack, Obama Interrupted by Heckling Reporter, Politico, June 15, 2012, at http://www.politico.com/politico44 /2012/06/obama-interrupted-by-heckling-reporter-126301.html; Joe Strupp, Past And Present White House Correspondents' Association Presidents Criticize "Discourteous" And "Rude" Daily Caller Reporter, Media Matters for America at http://mediamatters.org/blog/201206150014.

35. Martin Peretz, The New New Republic, Wall Street Journal, February 14, 2013, at A17.

36. John Dickerson, Go for the Throat!, Slate, January 18, 2013, at http:// www.slate.com/articles/news_and_politics/politics/2013/01/barack_obama_s _second_inaugural_address_the_president_should_declare_war.html.

37. Posner and Vermeule at 189–92.

38. Paul E. Peterson, Ludger Woessmann, Eric A. Hanushek and Carlos X. Lastra-Anadón, Globally Challenged: Are U.S. Students Ready to Compete? The latest on each state's international standing in math and reading viii (Taubman Center for State and Local Government, Harvard Kennedy School, PEPG Report No. 11-03, 2011).

39. Bryan Caplan, The Myth of the Rational Voter: Why Democracies Choose Bad Policies (Princeton U.P., 2007). For example, there is no evidence that voters reject politicians when the economy fares poorly. José Cheibub and Adam Przeworski, "Democracy, Elections, and Accountability for Economic Outcomes," in Democracy, Accountability, and Repression 222 (Adam Przeworski, Susan C. Stokes, and Bernard Manin, eds., Cambridge U.P., 1999).

40. Gerd Gigerenzer, "Bounded and Rational," in Contemporary Debates in Cognitive Science 124 (R. J. Stainton, ed., Oxford: Blackwell, 2006).

41. Anthony Downs, An Economic Theory of Democracy (New York: Harper & Row, 1957).

42. With perfect information, a voter would also know the intensity of a candidate's preferences. As such, the problem of indeterminacy associated with the Arrow Impossibility theorem would not arise, if we add a further assumption of costless bargaining over alternatives. Otherwise, political parties might

be seen as rough "solutions" to Arrovian impossibility, as suggested by Barry R. Weingast, A Rational Choice Perspective on Congressional Norms, 23 Am J. Pol. Sc. 245 (1979). See John H. Aldrich, Why Parties? The Origin and Transformation of Political Parties in America (U. Chicago P., 1995).

43. Seymour Martin Lipset and Gary Marks, It Didn't Happen Here: Why Socialism Failed in the United States 24–29 (New York: W. W. Norton, 2000).

44. Lipset and Marks at 282–83.

45. http://www.economicmobility.org/assets/pdfs/PEW_EMP_US -CANADA.pdf at Table 10.2.

46. World Bank at http://data.worldbank.org/indicator/NY.GDP.PCAP. CD.

47. Credit Suisse Research Institute Global Wealth Databook 2011 141 at Table 7.2, at https://infocus.credit-suisse.com/data/_product_documents /_shop/324292/2011_global_wealth_report_databook.pdf.

48. OECD.StatExtracts at http://stats.oecd.org/Index.aspx?DatasetCode =SNA_TABLE1.

49. IMF Bombshell: Age of America Nears End, in http://www .marketwatch.com/story/imf-bombshell-age-of-america-about-to-end-2011 -04-25?link=MW_home_latest_news.

50. Thomas L. Friedman, From WikiChina, New York Times, November 30, 2010; Andy Stern, China's Superior Economic Model, Wall Street Journal, December 1, 2011; Martin Jacques, When China Rules the World: The End of the Western World and the Birth of a New Global Order (New York: Penguin, 2009).

51. The Moment of Truth, Report of the National Commission on Fiscal Responsibility and Reform 11 (2010).

52. http://www.thesocialcontract.com/artman2/publish/tsc0804/article _755.shtml.

53. Elise Foley, Latino Voters in Election 2012 Help Sweep Obama to Reelection, Huffington Post, November 7, 2012. See Peter S. Canellos, Obama Victory Took Root in Kennedy-Inspired Immigration Act, Boston Globe, November 11, 2008.

54. See Jack Citrin, Amy Lerman, Michael Murakami, and Kathryn Pearson, Testing Huntington: Is Hispanic Immigration a Threat to American Identity?, 5 Perspectives on Politics 31 (2007).

55. The formula is Sum[(country intake/total intake)*FHcountry]/n. The data is taken from table 2 of the DHS 2011 Yearbook of Immigration Statistics, looking at the 1950–59 and 2000–09 periods. For the earlier period I excluded countries under Soviet control. For the Freedom House ranking I used the 2010 figure, since their rankings go back only to 1972.

56. Robert D. Putnam, Bowling Alone: The Collapse and Revival of American Community (New York: Simon & Schuster, 2000).

57. Charles Murray, Coming Apart: The State of White America, 1960–2010 (New York: Crown Forum, 2012).

58. Id. at 241.

59. Putnam at 341. See also Theda Skocpol, Diminished Democracy: From Membership to Management in American Civic Life ch. 3–4 (U. Oklahoma P., 2004).

60. Francis Fukuyama, The Great Disruption: Human Nature and the Reconstitution of Social Order (New York: Simon & Schuster, 1999).

61. Clinton v. City of New York, 524 U.S. 417 (1998).

62. [1998] 2 S.C.R. 217.

63. For evidence that referenda might usefully address the problem of excessive government spending, see John G. Matsusaka, For the Many or the Few: The Initiative, Public Policy, and American Democracy (U. Chicago P., 2004). As a device to empower Congress, a national referendum would backfire if the president could call for a referendum and set its terms. However, I do not think he could do so by executive order, without the authorization of funds from Congress—at least not without a further expansion of executive power.

64. David Freddoso, Pelosi on Health Care, San Francisco Examiner, March 9, 2010.

65. Dana Milbank, On health-care bill, Democratic senators are in states of denial, Washington Post, December 22, 2009; Chris Frates, Payoffs for states get Harry Reid to 60 votes, Politico at http://www.politico.com/news/stories/1209/30815.html.

66. Frates.

67. Milbank.

68. Bob Cusack, The 20 House Democrats who will decide the fate of the healthcare reform bill, The Hill, March 20, 2010.

69. Greg Hitt and Brody Mullins, Health-Bill Horse Trading, Wall Street Journal, March 19, 2010.

70. http://www.msnbc.msn.com/id/35764300/ns/msnbc_tv-rachel _maddow_show/.

71. Mann and Ornstein, It's Even Worse than It Looks at 85.

72. For recent examples, see Walter J. Oleszek, Congressional Procedures and the Policy Process 57–58 (Washington: CQ Press, 8th ed., 2011).

73. John F. Kennedy, Profiles in Courage 146 (New York: Harper & Row, 1964).

74. David O. Stewart, Impeached: The Trial of President Andrew Johnson and the Fight for Lincoln's Legacy 294–99 (New York: Simon & Schuster, 2009).

APPENDIX A: THE FRAMERS

1. The STATA command is ologit y x_1 x_2 x_3.

2. The STATA command is regress y x_1 x_2 x_3, cluster (state).

3. I.163. Delegate preferences on Veto are taken from McGuire at 55–56, 86, which in turn are largely derived from Forrest McDonald's We the People: The Economic Origins of the Constitution 98–99 (U. Chicago P., 1958). For a closer analysis of delegate voting patterns, see F. H. Buckley, The Efficient Secret: How America Nearly Adopted a Parliamentary System, and Why It Should Have Done So, 1 British J. Am. Legal Stud. 349, 396–403, 406 (2012).

4. I constructed for the Rich variable from the description of the economic interests of the delegates in McDonald, We the People.

5. Charles A. Beard, An Economic Interpretation of the Constitution of the United States (New York: Macmillan, 1935) [1913]. See Gordon S. Wood, Revolutionary Characters: What Made the Founders Different 6 (New York: Penguin, 2006).

6. See Robert E. Brown, Charles Beard and the Constitution (Princeton U.P., 1956); McDonald, We the People. See also Alan Gibson, Understanding the Founding: The Crucial Questions ch. 1 (U.P. Kansas, 2010).

7. Beard at 324. Beard tried to have it both ways. While denying that he claimed the members of the Convention were self-interested (Heaven forfend), he went on to say that he did not want to ask "how many hundred thousand dollars accrued to them as a result of the foundation of the new government." Id. at 73.

8. Robert A. McGuire, To Form a More Perfect Union: A New Economic Interpretation of the United States Constitution (Oxford U.P., 2003). See also Jac C. Heckelman and Keith L. Dougherty, Personality Interests in the Constitutional Convention: New Tests of the Beard Thesis, 4 Cliometrica 207 (2010).

9. Roll call 164 at II.24 and II.401.

10. I.79.

11. See II.114.

12. III.253.

13. The figures are taken from Pinckney at III.253.

14. McDonald, We the People. See also William H. Riker, The Senate and American Federalism, 49 Am. Pol. Sc. Rev. 452 (1955); Clinton Rossiter, 1787: The Grand Convention (New York: Macmillan, 1966); Forrest Macdonald, E Pluribus Unum: The Formation of the American Republic 1776–1790 (Indianapolis: Liberty Fund, 1979).

15. See generally McGuire at 49–64 on regression analyses of voting patterns at the Convention.

APPENDIX B: PRESIDENTIALISM AND LIBERTY

1. Nathaniel Beck and Jonathan N. Katz, What To Do (and Not To Do) with Time-Series–Cross-Section Data in Comparative Politics, 89 Am. Pol. Sci. Rev. 634 (1995).

2. Adam Przeworski, Michael E. Alvarez, José Cheibub, and Fernando Limongi, Democracy and Development: Political Institutions and Well-Being

in the World, 1950–1990 (Cambridge U.P., 2000); David L. Epstein, Robert Bates, Jack Goldstone, Ida Kristensen, and Sharyn O'Halloran, Democratic Transitions, 50 Am. J. Pol. Sc. 551 (2006).

APPENDIX C: PRESIDENTS AND CORRUPTION

1. Robert Klitgaard, Controlling Corruption 75 (U. California P., 1988).

2. Jeffrey D. Sachs and Andrew M. Warner, Natural Resource Abundance and Economic Growth, Development Discussion Paper 517a, Harvard Institute for International Development 1995; Paul Collier and Anke Hoeffer, On Economic Causes of Civil War, 50 Oxford Econ. Papers 563 (1998).

3. Michael L. Ross, The Oil Curse: How Petroleum Wealth Shapes the Development of Nations 229 (Princeton U.P., 2012).

4. Ross at 15–16.

5. As is done in Timothy Hellwig and David Samuels, Electoral Accountability and the Variety of Democratic Regimes, 37 British J. Pol. Sc. 65 (2008).

6. Lorenz Blume, Jens Müller, Stefan Voigt, and Carsten Wolf, The Economic Effects of Constitutions: Replicating—and Extending—Persson and Tabellini, 139 Public Choice 197, 212–14 (2009).

7. Daniel Lederman, Norman V. Loayza and Rodrigo R. Soares, Accountability and Corruption: Political Institutions Matter, 17 Econ. & Politics 1 (2005) (presidential systems increase corruption by 0.8 points on the 0 to 6 International Country Risk Guide corruption index).

8. Jana Kunicova and Susan Rose-Ackerman, Electoral Rules and Constitutional Structures as Constraints on Corruption, 35 British J. Pol. Sc. 573 (2005).

9. John Gerring and Strom C. Thacker, Political Institutions and Corruption: The Role of Unitarism and Parliamentarism, 34 British Journal of Political Science 295, 306 (2004).

10. John Gerring, Strom C. Thacker, and Carola Moreno, Are Parliamentary Systems Better?, 42 Comparative Political Studies 327 (2009).

11. Torsten Persson and Guido Tabellini, The Economic Effects of Constitutions 23–24 (MIT Press, 2003).

Index